The Law of Ueki™

うえきの法則

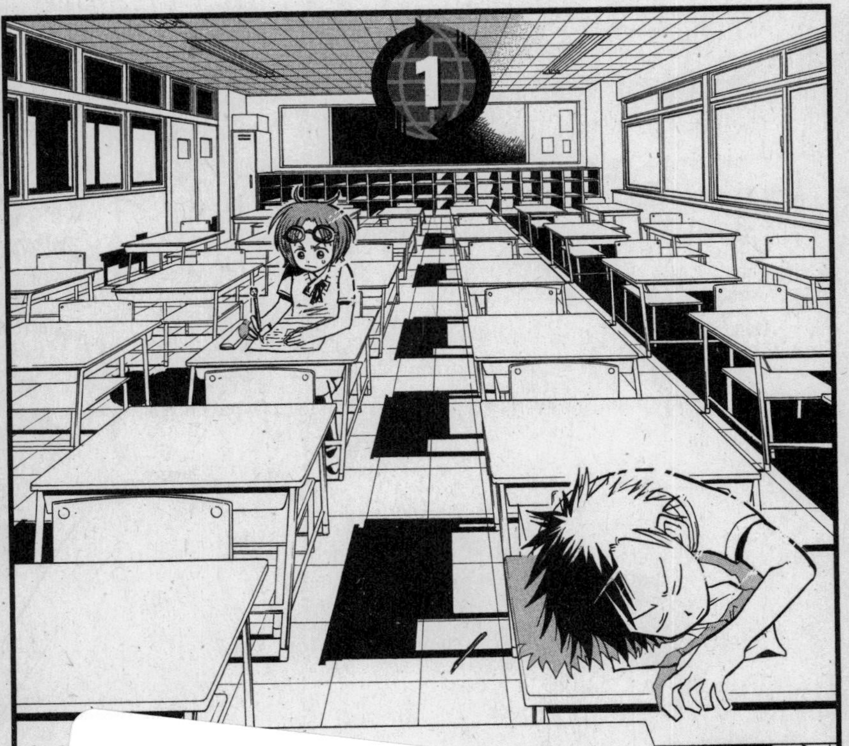
1
翼
UCHI PRESENTS

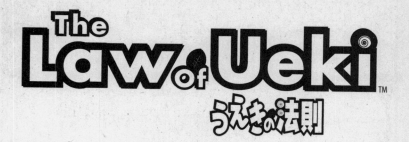

The Law of Ueki™

うえきの法則

Table of Contents

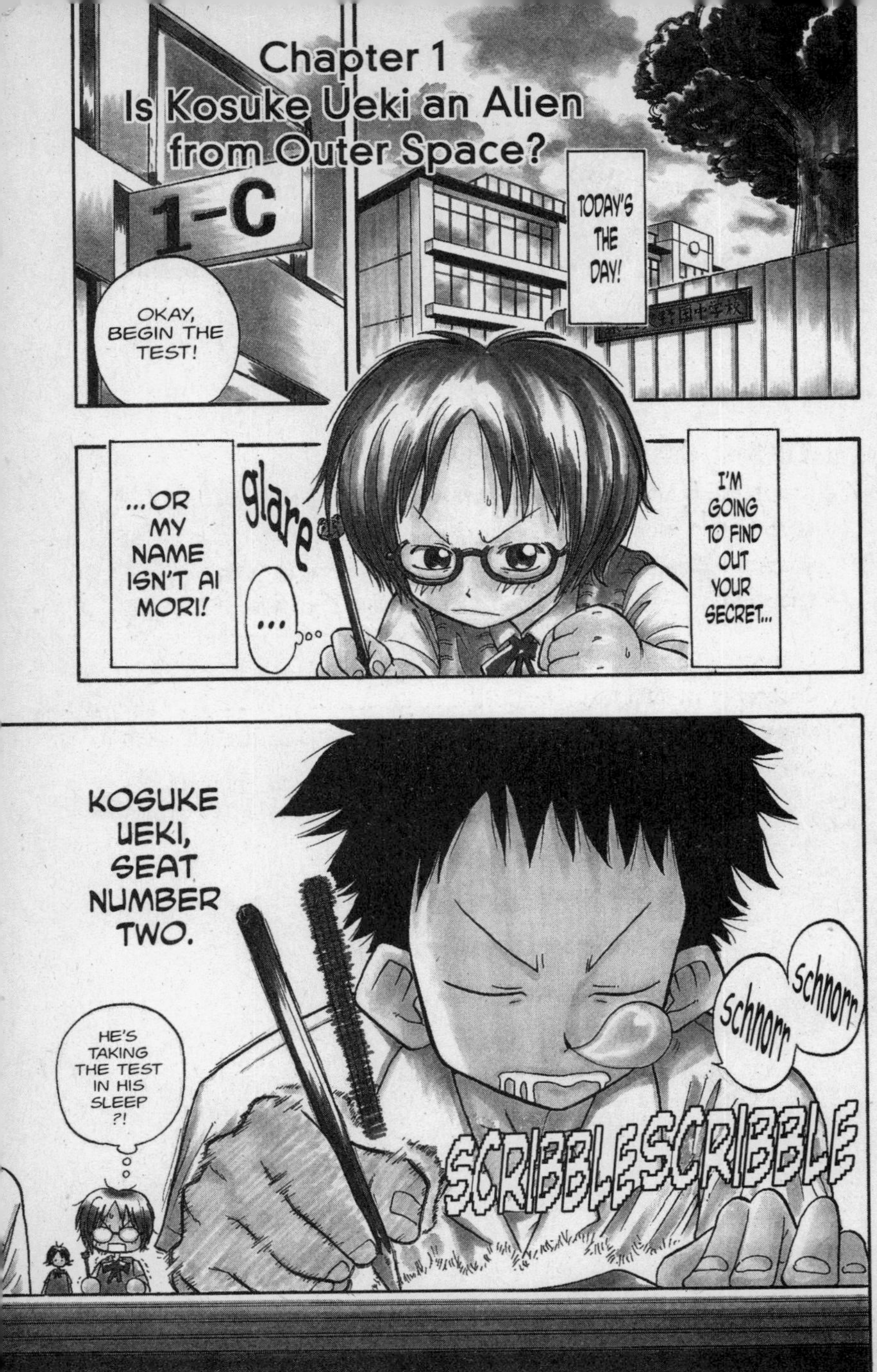
Chapter 1
Is Kosuke Ueki an Alien from Outer Space?
1-C
TODAY'S THE DAY!
OKAY, BEGIN THE TEST!
I'M GOING TO FIND OUT YOUR SECRET...
glare
...
...OR MY NAME ISN'T AI MORI!
schnorr
schnorr
SCRIBBLESCRIBBLE
KOSUKE UEKI, SEAT NUMBER TWO.
HE'S TAKING THE TEST IN HIS SLEEP?!

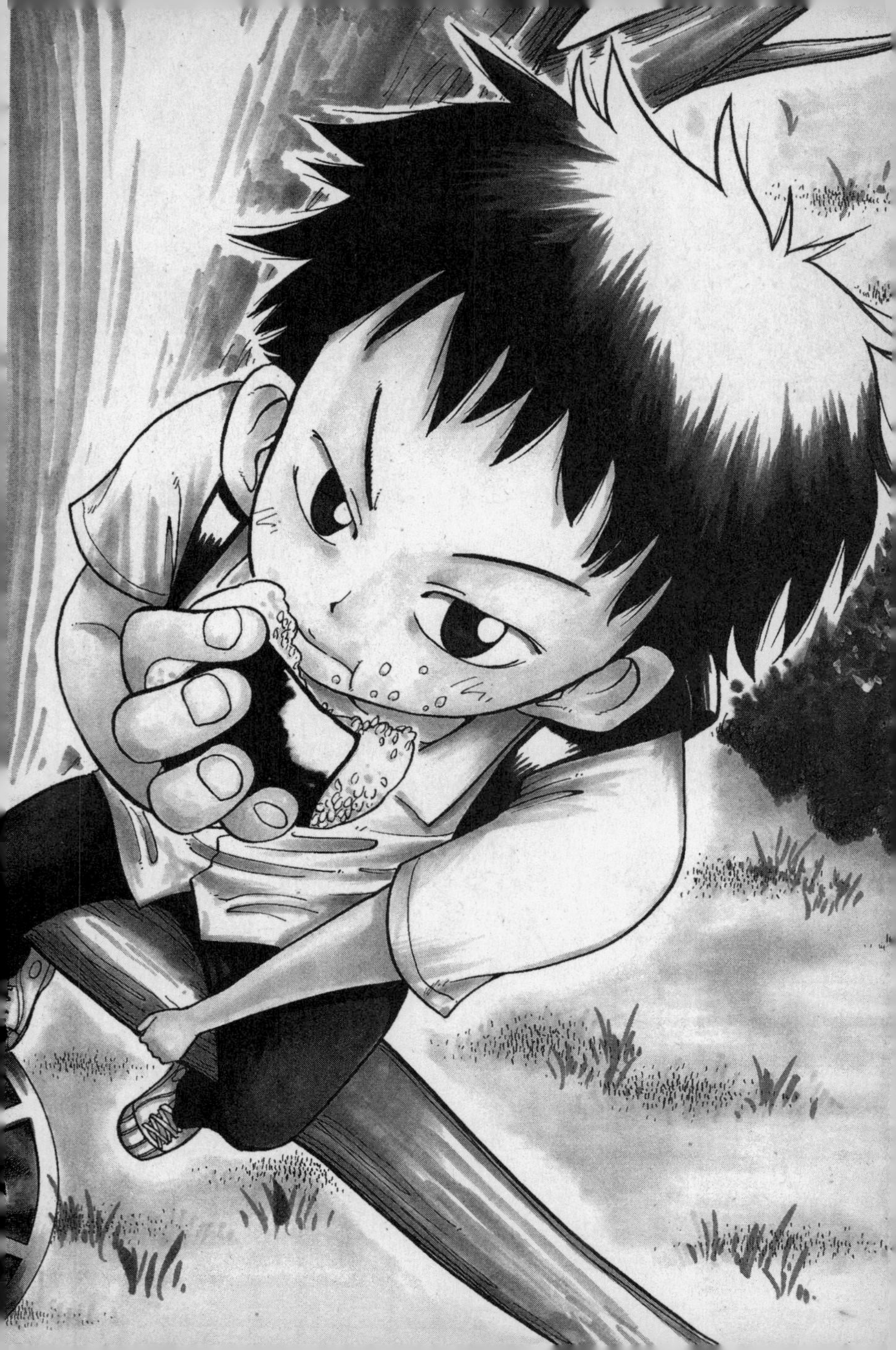

Chapter 1
Is Kosuke Ueki an Alien from Outer Space?

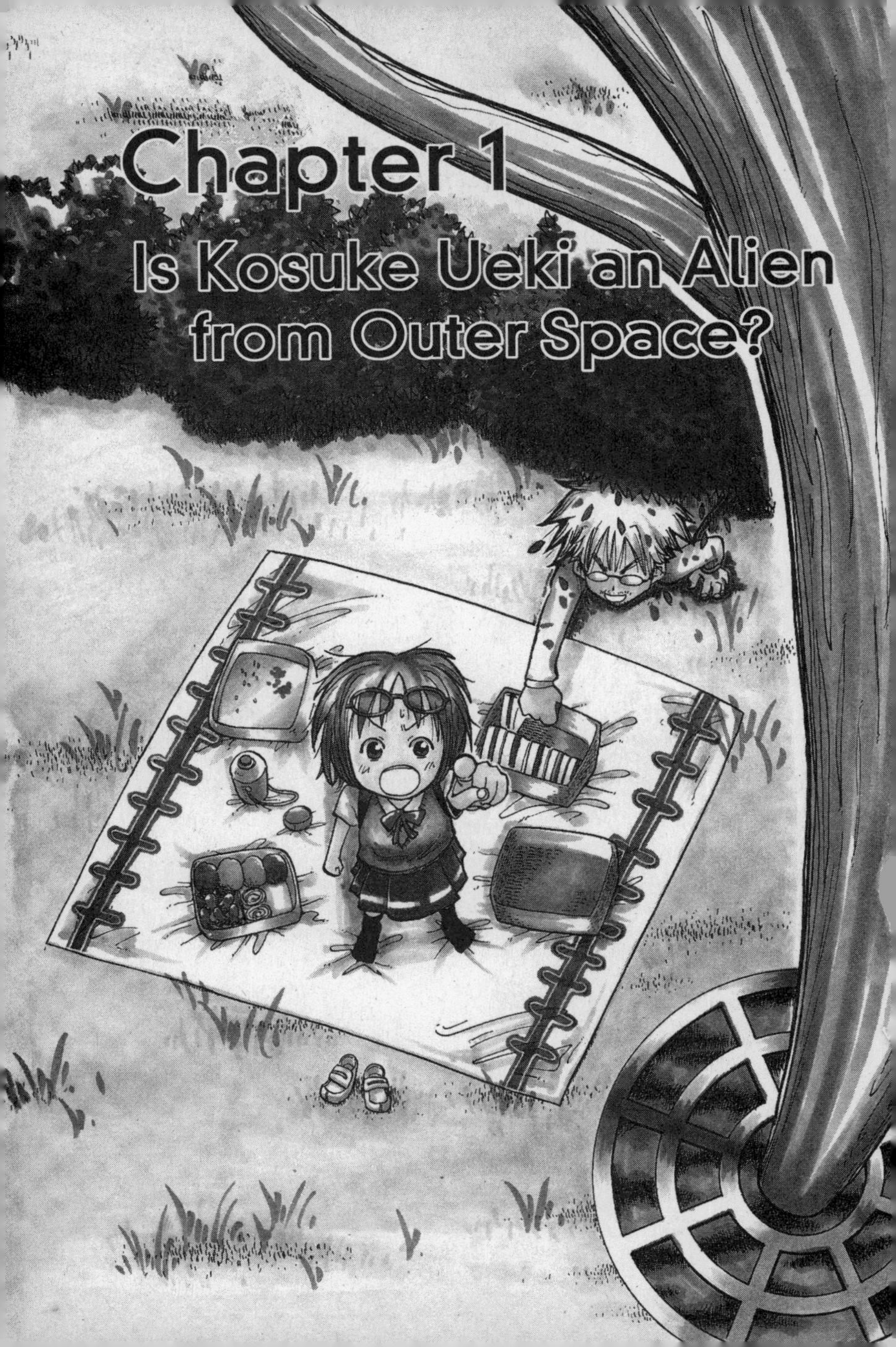

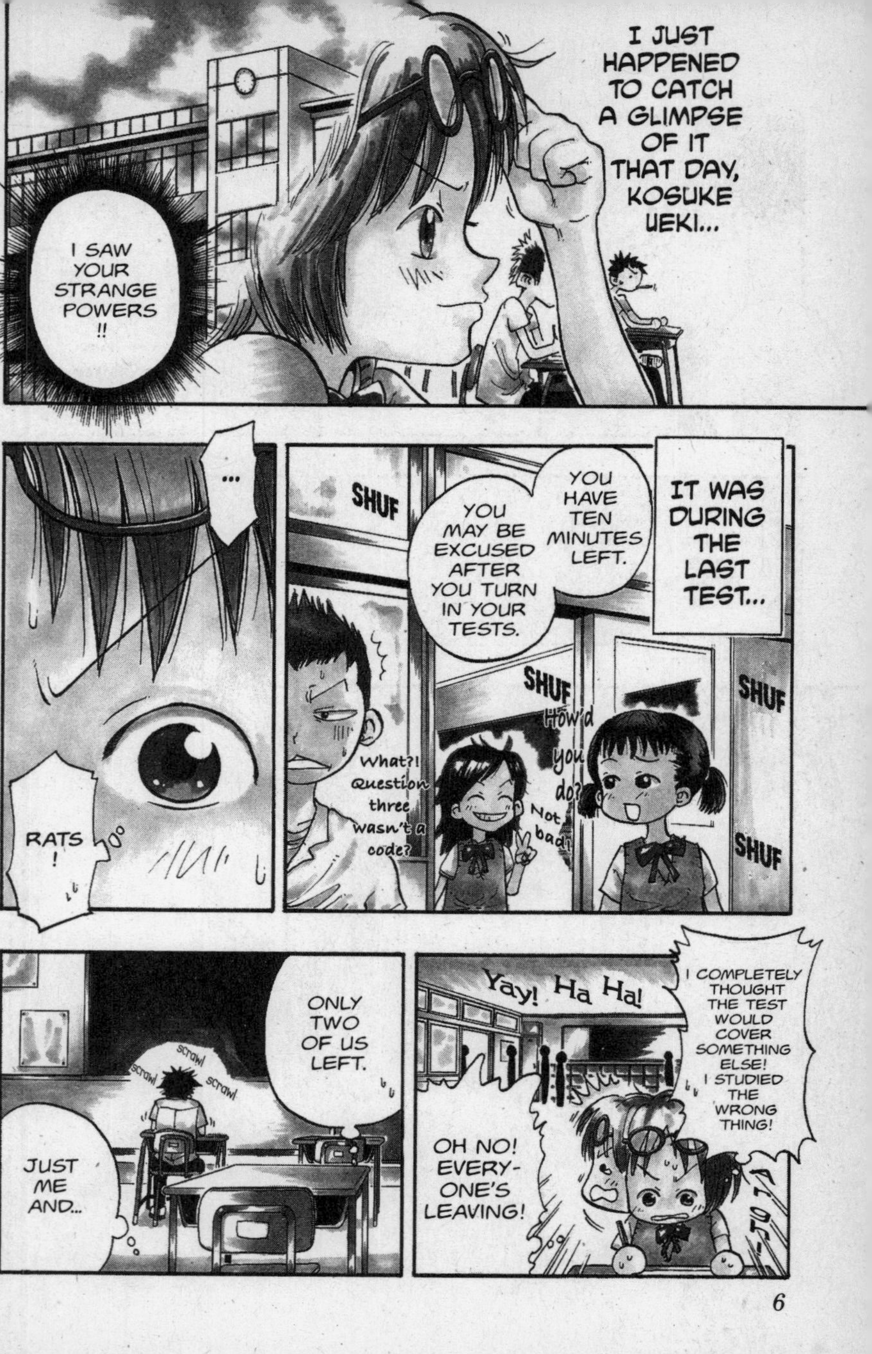
I JUST HAPPENED TO CATCH A GLIMPSE OF IT THAT DAY, KOSUKE UEKI...
I SAW YOUR STRANGE POWERS !!
IT WAS DURING THE LAST TEST...
YOU HAVE TEN MINUTES LEFT.
YOU MAY BE EXCUSED AFTER YOU TURN IN YOUR TESTS.
SHUF
SHUF
SHUF
SHUF
How'd you do?
Not bad!
What?! Question three wasn't a code?
...
RATS !
I COMPLETELY THOUGHT THE TEST WOULD COVER SOMETHING ELSE! I STUDIED THE WRONG THING!
Yay! Ha Ha!
OH NO! EVERY-ONE'S LEAVING!
ONLY TWO OF US LEFT.
scrawl scrawl scrawl
JUST ME AND...

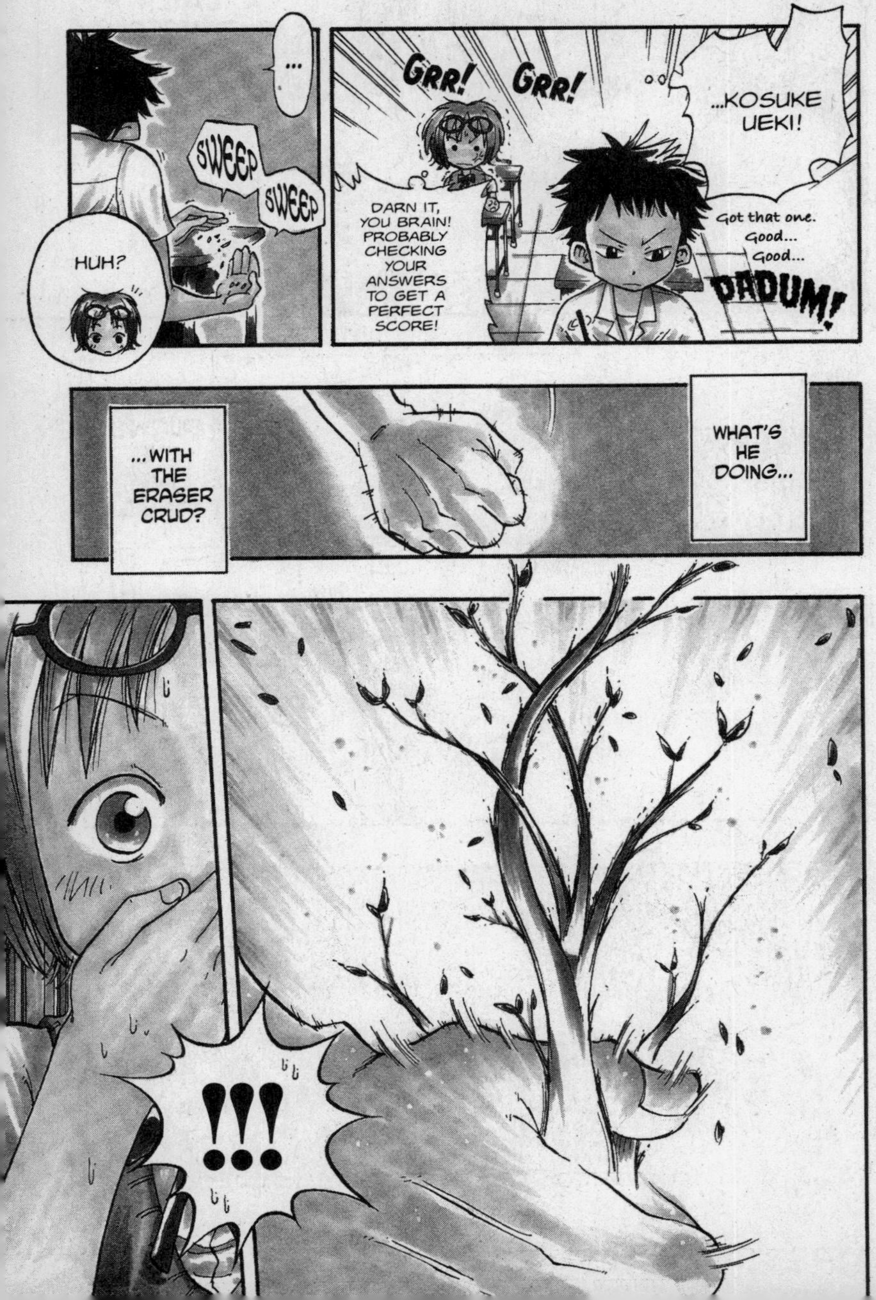
...KOSUKE UEKI!
Got that one. Good... Good...
DADUM!
GRR!
GRR!
DARN IT, YOU BRAIN! PROBABLY CHECKING YOUR ANSWERS TO GET A PERFECT SCORE!
...
SWEEP
SWEEP
HUH?
WHAT'S HE DOING...
...WITH THE ERASER CRUD?
!!!

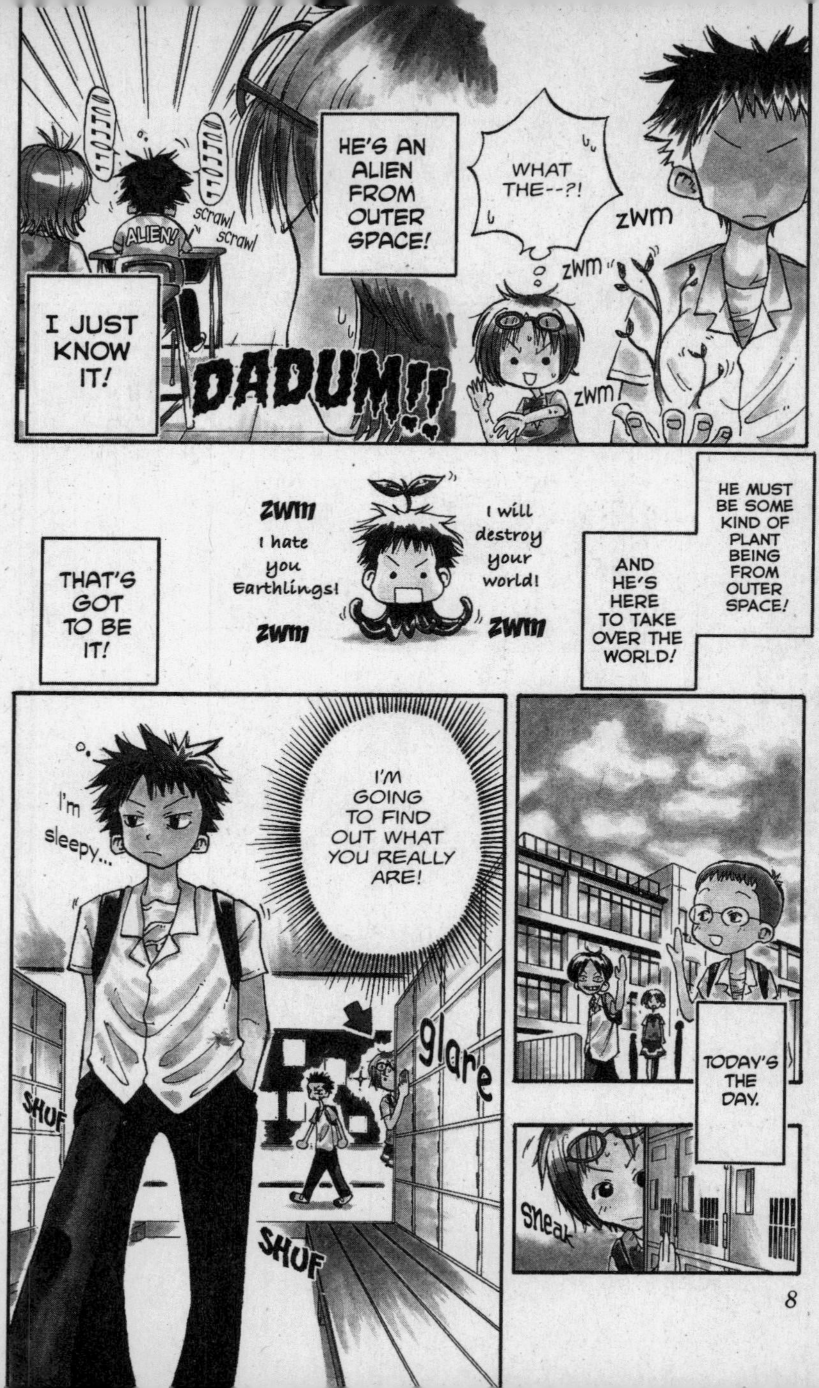
WHAT THE--?!
zwm
zwm
zwm
HE'S AN ALIEN FROM OUTER SPACE!
ALIEN!
scrawl
scrawl
I JUST KNOW IT!
DADUM!!
HE MUST BE SOME KIND OF PLANT BEING FROM OUTER SPACE!
AND HE'S HERE TO TAKE OVER THE WORLD!
zwm
I will destroy your world!
zwm
I hate you Earthlings!
zwm
zwm
THAT'S GOT TO BE IT!
TODAY'S THE DAY.
sneak
I'M GOING TO FIND OUT WHAT YOU REALLY ARE!
glare
I'm sleepy...
SHUF
SHUF

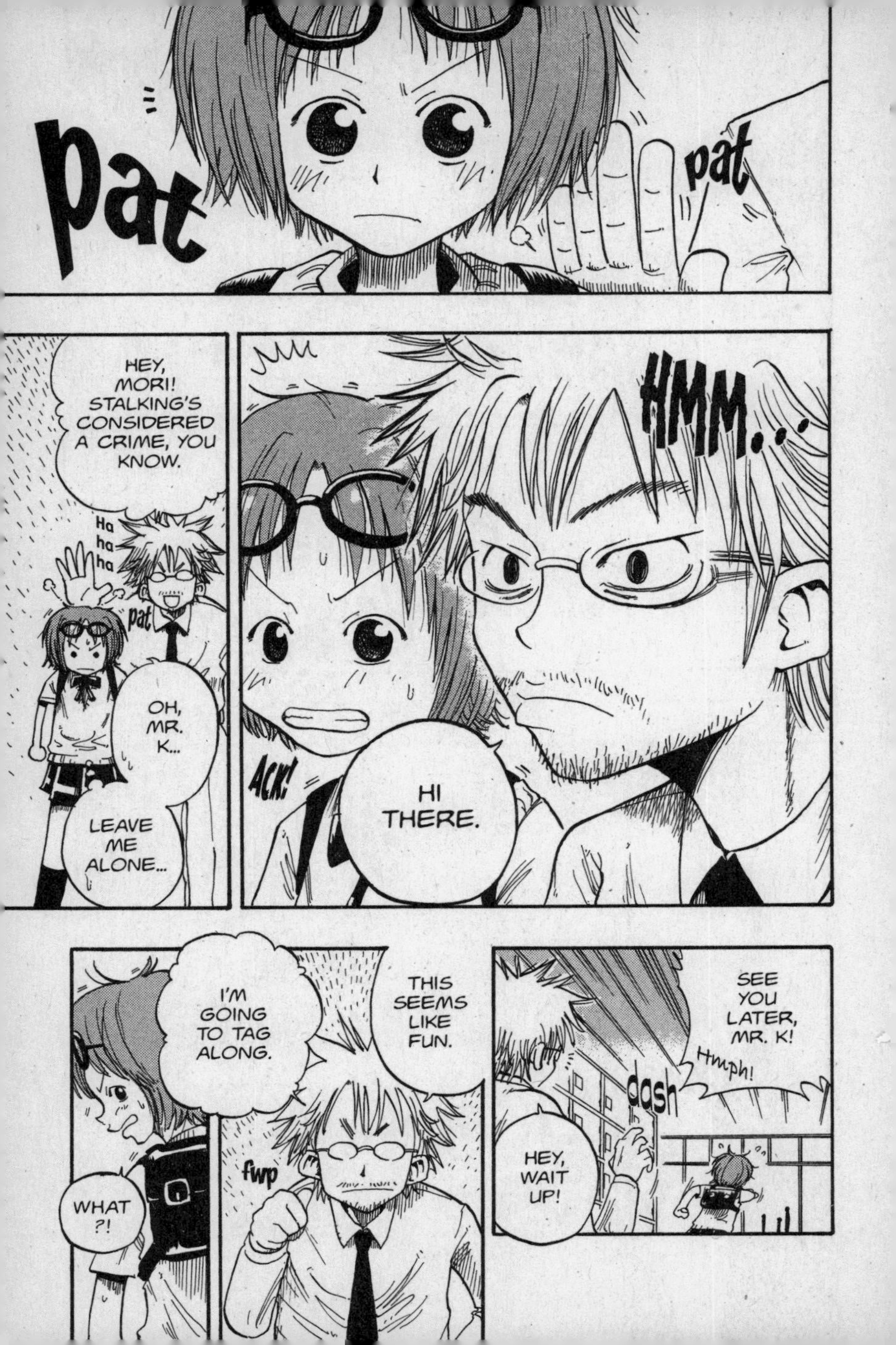
pat
pat
HMM...
ACK!
HI THERE.
HEY, MORI! STALKING'S CONSIDERED A CRIME, YOU KNOW.
Ha ha ha
pat
OH, MR. K...
LEAVE ME ALONE...
SEE YOU LATER, MR. K!
Hmph!
dash
HEY, WAIT UP!
THIS SEEMS LIKE FUN.
I'M GOING TO TAG ALONG.
fwp
WHAT?!

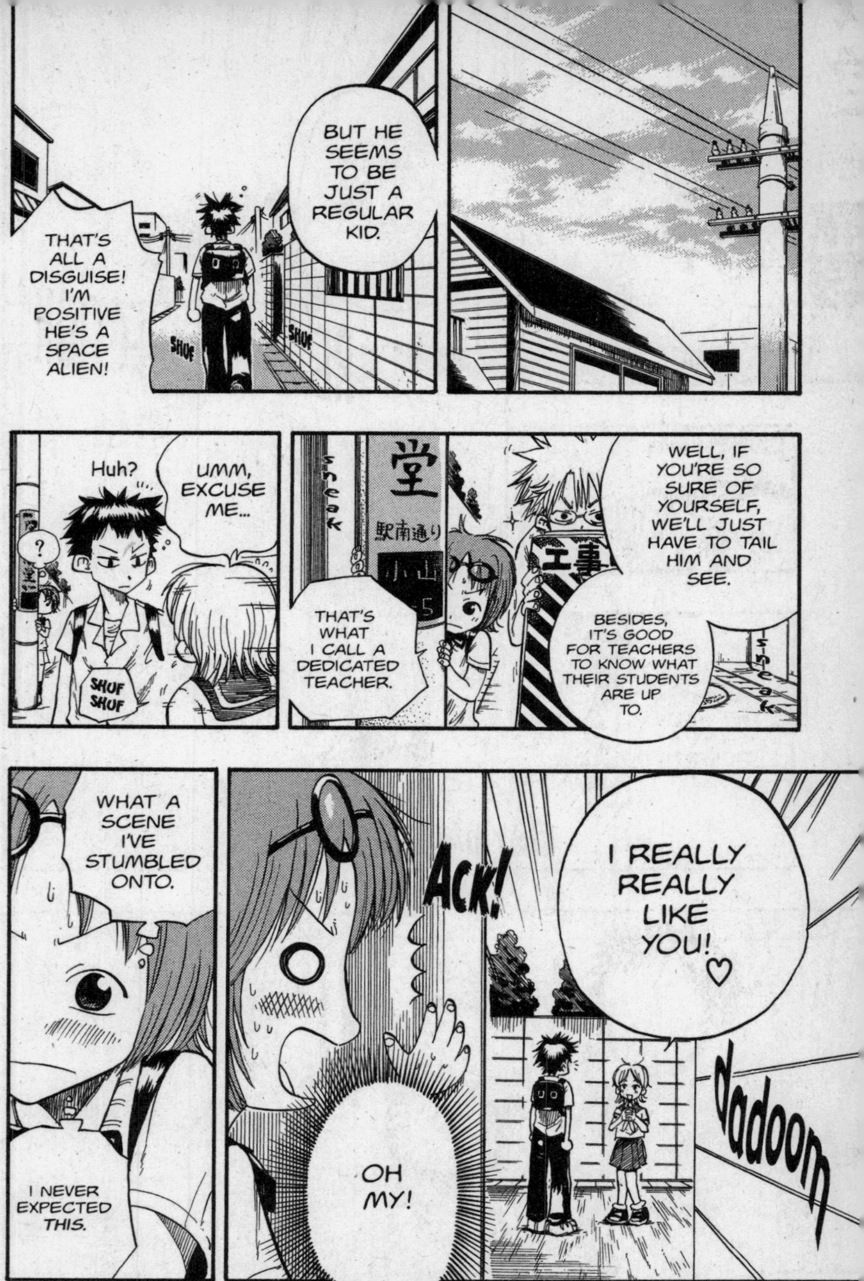
BUT HE SEEMS TO BE JUST A REGULAR KID.
THAT'S ALL A DISGUISE! I'M POSITIVE HE'S A SPACE ALIEN!
SHUF
SHUF
sneak
WELL, IF YOU'RE SO SURE OF YOURSELF, WE'LL JUST HAVE TO TAIL HIM AND SEE.
BESIDES, IT'S GOOD FOR TEACHERS TO KNOW WHAT THEIR STUDENTS ARE UP TO.
sneak
堂
駅南通り
小山
工事
THAT'S WHAT I CALL A DEDICATED TEACHER.
UMM, EXCUSE ME...
Huh?
?
SHUF SHUF
I REALLY REALLY LIKE YOU! ♥
dadoom
ACK!
OH MY!
WHAT A SCENE I'VE STUMBLED ONTO.
I NEVER EXPECTED THIS.

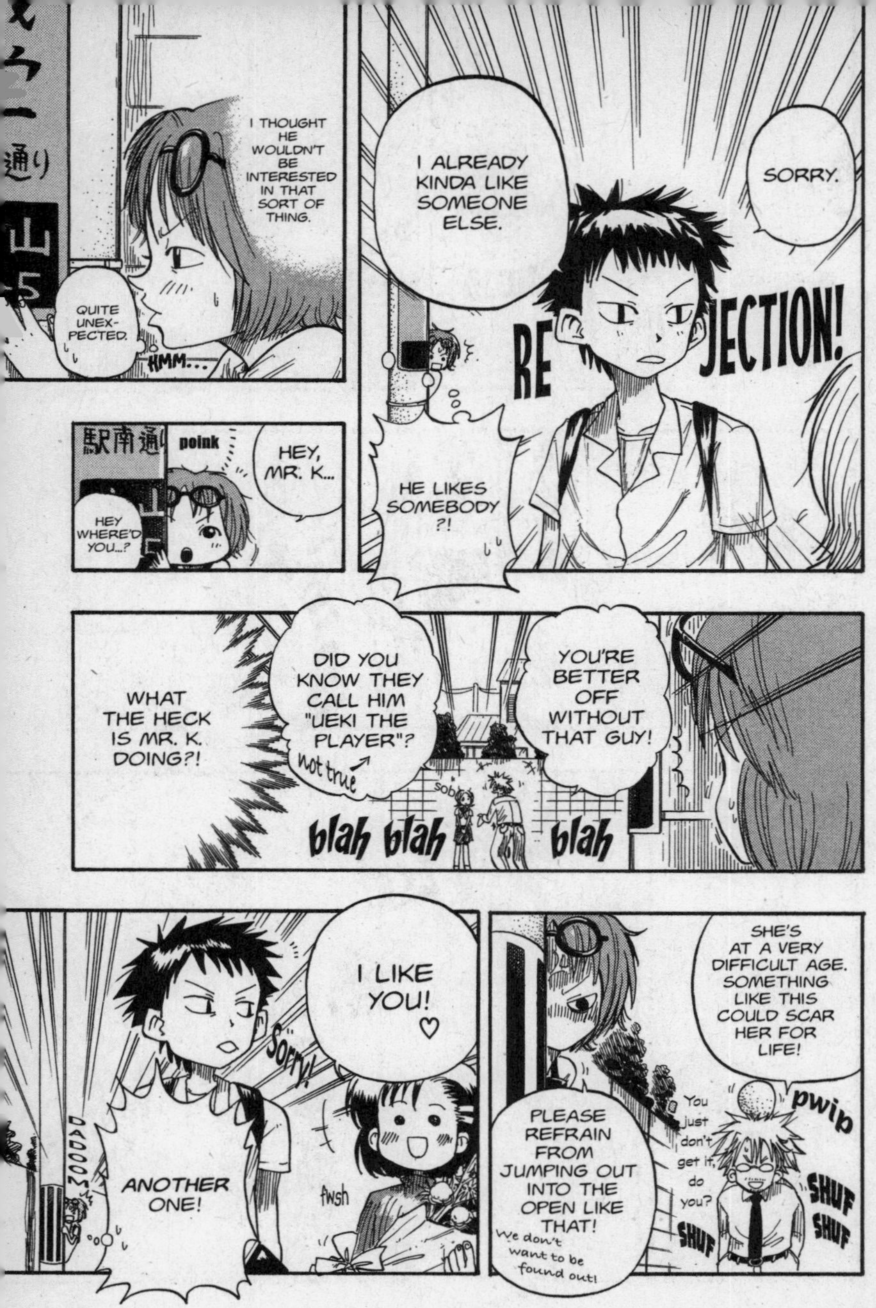
SORRY.
I ALREADY KINDA LIKE SOMEONE ELSE.
REJECTION!
HE LIKES SOMEBODY?!
I THOUGHT HE WOULDN'T BE INTERESTED IN THAT SORT OF THING.
QUITE UNEXPECTED.
HMM...
駅南通り
poink
HEY, MR. K...
HEY WHERE'D YOU...?
YOU'RE BETTER OFF WITHOUT THAT GUY!
DID YOU KNOW THEY CALL HIM "UEKI THE PLAYER"?
not true
sob
blah blah blah
WHAT THE HECK IS MR. K. DOING?!
SHE'S AT A VERY DIFFICULT AGE. SOMETHING LIKE THIS COULD SCAR HER FOR LIFE!
pwip
You just don't get it, do you?
PLEASE REFRAIN FROM JUMPING OUT INTO THE OPEN LIKE THAT!
We don't want to be found out!
SHUF SHUF SHUF
I LIKE YOU! ♥
Sorry!
ANOTHER ONE!
DADOOOM
fwsh

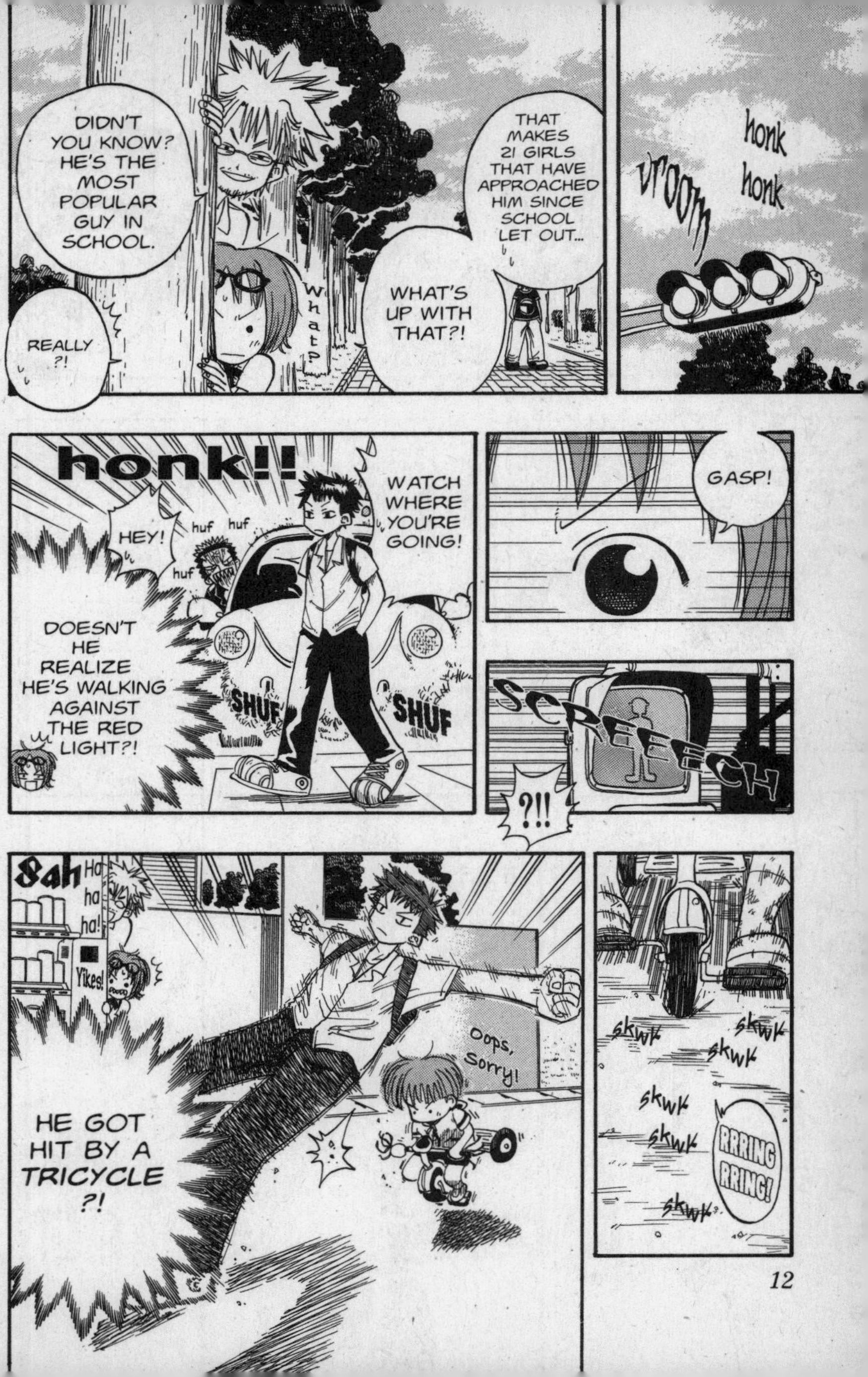

honk
honk
vroom
THAT MAKES 21 GIRLS THAT HAVE APPROACHED HIM SINCE SCHOOL LET OUT...
WHAT'S UP WITH THAT?!
What?
DIDN'T YOU KNOW? HE'S THE MOST POPULAR GUY IN SCHOOL.
REALLY?!
GASP!
SCREEECH
?!!
honk!!
WATCH WHERE YOU'RE GOING!
HEY!
huf huf
huf
DOESN'T HE REALIZE HE'S WALKING AGAINST THE RED LIGHT?!
SHUF
SHUF
skwk
skwk
skwk
skwk
skwk
skwk
RRRING RRING!
Sah
Ha ha ha!
Yikes!
Oops, Sorry!
HE GOT HIT BY A TRICYCLE?!

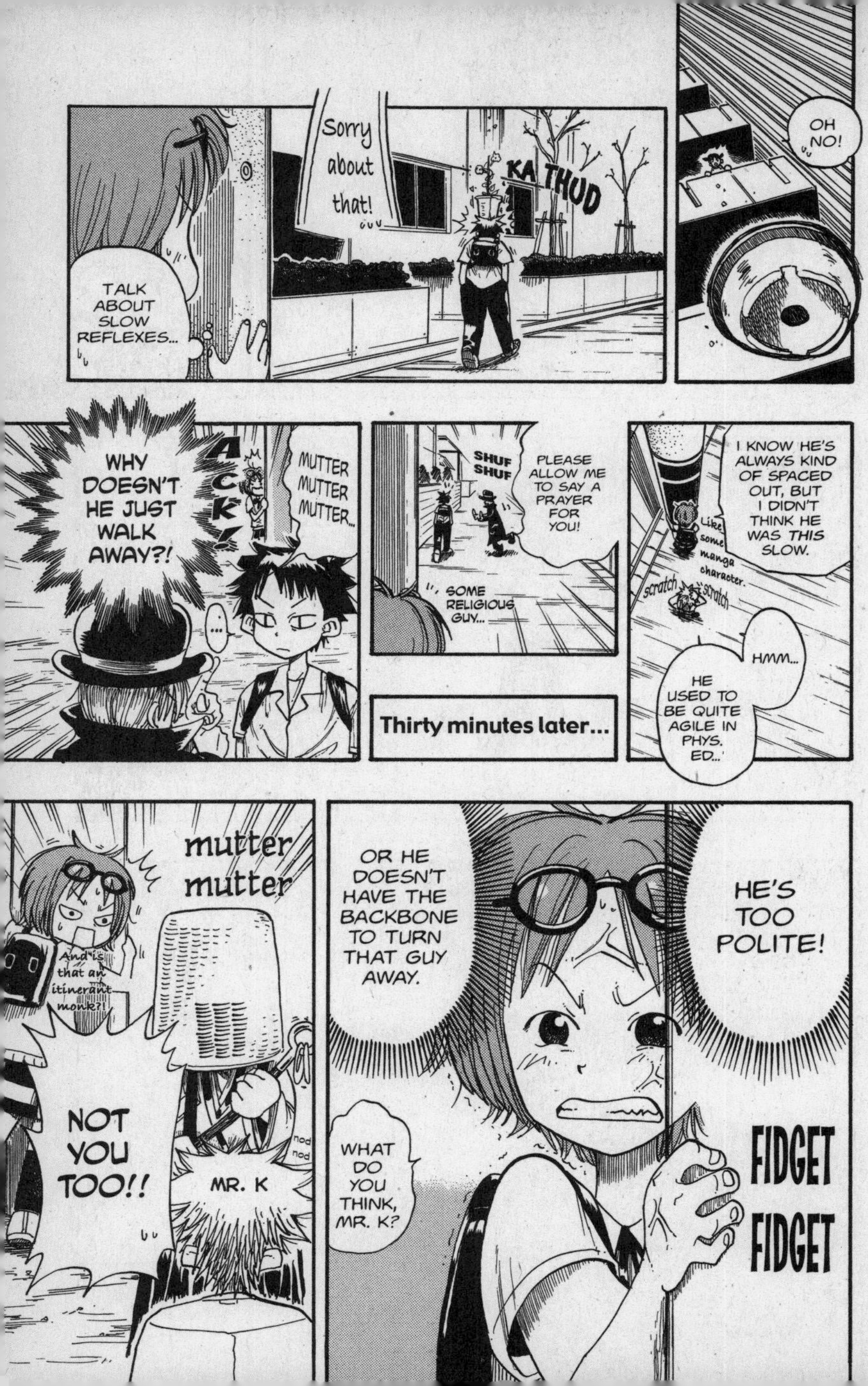
OH NO!
Sorry about that!
KA THUD
TALK ABOUT SLOW REFLEXES...
I KNOW HE'S ALWAYS KIND OF SPACED OUT, BUT I DIDN'T THINK HE WAS THIS SLOW.
Like some manga character.
scratch scratch
HMM...
HE USED TO BE QUITE AGILE IN PHYS. ED...
SHUF SHUF
PLEASE ALLOW ME TO SAY A PRAYER FOR YOU!
SOME RELIGIOUS GUY...
Thirty minutes later...
MUTTER MUTTER MUTTER...
ACK!
WHY DOESN'T HE JUST WALK AWAY?!
...
HE'S TOO POLITE!
OR HE DOESN'T HAVE THE BACKBONE TO TURN THAT GUY AWAY.
FIDGET FIDGET
WHAT DO YOU THINK, MR. K?
mutter mutter
And is that an itinerant monk?!
NOT YOU TOO!!
nod nod
MR. K

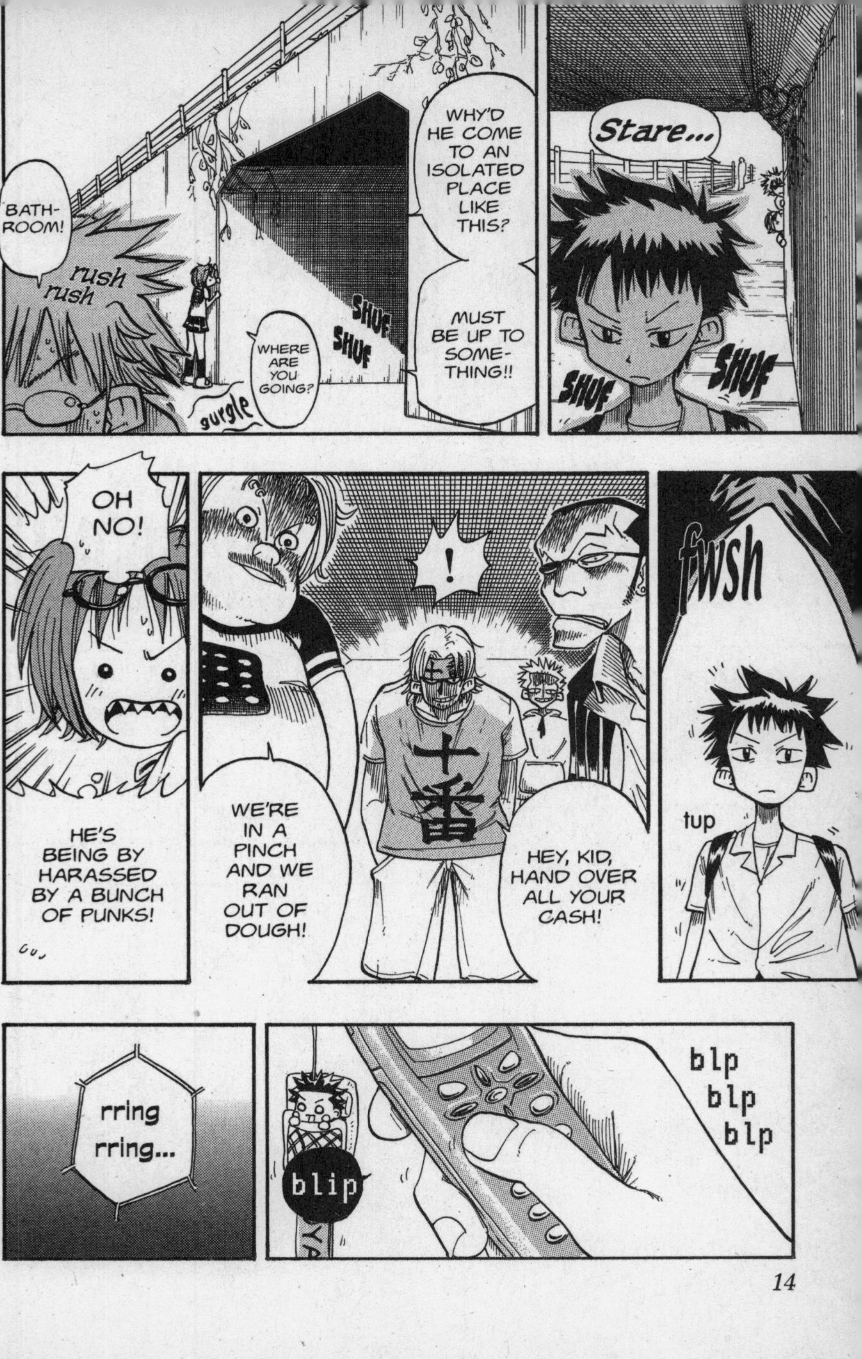
Stare...
SHUF
SHUF
WHY'D HE COME TO AN ISOLATED PLACE LIKE THIS?
MUST BE UP TO SOME-THING!!
SHUF
SHUF
WHERE ARE YOU GOING?
BATH-ROOM!
rush rush
gurgle
fwsh
tup
!
十番
HEY, KID, HAND OVER ALL YOUR CASH!
WE'RE IN A PINCH AND WE RAN OUT OF DOUGH!
OH NO!
HE'S BEING BY HARASSED BY A BUNCH OF PUNKS!
blp
blp
blp
blip
rring
rring...

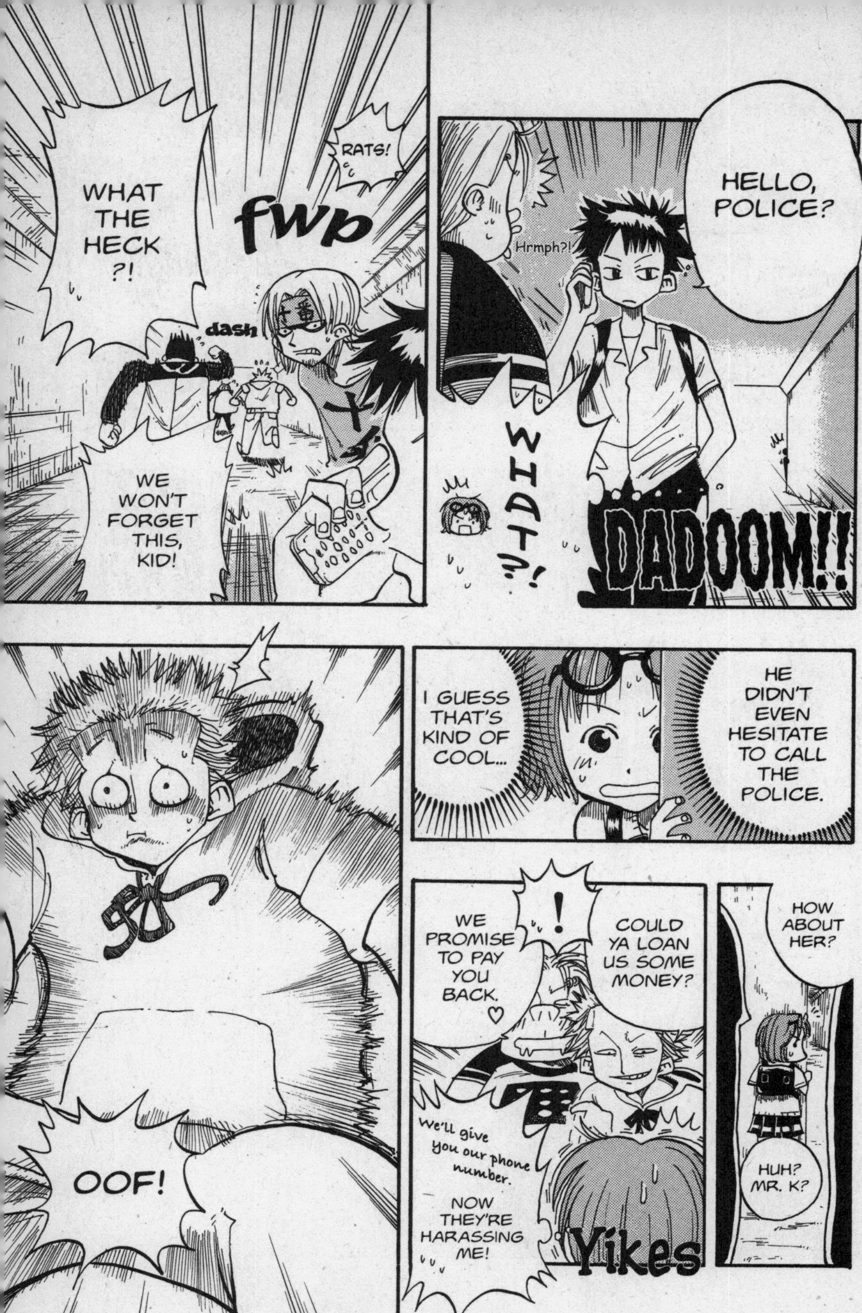
HELLO, POLICE?
Hrmph?!
WHAT?!
DADOOM!!
RATS!
fwp
WHAT THE HECK ?!
dash
WE WON'T FORGET THIS, KID!
HE DIDN'T EVEN HESITATE TO CALL THE POLICE.
I GUESS THAT'S KIND OF COOL...
HOW ABOUT HER?
HUH? MR. K?
!
COULD YA LOAN US SOME MONEY?
WE PROMISE TO PAY YOU BACK. ♡
We'll give you our phone number.
NOW THEY'RE HARASSING ME!
Yikes
OOF!

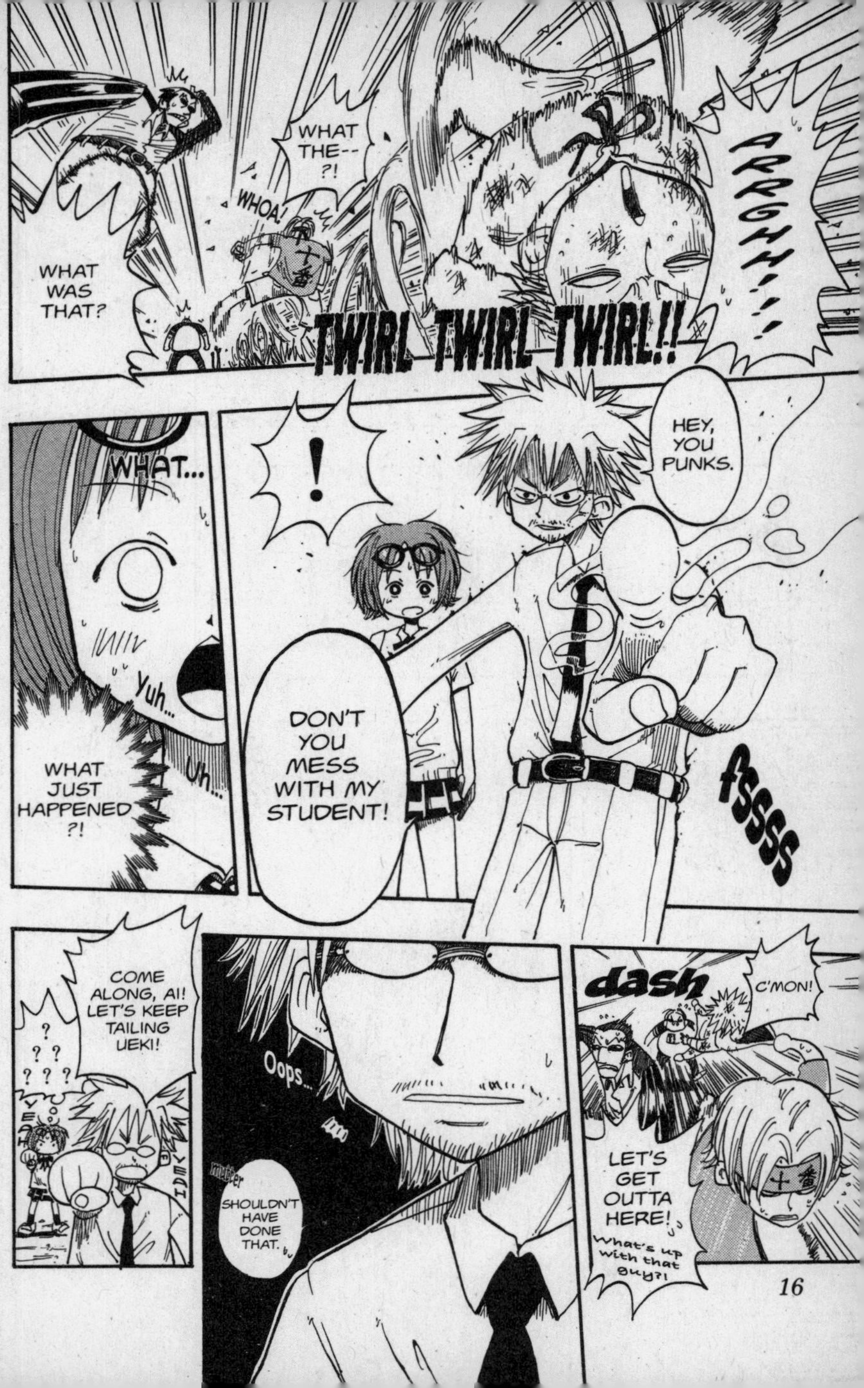
ARRGHH!!!
WHAT THE-- ?!
WHOA!
TWIRL TWIRL TWIRL!!
WHAT WAS THAT?
HEY, YOU PUNKS.
!
DON'T YOU MESS WITH MY STUDENT!
fssss
WHAT...
Yuh...
Uh...
WHAT JUST HAPPENED ?!
C'MON!
dash
LET'S GET OUTTA HERE!
What's up with that guy?!
Oops...
mutter
SHOULDN'T HAVE DONE THAT.
COME ALONG, AI! LET'S KEEP TAILING UEKI!
? ? ? ? ? ?
YEAH
YEAH

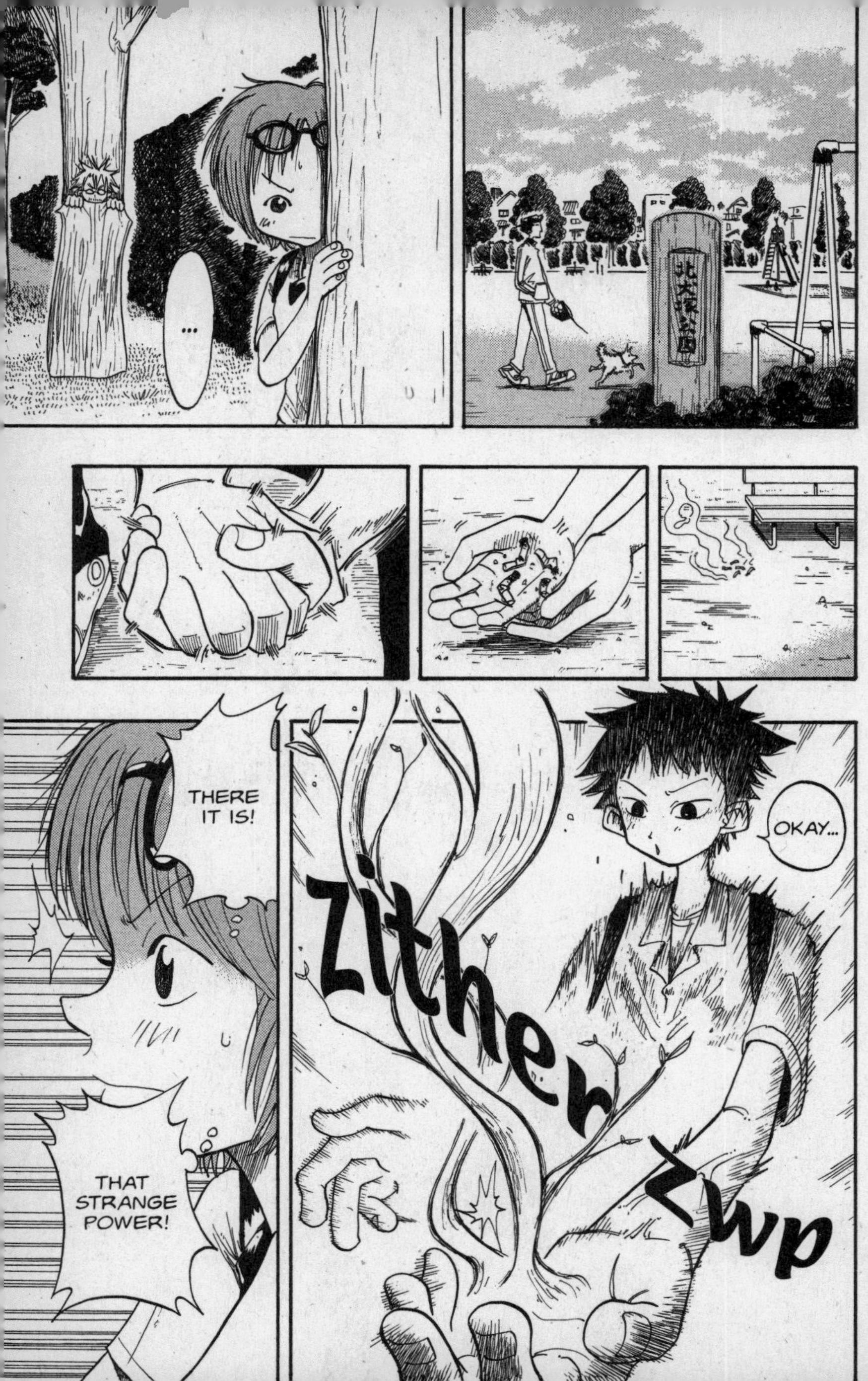
...
OKAY...
Zither
Zwp
THERE IT IS!
THAT STRANGE POWER!

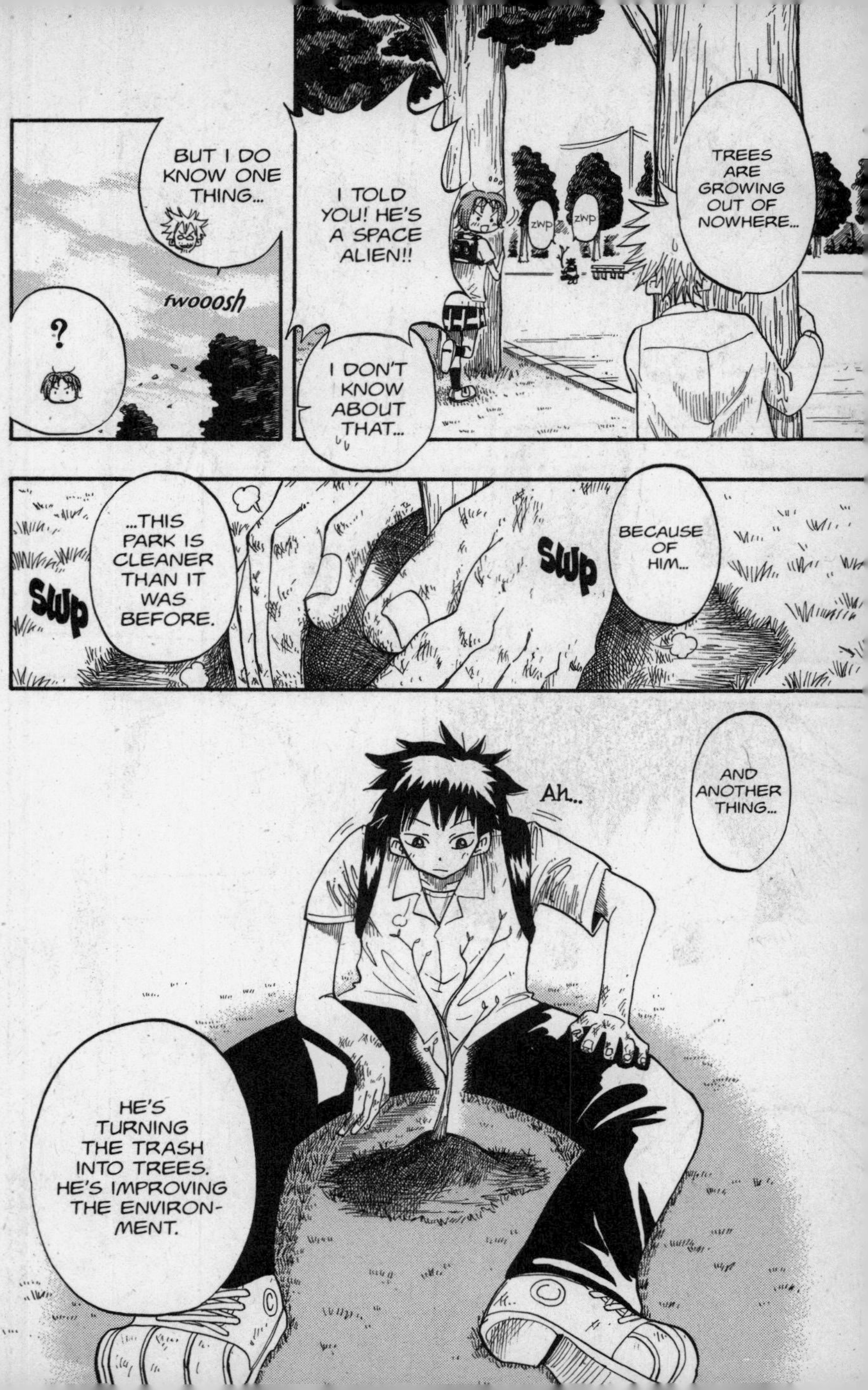
TREES ARE GROWING OUT OF NOWHERE...
zwp
zwp
I TOLD YOU! HE'S A SPACE ALIEN!!
I DON'T KNOW ABOUT THAT...
BUT I DO KNOW ONE THING...
fwooosh
?
BECAUSE OF HIM...
SWP
...THIS PARK IS CLEANER THAN IT WAS BEFORE.
SWP
AND ANOTHER THING...
Ah...
HE'S TURNING THE TRASH INTO TREES. HE'S IMPROVING THE ENVIRON-MENT.

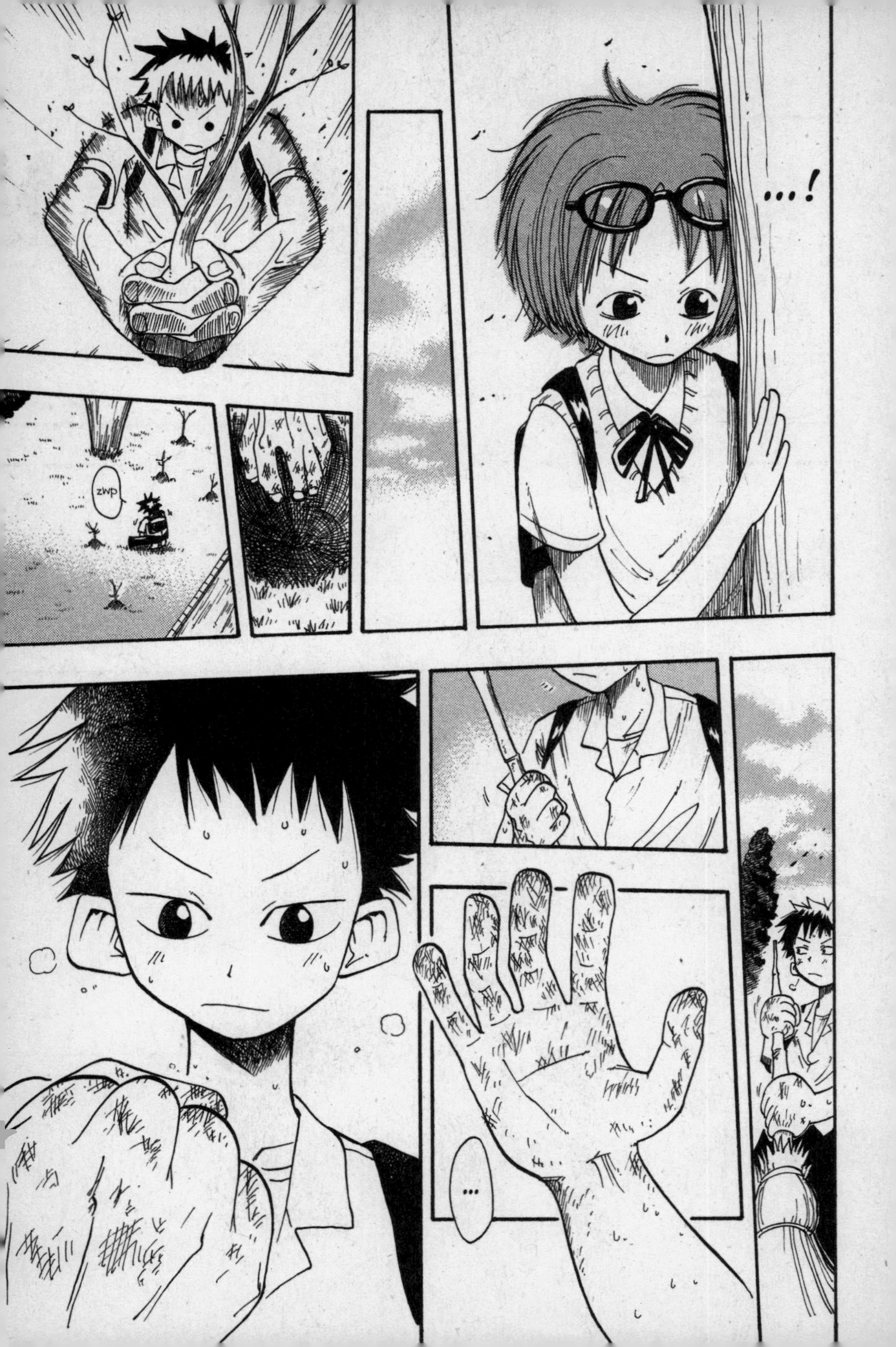
...!
zwp
...

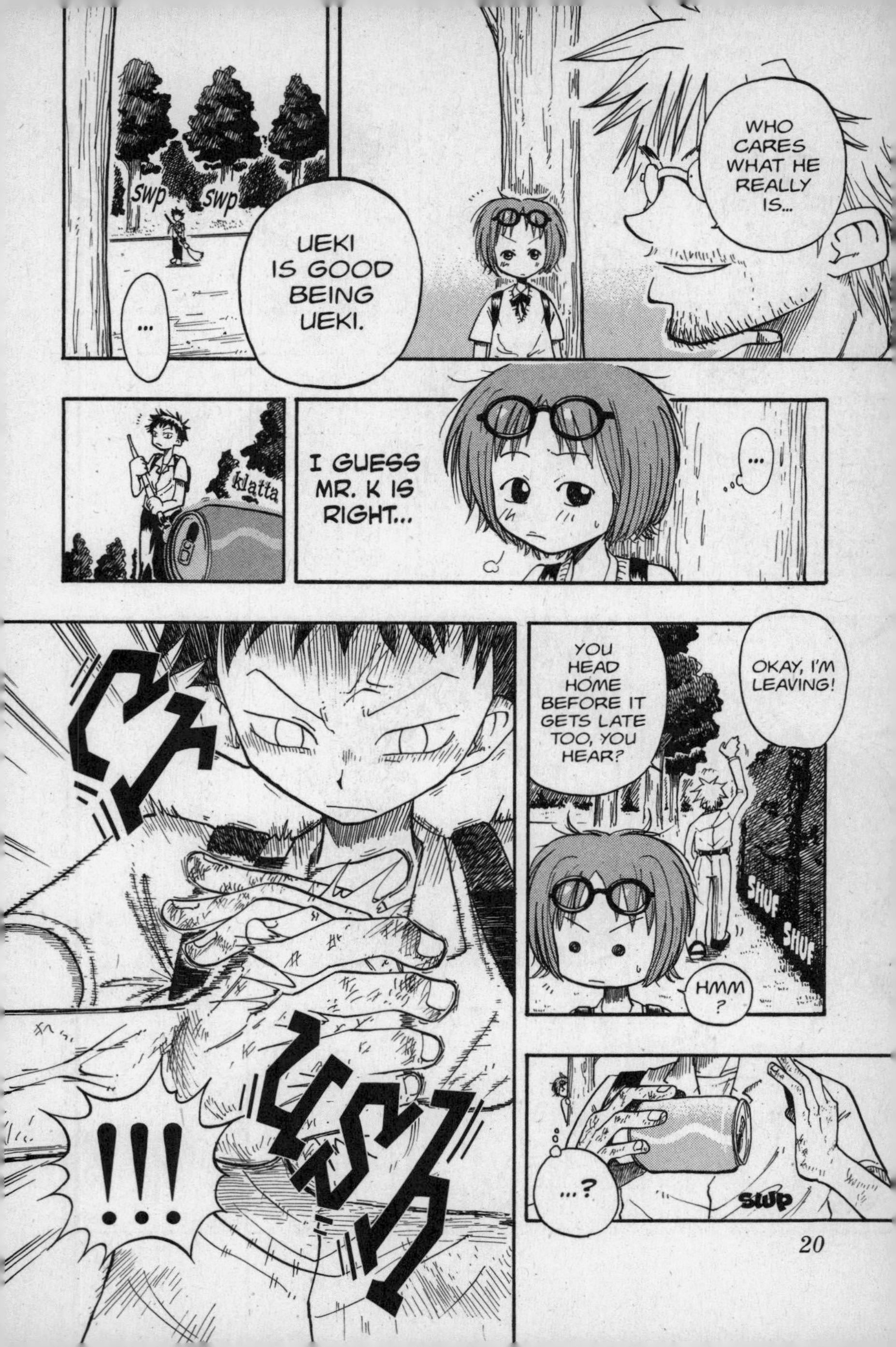
WHO CARES WHAT HE REALLY IS...
UEKI IS GOOD BEING UEKI.
swp
swp
...
...
I GUESS MR. K IS RIGHT...
klatta
OKAY, I'M LEAVING!
YOU HEAD HOME BEFORE IT GETS LATE TOO, YOU HEAR?
SHUF
SHUF
HMM ?
SLUP
...?
!!!

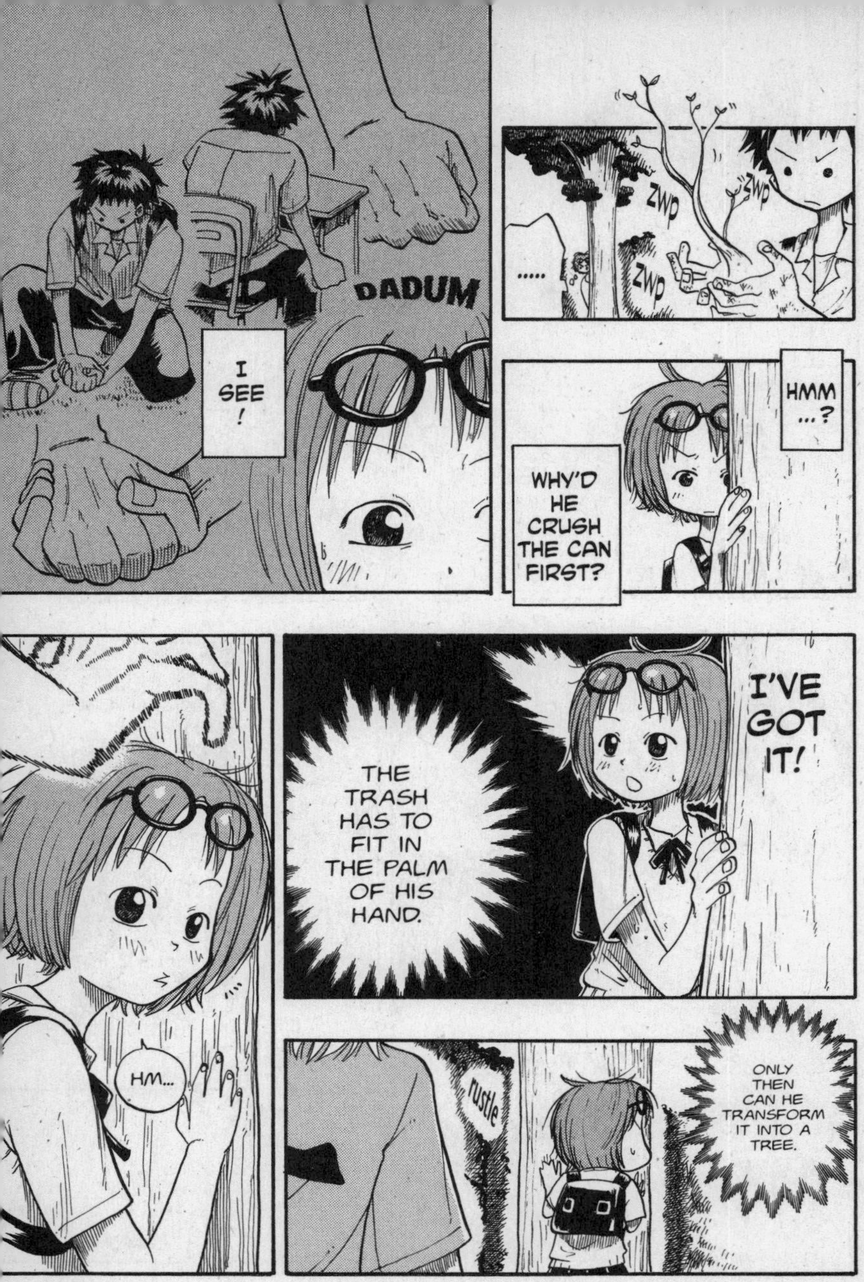
ZWP
ZWP
ZWP
.....
HMM ...?
WHY'D HE CRUSH THE CAN FIRST?
DADUM
I SEE!
I'VE GOT IT!
THE TRASH HAS TO FIT IN THE PALM OF HIS HAND.
ONLY THEN CAN HE TRANSFORM IT INTO A TREE.
rustle
HM...

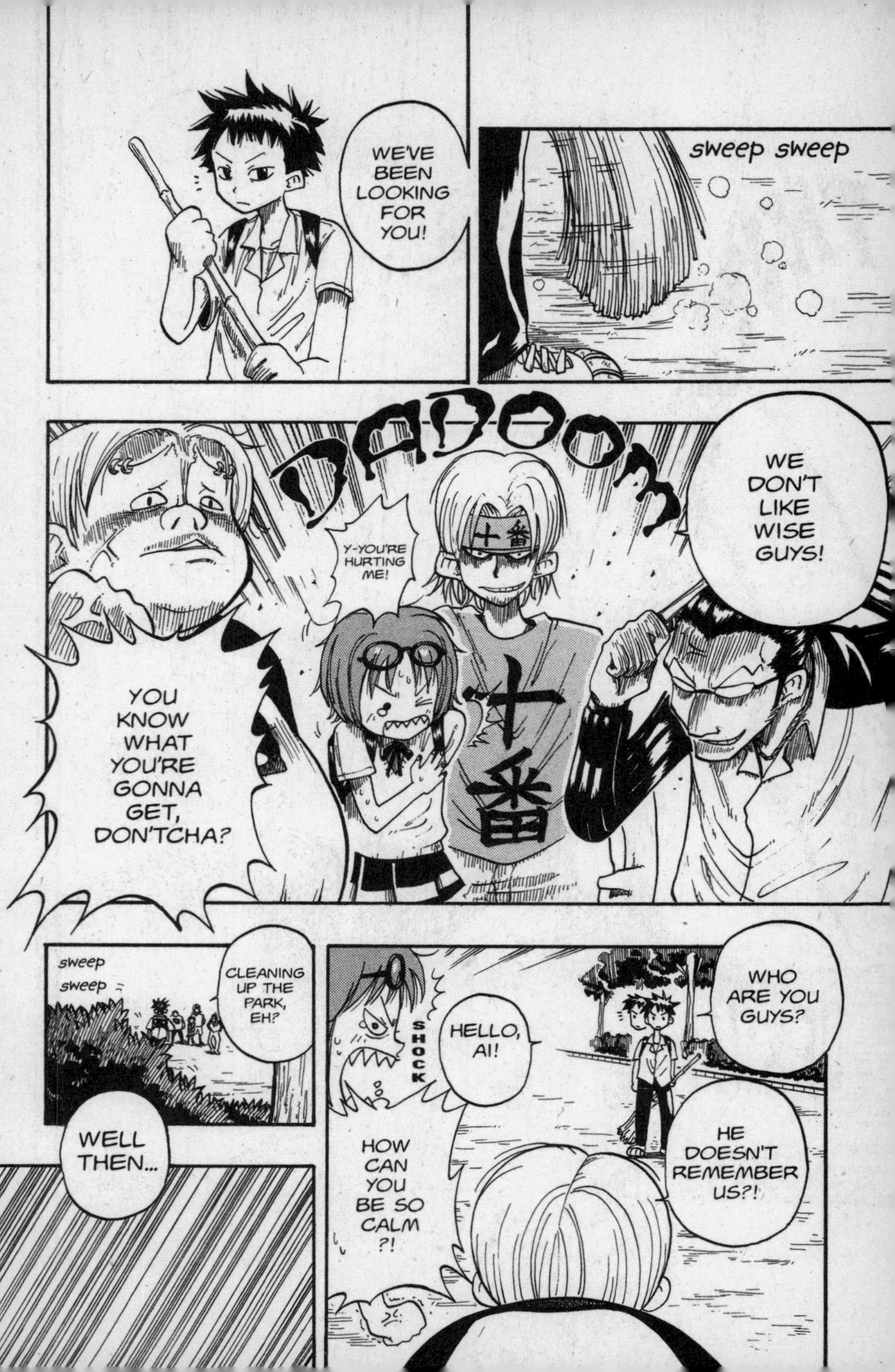
sweep sweep
WE'VE BEEN LOOKING FOR YOU!
DADOOM
WE DON'T LIKE WISE GUYS!
Y-YOU'RE HURTING ME!
YOU KNOW WHAT YOU'RE GONNA GET, DON'TCHA?
WHO ARE YOU GUYS?
HE DOESN'T REMEMBER US?!
HELLO, AI!
SHOCK
HOW CAN YOU BE SO CALM?!
sweep sweep
CLEANING UP THE PARK, EH?
WELL THEN...

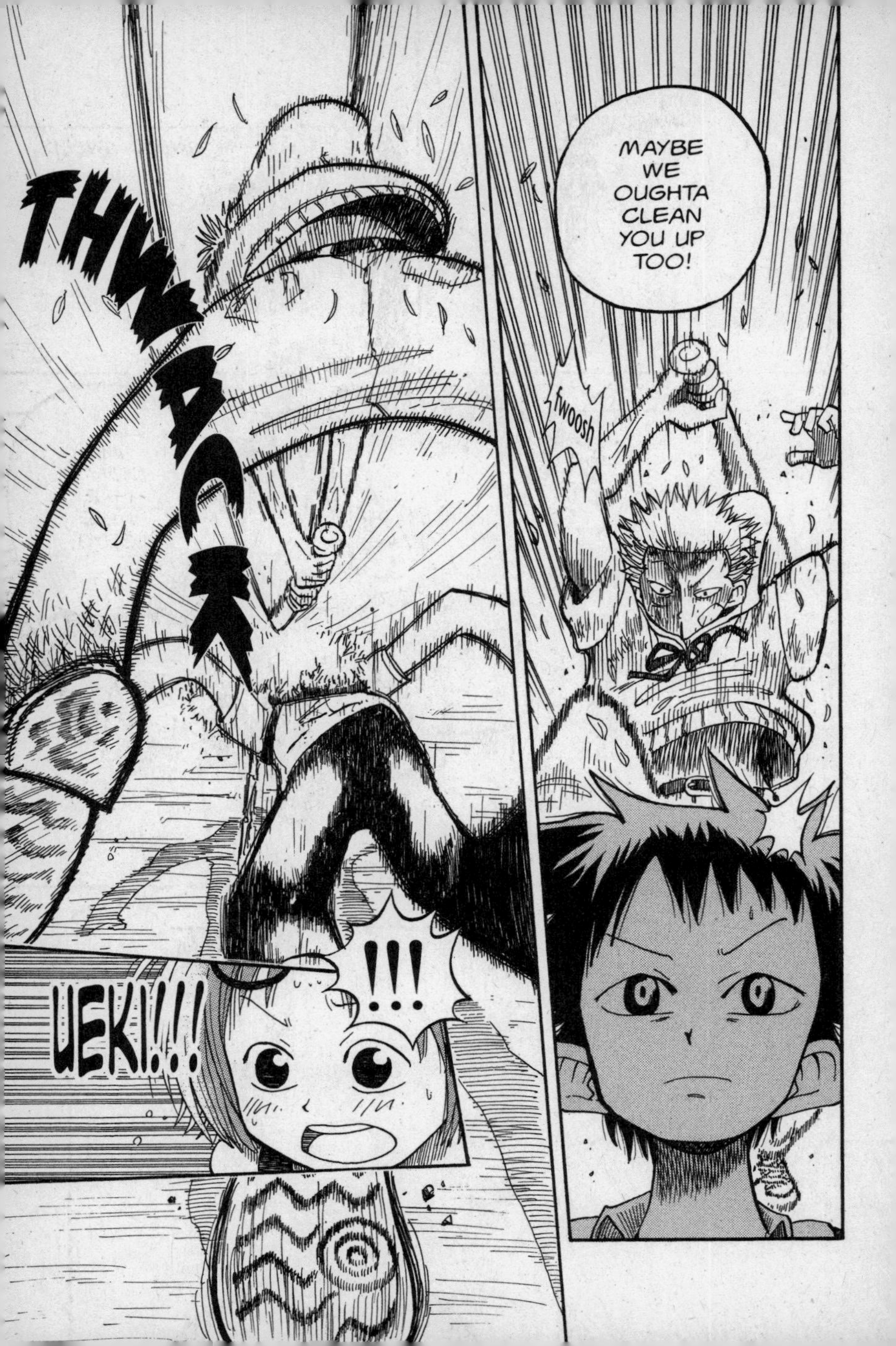
MAYBE WE OUGHTA CLEAN YOU UP TOO!
fwoosh
THWACK
!!!
UEKI!!!

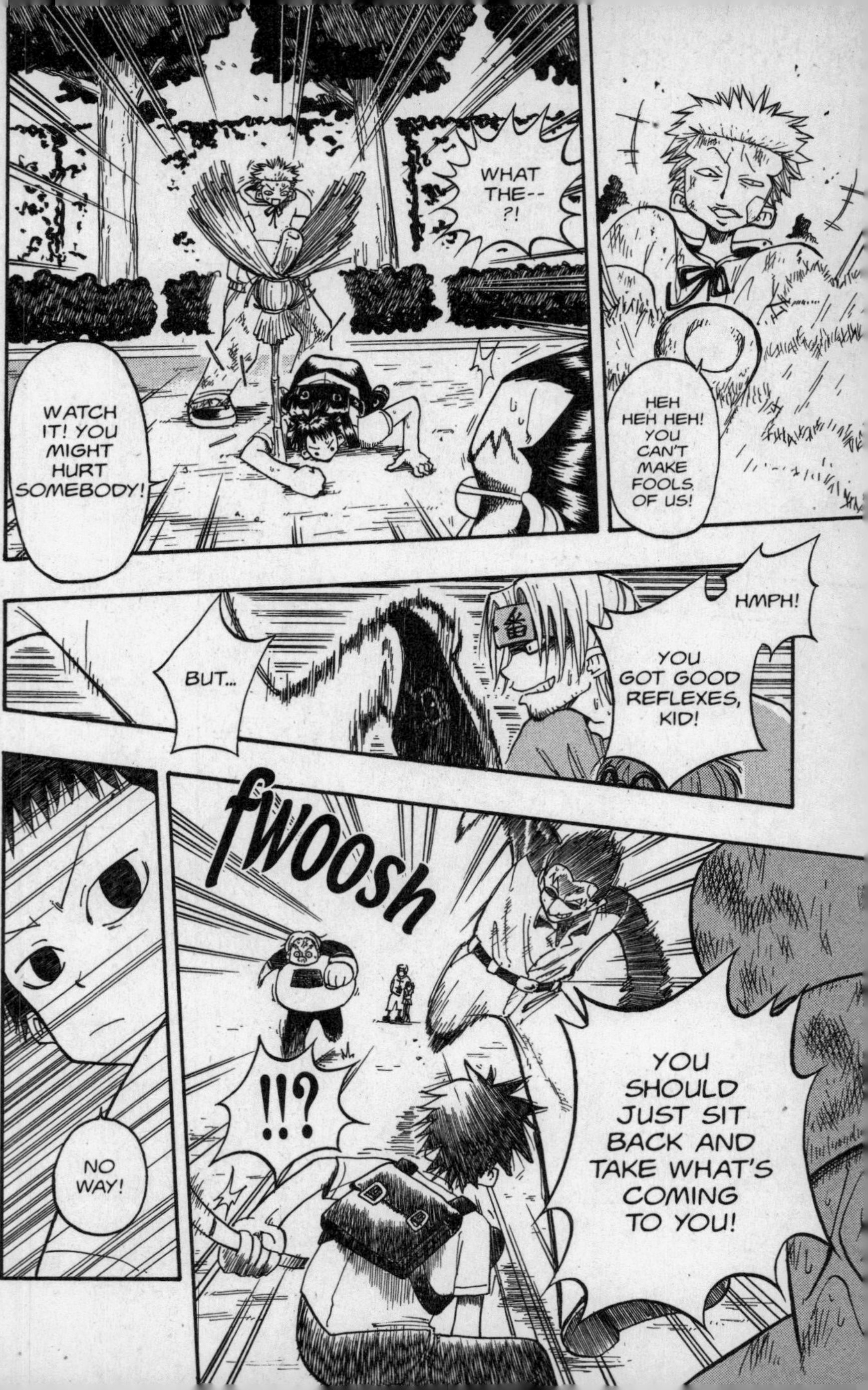
HEH HEH HEH! YOU CAN'T MAKE FOOLS OF US!
WHAT THE-- ?!
WATCH IT! YOU MIGHT HURT SOMEBODY!
HMPH!
YOU GOT GOOD REFLEXES, KID!
BUT...
fwoosh
YOU SHOULD JUST SIT BACK AND TAKE WHAT'S COMING TO YOU!
!!?
NO WAY!

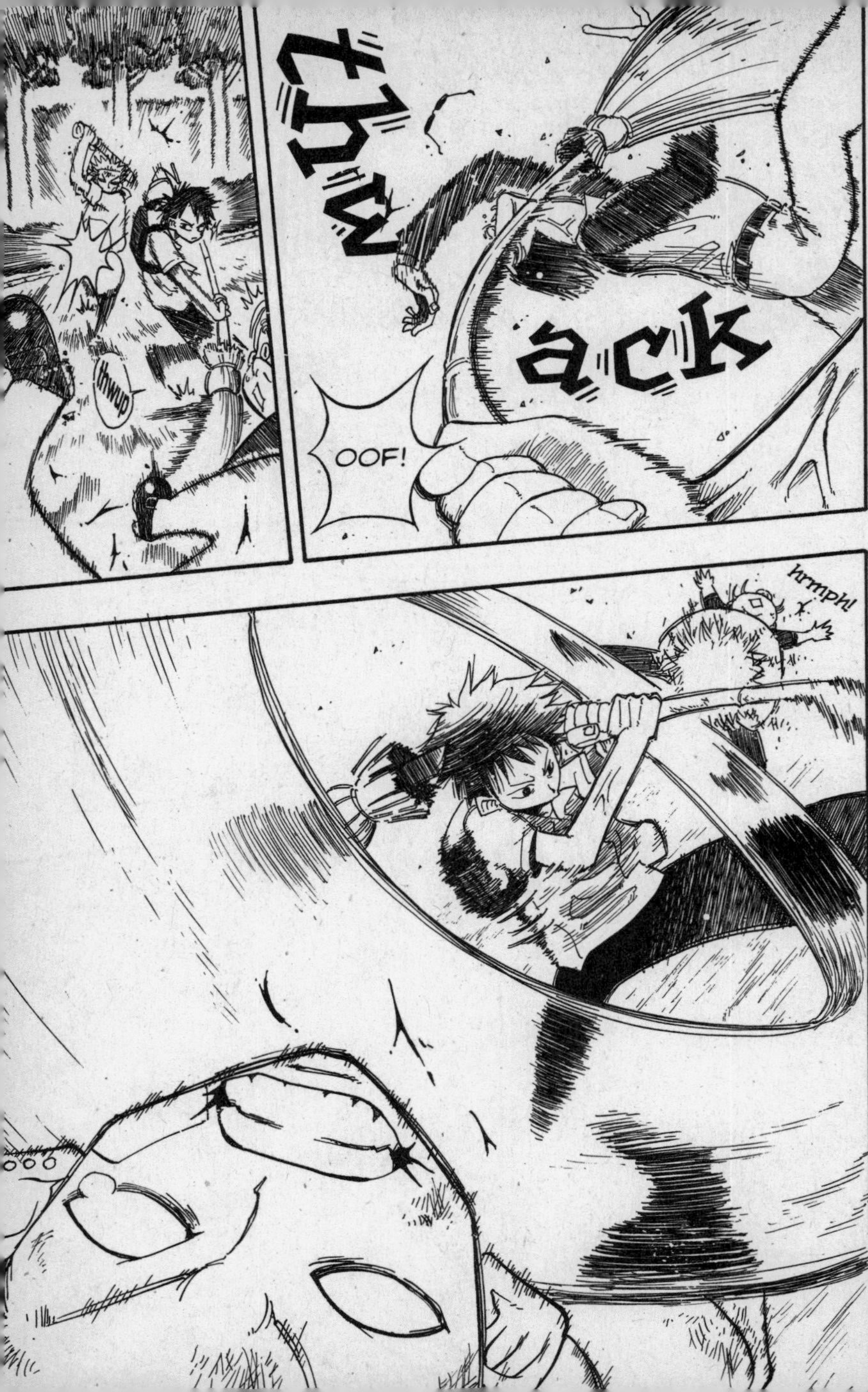
thw
ack
OOF!
thwup
hrmph!

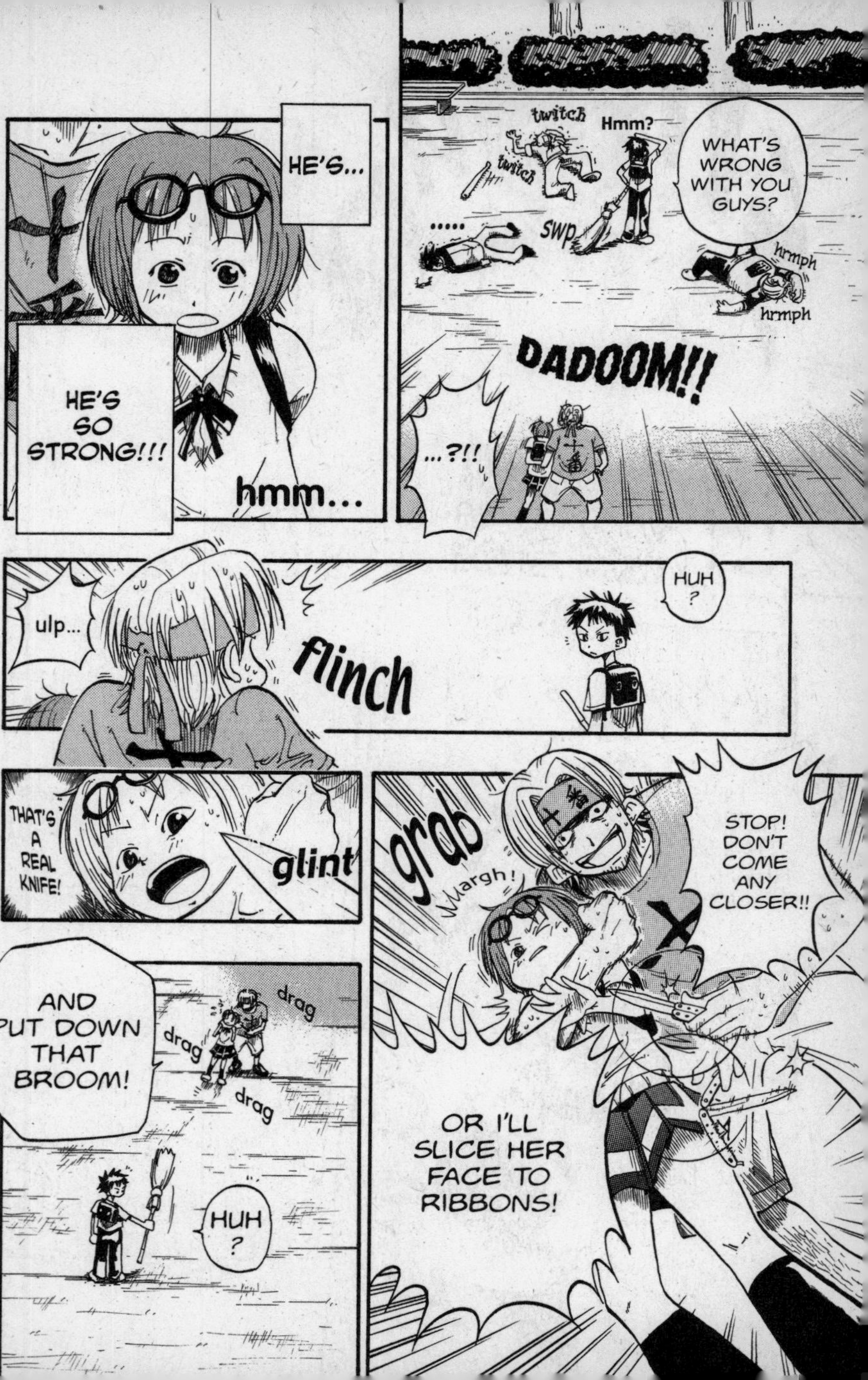

twitch
Hmm?
twitch
.....
swp
WHAT'S WRONG WITH YOU GUYS?
hrmph
hrmph
DADOOM!!
...?!!
HE'S...
HE'S SO STRONG!!!
hmm...
HUH?
flinch
ulp...
grab
urargh!
STOP! DON'T COME ANY CLOSER!!
OR I'LL SLICE HER FACE TO RIBBONS!
THAT'S A REAL KNIFE!
glint
AND PUT DOWN THAT BROOM!
drag
drag
drag
HUH?

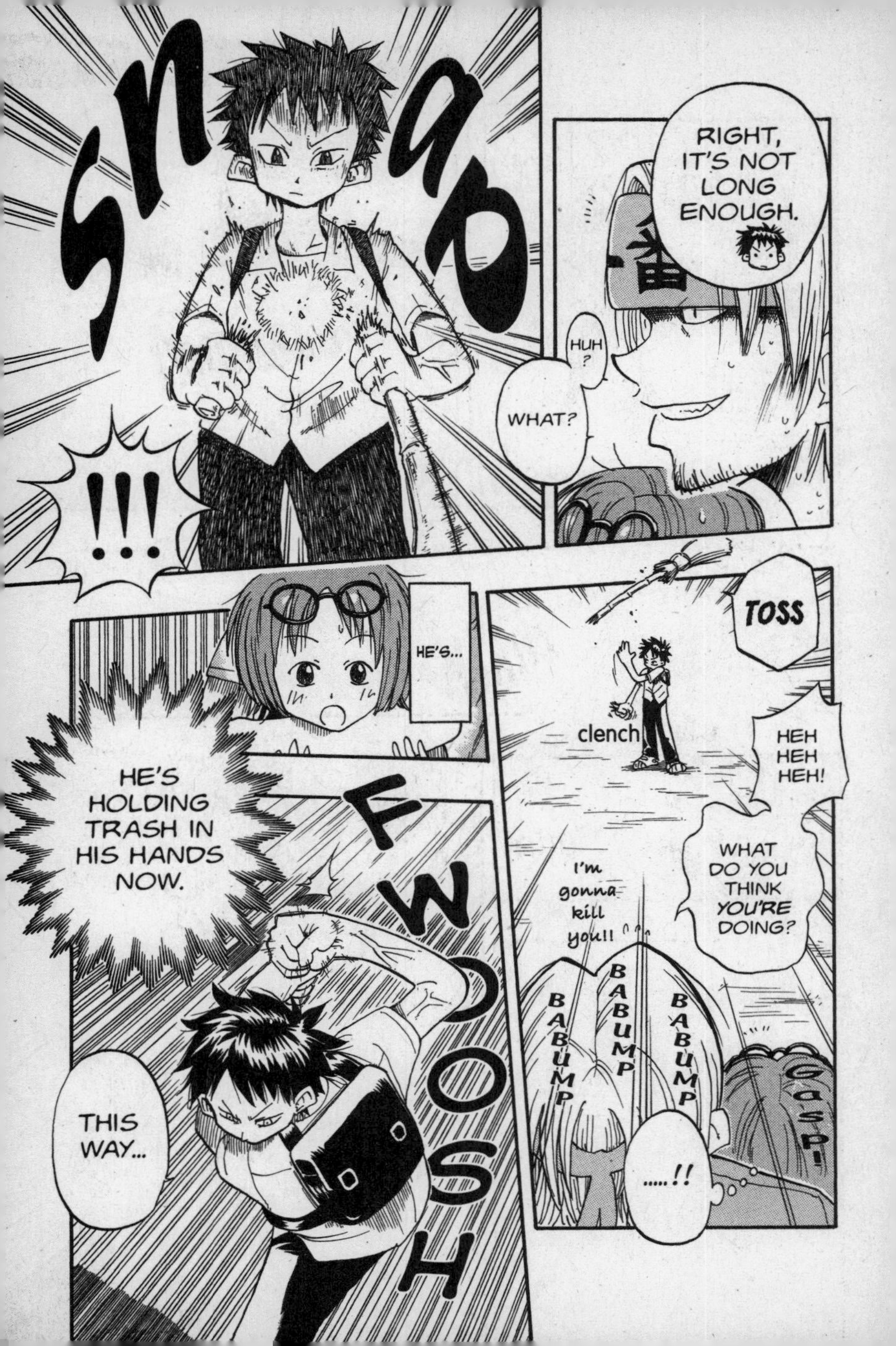
RIGHT, IT'S NOT LONG ENOUGH.
HUH?
WHAT?
SNAP
!!!
TOSS
clench
HEH HEH HEH!
WHAT DO YOU THINK YOU'RE DOING?
I'm gonna kill you!!
BABUMP
BABUMP
BABUMP
GASP!
.....!!
HE'S...
HE'S HOLDING TRASH IN HIS HANDS NOW.
FWOOSH
THIS WAY...

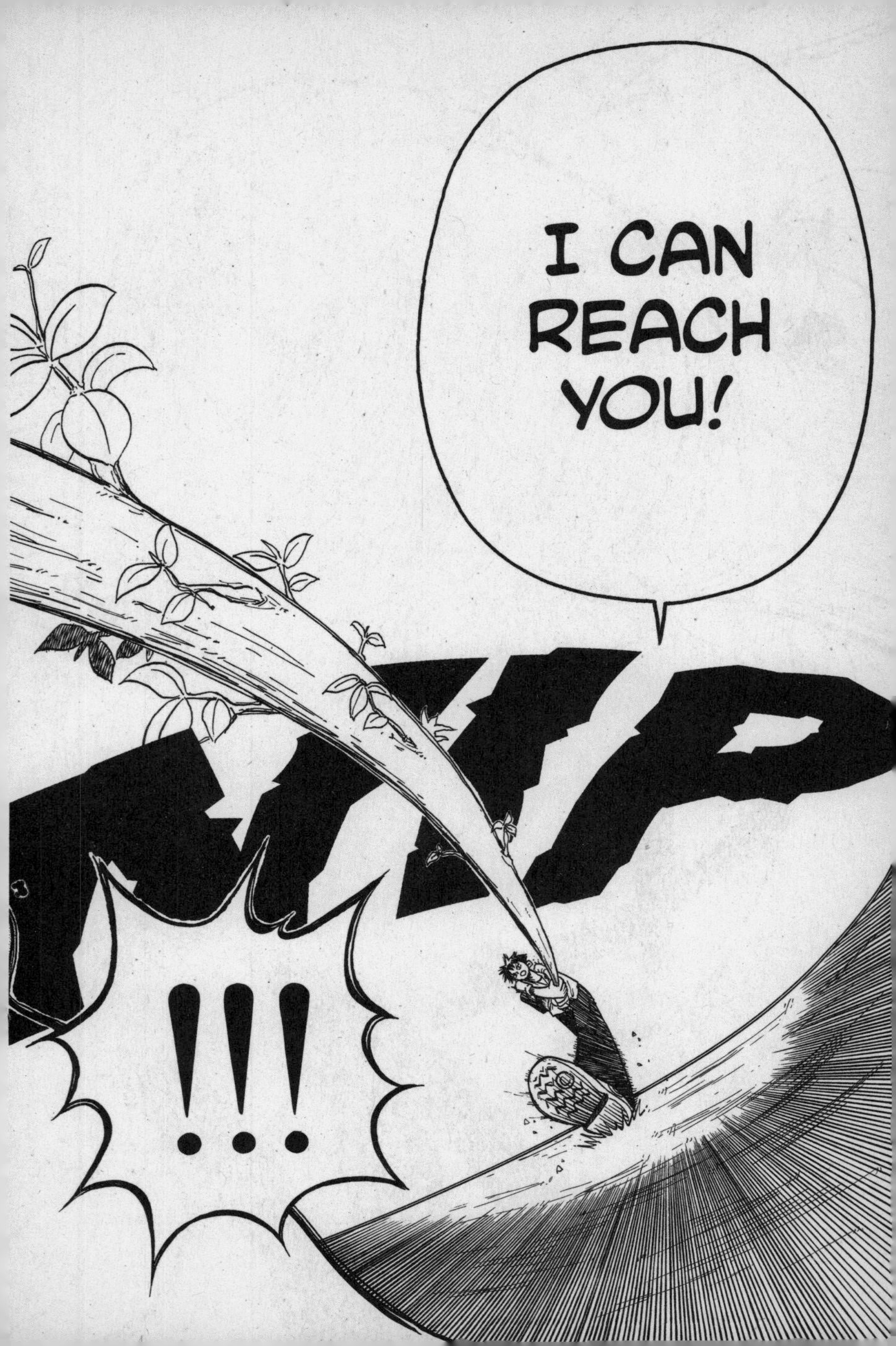
I CAN REACH YOU!
!!!

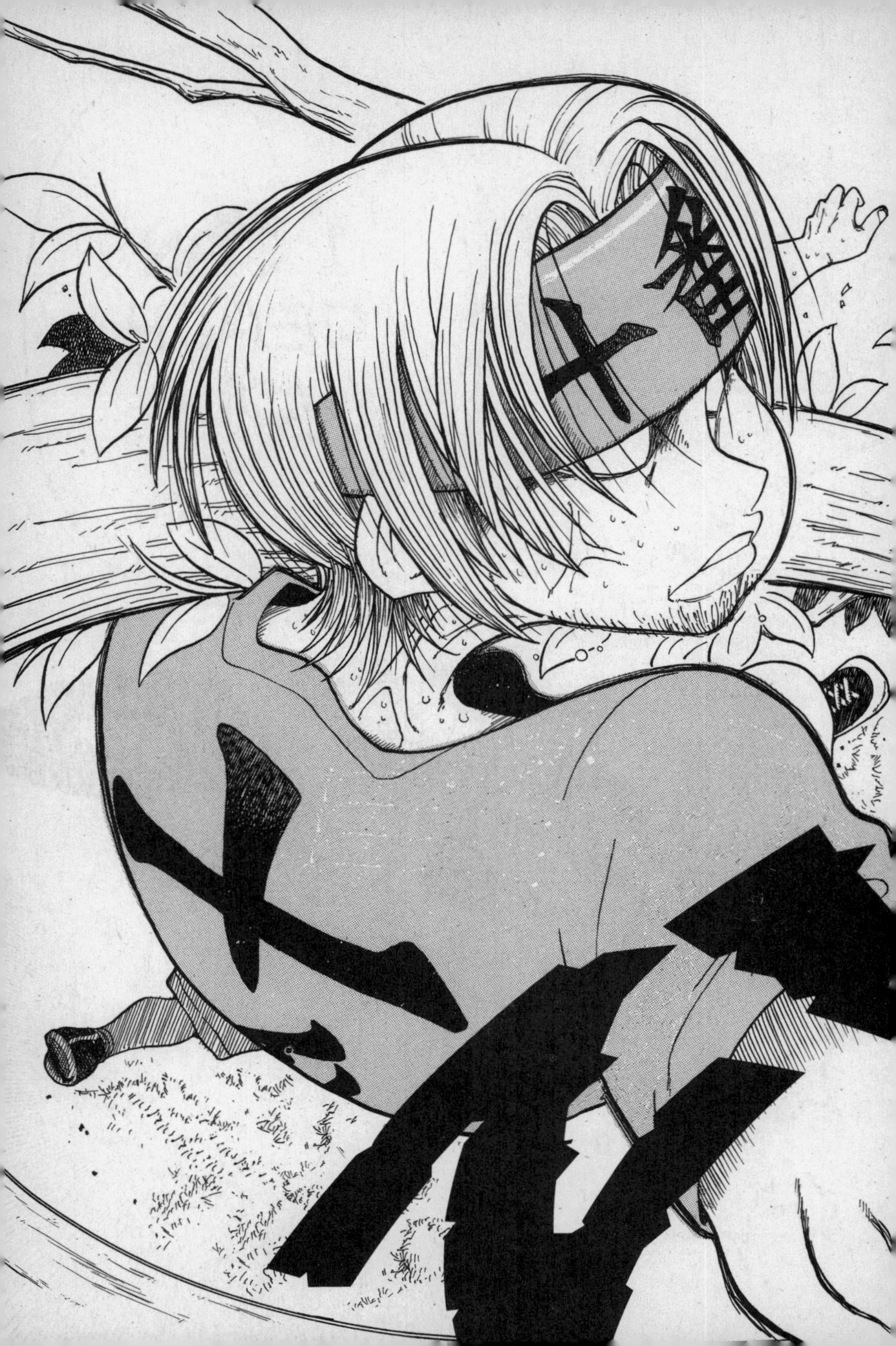

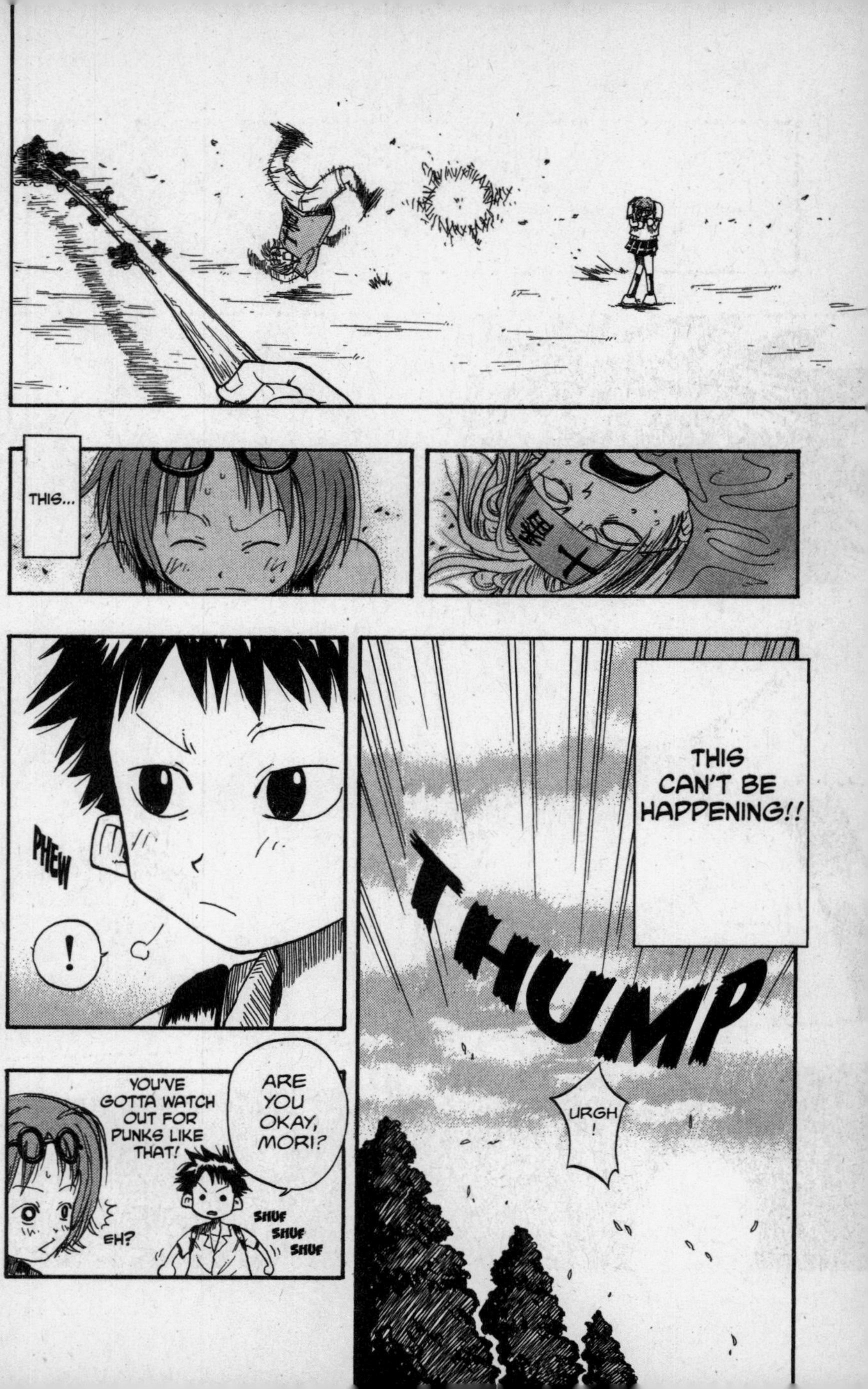
THIS...
THIS CAN'T BE HAPPENING!!
THUMP
URGH!
PHEW
!
ARE YOU OKAY, MORI?
YOU'VE GOTTA WATCH OUT FOR PUNKS LIKE THAT!
SHUF SHUF SHUF
EH?

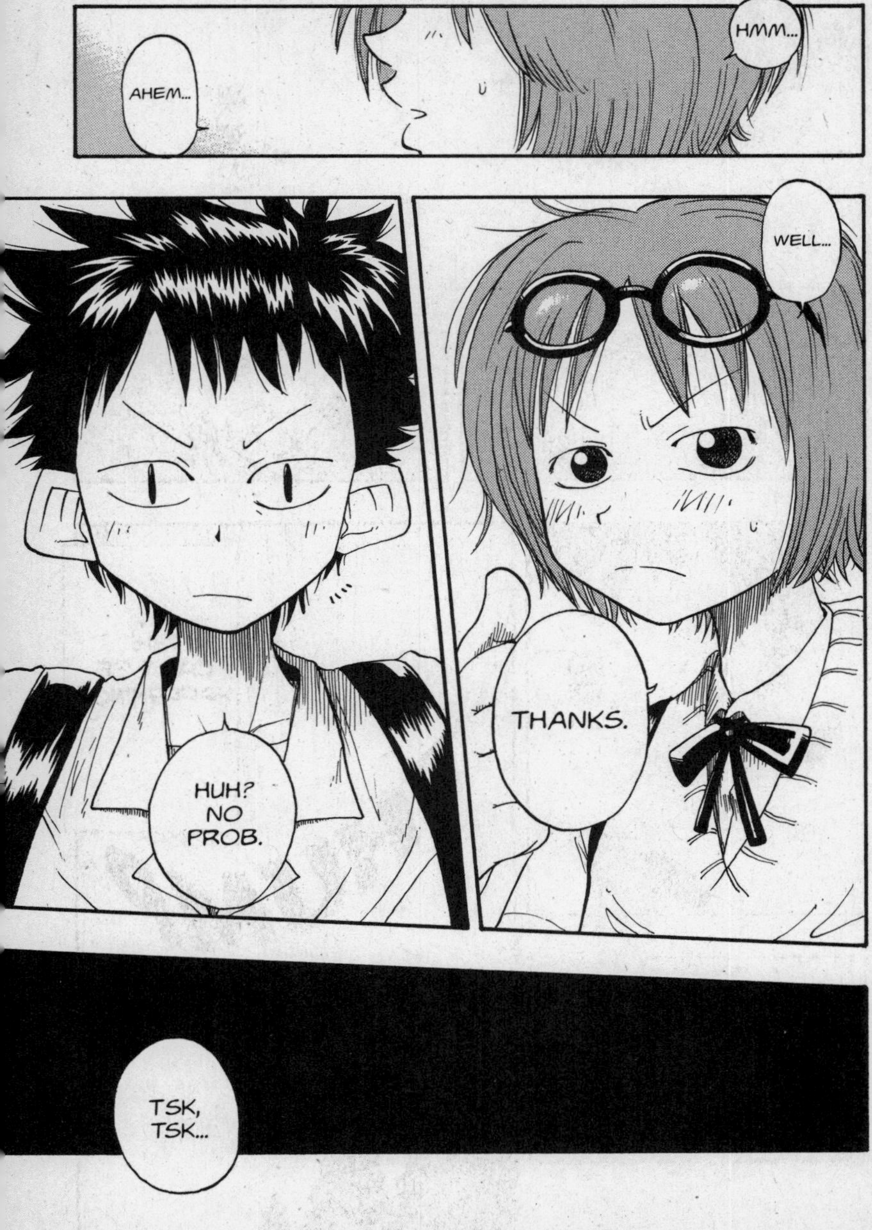
HMM...
AHEM...
WELL...
THANKS.
HUH? NO PROB.
TSK, TSK...

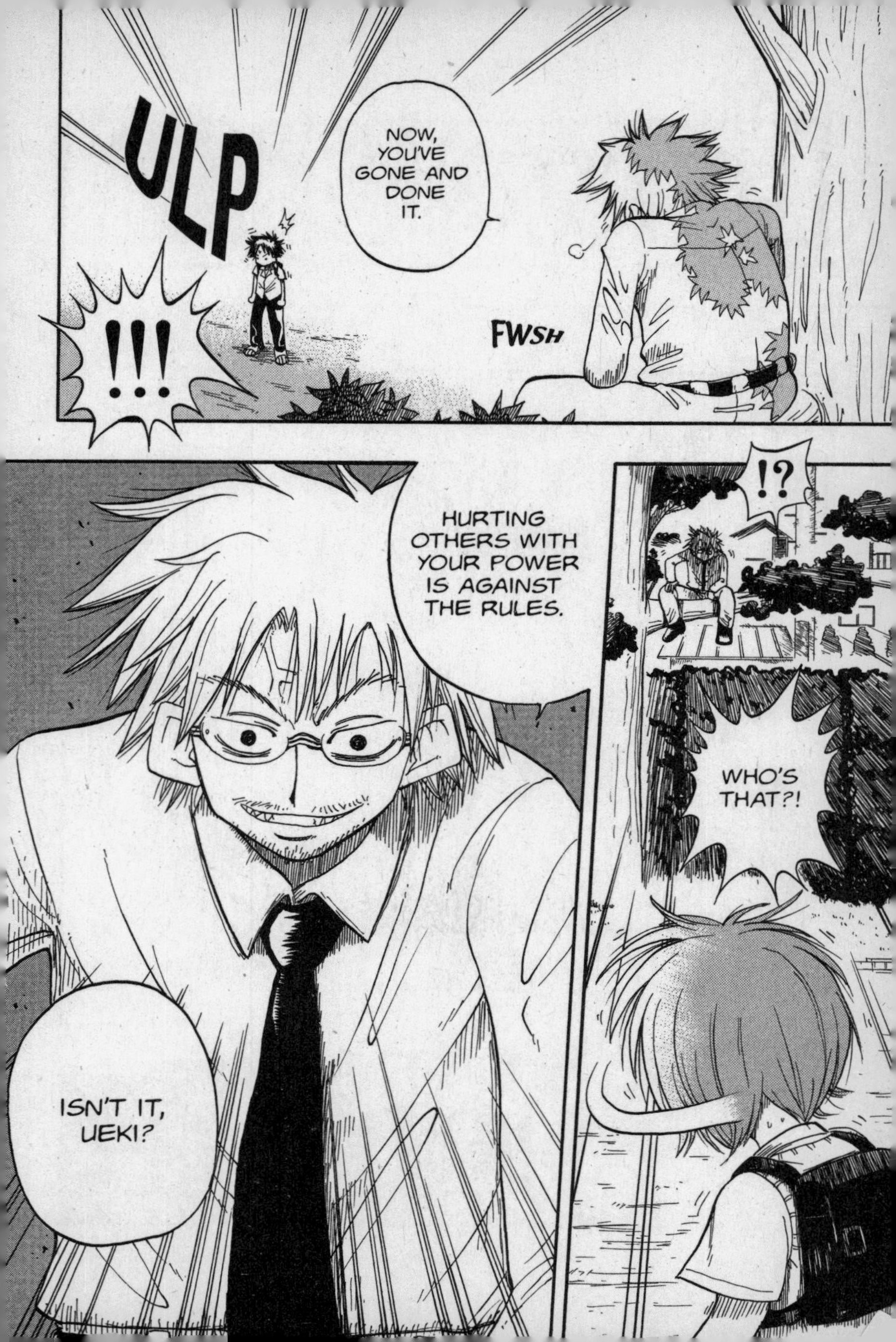
NOW, YOU'VE GONE AND DONE IT.
FWSH
ULP
!!!
!?
WHO'S THAT?!
HURTING OTHERS WITH YOUR POWER IS AGAINST THE RULES.
ISN'T IT, UEKI?

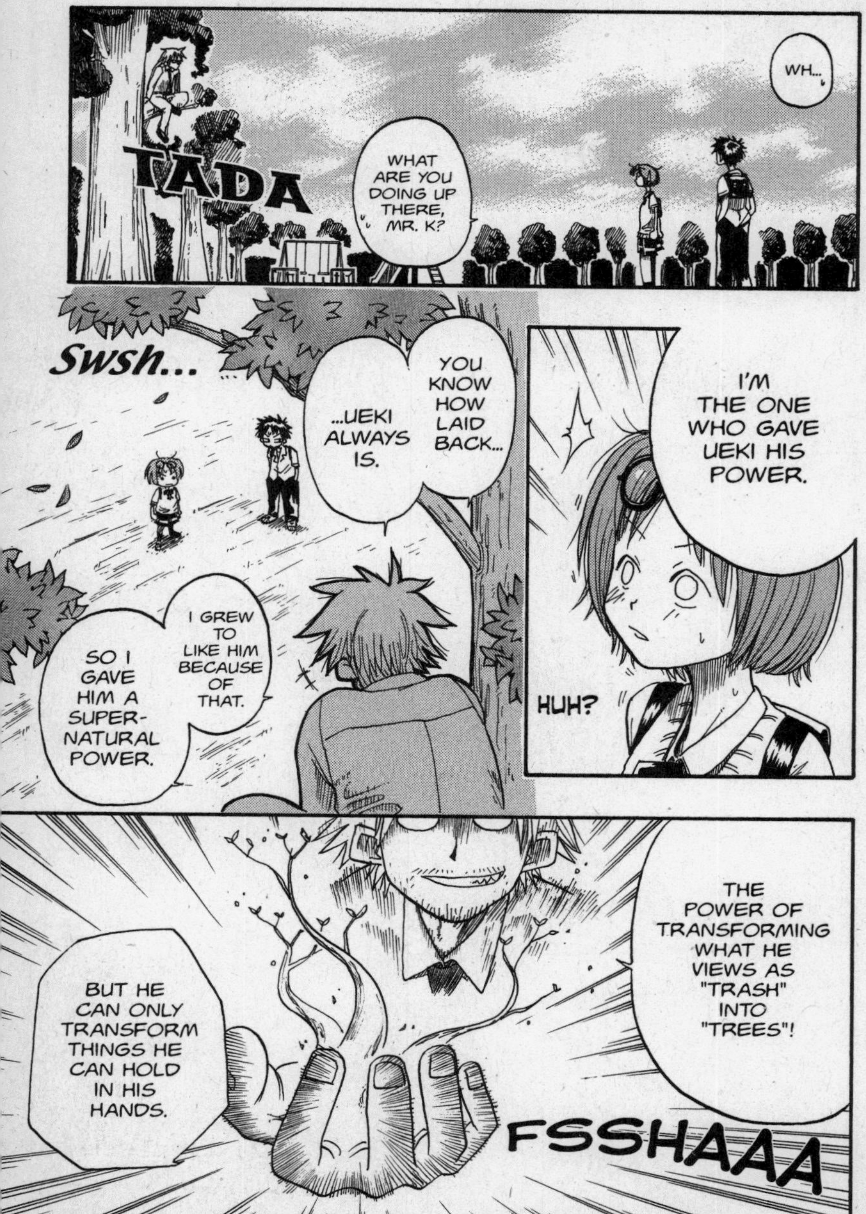
WH...
WHAT ARE YOU DOING UP THERE, MR. K?
TADA
I'M THE ONE WHO GAVE UEKI HIS POWER.
HUH?
YOU KNOW HOW LAID BACK...
...UEKI ALWAYS IS.
Swsh...
I GREW TO LIKE HIM BECAUSE OF THAT.
SO I GAVE HIM A SUPER-NATURAL POWER.
THE POWER OF TRANSFORMING WHAT HE VIEWS AS "TRASH" INTO "TREES"!
FSSHAAA
BUT HE CAN ONLY TRANSFORM THINGS HE CAN HOLD IN HIS HANDS.

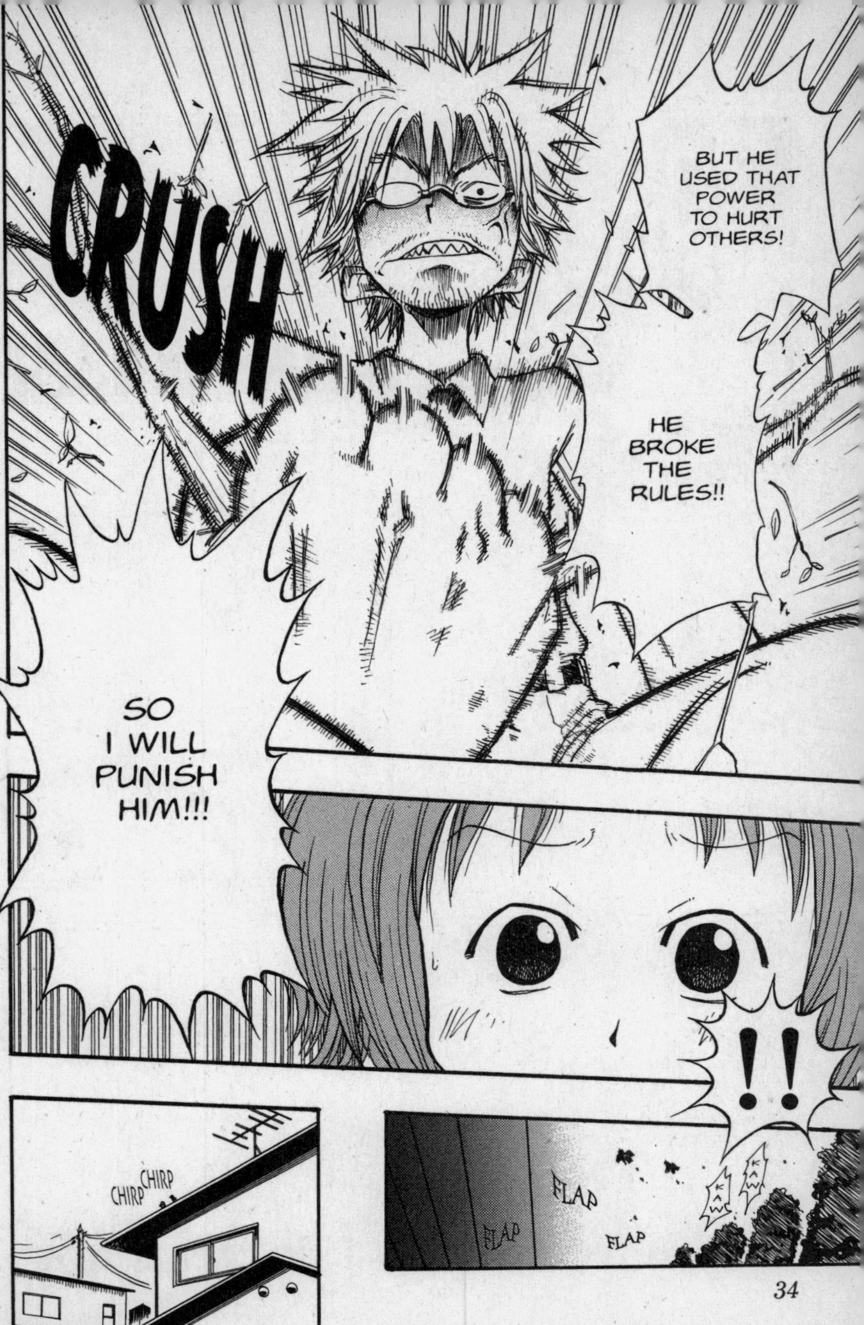
BUT HE USED THAT POWER TO HURT OTHERS!
HE BROKE THE RULES!!
CRUSH
SO I WILL PUNISH HIM!!!
!!
KAW
KAW
FLAP
FLAP
FLAP
CHIRP CHIRP

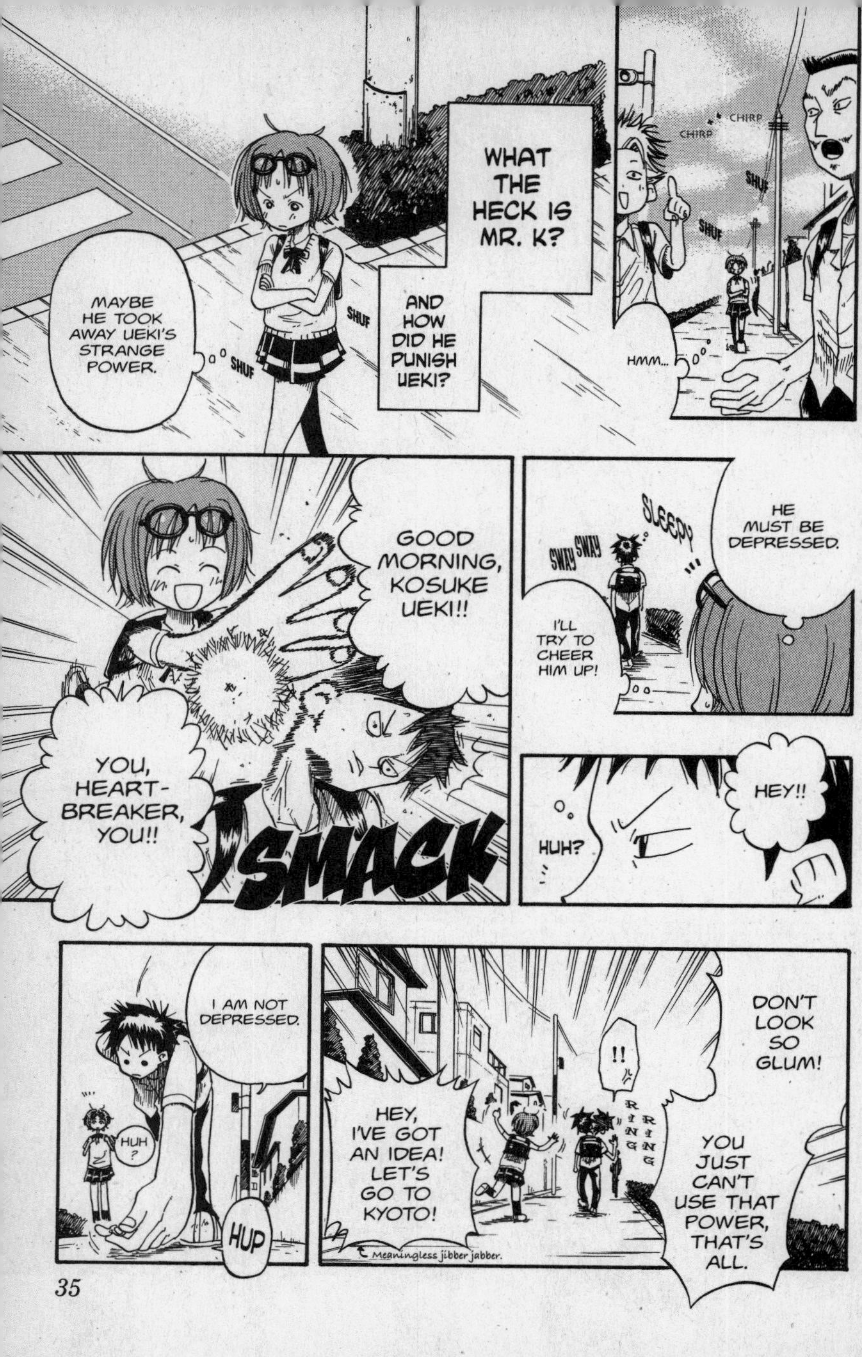
CHIRP
CHIRP
SHUF
SHUF
HMM...
WHAT THE HECK IS MR. K?
AND HOW DID HE PUNISH UEKI?
MAYBE HE TOOK AWAY UEKI'S STRANGE POWER.
SHUF
SHUF
HE MUST BE DEPRESSED.
SLEEPY
SWAY SWAY
I'LL TRY TO CHEER HIM UP!
HEY!!
HUH?
GOOD MORNING, KOSUKE UEKI!!
YOU, HEART-BREAKER, YOU!!
SMACK
DON'T LOOK SO GLUM!
!!
RING RING
YOU JUST CAN'T USE THAT POWER, THAT'S ALL.
HEY, I'VE GOT AN IDEA! LET'S GO TO KYOTO!
Meaningless jibber jabber.
I AM NOT DEPRESSED.
HUH?
HUP

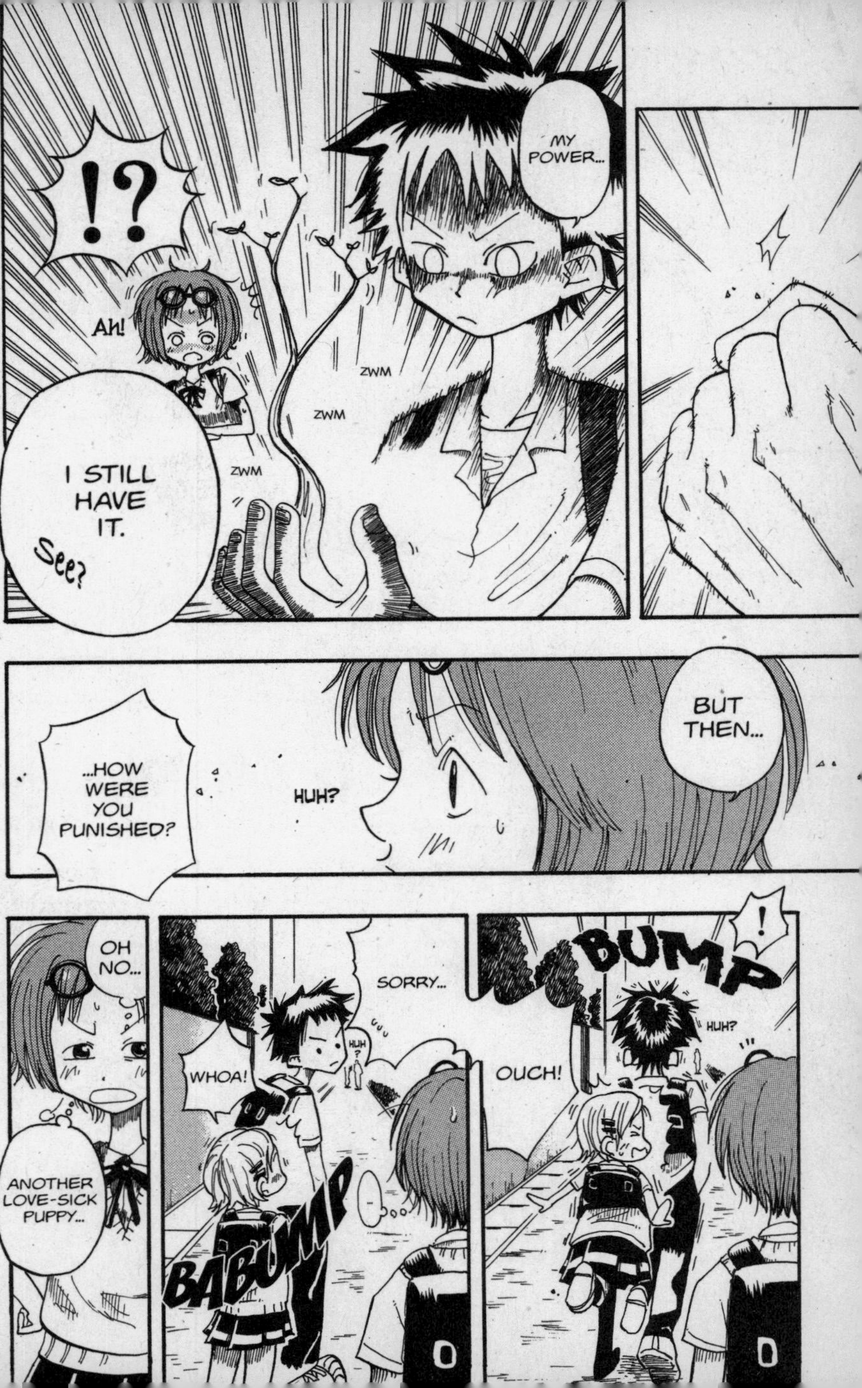
MY POWER...
!?
Ah!
ZWM
ZWM
ZWM
I STILL HAVE IT.
See?
BUT THEN...
HUH?
...HOW WERE YOU PUNISHED?
!
BUMP
HUH?
OUCH!
SORRY...
HUH?
WHOA!
BABUMP
...
OH NO...
ANOTHER LOVE-SICK PUPPY...

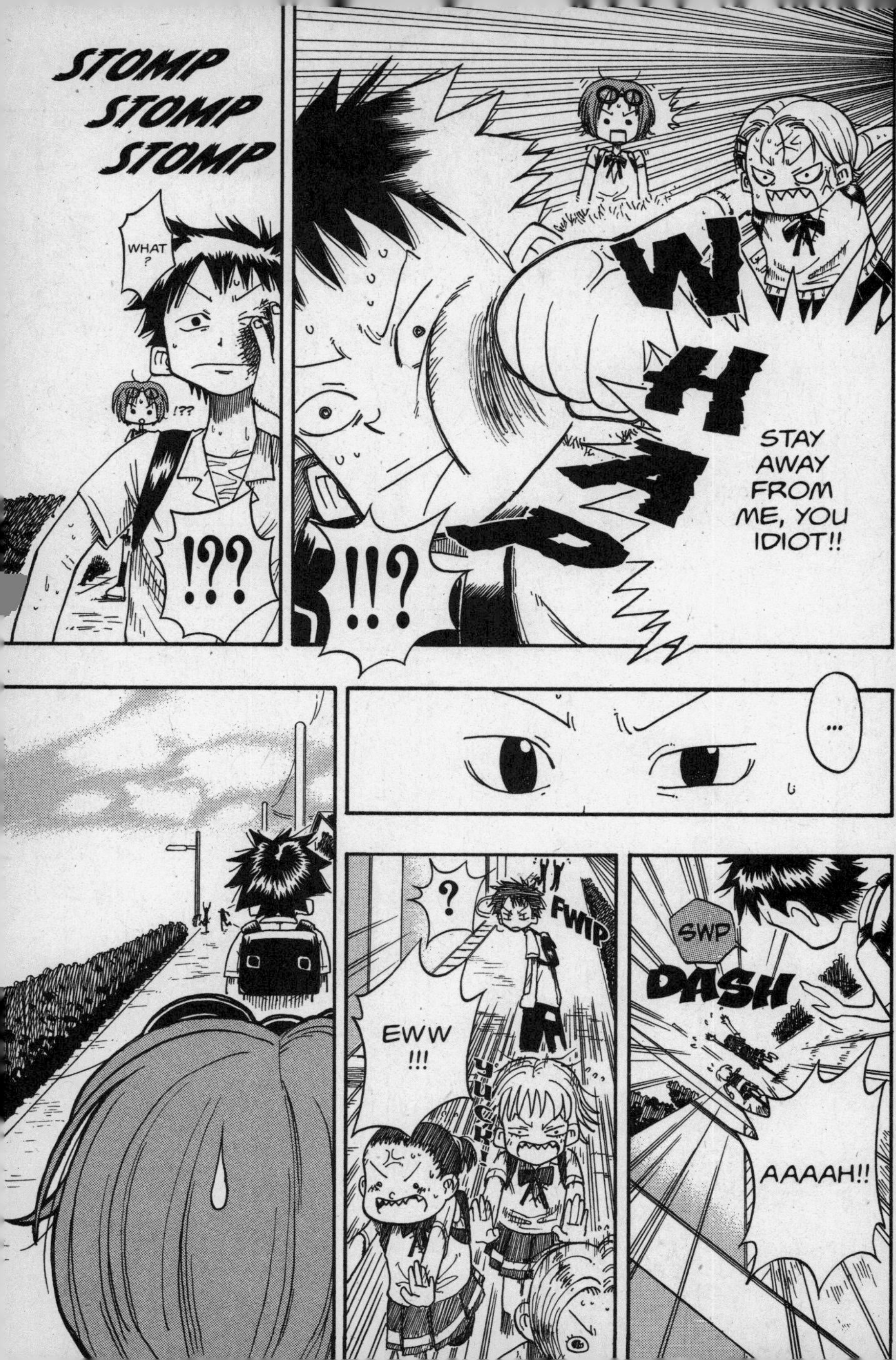
WHAP
STAY AWAY FROM ME, YOU IDIOT!!
!!?
STOMP STOMP STOMP
WHAT?
!??
!??
...
SWP
DASH
AAAAH!!
?
FWIP
EWW !!!
YUCK!

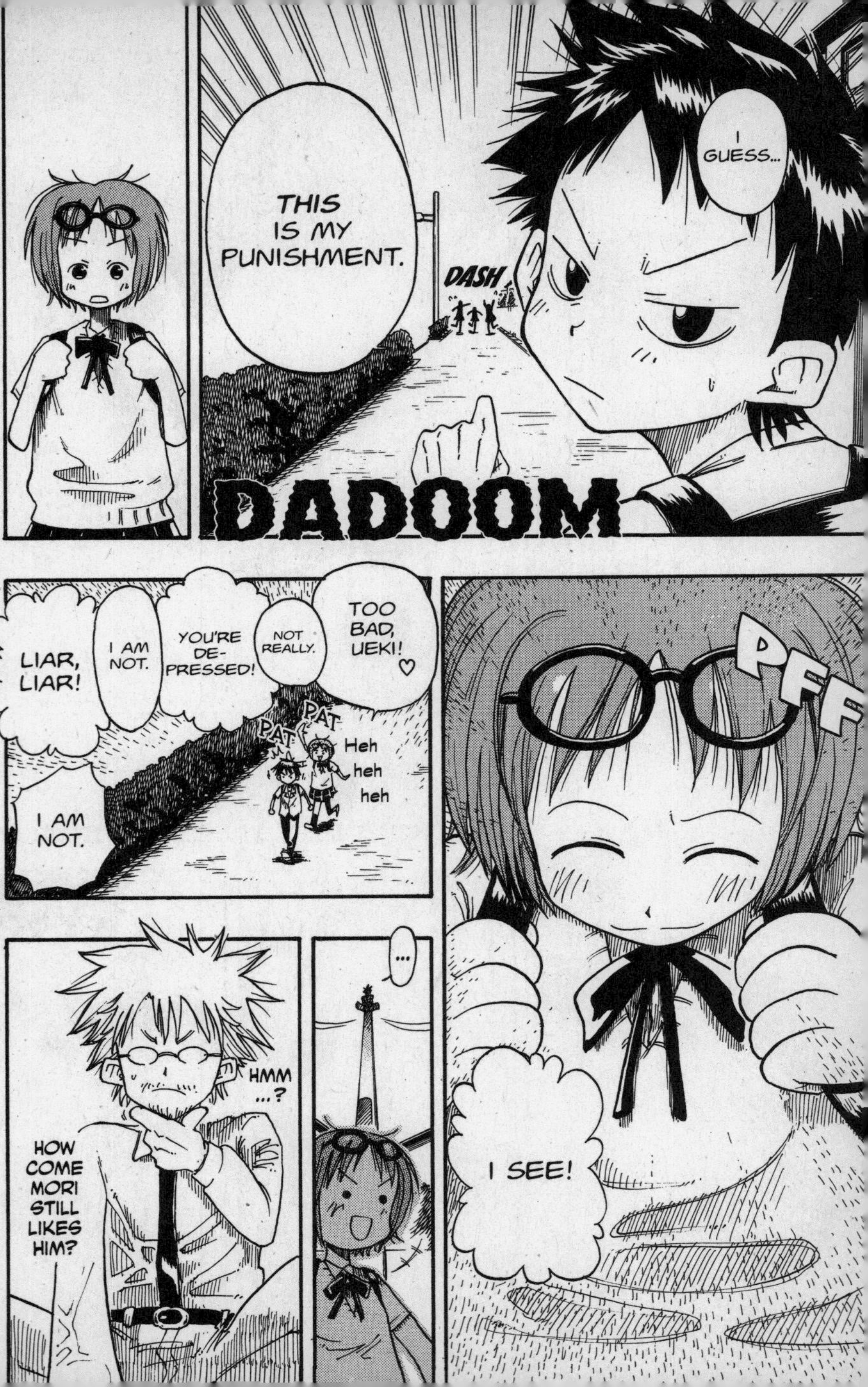
I GUESS...
THIS IS MY PUNISHMENT.
DASH
DADOOM
PFF
I SEE!
TOO BAD, UEKI! ♡
NOT REALLY.
YOU'RE DE-PRESSED!
I AM NOT.
LIAR, LIAR!
PAT PAT
Heh heh heh
I AM NOT.
...
HMM ...?
HOW COME MORI STILL LIKES HIM?

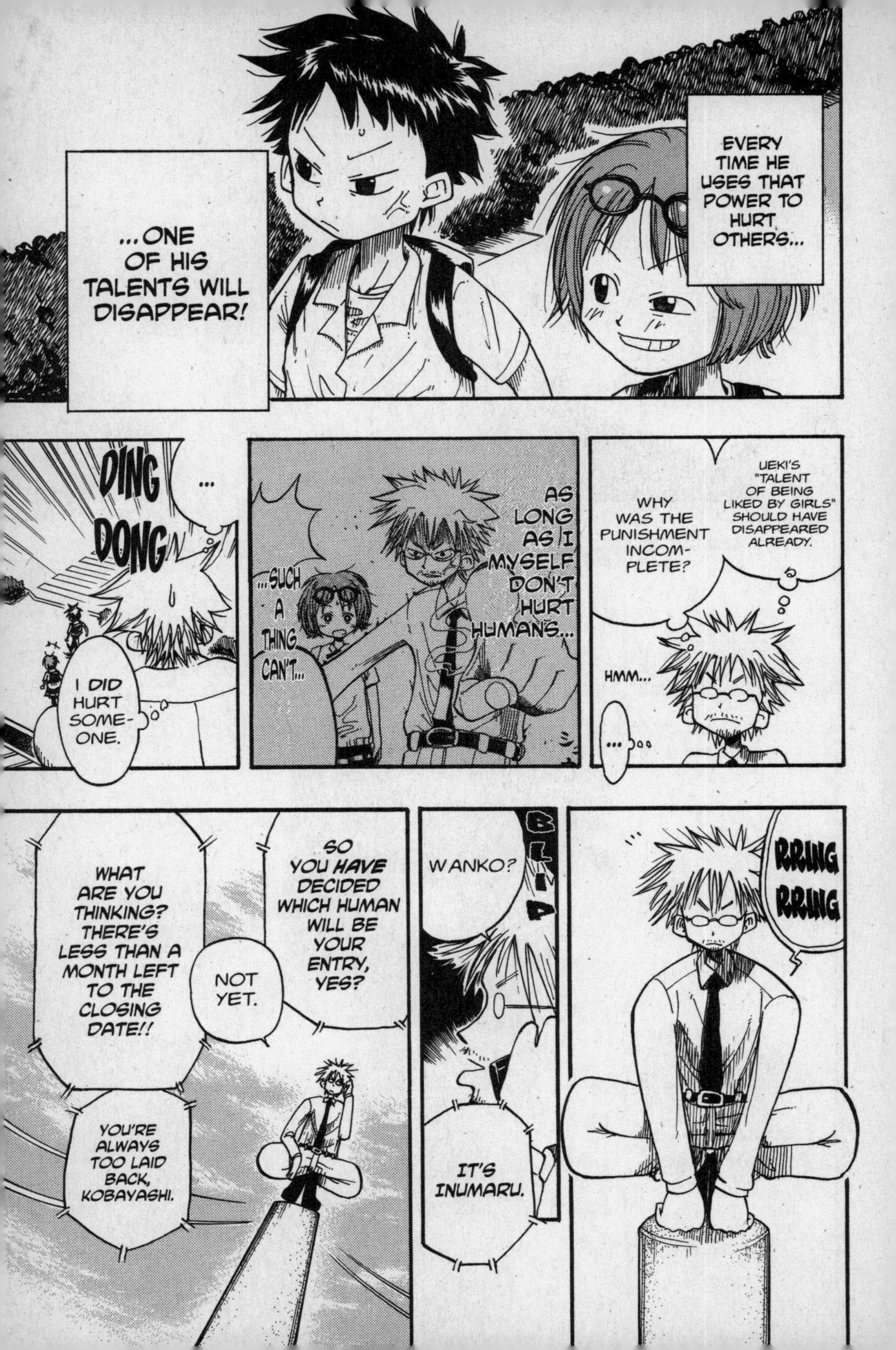
EVERY TIME HE USES THAT POWER TO HURT OTHERS...
...ONE OF HIS TALENTS WILL DISAPPEAR!
UEKI'S "TALENT OF BEING LIKED BY GIRLS" SHOULD HAVE DISAPPEARED ALREADY.
WHY WAS THE PUNISHMENT INCOMPLETE?
HMM...
...
AS LONG AS I MYSELF DON'T HURT HUMANS...
...SUCH A THING CAN'T...
DING DONG
...
I DID HURT SOMEONE.
RRING RRING
BLIP
WANKO?
IT'S INUMARU.
SO YOU *HAVE* DECIDED WHICH HUMAN WILL BE YOUR ENTRY, YES?
NOT YET.
WHAT ARE YOU THINKING? THERE'S LESS THAN A MONTH LEFT TO THE CLOSING DATE!!
YOU'RE ALWAYS TOO LAID BACK, KOBAYASHI.

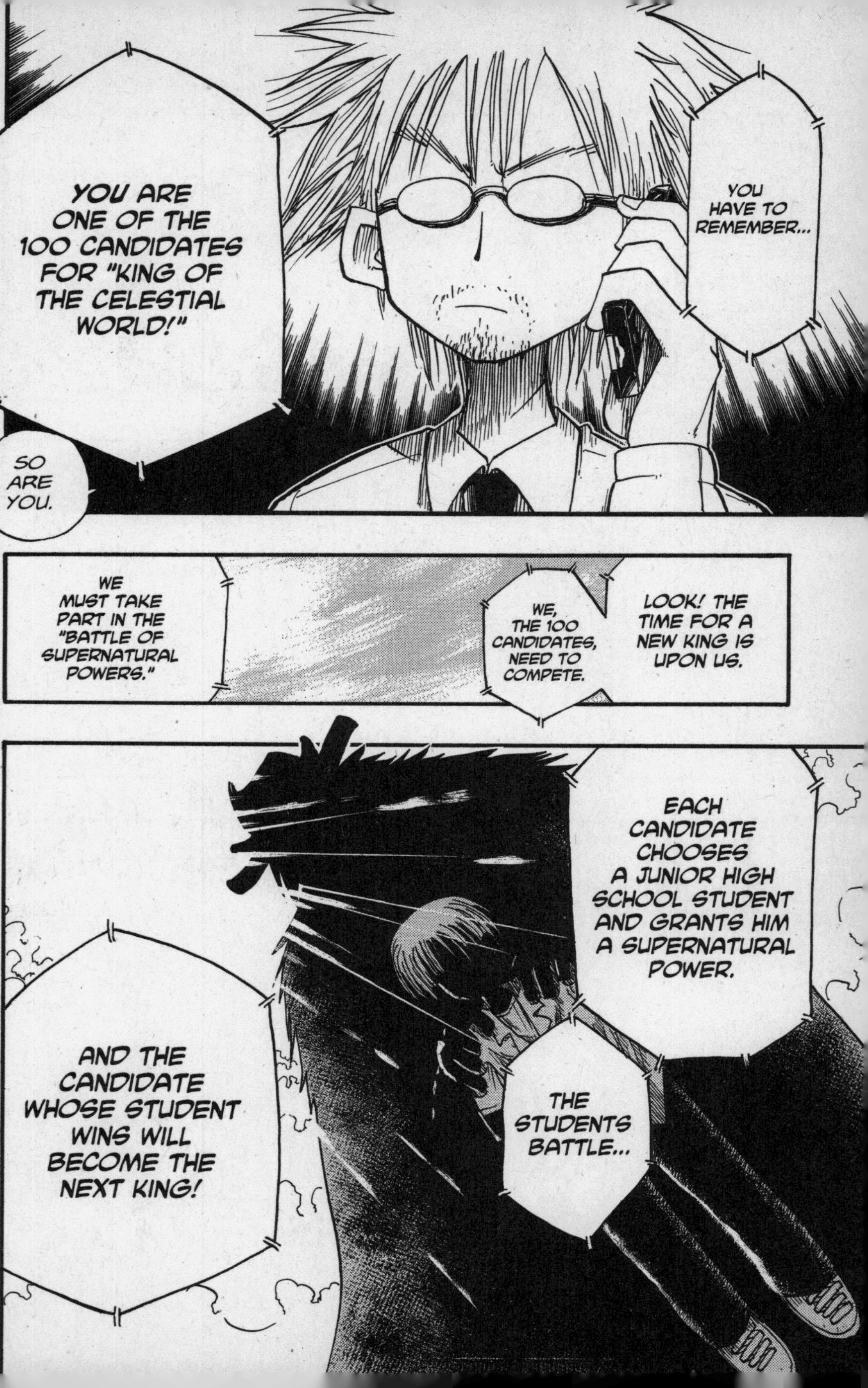
YOU HAVE TO REMEMBER...
YOU ARE ONE OF THE 100 CANDIDATES FOR "KING OF THE CELESTIAL WORLD!"
SO ARE YOU.
LOOK! THE TIME FOR A NEW KING IS UPON US.
WE, THE 100 CANDIDATES, NEED TO COMPETE.
WE MUST TAKE PART IN THE "BATTLE OF SUPERNATURAL POWERS."
EACH CANDIDATE CHOOSES A JUNIOR HIGH SCHOOL STUDENT AND GRANTS HIM A SUPERNATURAL POWER.
THE STUDENTS BATTLE...
AND THE CANDIDATE WHOSE STUDENT WINS WILL BECOME THE NEXT KING!

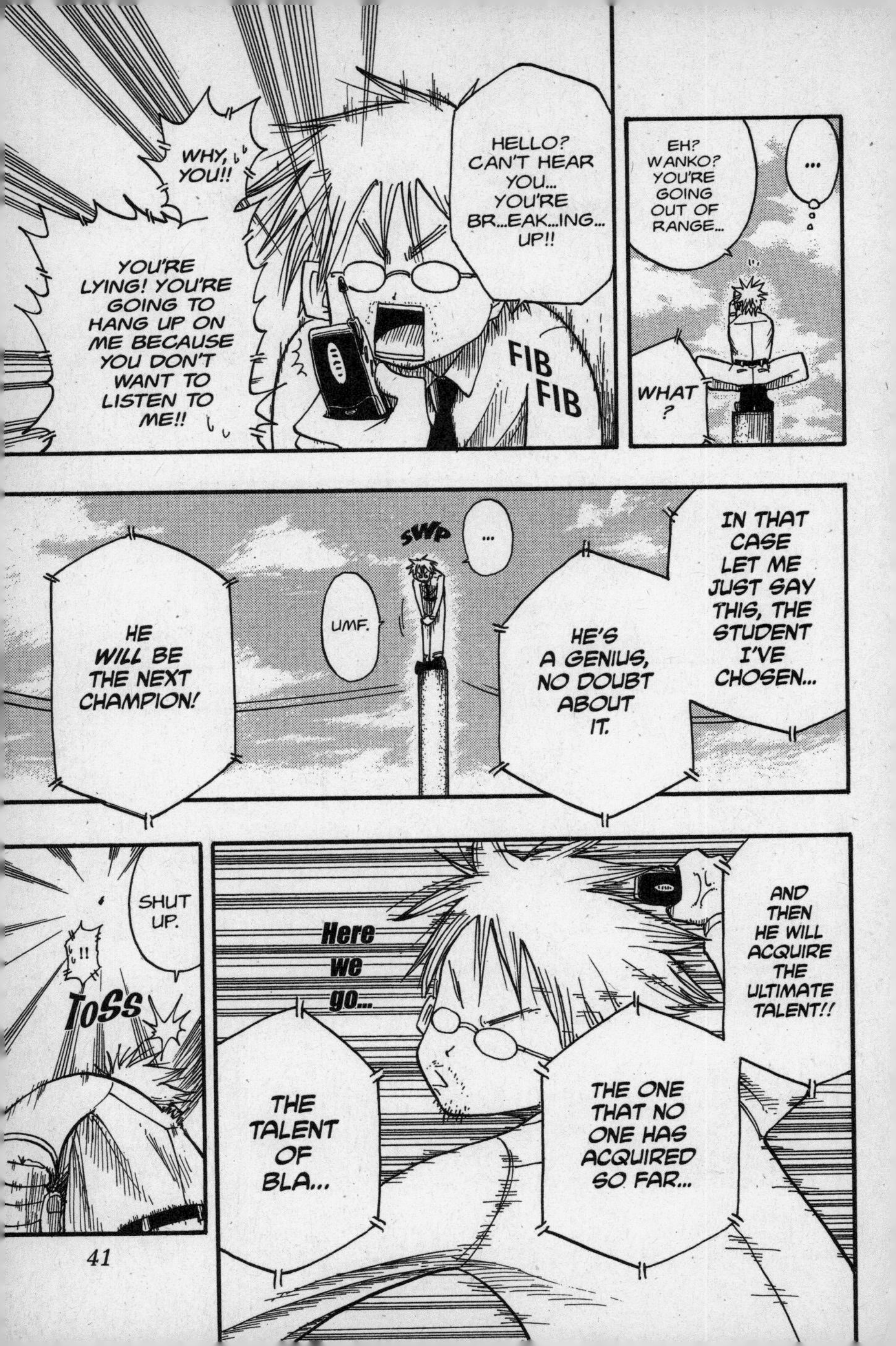
...
EH? WANKO? YOU'RE GOING OUT OF RANGE...
WHAT?
HELLO? CAN'T HEAR YOU... YOU'RE BR...EAK...ING... UP!!
FIB FIB
WHY, YOU!!
YOU'RE LYING! YOU'RE GOING TO HANG UP ON ME BECAUSE YOU DON'T WANT TO LISTEN TO ME!!
IN THAT CASE LET ME JUST SAY THIS, THE STUDENT I'VE CHOSEN...
HE'S A GENIUS, NO DOUBT ABOUT IT.
...
SWP
UMF.
HE WILL BE THE NEXT CHAMPION!
AND THEN HE WILL ACQUIRE THE ULTIMATE TALENT!!
THE ONE THAT NO ONE HAS ACQUIRED SO FAR...
Here we go...
THE TALENT OF BLA...
SHUT UP.
!!
TOSS

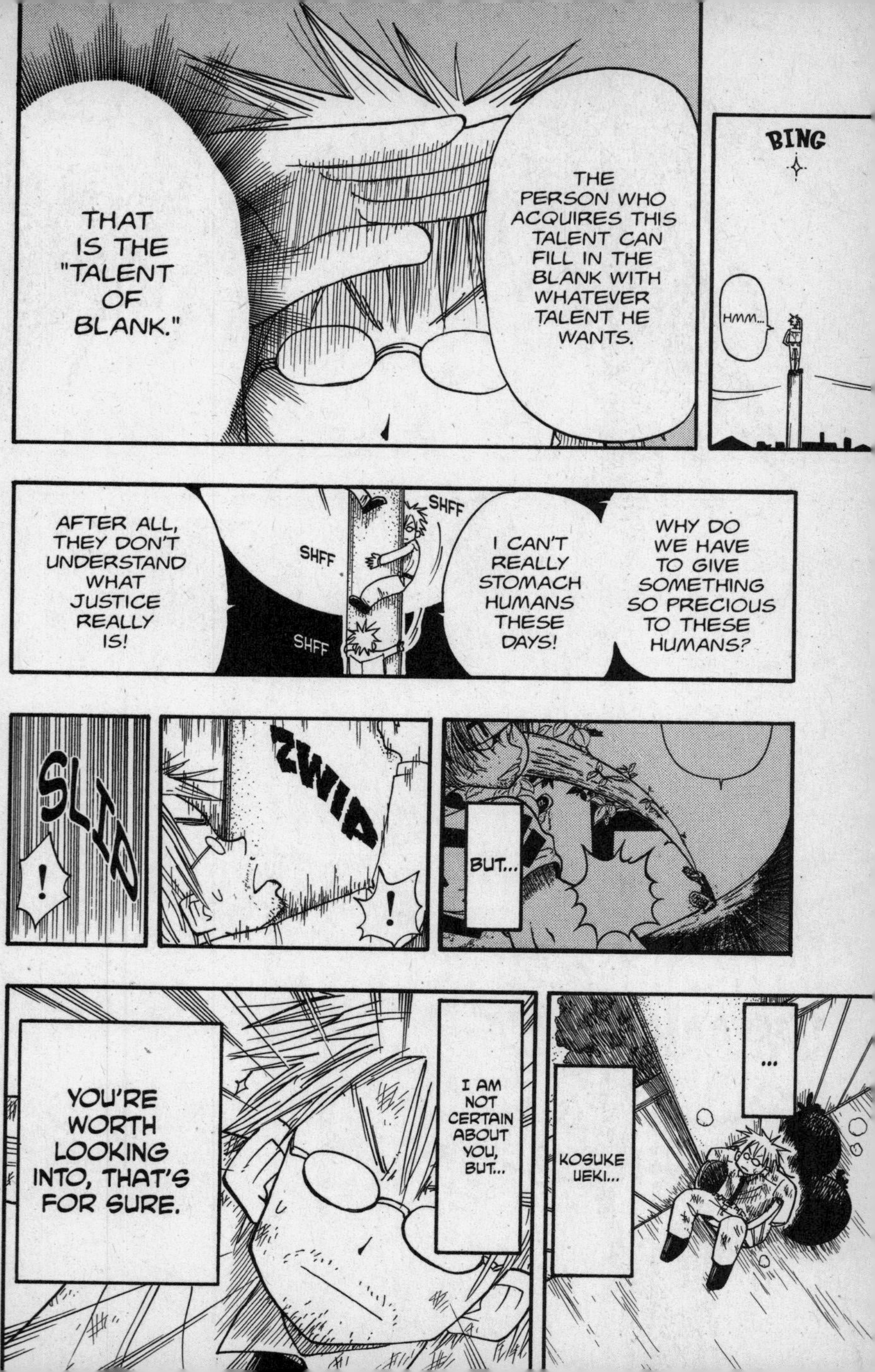
BING
HMM...
THE PERSON WHO ACQUIRES THIS TALENT CAN FILL IN THE BLANK WITH WHATEVER TALENT HE WANTS.
THAT IS THE "TALENT OF BLANK."
WHY DO WE HAVE TO GIVE SOMETHING SO PRECIOUS TO THESE HUMANS?
I CAN'T REALLY STOMACH HUMANS THESE DAYS!
SHFF
SHFF
SHFF
AFTER ALL, THEY DON'T UNDERSTAND WHAT JUSTICE REALLY IS!
BUT...
ZWIP
!
SLIP
!
...
KOSUKE UEKI...
I AM NOT CERTAIN ABOUT YOU, BUT...
YOU'RE WORTH LOOKING INTO, THAT'S FOR SURE.

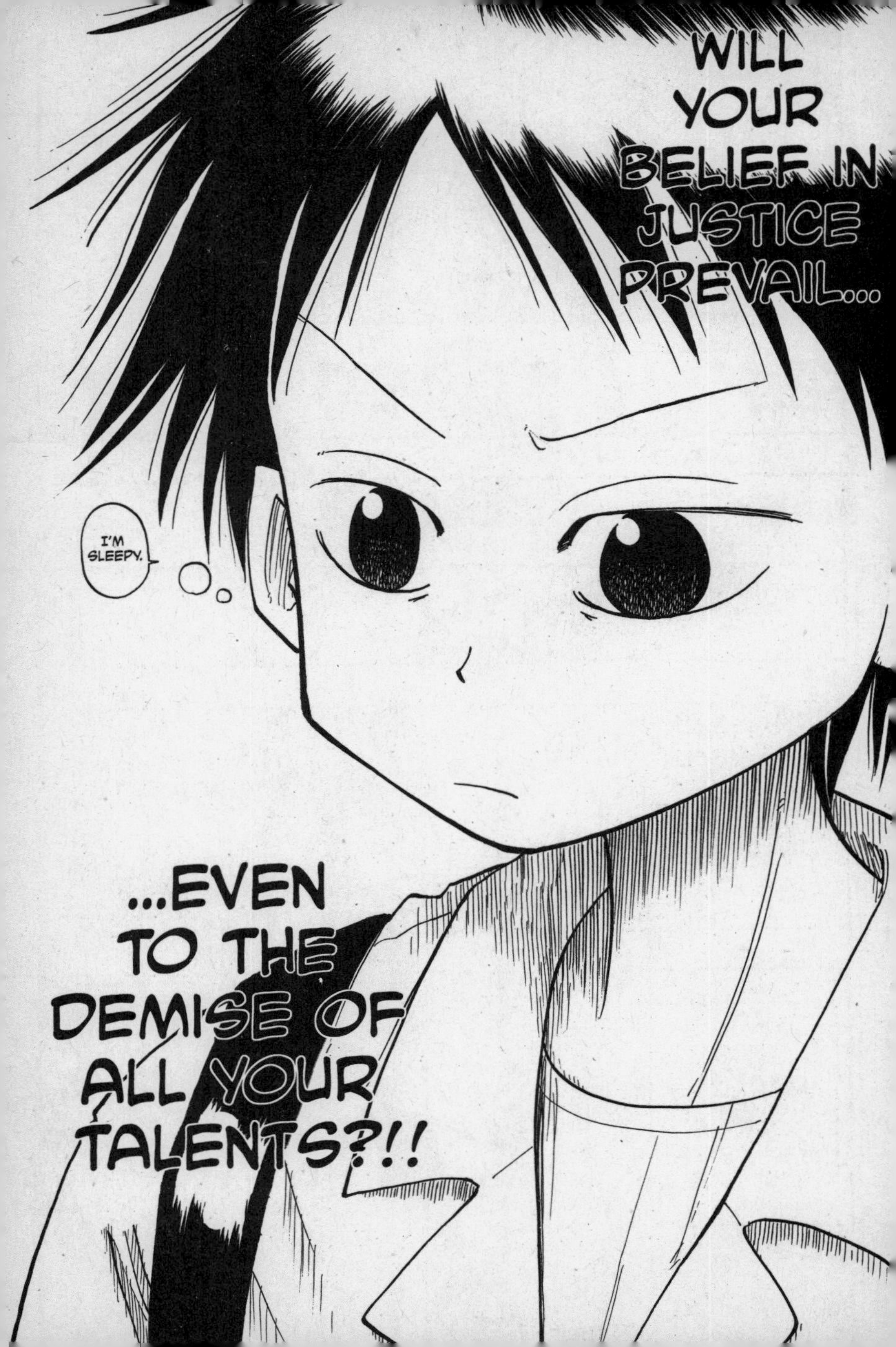
WILL YOUR BELIEF IN JUSTICE PREVAIL...
I'M SLEEPY.
...EVEN TO THE DEMISE OF ALL YOUR TALENTS?!!

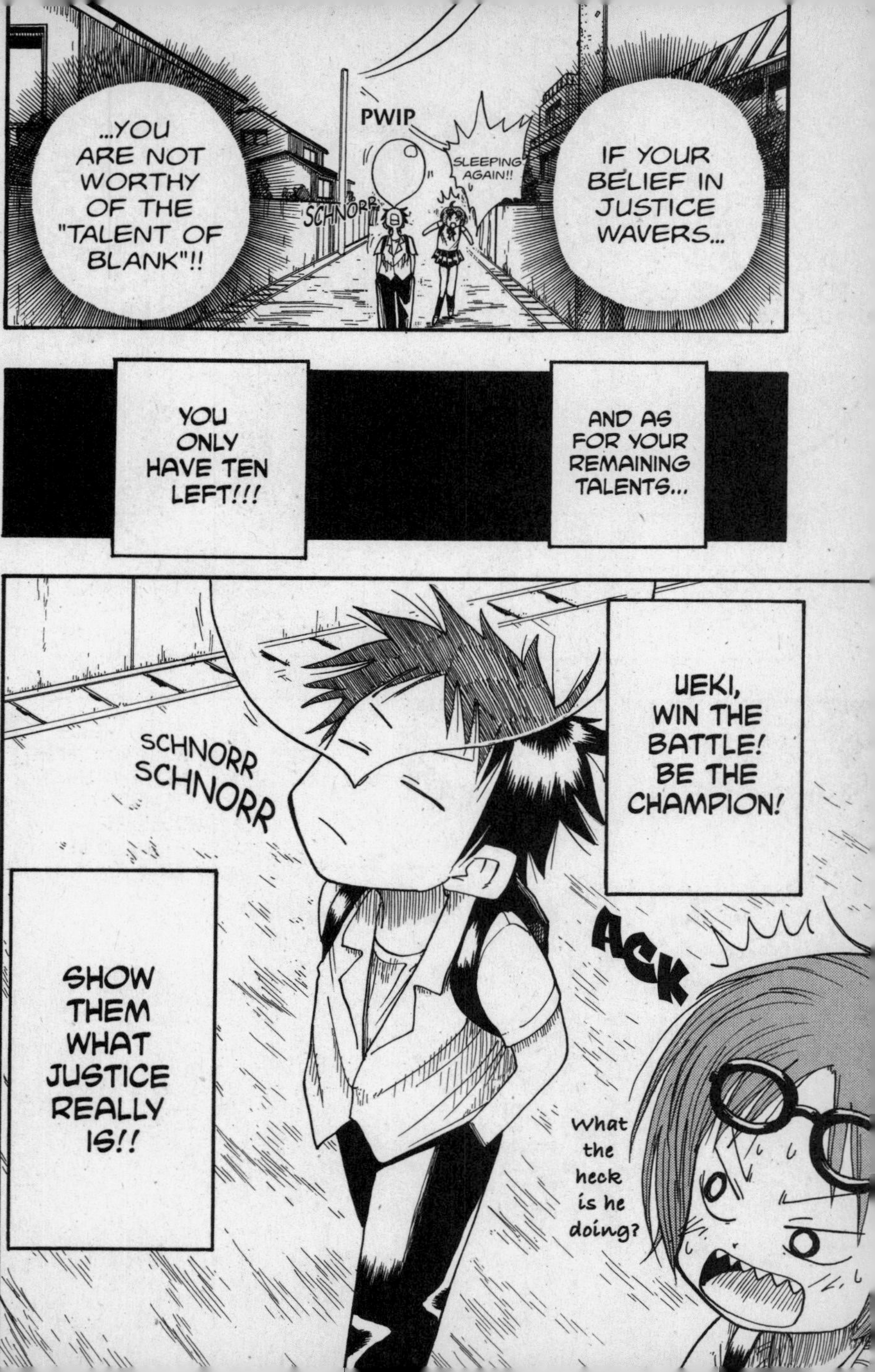
IF YOUR BELIEF IN JUSTICE WAVERS...
PWIP
SLEEPING AGAIN!!
SCHNORR
...YOU ARE NOT WORTHY OF THE "TALENT OF BLANK"!!
AND AS FOR YOUR REMAINING TALENTS...
YOU ONLY HAVE TEN LEFT!!!
UEKI, WIN THE BATTLE! BE THE CHAMPION!
SCHNORR SCHNORR
ACK
What the heck is he doing?
SHOW THEM WHAT JUSTICE REALLY IS!!

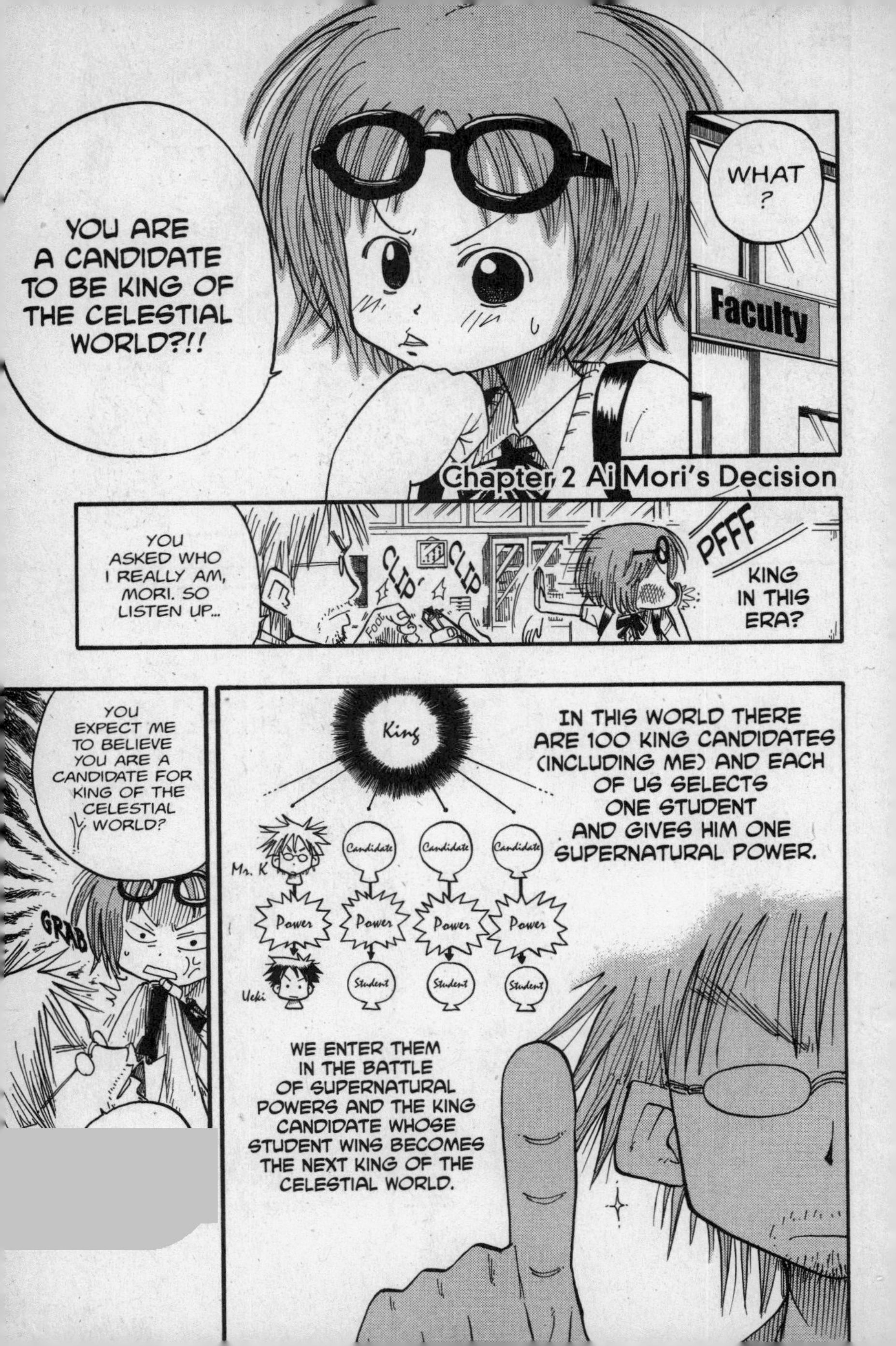
WHAT?
Faculty
YOU ARE A CANDIDATE TO BE KING OF THE CELESTIAL WORLD?!!
Chapter 2 Ai Mori's Decision
PFFF
KING IN THIS ERA?
CLIP CLIP
YOU ASKED WHO I REALLY AM, MORI. SO LISTEN UP...
IN THIS WORLD THERE ARE 100 KING CANDIDATES (INCLUDING ME) AND EACH OF US SELECTS ONE STUDENT AND GIVES HIM ONE SUPERNATURAL POWER.
King
Candidate
Candidate
Candidate
Mr. K
Power
Power
Power
Power
Ueki
Student
Student
Student
WE ENTER THEM IN THE BATTLE OF SUPERNATURAL POWERS AND THE KING CANDIDATE WHOSE STUDENT WINS BECOMES THE NEXT KING OF THE CELESTIAL WORLD.
YOU EXPECT ME TO BELIEVE YOU ARE A CANDIDATE FOR KING OF THE CELESTIAL WORLD?
GRAB

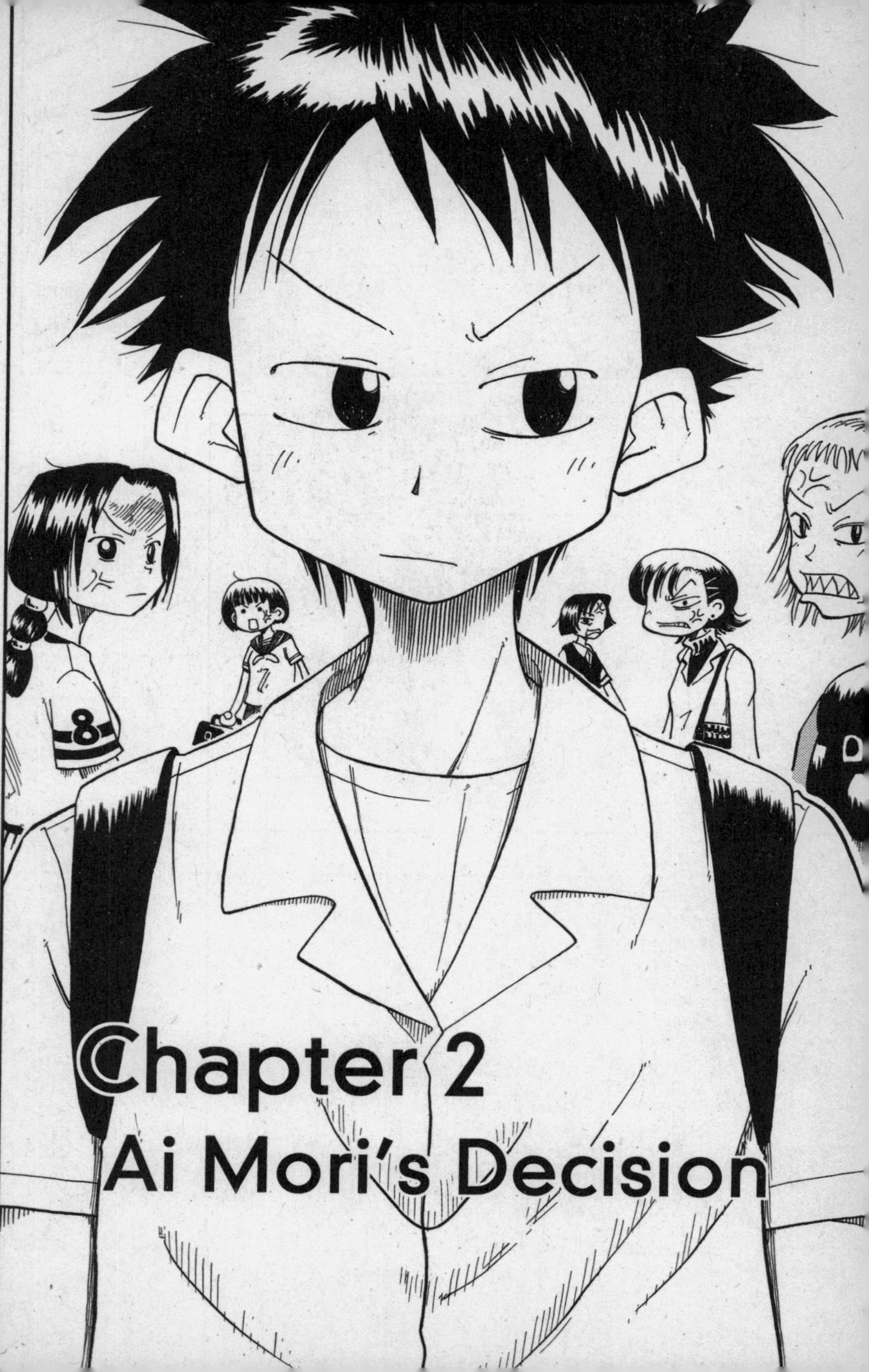
Chapter 2
Ai Mori's Decision

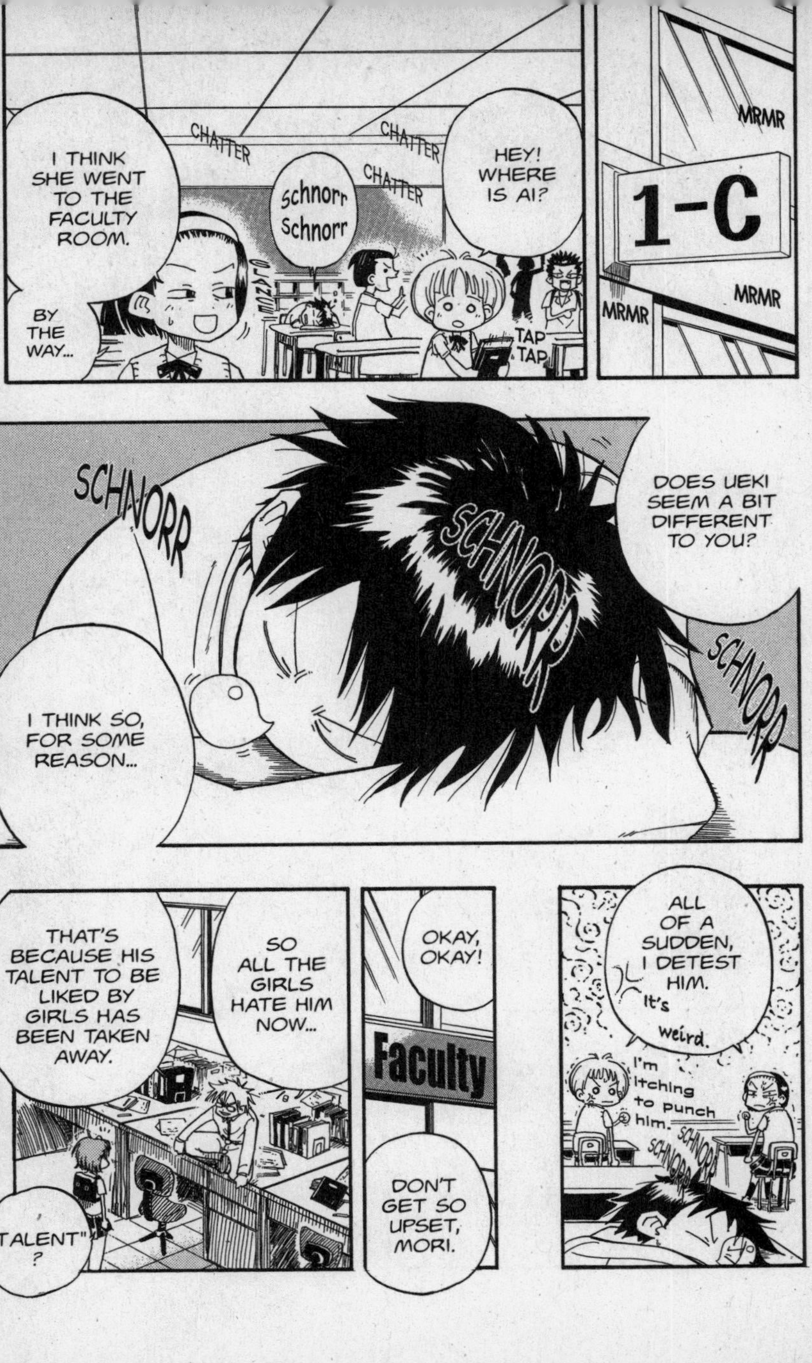
MRMR
1-C
MRMR
MRMR
HEY! WHERE IS AI?
CHATTER
CHATTER
CHATTER
Schnorr Schnorr
GLANCE
I THINK SHE WENT TO THE FACULTY ROOM.
TAP TAP
BY THE WAY...
DOES UEKI SEEM A BIT DIFFERENT TO YOU?
SCHNORR
SCHNORR
SCHNORR
I THINK SO, FOR SOME REASON...
ALL OF A SUDDEN, I DETEST HIM.
It's weird.
I'm itching to punch him.
SCHNORR
SCHNORR
OKAY, OKAY!
Faculty
DON'T GET SO UPSET, MORI.
SO ALL THE GIRLS HATE HIM NOW...
THAT'S BECAUSE HIS TALENT TO BE LIKED BY GIRLS HAS BEEN TAKEN AWAY.
"TALENT"?

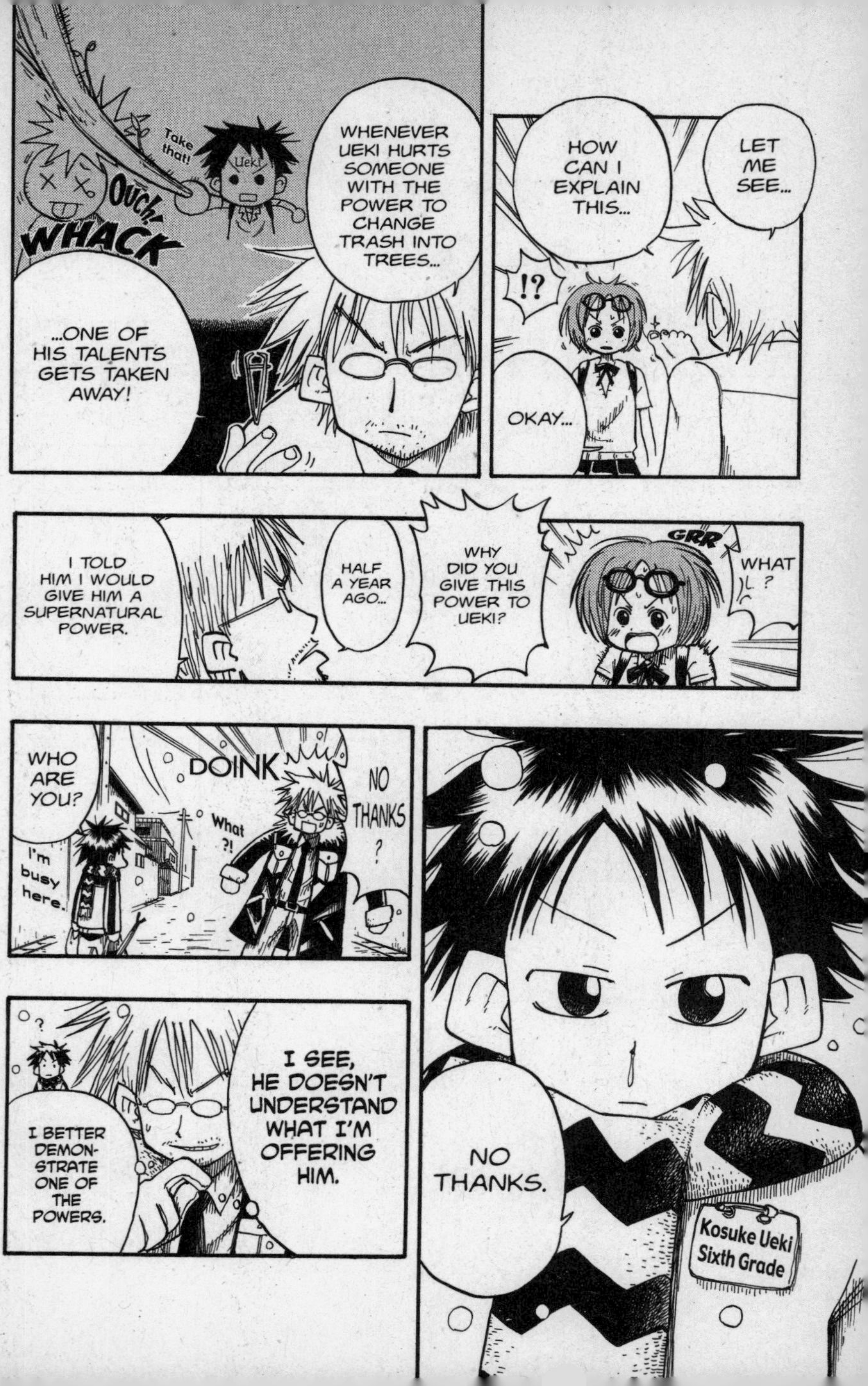
LET ME SEE...
HOW CAN I EXPLAIN THIS...
!?
OKAY...
WHENEVER UEKI HURTS SOMEONE WITH THE POWER TO CHANGE TRASH INTO TREES...
Take that!
Ueki
OUCH!
WHACK
...ONE OF HIS TALENTS GETS TAKEN AWAY!
WHAT!?
GRR
WHY DID YOU GIVE THIS POWER TO UEKI?
HALF A YEAR AGO...
I TOLD HIM I WOULD GIVE HIM A SUPERNATURAL POWER.
NO THANKS.
Kosuke Ueki Sixth Grade
NO THANKS?
DOINK
What?!
WHO ARE YOU?
I'm busy here.
I SEE, HE DOESN'T UNDERSTAND WHAT I'M OFFERING HIM.
I BETTER DEMONSTRATE ONE OF THE POWERS.

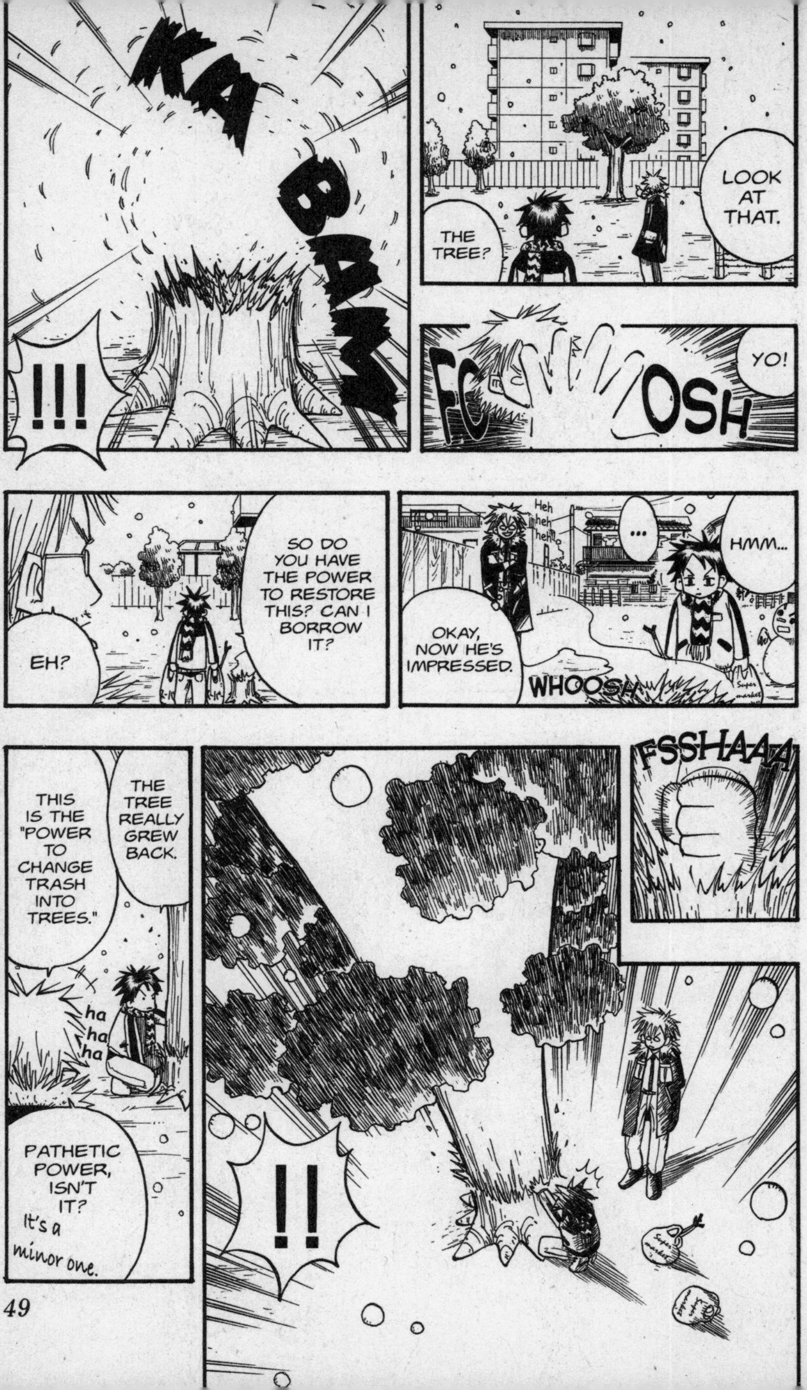
LOOK AT THAT.
THE TREE?
YO!
FOOSH
KA
BAM
!!!
HMM...
...
Heh heh heh
OKAY, NOW HE'S IMPRESSED.
WHOOSH
SO DO YOU HAVE THE POWER TO RESTORE THIS? CAN I BORROW IT?
EH?
FSSHAAA
!!
THE TREE REALLY GREW BACK.
THIS IS THE "POWER TO CHANGE TRASH INTO TREES."
ha ha ha
PATHETIC POWER, ISN'T IT?
It's a minor one.

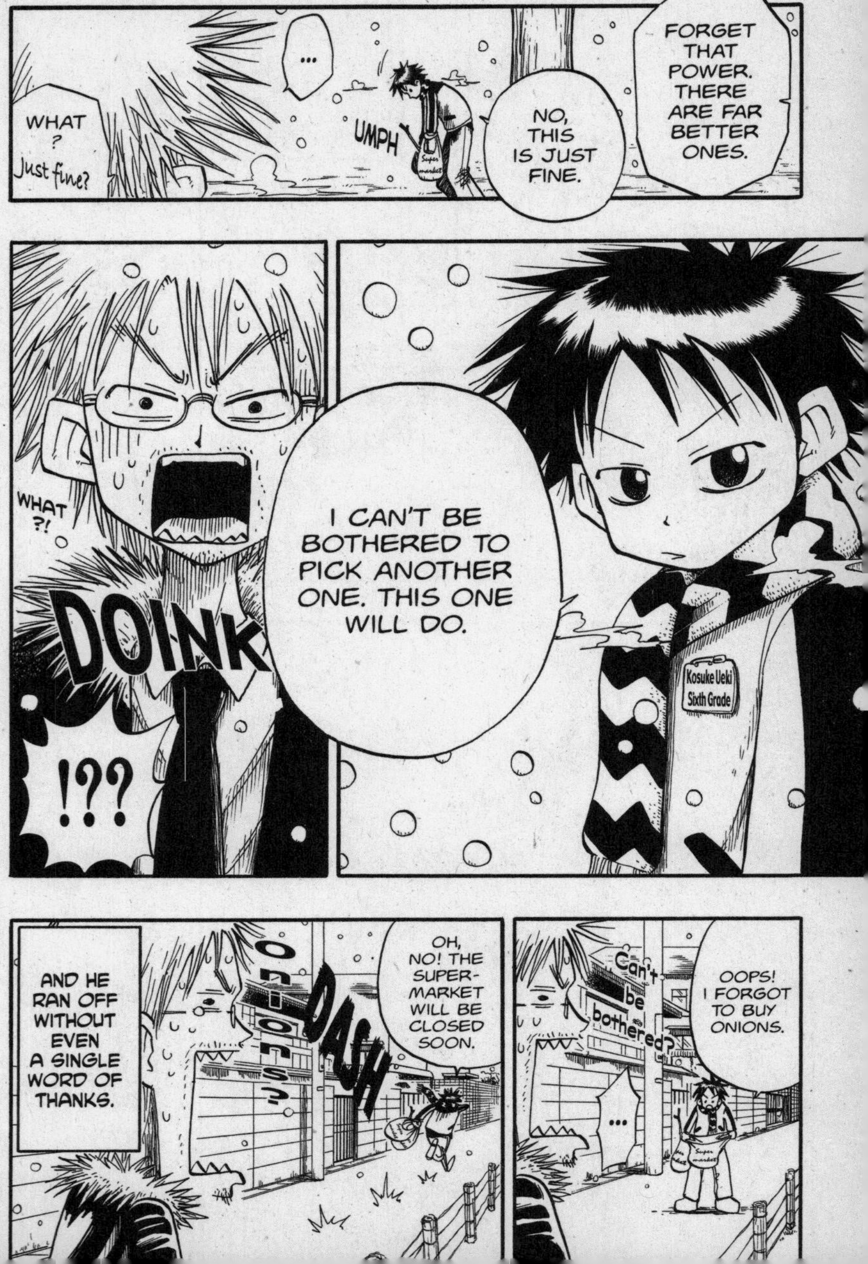
FORGET THAT POWER. THERE ARE FAR BETTER ONES.
NO, THIS IS JUST FINE.
UMPH
Super market
...
WHAT? Just fine?
I CAN'T BE BOTHERED TO PICK ANOTHER ONE. THIS ONE WILL DO.
Kosuke Ueki Sixth Grade
WHAT?!
DOINK
!??
OOPS! I FORGOT TO BUY ONIONS.
Can't be bothered?
...
OH, NO! THE SUPER-MARKET WILL BE CLOSED SOON.
DASH
Onions?
AND HE RAN OFF WITHOUT EVEN A SINGLE WORD OF THANKS.

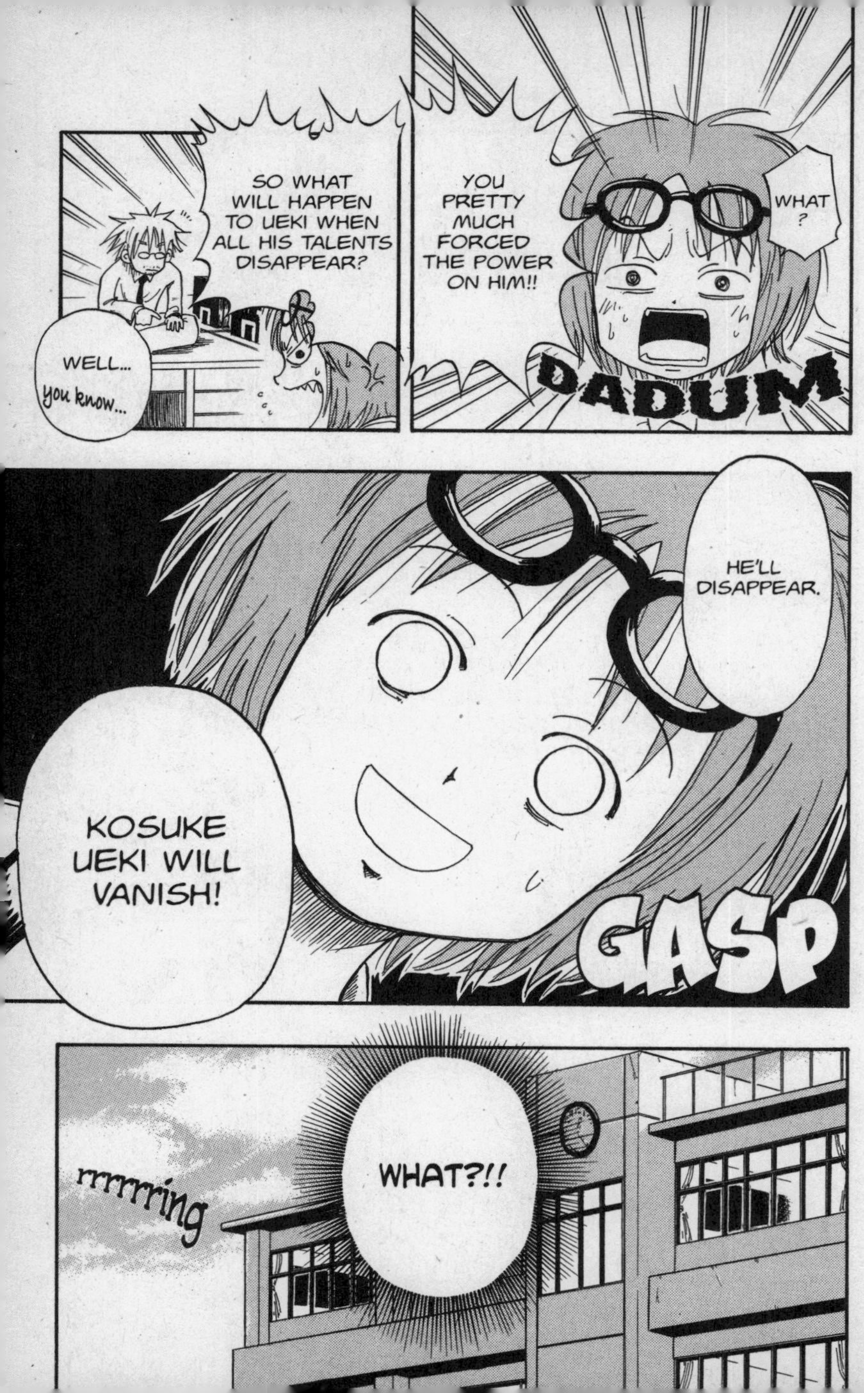
YOU PRETTY MUCH FORCED THE POWER ON HIM!!
WHAT?
DADUM
SO WHAT WILL HAPPEN TO UEKI WHEN ALL HIS TALENTS DISAPPEAR?
WELL... you know...
HE'LL DISAPPEAR.
KOSUKE UEKI WILL VANISH!
GASP
WHAT?!!
rrrrrring

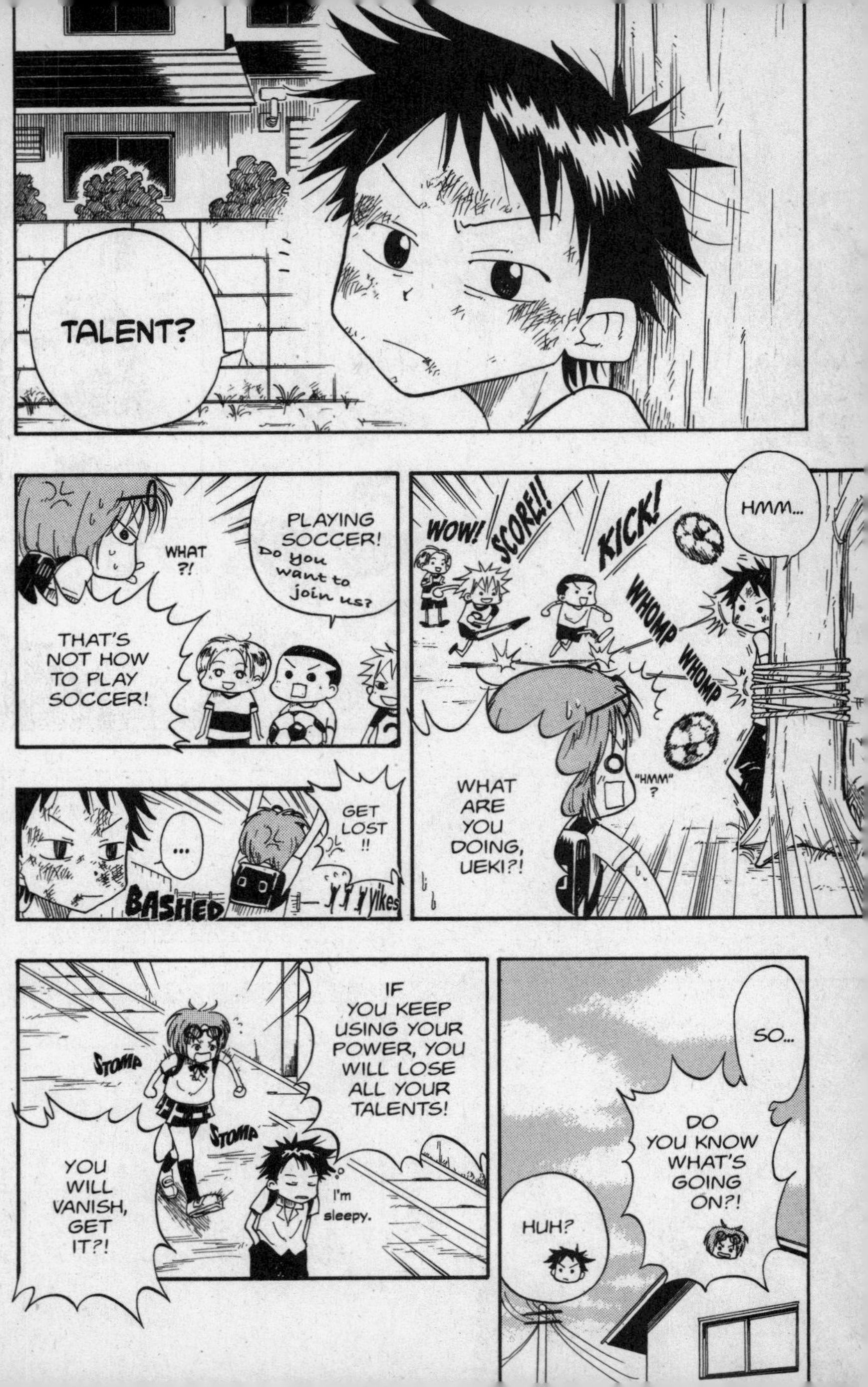
TALENT?
HMM...
KICK!
SCORE!!
WOW!
WHOMP
WHOMP
"HMM"?
WHAT ARE YOU DOING, UEKI?!
PLAYING SOCCER! Do you want to join us?
WHAT?!
THAT'S NOT HOW TO PLAY SOCCER!
GET LOST!!
yikes
...
BASHED
SO...
DO YOU KNOW WHAT'S GOING ON?!
HUH?
IF YOU KEEP USING YOUR POWER, YOU WILL LOSE ALL YOUR TALENTS!
STOMP
STOMP
I'm sleepy.
YOU WILL VANISH, GET IT?!

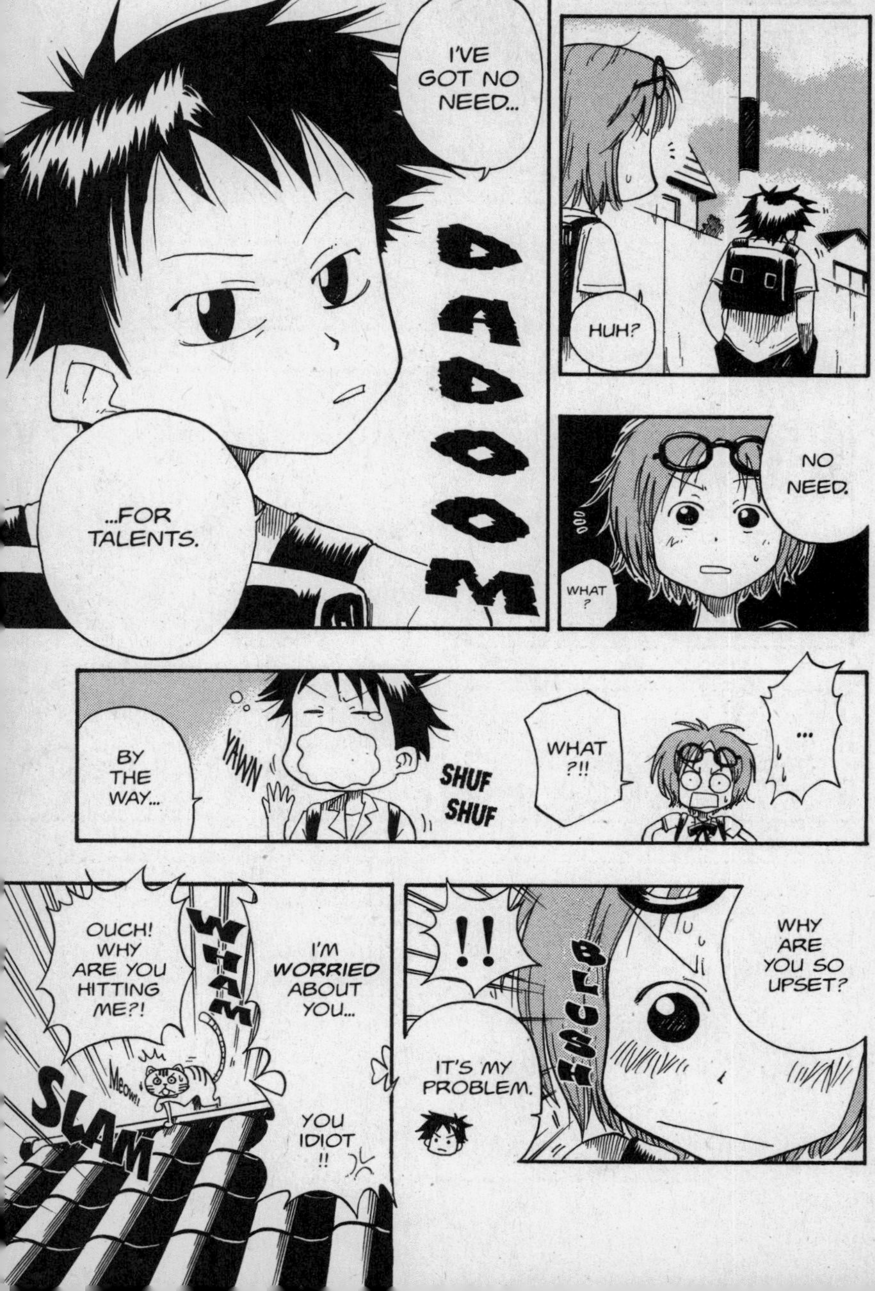
HUH?
NO NEED.
WHAT ?
I'VE GOT NO NEED...
DADOOOM
...FOR TALENTS.
...
WHAT ?!!
SHUF SHUF
YAWN
BY THE WAY...
WHY ARE YOU SO UPSET?
!!
BLUSH
IT'S MY PROBLEM.
I'M WORRIED ABOUT YOU...
WHAM
OUCH! WHY ARE YOU HITTING ME?!
YOU IDIOT !!
Meow!!
SLAM

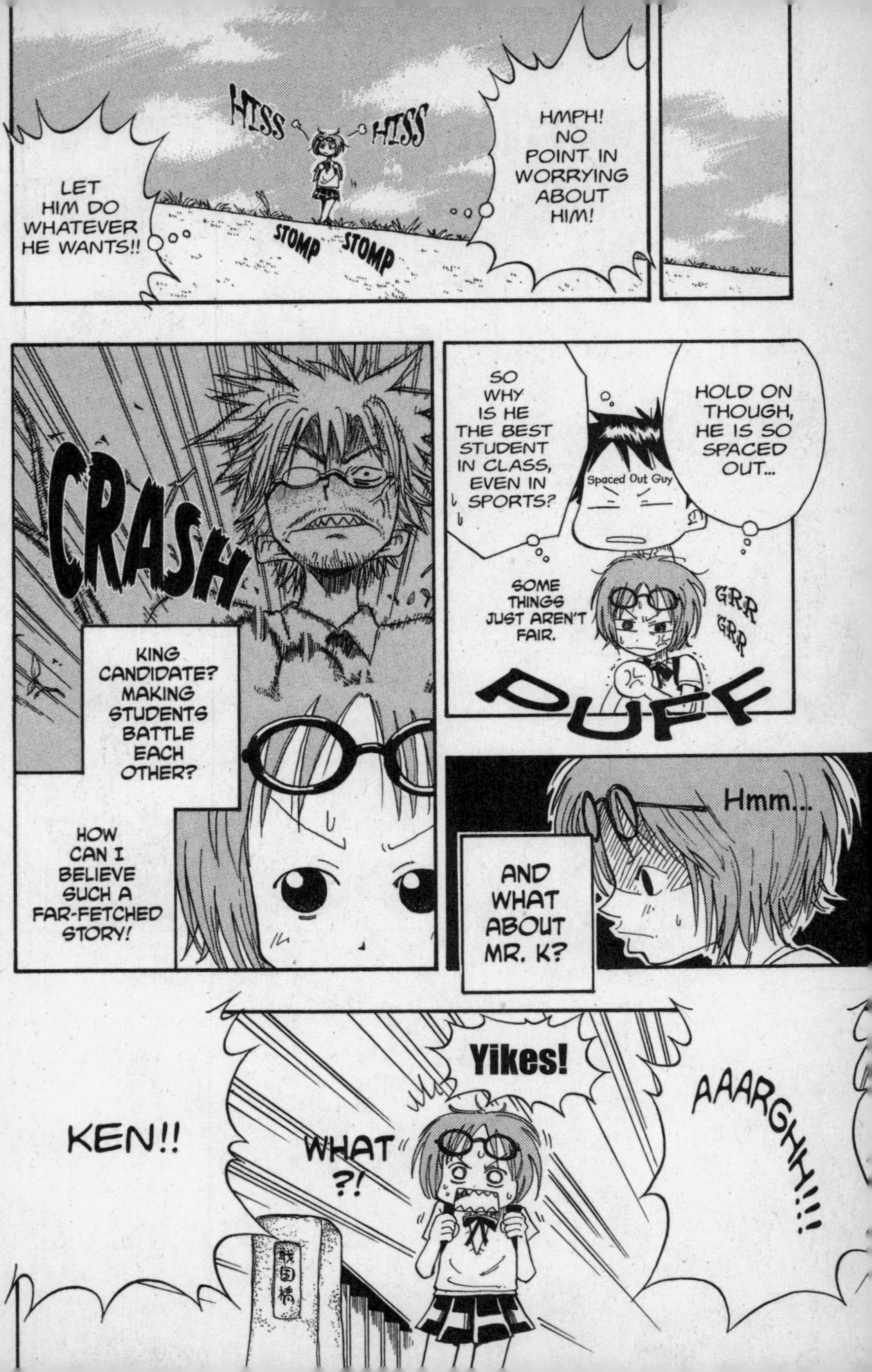
HMPH! NO POINT IN WORRYING ABOUT HIM!
HISS
HISS
LET HIM DO WHATEVER HE WANTS!!
STOMP
STOMP
HOLD ON THOUGH, HE IS SO SPACED OUT...
SO WHY IS HE THE BEST STUDENT IN CLASS, EVEN IN SPORTS?
Spaced Out Guy
GRR
GRR
SOME THINGS JUST AREN'T FAIR.
PUFF
Hmm...
AND WHAT ABOUT MR. K?
CRASH
KING CANDIDATE? MAKING STUDENTS BATTLE EACH OTHER?
HOW CAN I BELIEVE SUCH A FAR-FETCHED STORY!
AAARGHH!!!
Yikes!
WHAT ?!
戦国橋
KEN!!

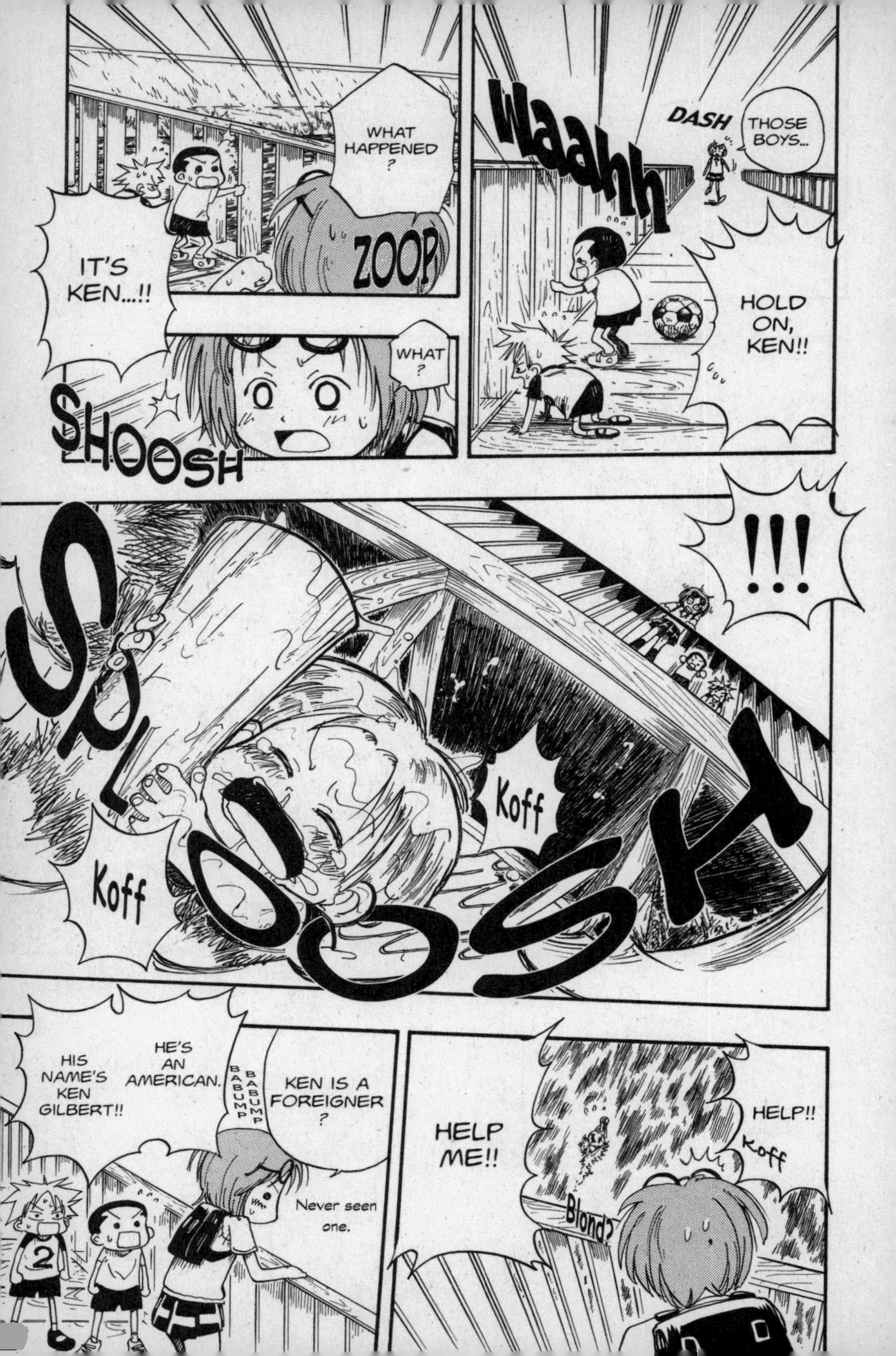
DASH
THOSE BOYS...
Waaahh
HOLD ON, KEN!!
WHAT HAPPENED?
ZOOP
IT'S KEN...!!
WHAT?
SHOOSH
!!!
SPLOOSH
Koff
Koff
HELP!!
Koff
HELP ME!!
Blond?
KEN IS A FOREIGNER?
BABUMP BABUMP
HE'S AN AMERICAN.
HIS NAME'S KEN GILBERT!!
Never seen one.

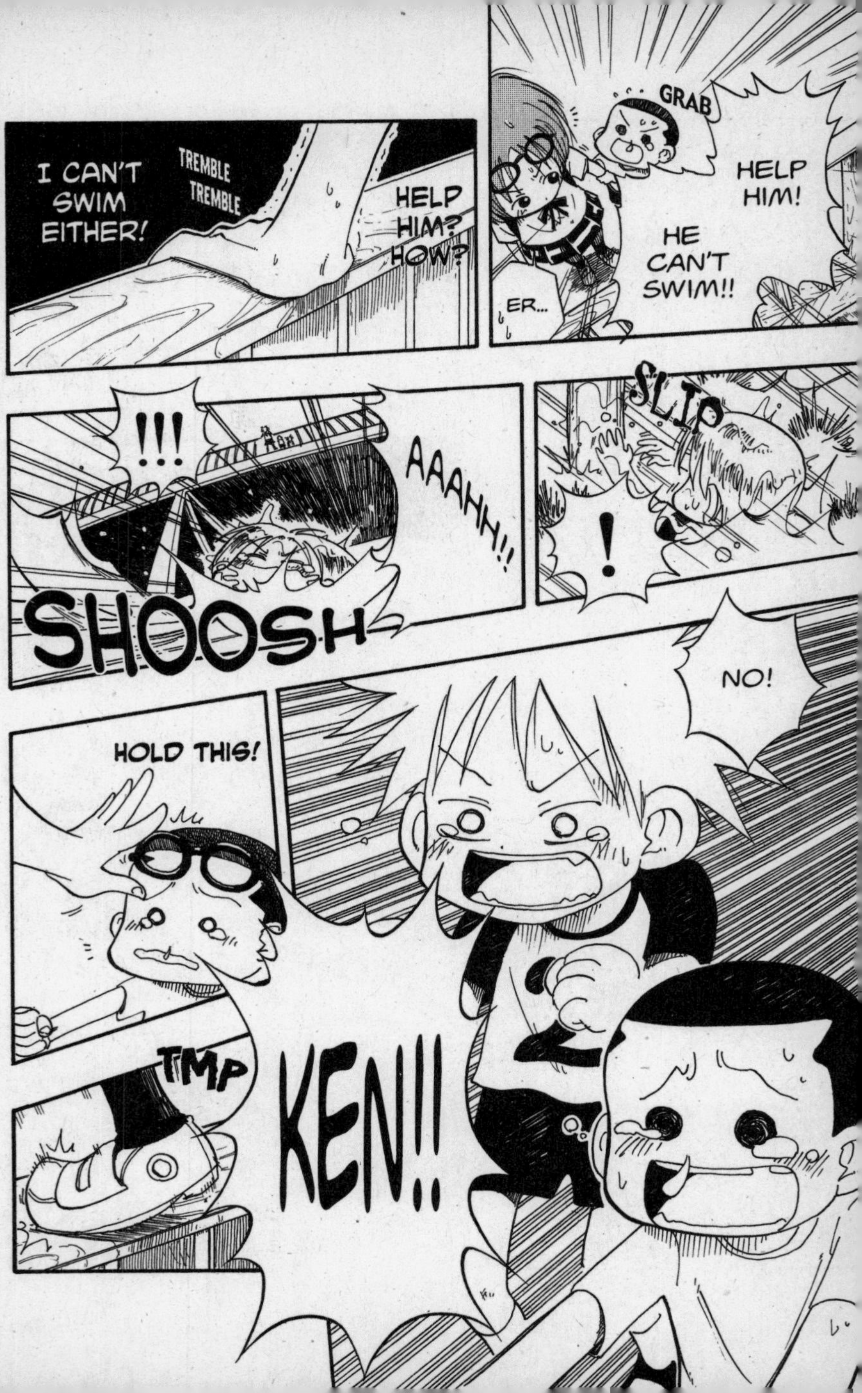
GRAB
HELP HIM!
HE CAN'T SWIM!!
ER...
HELP HIM? HOW?
I CAN'T SWIM EITHER!
TREMBLE TREMBLE
SLIP
!
!!!
AAAHH!!
SHOOSH
NO!
KEN!!
HOLD THIS!
TMP

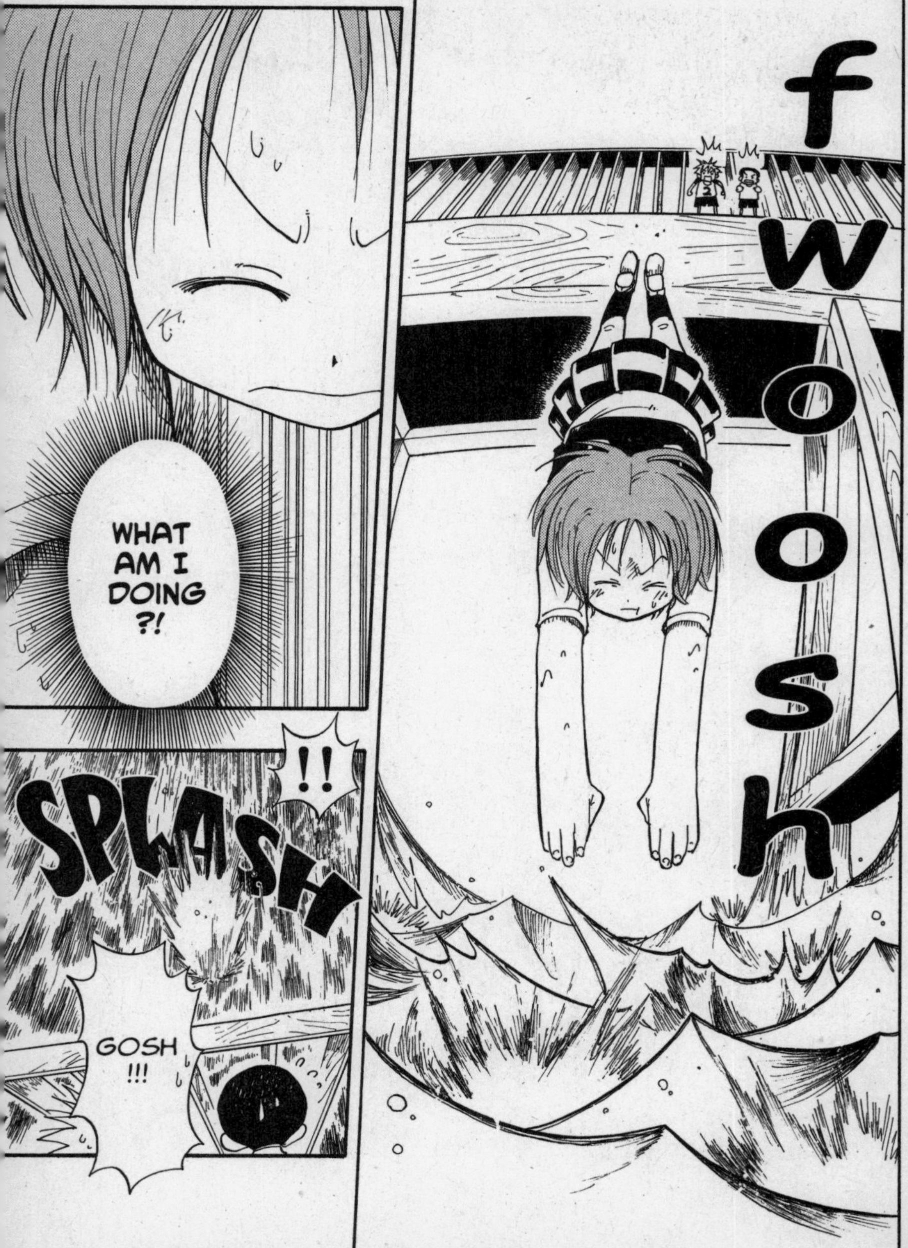
fwoosh
WHAT AM I DOING ?!
!!
SPLASH
GOSH !!!

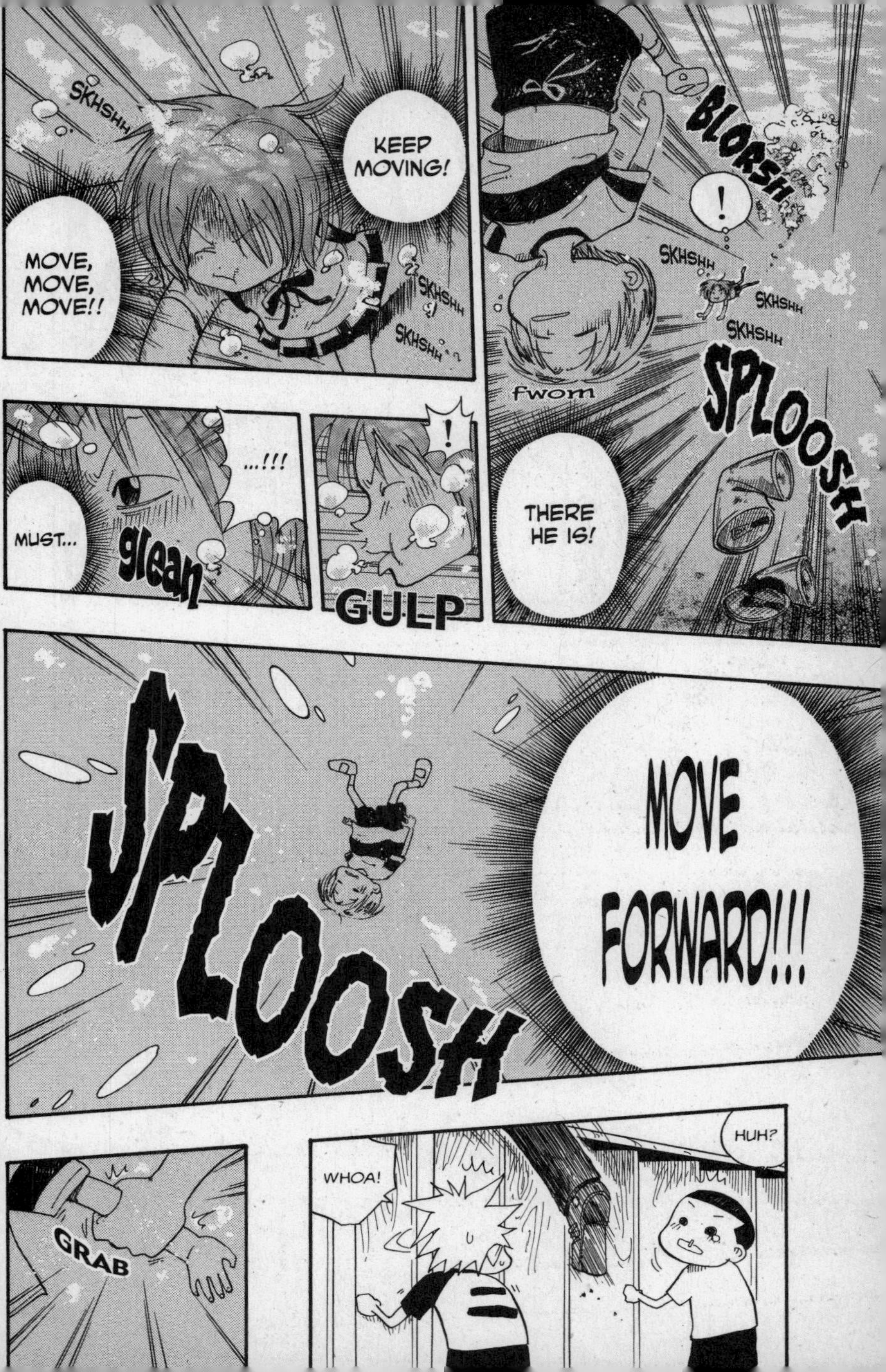
BLORSH
!
SKHSHH
SKHSHH
SKHSHH
fwom
SPLOOSH
THERE HE IS!
KEEP MOVING!
SKHSHH
MOVE, MOVE, MOVE!!
SKHSHH
SKHSHH
!
GULP
...!!!
MUST...
glean
MOVE FORWARD!!!
SPLOOSH
HUH?
WHOA!
GRAB

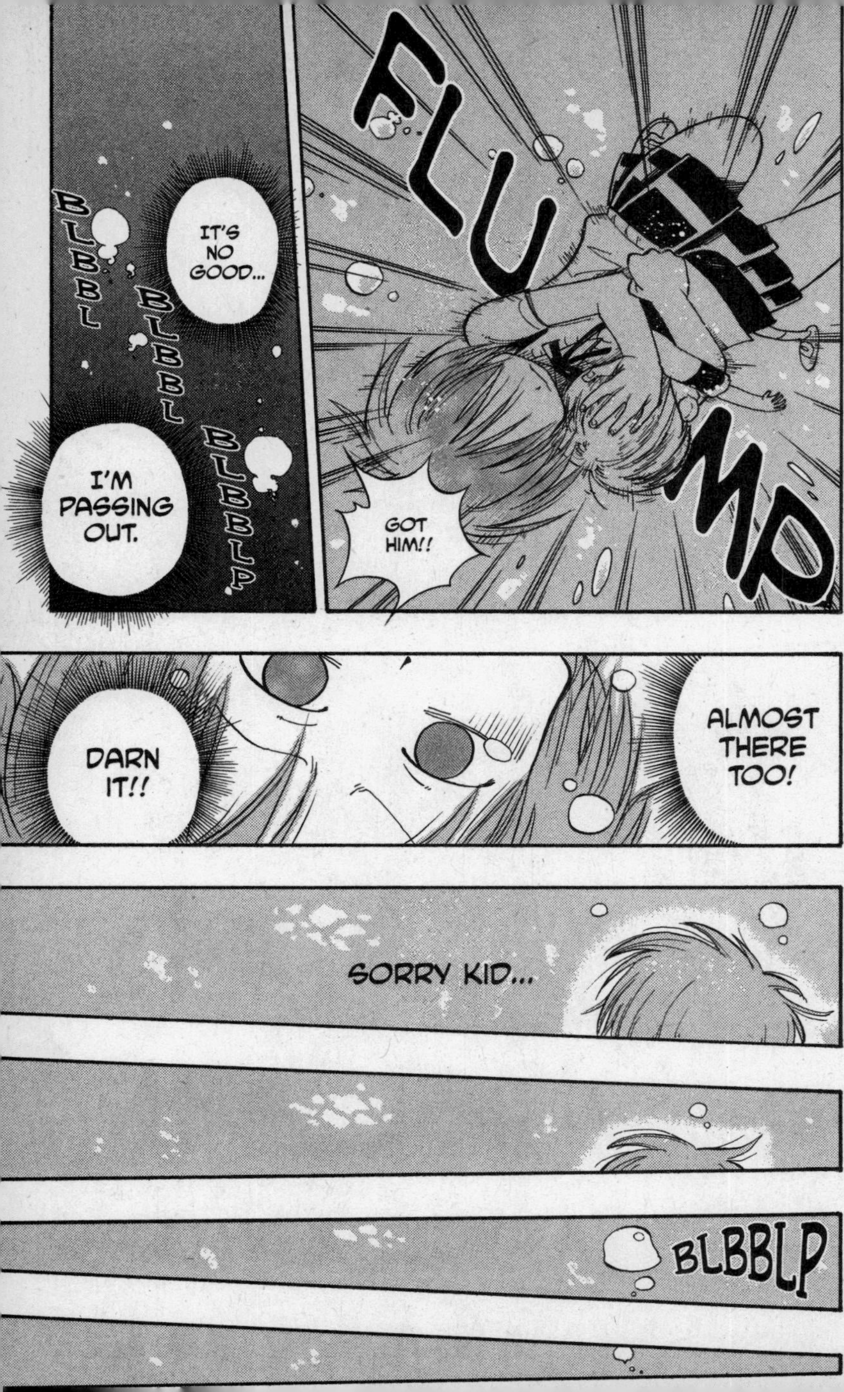
FLUMP
GOT HIM!!
IT'S NO GOOD...
BLBBL
BLBBL
BLBBBLP
I'M PASSING OUT.
ALMOST THERE TOO!
DARN IT!!
SORRY KID...
BLBBLP

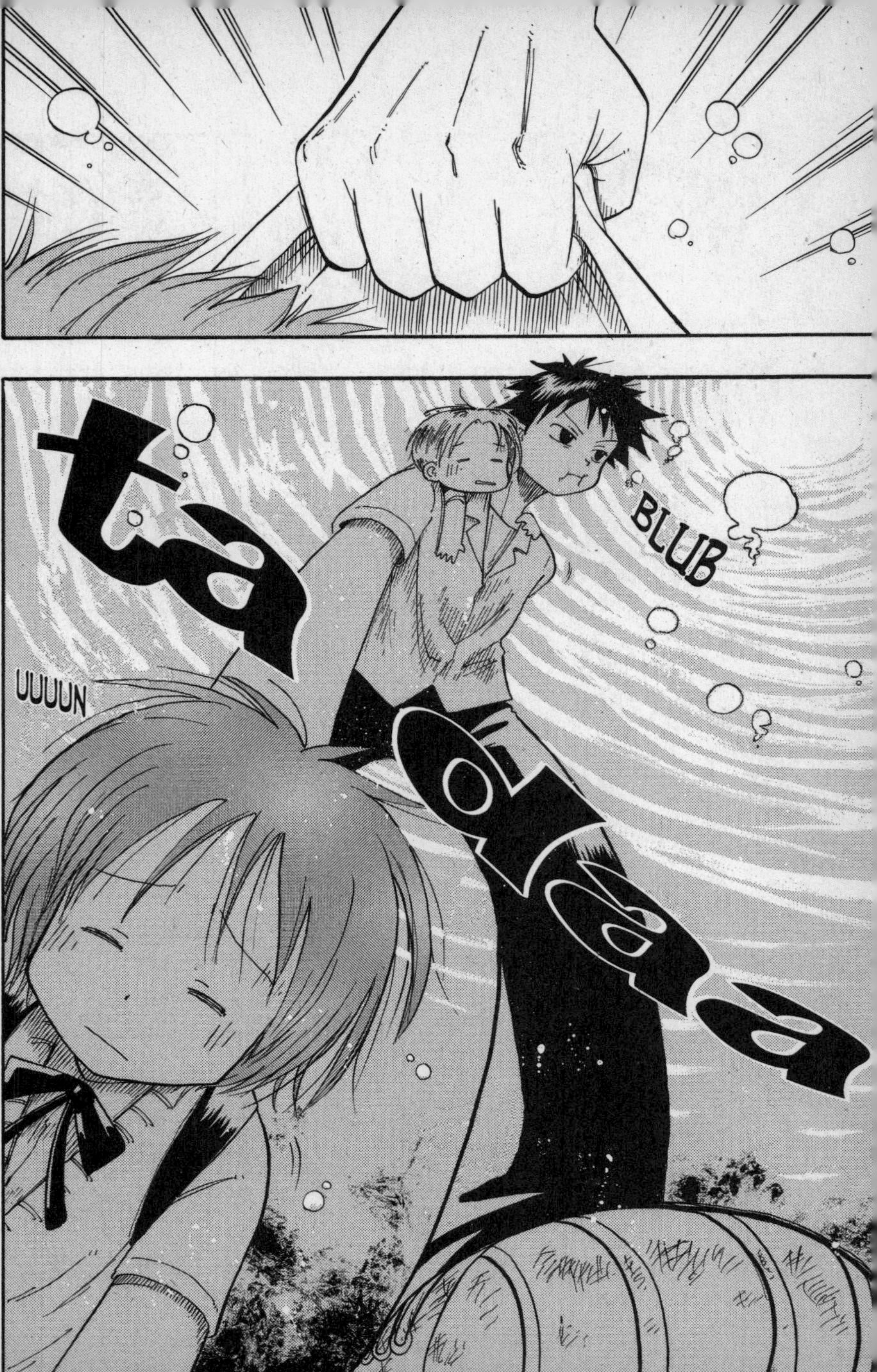
BLUB
taaaa
UUUUN

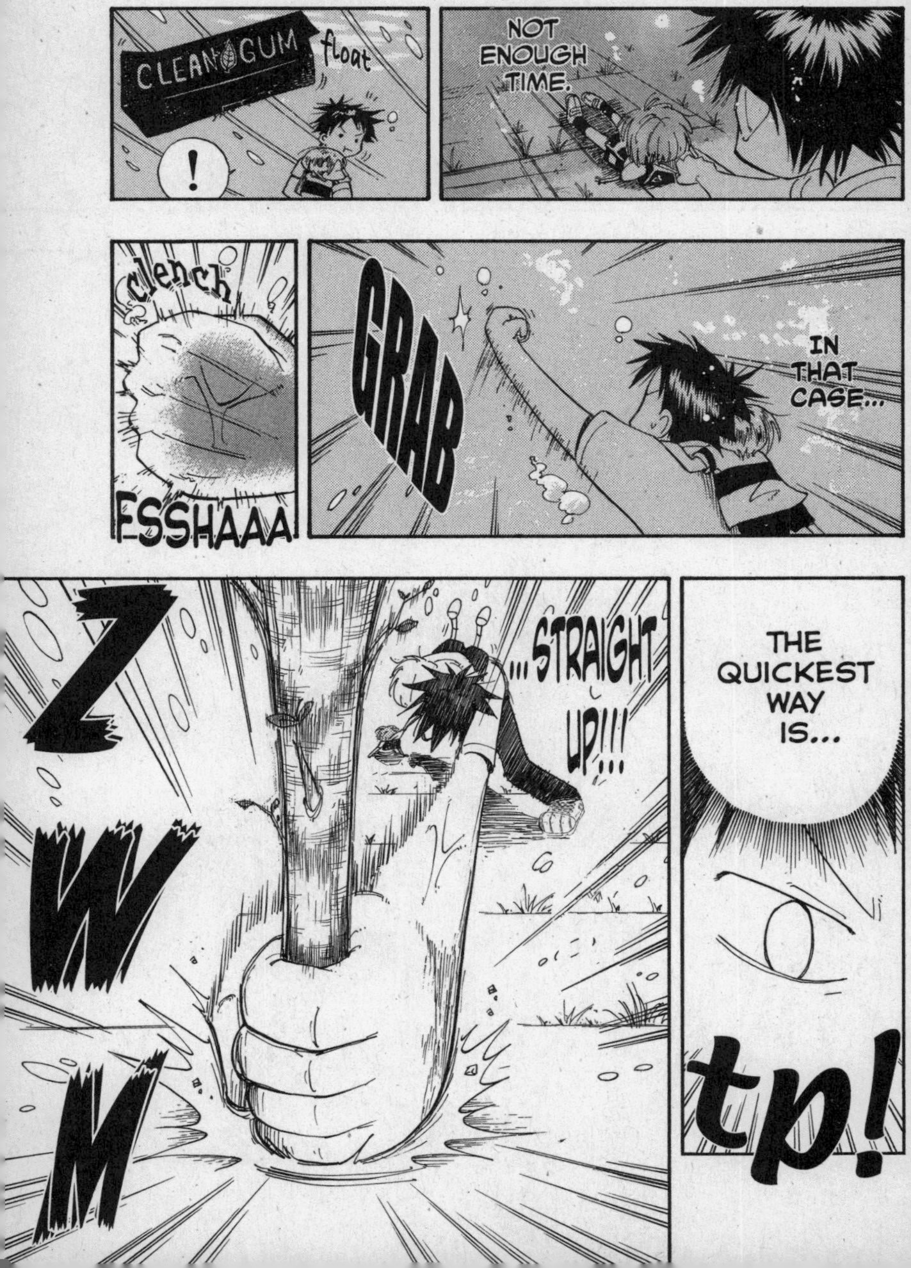
NOT ENOUGH TIME.
CLEAN GUM
float
!
IN THAT CASE...
GRAB
clench
FSSHAAA
THE QUICKEST WAY IS...
tp!
...STRAIGHT UP!!!
ZWM

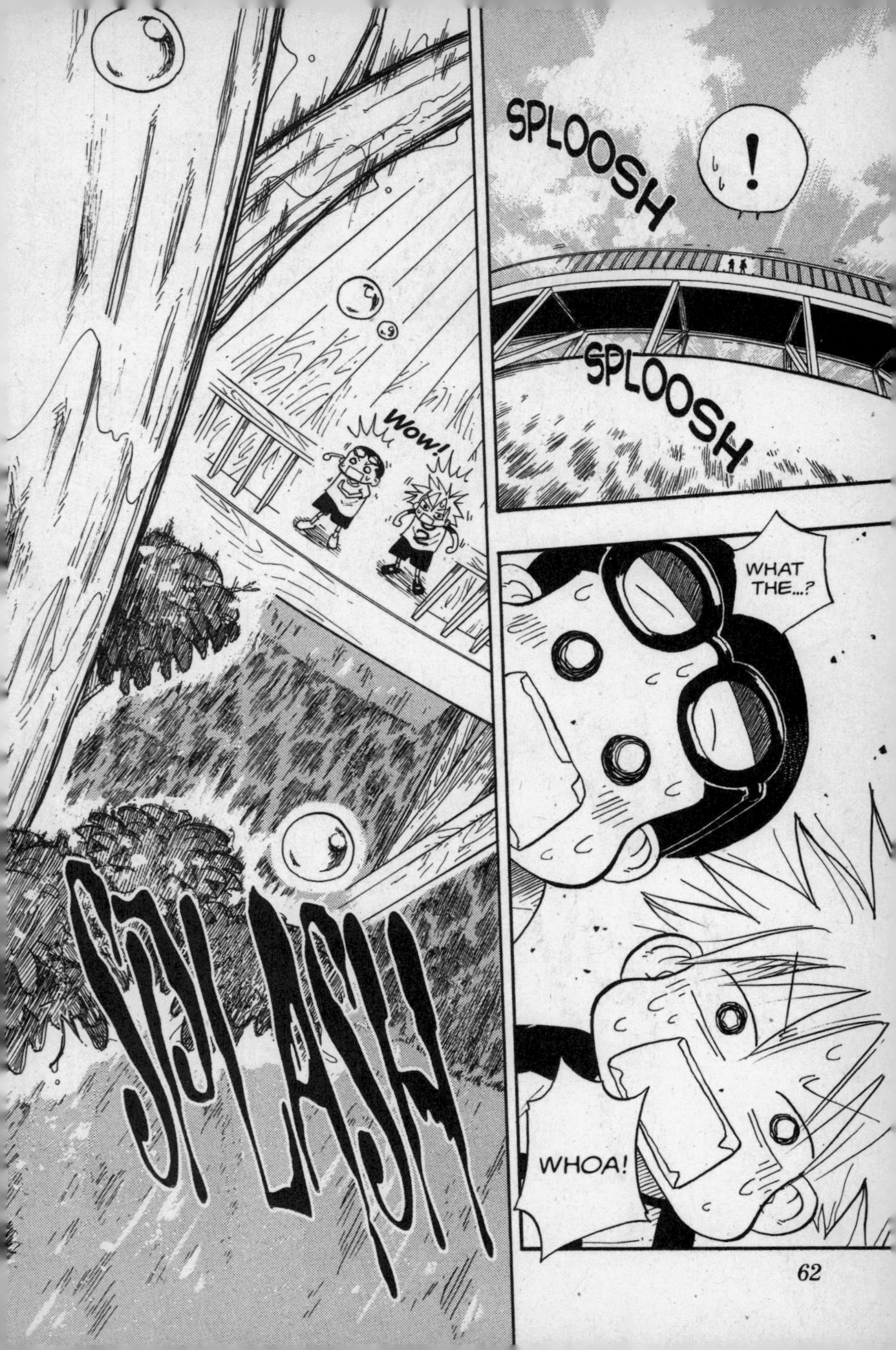
SPLOOSH
!
SPLOOSH
WHAT THE...?
WHOA!
Wow!
SPLASH

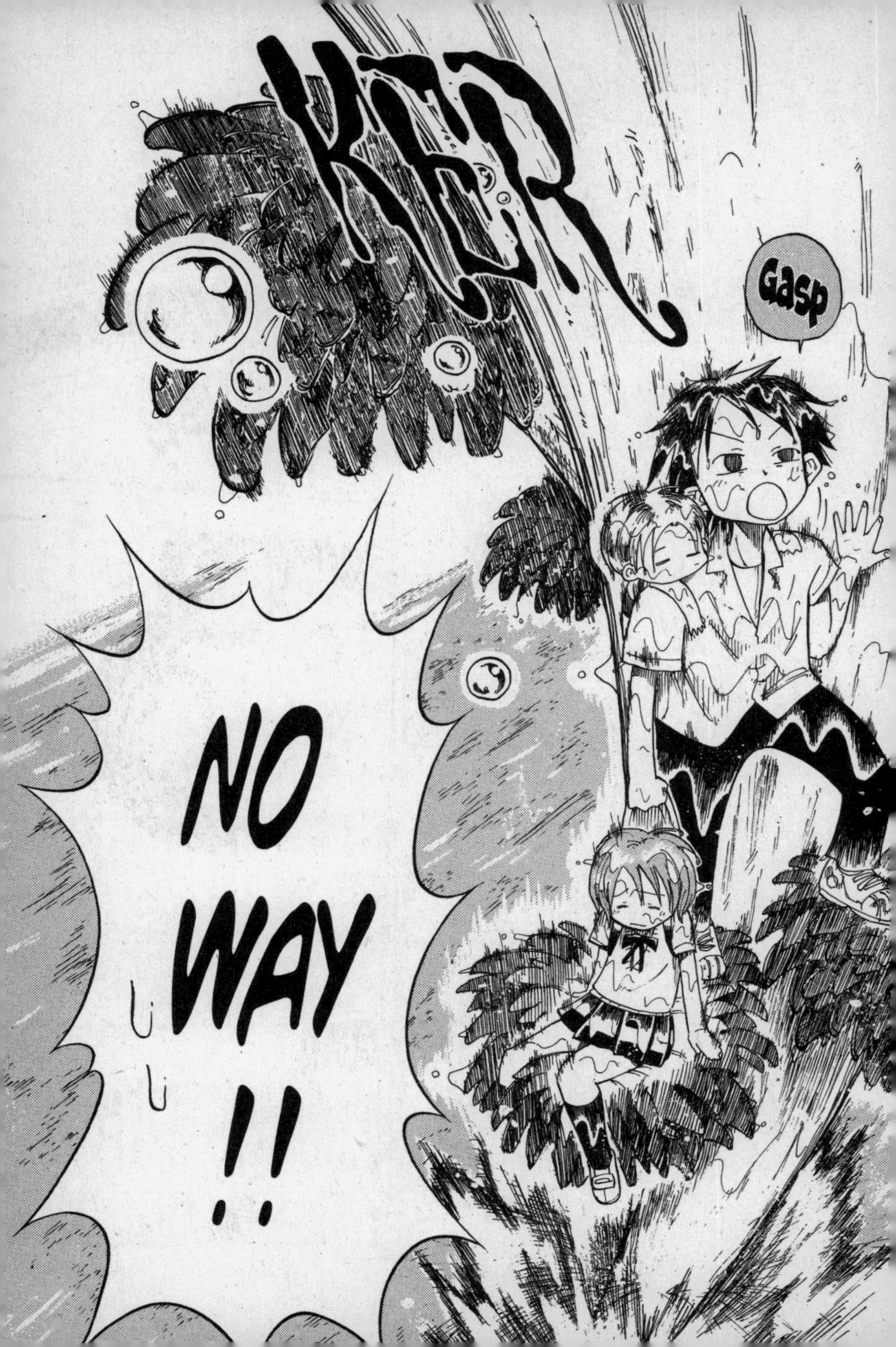
Gasp
NO WAY!!

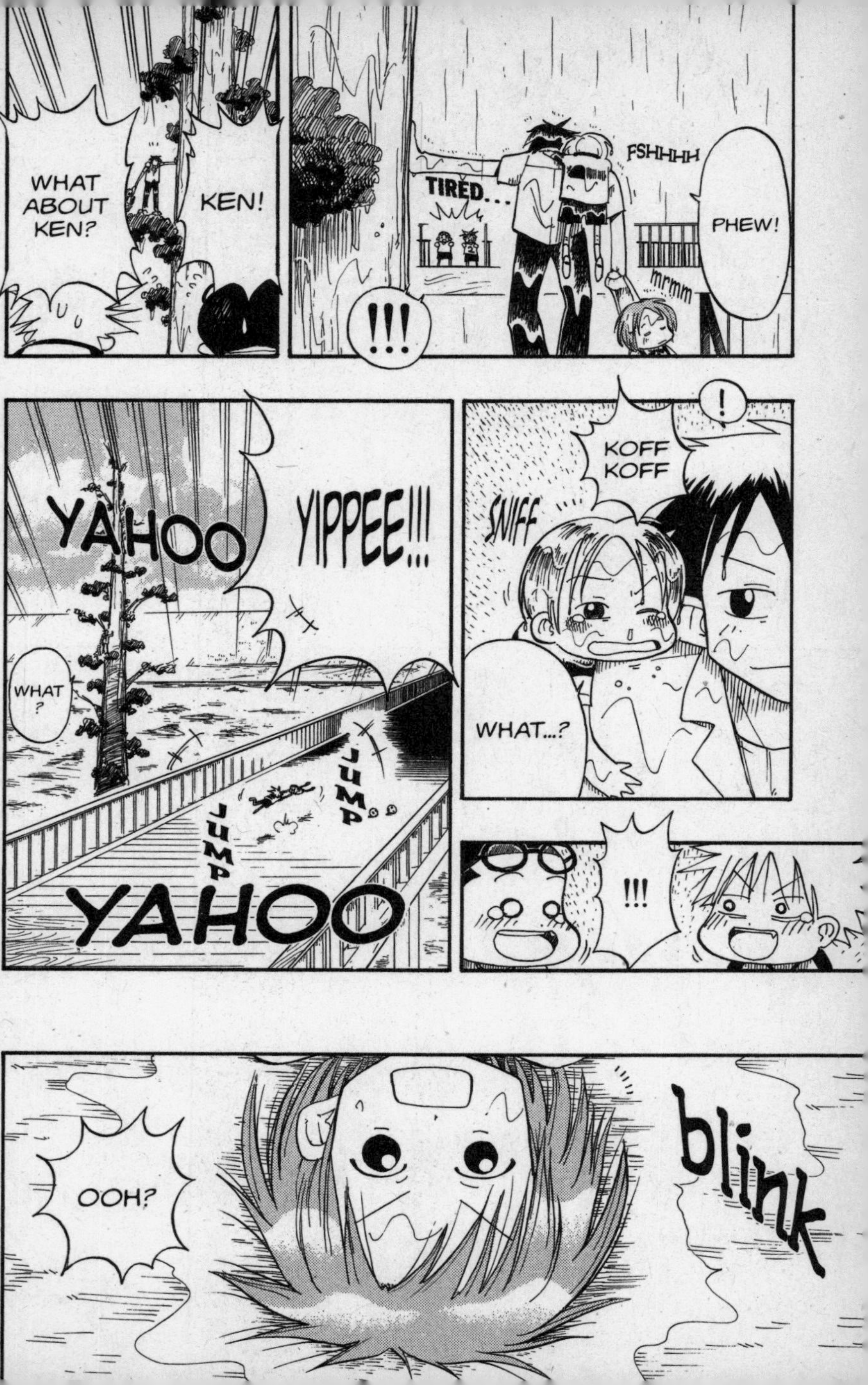
PHEW!
FSHHHH
TIRED...
mrmm
!!!
KEN!
WHAT ABOUT KEN?
!
KOFF KOFF
SNIFF
WHAT...?
!!!
YIPPEE!!!
YAHOO
WHAT?
JUMP
JUMP
YAHOO
blink
OOH?

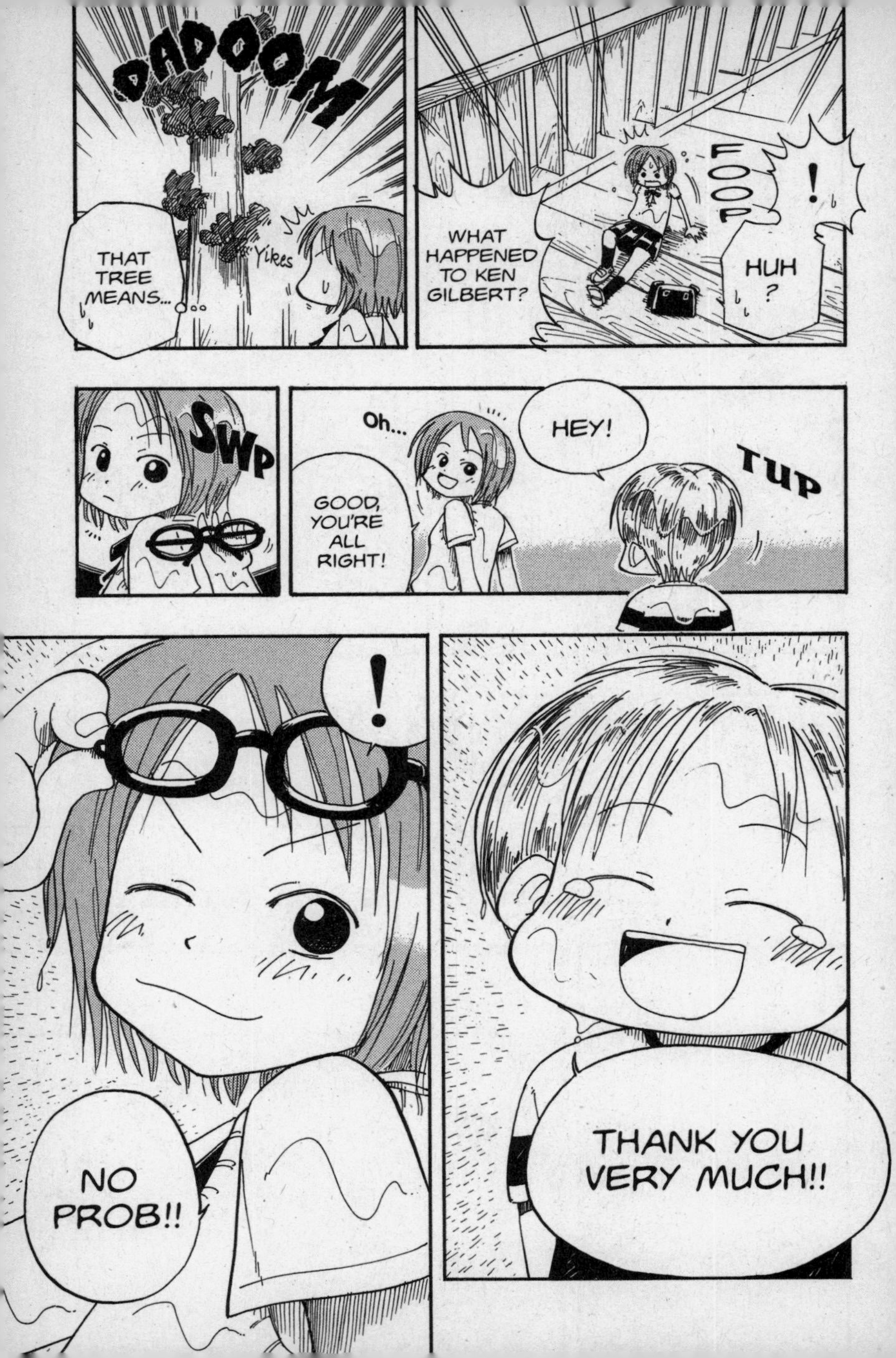
!
HUH ?
FOOP
WHAT HAPPENED TO KEN GILBERT?
DADOOM
Yikes
THAT TREE MEANS...
TUP
HEY!
Oh...
GOOD, YOU'RE ALL RIGHT!
SWP
THANK YOU VERY MUCH!!
!
NO PROB!!

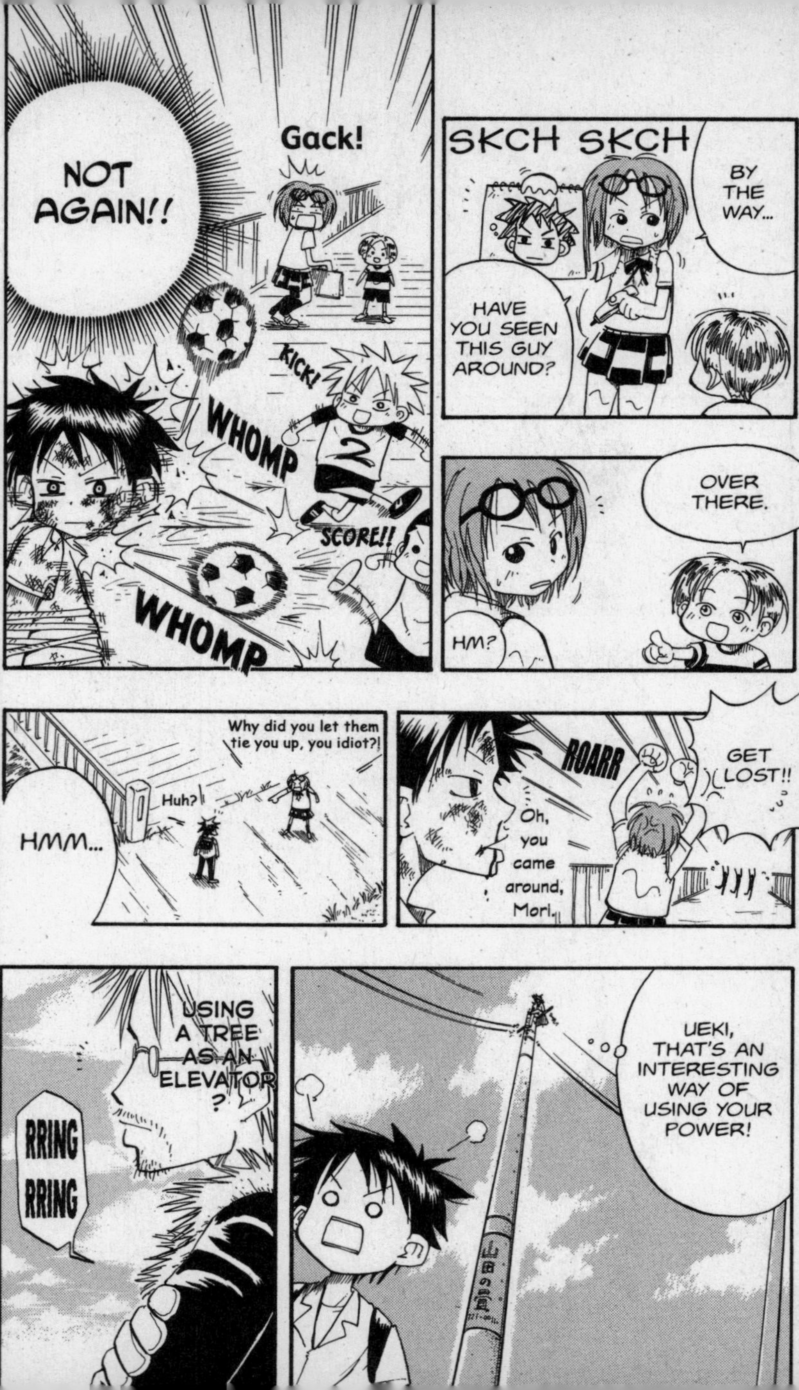
SKCH SKCH
BY THE WAY...
HAVE YOU SEEN THIS GUY AROUND?
OVER THERE.
HM?
Gack!
NOT AGAIN!!
KICK!
WHOMP
SCORE!!
WHOMP
GET LOST!!
ROARR
Oh, you came around, Mori.
Why did you let them tie you up, you idiot?!
Huh?
HMM...
UEKI, THAT'S AN INTERESTING WAY OF USING YOUR POWER!
USING A TREE AS AN ELEVATOR?
RRING RRING

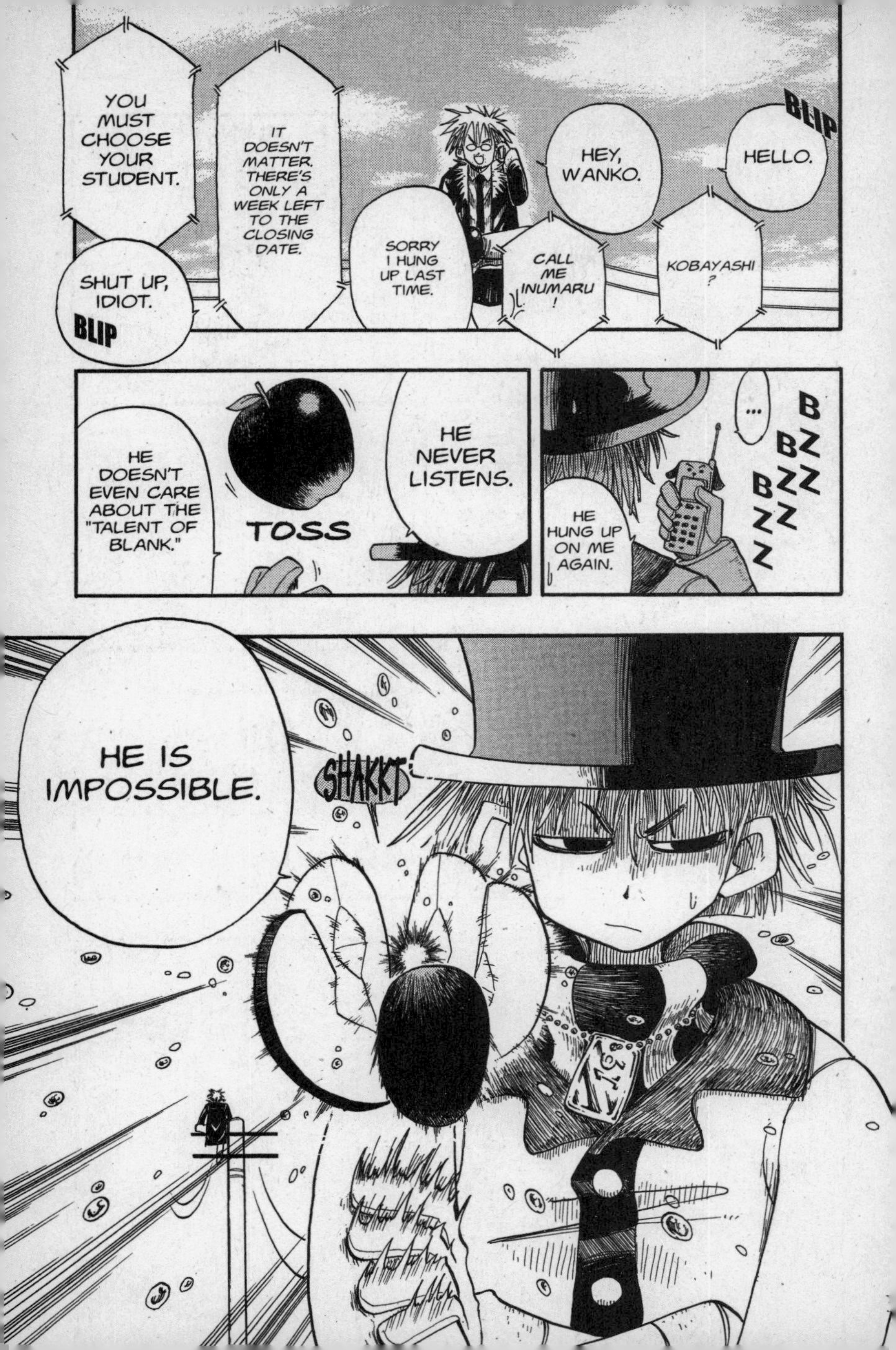
BLIP
HELLO.
KOBAYASHI?
HEY, WANKO.
CALL ME INUMARU!
SORRY I HUNG UP LAST TIME.
IT DOESN'T MATTER. THERE'S ONLY A WEEK LEFT TO THE CLOSING DATE.
YOU MUST CHOOSE YOUR STUDENT.
SHUT UP, IDIOT.
BLIP
...
BZZ BZZ BZZ
HE HUNG UP ON ME AGAIN.
HE NEVER LISTENS.
TOSS
HE DOESN'T EVEN CARE ABOUT THE "TALENT OF BLANK."
SHAKKT
HE IS IMPOSSIBLE.

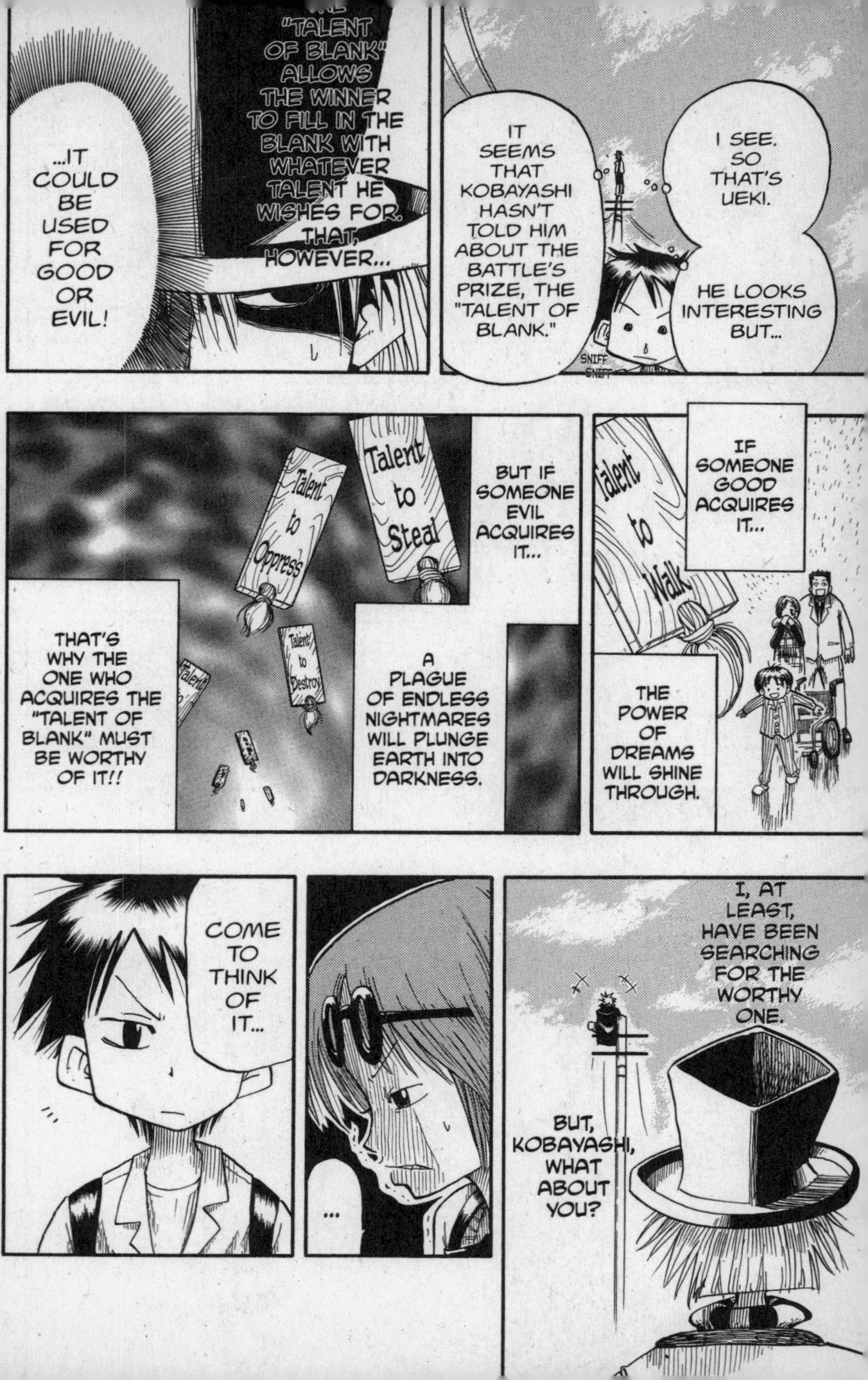
I SEE. SO THAT'S UEKI.
HE LOOKS INTERESTING BUT...
IT SEEMS THAT KOBAYASHI HASN'T TOLD HIM ABOUT THE BATTLE'S PRIZE, THE "TALENT OF BLANK."
SNIFF SNIFF
"TALENT OF BLANK" ALLOWS THE WINNER TO FILL IN THE BLANK WITH WHATEVER TALENT HE WISHES FOR. THAT, HOWEVER...
...IT COULD BE USED FOR GOOD OR EVIL!
IF SOMEONE GOOD ACQUIRES IT...
Talent to Walk
THE POWER OF DREAMS WILL SHINE THROUGH.
BUT IF SOMEONE EVIL ACQUIRES IT...
Talent to Steal
Talent to Oppress
Talent to Destroy
A PLAGUE OF ENDLESS NIGHTMARES WILL PLUNGE EARTH INTO DARKNESS.
THAT'S WHY THE ONE WHO ACQUIRES THE "TALENT OF BLANK" MUST BE WORTHY OF IT!!
I, AT LEAST, HAVE BEEN SEARCHING FOR THE WORTHY ONE.
BUT, KOBAYASHI, WHAT ABOUT YOU?
...
COME TO THINK OF IT...

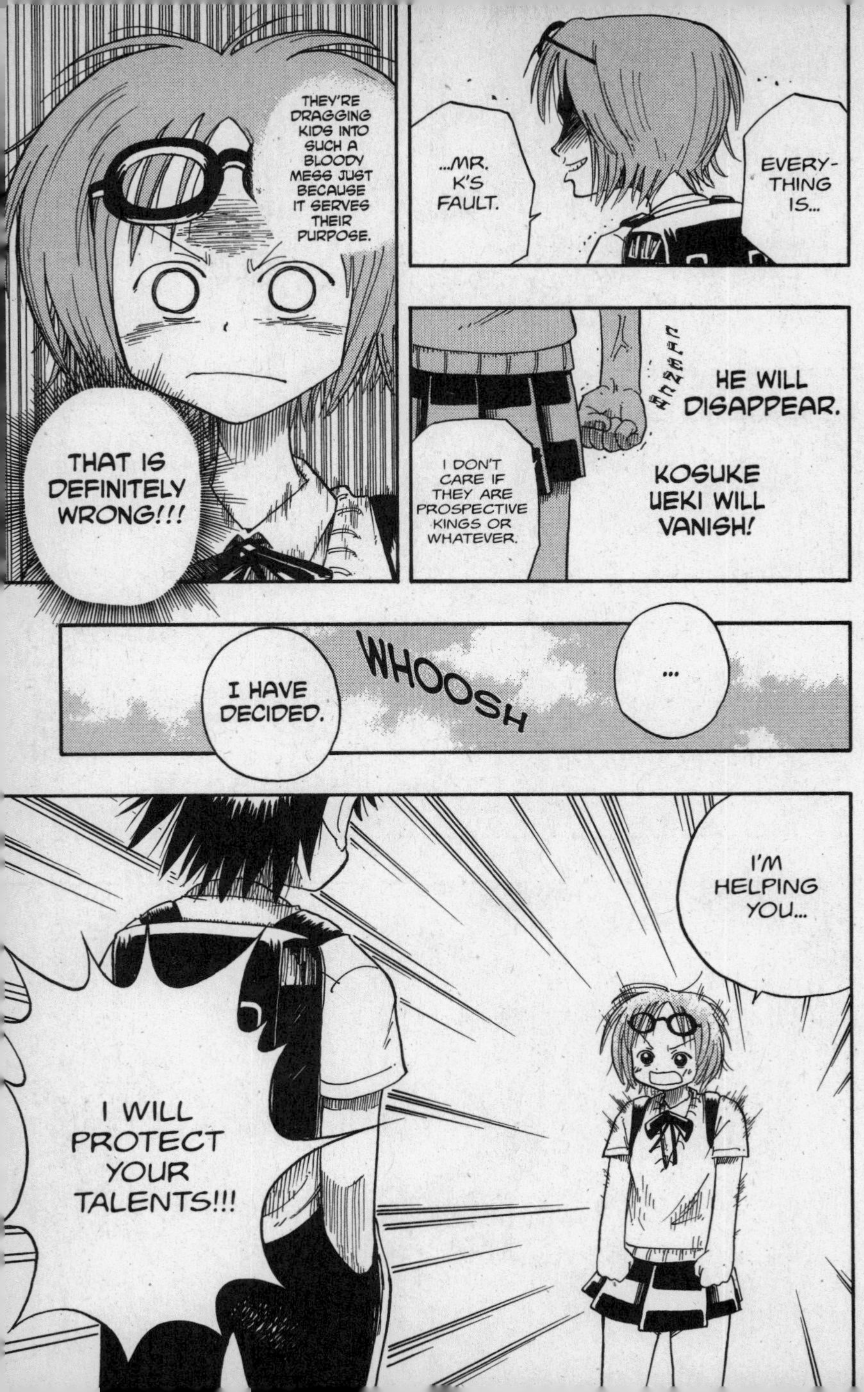
EVERYTHING IS...
...MR. K'S FAULT.
HE WILL DISAPPEAR.
CLENCH
KOSUKE UEKI WILL VANISH!
I DON'T CARE IF THEY ARE PROSPECTIVE KINGS OR WHATEVER.
THEY'RE DRAGGING KIDS INTO SUCH A BLOODY MESS JUST BECAUSE IT SERVES THEIR PURPOSE.
THAT IS DEFINITELY WRONG!!!
...
WHOOSH
I HAVE DECIDED.
I'M HELPING YOU...
I WILL PROTECT YOUR TALENTS!!!

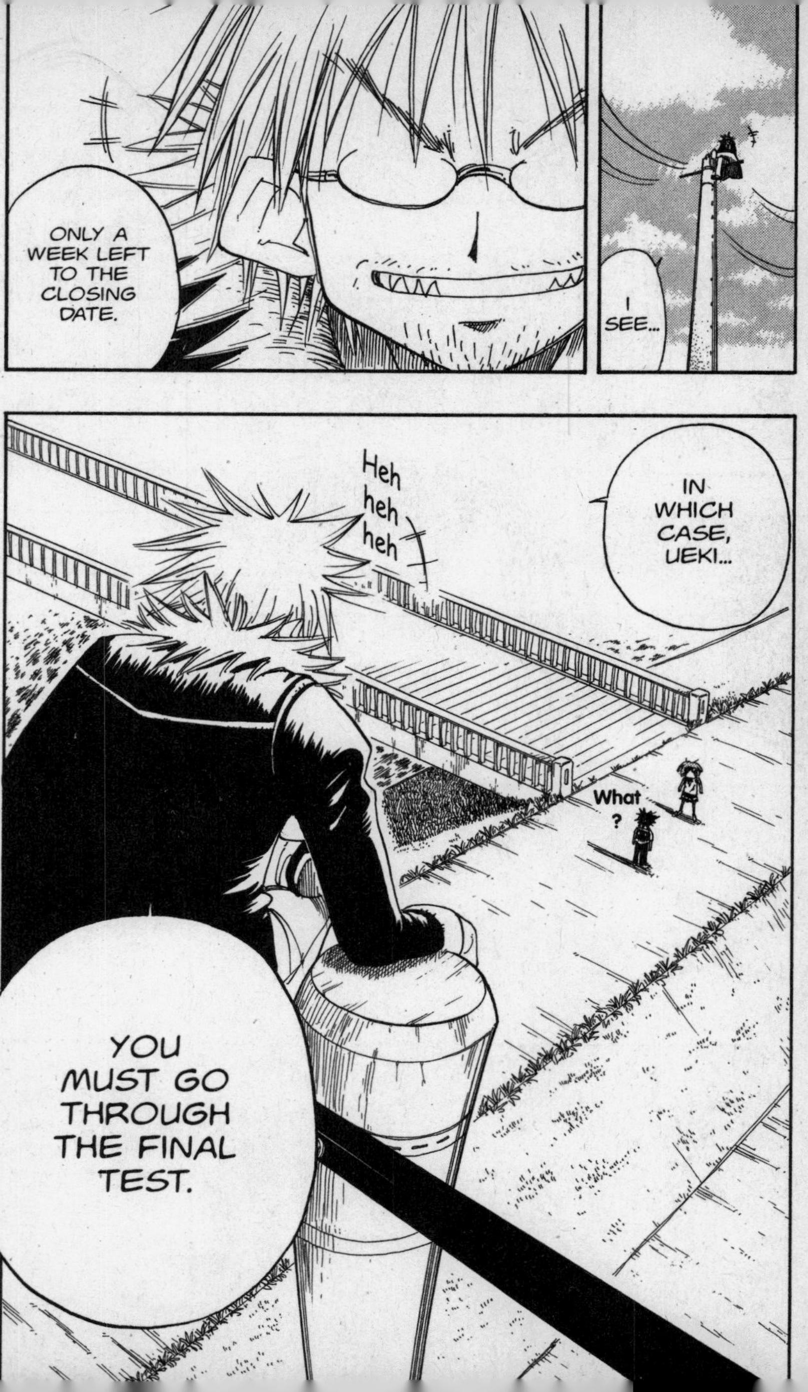
I SEE...
ONLY A WEEK LEFT TO THE CLOSING DATE.
IN WHICH CASE, UEKI...
Heh heh heh
What?
YOU MUST GO THROUGH THE FINAL TEST.

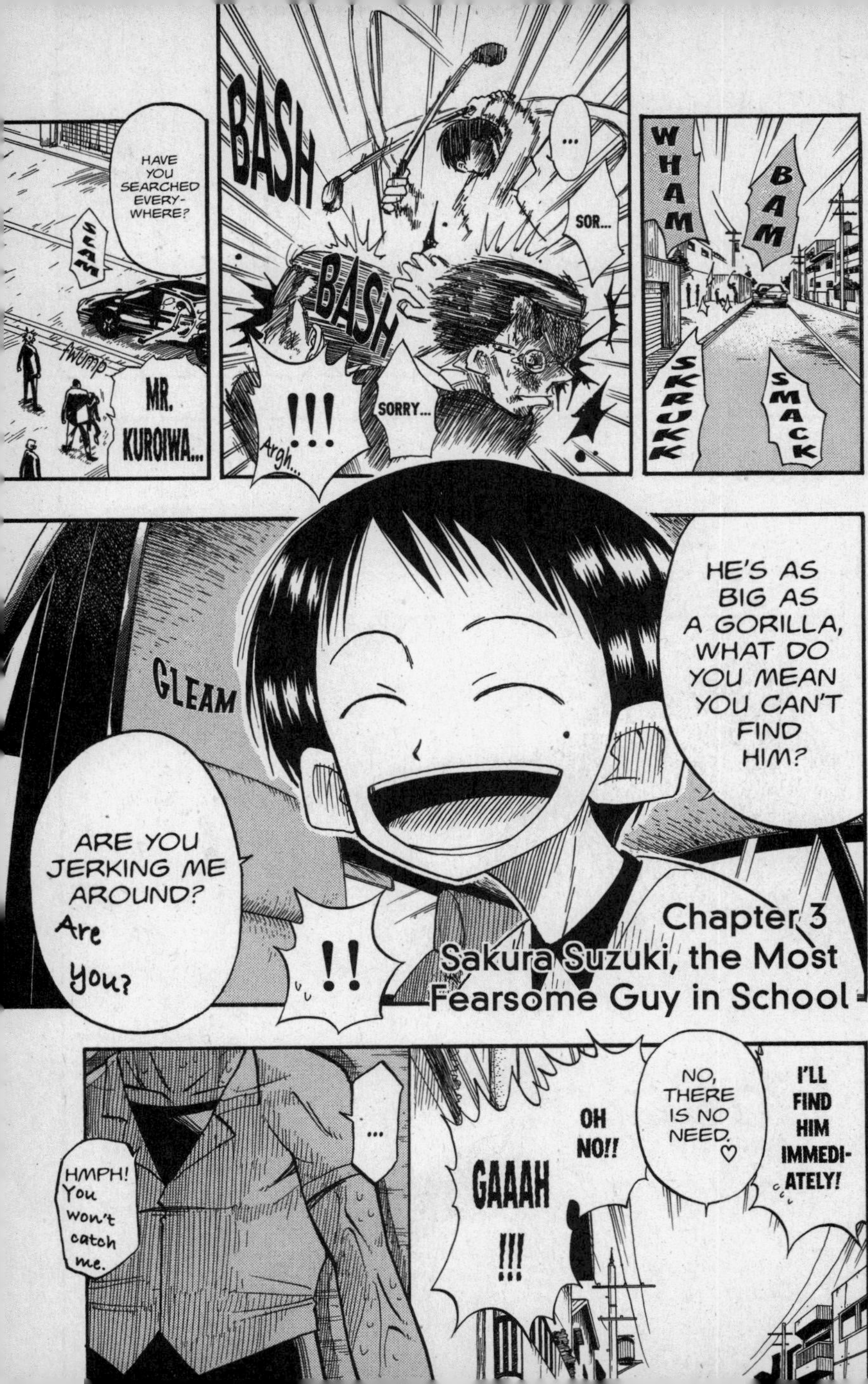
WHAM
BAM
SKRUKK
SMACK
BASH
...
SOR...
BASH
!!!
Argh...
SORRY...
HAVE YOU SEARCHED EVERY-WHERE?
SLAM
fwump
MR. KUROIWA...
HE'S AS BIG AS A GORILLA, WHAT DO YOU MEAN YOU CAN'T FIND HIM?
GLEAM
ARE YOU JERKING ME AROUND? Are you?
!!
Chapter 3
Sakura Suzuki, the Most Fearsome Guy in School
I'LL FIND HIM IMMEDI-ATELY!
NO, THERE IS NO NEED. ♡
OH NO!!
GAAAH!!!
...
HMPH! You won't catch me.

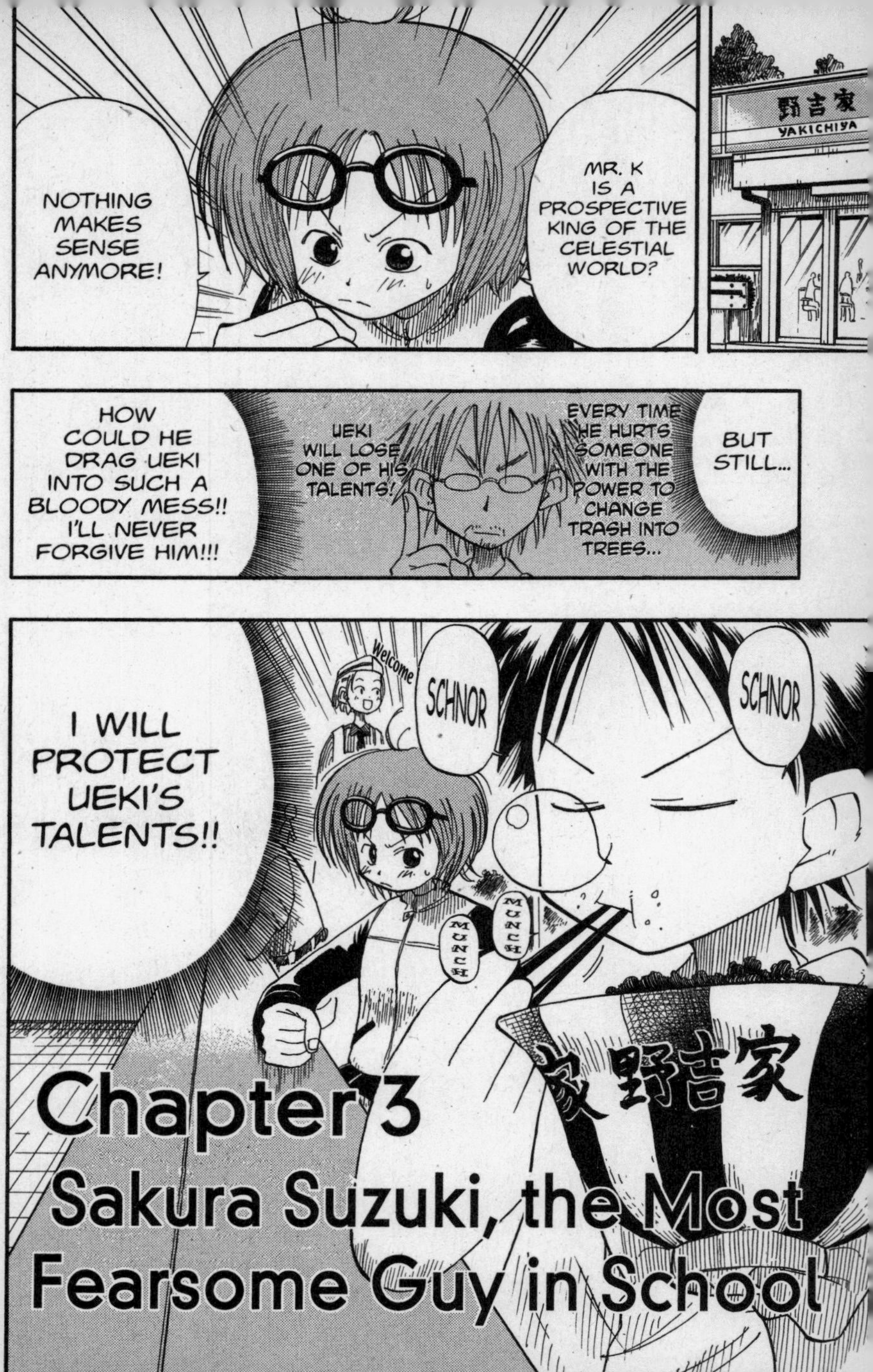

野吉家
YAKICHIYA
MR. K IS A PROSPECTIVE KING OF THE CELESTIAL WORLD?
NOTHING MAKES SENSE ANYMORE!
BUT STILL...
EVERY TIME HE HURTS SOMEONE WITH THE POWER TO CHANGE TRASH INTO TREES...
UEKI WILL LOSE ONE OF HIS TALENTS!
HOW COULD HE DRAG UEKI INTO SUCH A BLOODY MESS!! I'LL NEVER FORGIVE HIM!!!
SCHNOR
SCHNOR
Welcome
MUNCH
MUNCH
I WILL PROTECT UEKI'S TALENTS!!
家野吉家
Chapter 3
Sakura Suzuki, the Most Fearsome Guy in School

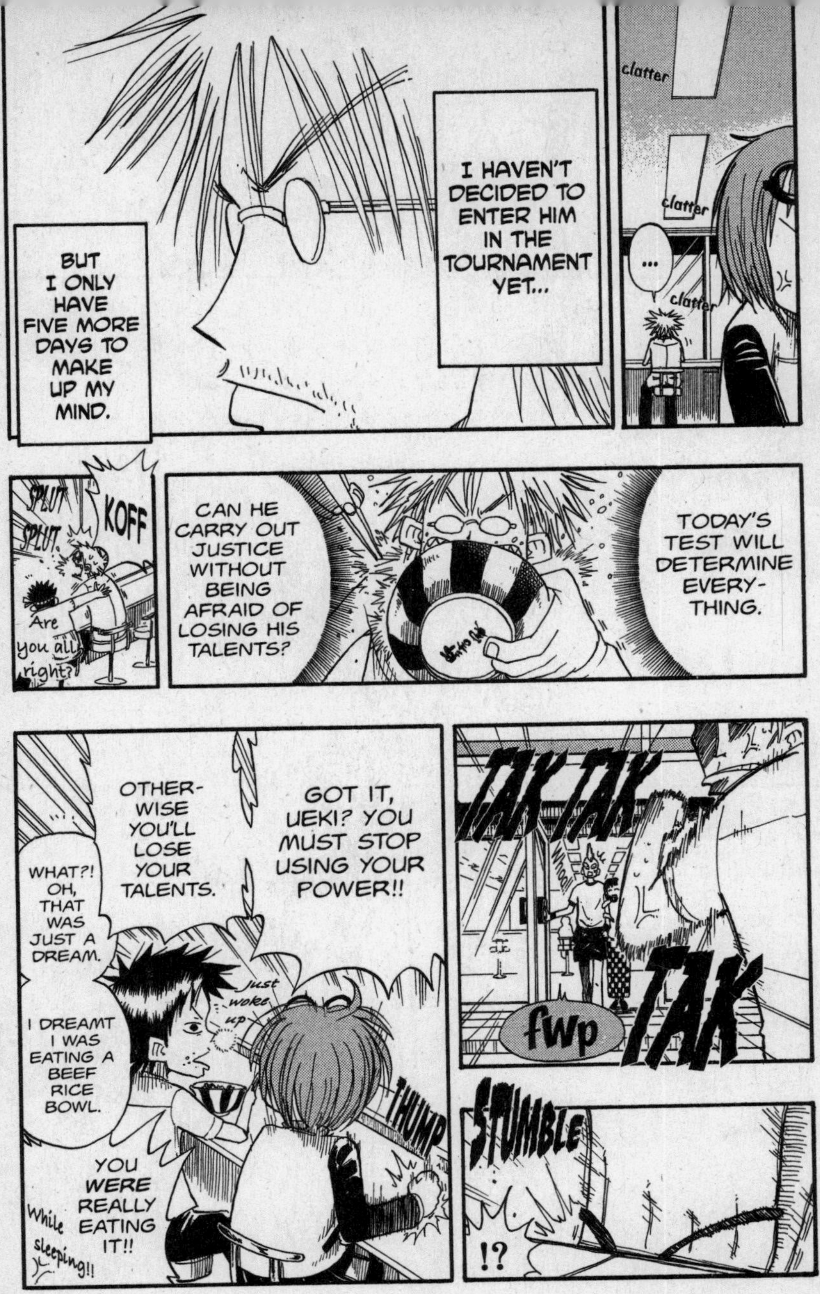
clatter
clatter
...
clatter
I HAVEN'T DECIDED TO ENTER HIM IN THE TOURNAMENT YET...
BUT I ONLY HAVE FIVE MORE DAYS TO MAKE UP MY MIND.
TODAY'S TEST WILL DETERMINE EVERY-THING.
CAN HE CARRY OUT JUSTICE WITHOUT BEING AFRAID OF LOSING HIS TALENTS?
KOFF
SPLUT
SPLUT
Are you all right?
TAK TAK
Whoa!!
fwp
TAK
STUMBLE
!?
GOT IT, UEKI? YOU MUST STOP USING YOUR POWER!!
OTHER-WISE YOU'LL LOSE YOUR TALENTS.
WHAT?! OH, THAT WAS JUST A DREAM.
just woke up
I DREAMT I WAS EATING A BEEF RICE BOWL.
THUMP
YOU WERE REALLY EATING IT!!
While sleeping!!

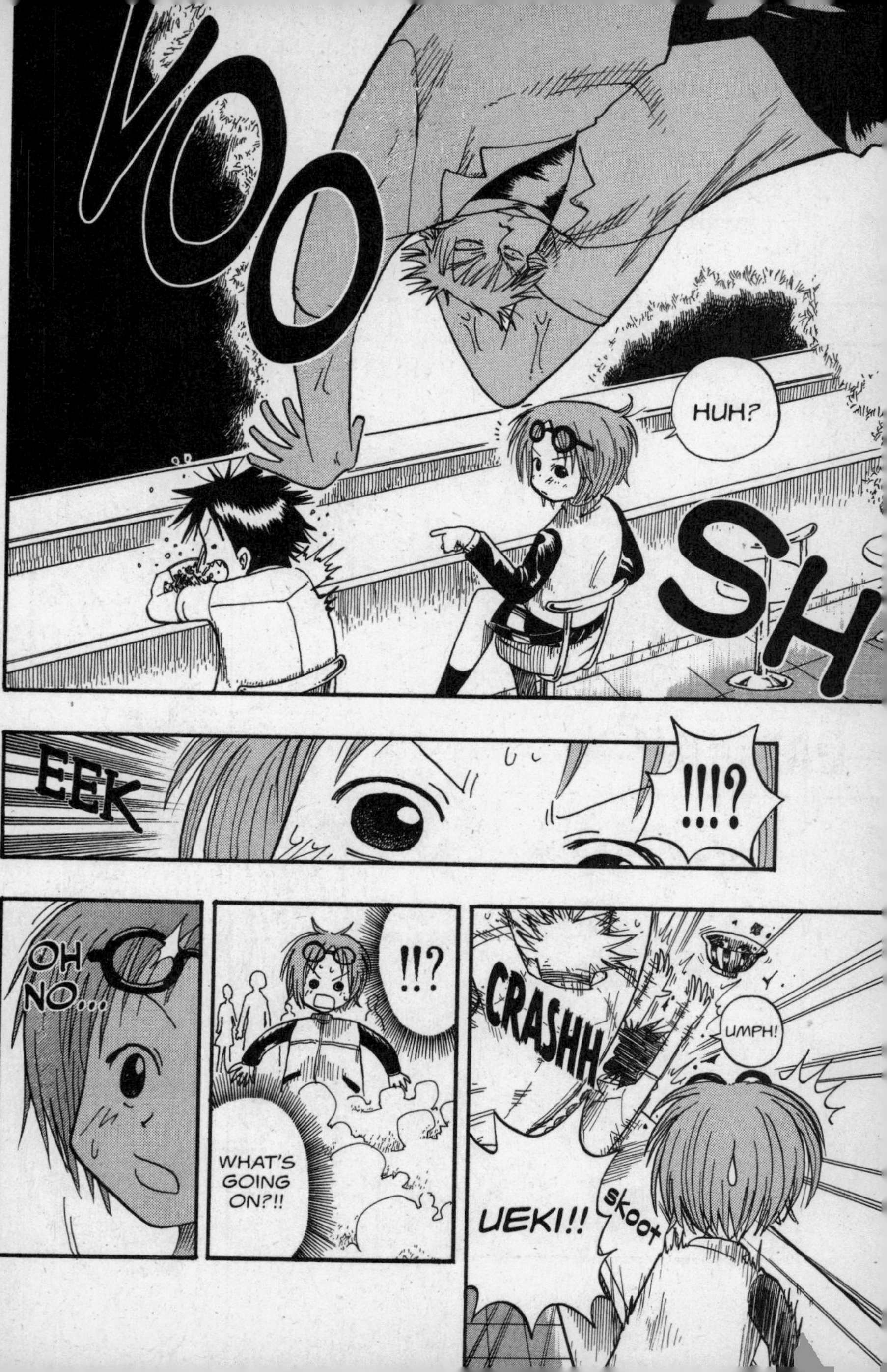
VOOO
HUH?
SH
!!!?
EEK
UMPH!
CRASHH
skoot
UEKI!!
!!?
WHAT'S GOING ON?!!
OH NO...

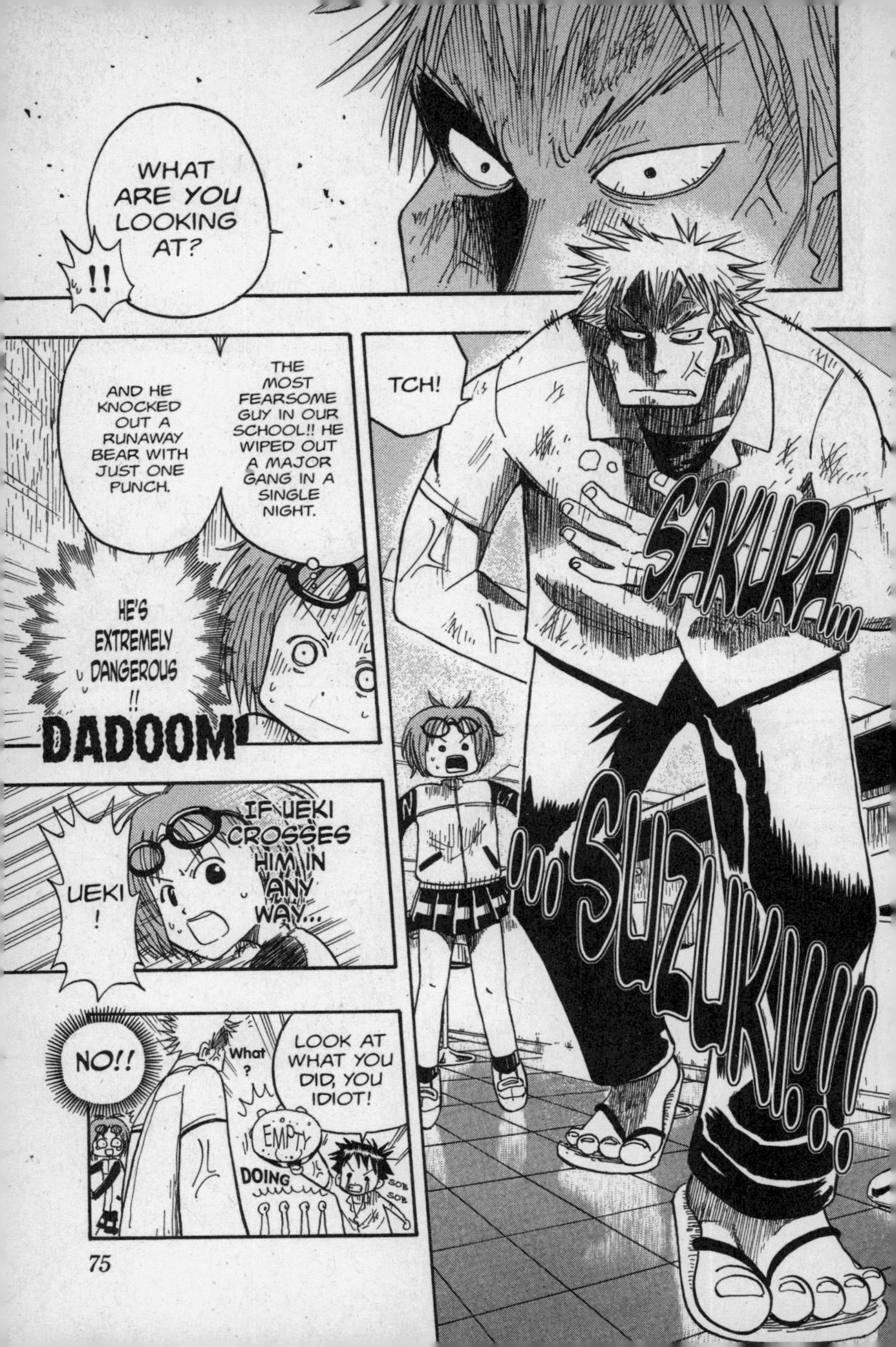
WHAT ARE YOU LOOKING AT?
!!
TCH!
SAKURA...
...SUZUKI!!!!
THE MOST FEARSOME GUY IN OUR SCHOOL!! HE WIPED OUT A MAJOR GANG IN A SINGLE NIGHT.
AND HE KNOCKED OUT A RUNAWAY BEAR WITH JUST ONE PUNCH.
HE'S EXTREMELY DANGEROUS!!
DADOOM
IF UEKI CROSSES HIM IN ANY WAY...
UEKI!
LOOK AT WHAT YOU DID, YOU IDIOT!
What?
NO!!
EMPTY
DOING
SOB SOB

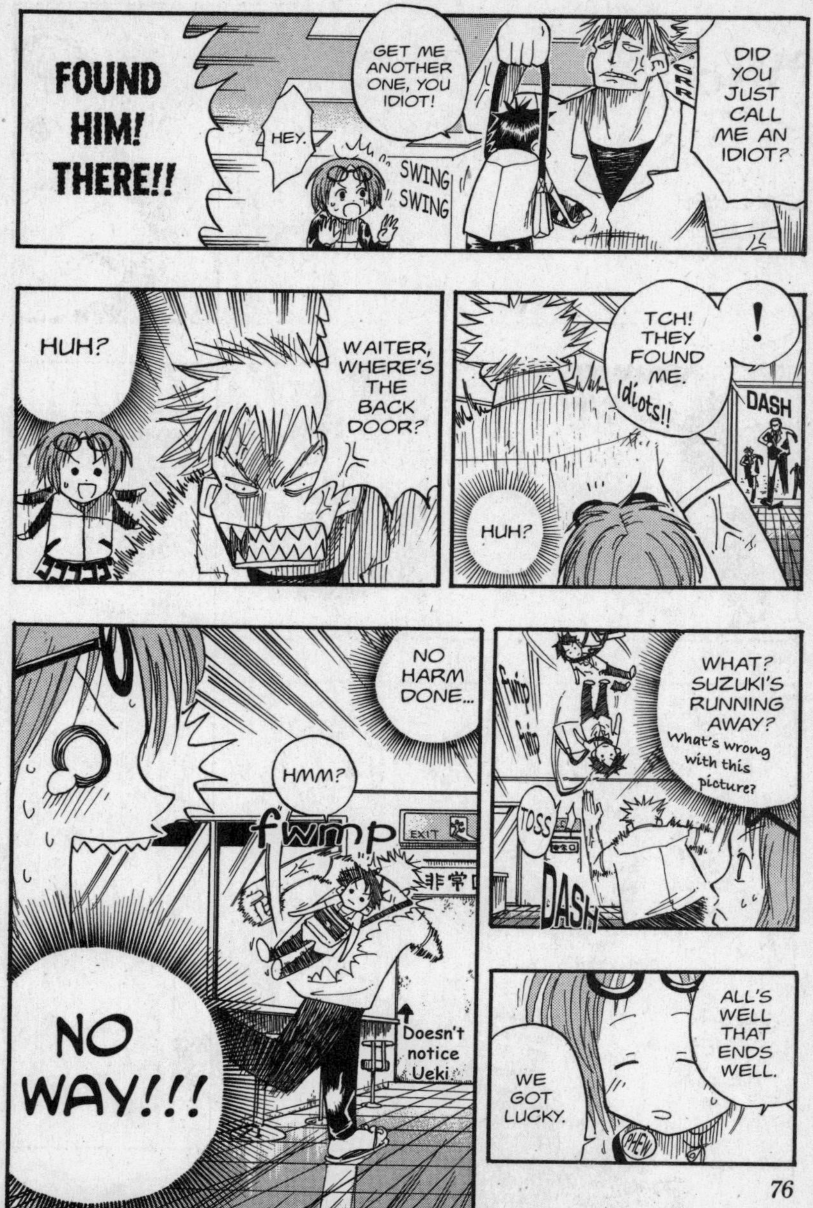
GRR
DID YOU JUST CALL ME AN IDIOT?
GET ME ANOTHER ONE, YOU IDIOT!
SWING SWING
HEY.
FOUND HIM! THERE!!
!
TCH! THEY FOUND ME. Idiots!!
DASH
HUH?
WAITER, WHERE'S THE BACK DOOR?
HUH?
WHAT? SUZUKI'S RUNNING AWAY? What's wrong with this picture?
fwip fwip
TOSS
DASH
ALL'S WELL THAT ENDS WELL.
WE GOT LUCKY.
PHEW
NO HARM DONE...
HMM?
fwmp
EXIT
非常口
Doesn't notice Ueki.
NO WAY!!!

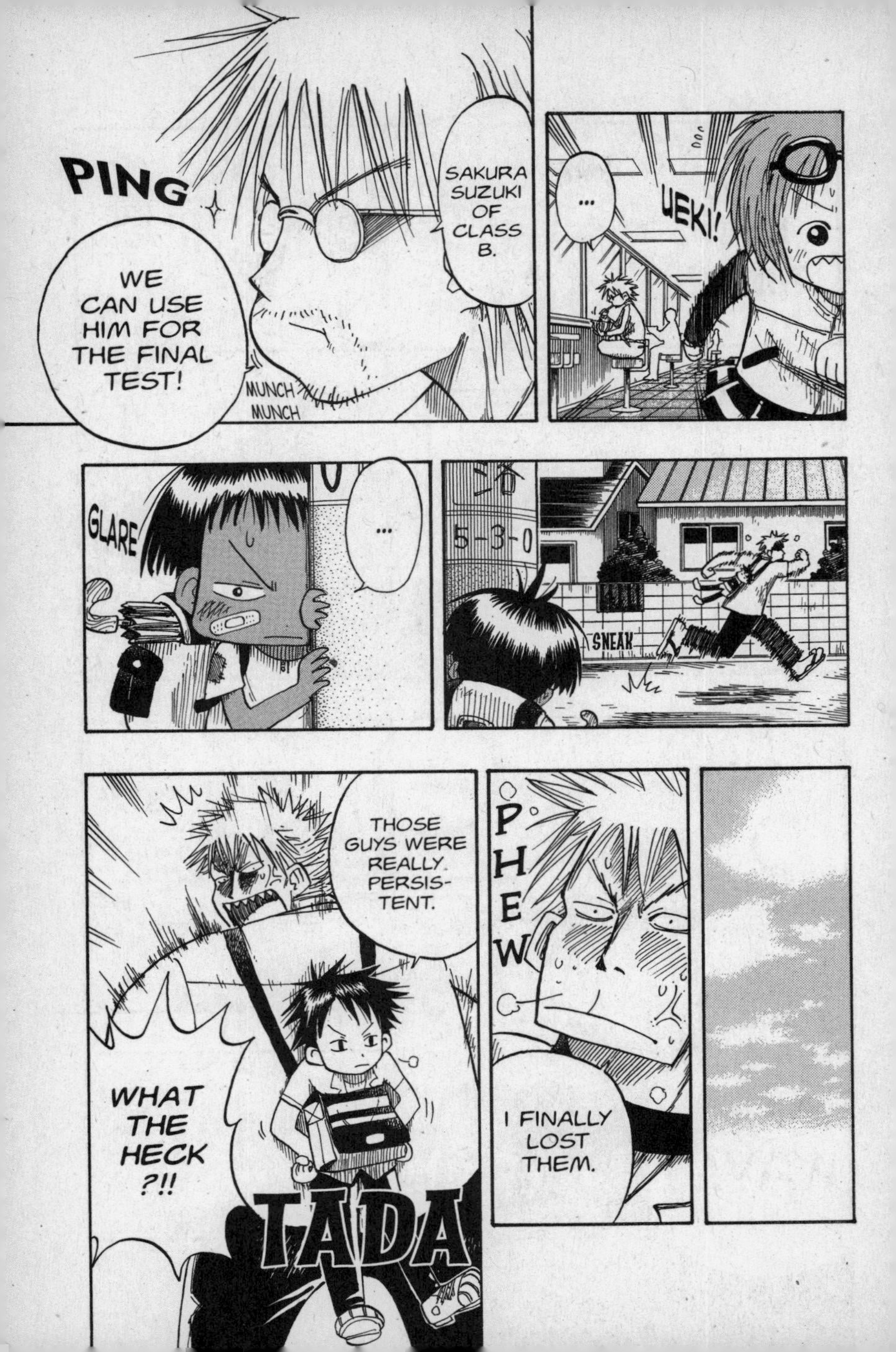

UEKI!
...
SAKURA SUZUKI OF CLASS B.
PING
WE CAN USE HIM FOR THE FINAL TEST!
MUNCH MUNCH
5-3-0
SNEAK
...
GLARE
PHEW
I FINALLY LOST THEM.
THOSE GUYS WERE REALLY PERSIS-TENT.
WHAT THE HECK ?!!
TADA

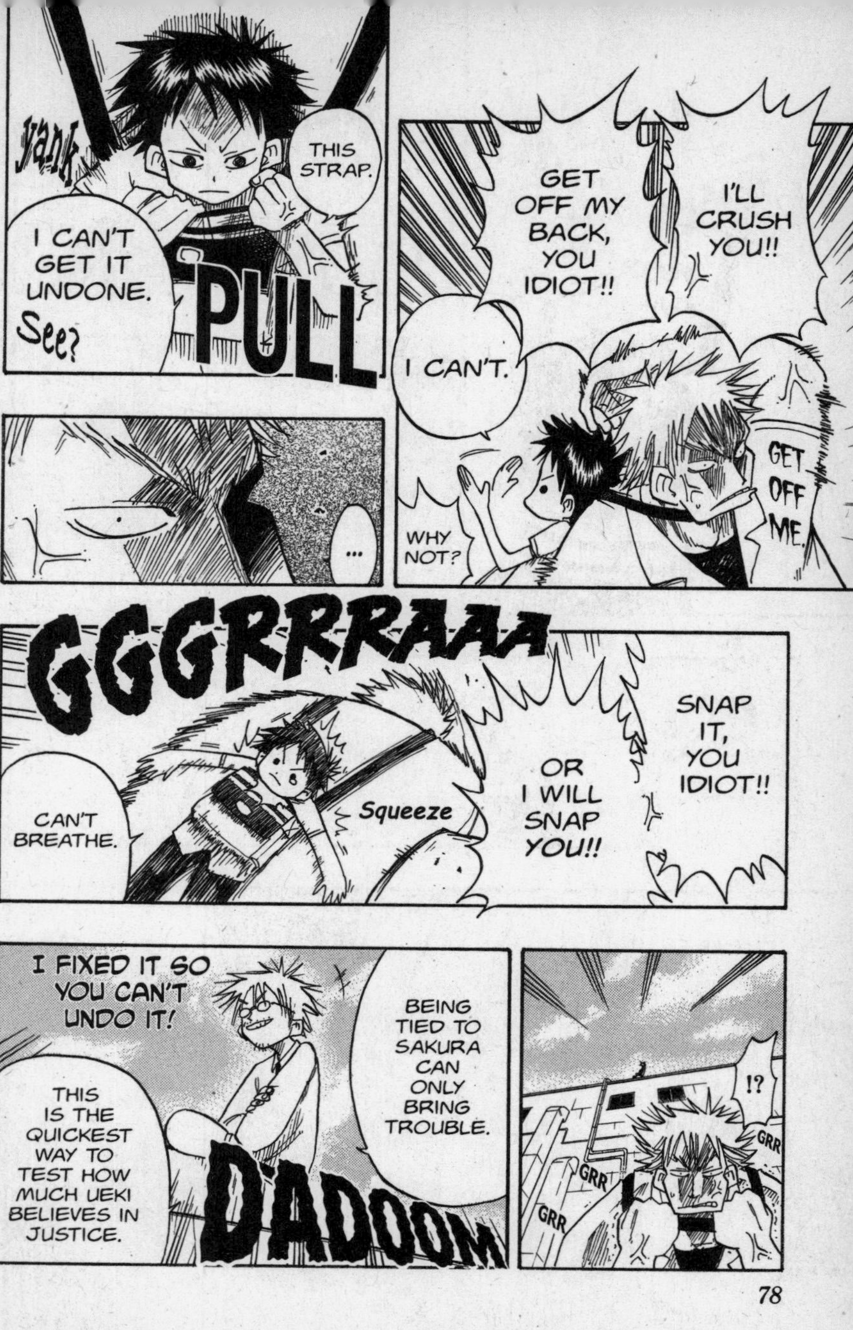
I'LL CRUSH YOU!!
GET OFF MY BACK, YOU IDIOT!!
GET OFF ME.
I CAN'T.
WHY NOT?
yank
THIS STRAP.
PULL
I CAN'T GET IT UNDONE.
See?
...
SNAP IT, YOU IDIOT!!
OR I WILL SNAP YOU!!
GGGRRRAAA
Squeeze
CAN'T BREATHE.
!?
GRR
GRR
GRR
BEING TIED TO SAKURA CAN ONLY BRING TROUBLE.
I FIXED IT SO YOU CAN'T UNDO IT!
THIS IS THE QUICKEST WAY TO TEST HOW MUCH UEKI BELIEVES IN JUSTICE.
DADOOM

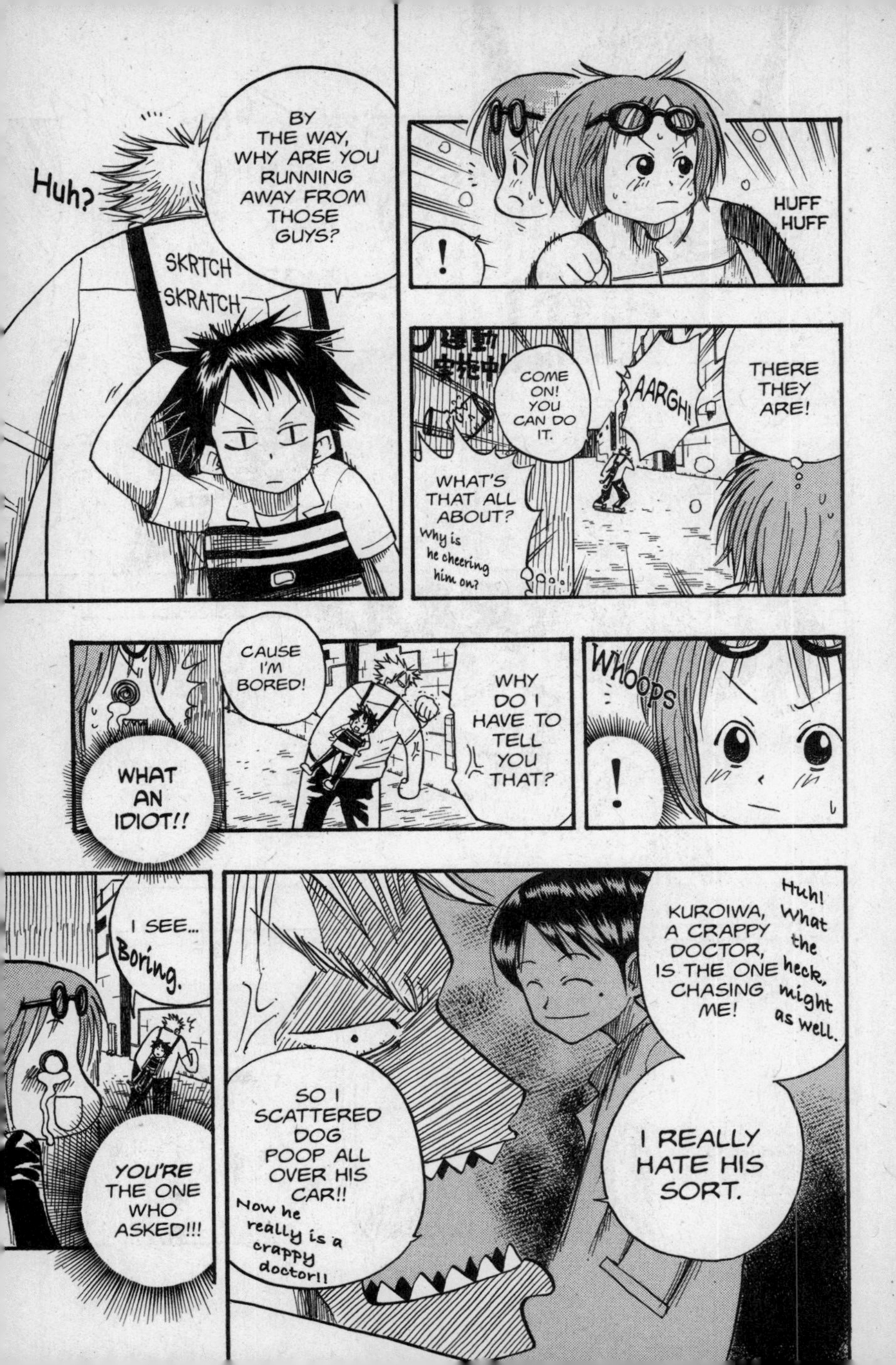

HUFF HUFF
!
THERE THEY ARE!
AARGH!
COME ON! YOU CAN DO IT.
運動実施中
WHAT'S THAT ALL ABOUT?
Why is he cheering him on?
Huh?
BY THE WAY, WHY ARE YOU RUNNING AWAY FROM THOSE GUYS?
SKRTCH SKRATCH
Whoops
!
WHY DO I HAVE TO TELL YOU THAT?
CAUSE I'M BORED!
WHAT AN IDIOT!!
KUROIWA, A CRAPPY DOCTOR, IS THE ONE CHASING ME!
Huh! What the heck, might as well.
I REALLY HATE HIS SORT.
SO I SCATTERED DOG POOP ALL OVER HIS CAR!!
Now he really is a crappy doctor!!
I SEE...
Boring.
YOU'RE THE ONE WHO ASKED!!!

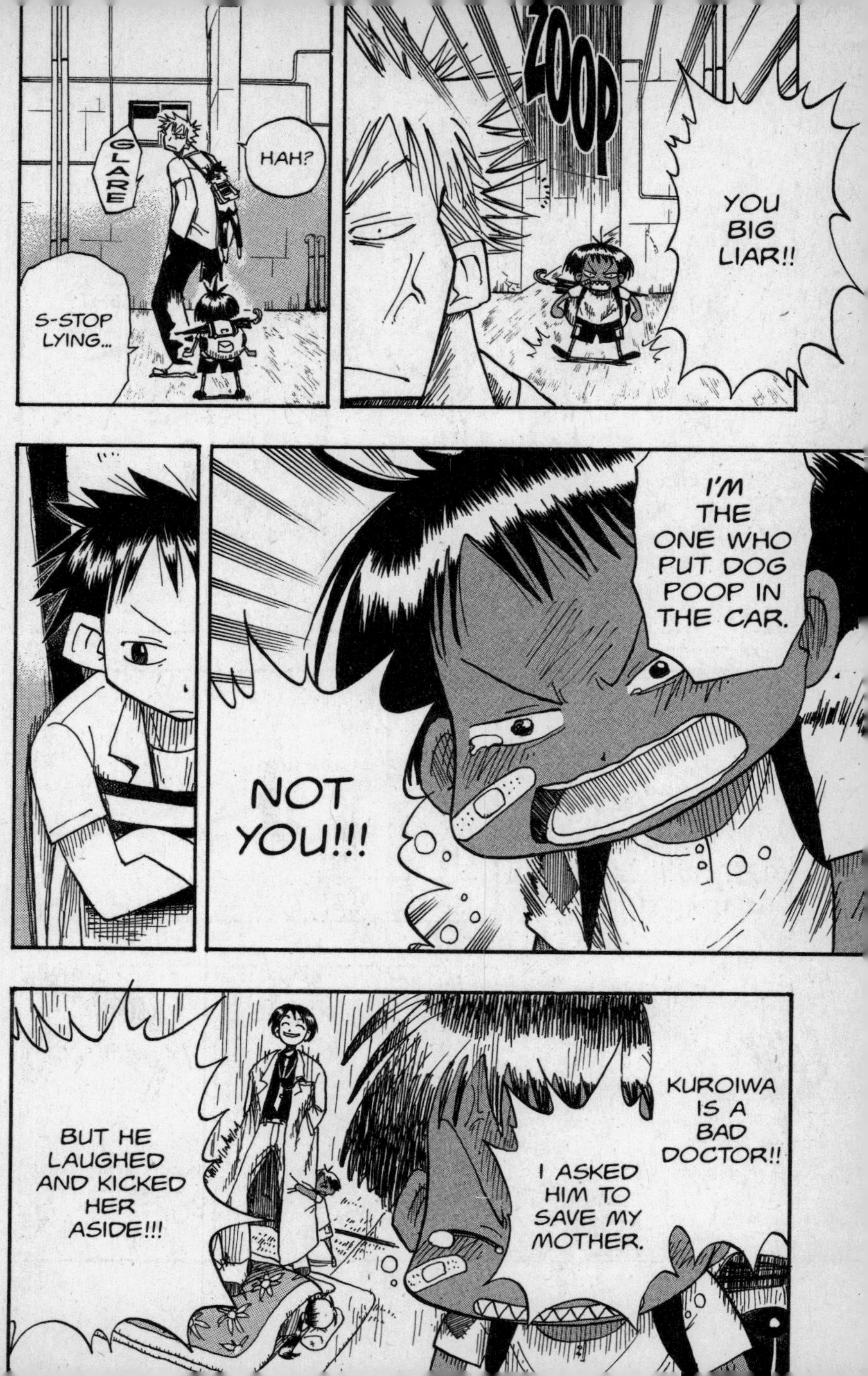
ZOOP
YOU BIG LIAR!!
HAH?
GLARE
S-STOP LYING...
I'M THE ONE WHO PUT DOG POOP IN THE CAR.
NOT YOU!!!
...
KUROIWA IS A BAD DOCTOR!!
I ASKED HIM TO SAVE MY MOTHER.
BUT HE LAUGHED AND KICKED HER ASIDE!!!

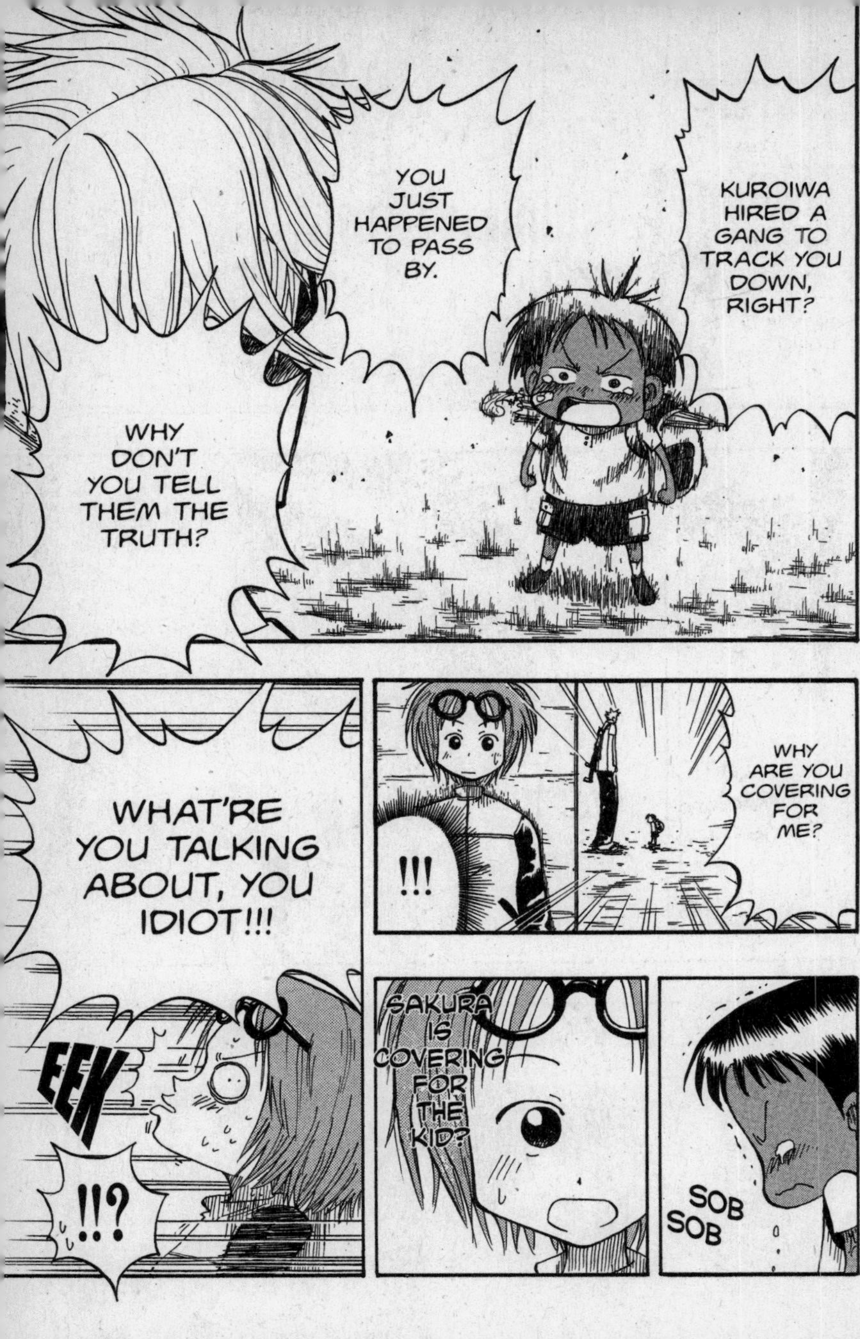
KUROIWA HIRED A GANG TO TRACK YOU DOWN, RIGHT?
YOU JUST HAPPENED TO PASS BY.
WHY DON'T YOU TELL THEM THE TRUTH?
WHY ARE YOU COVERING FOR ME?
!!!
SOB SOB
SAKURA IS COVERING FOR THE KID?
WHAT'RE YOU TALKING ABOUT, YOU IDIOT!!!
EEK
!!?

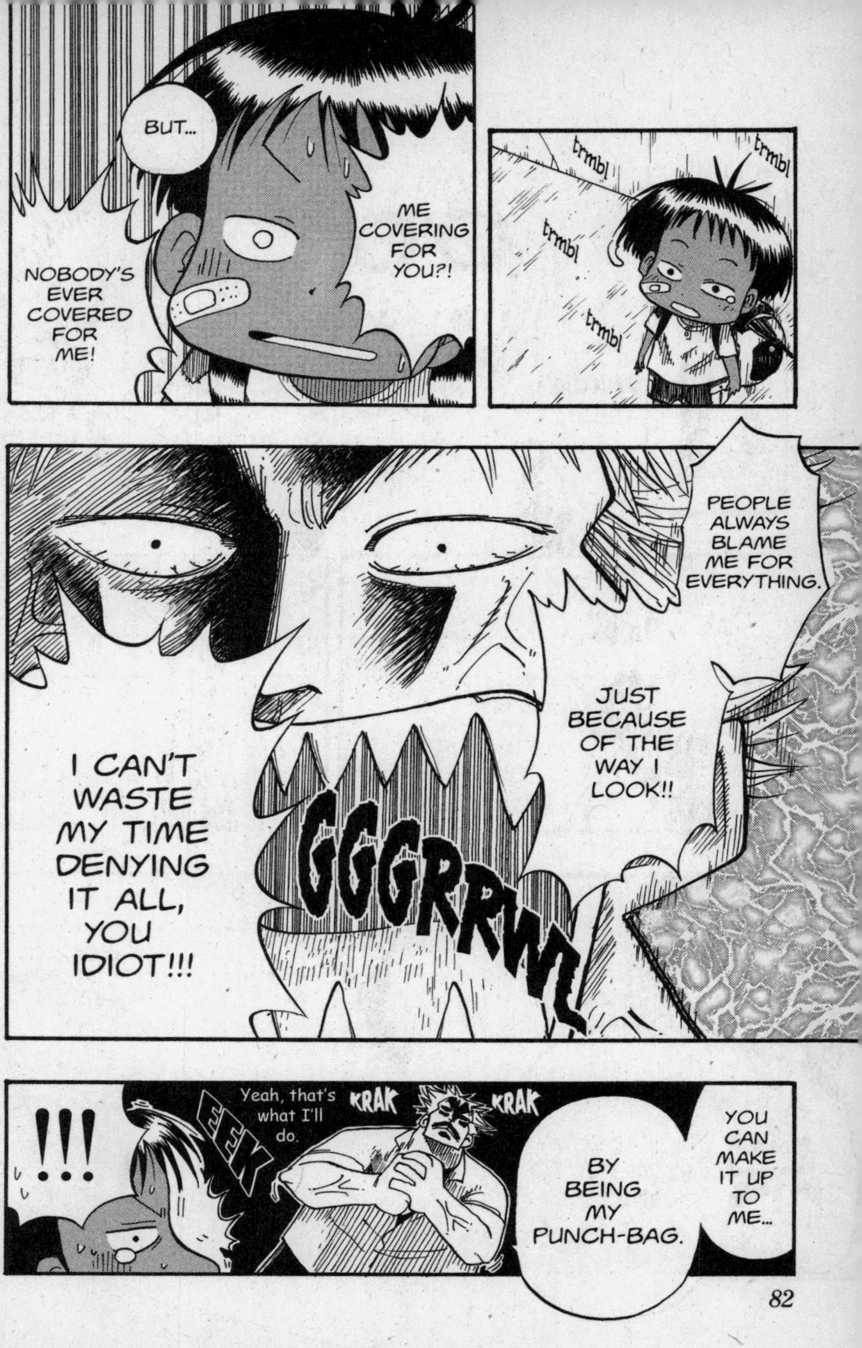
trmbl
trmbl
trmbl
trmbl
BUT...
ME COVERING FOR YOU?!
NOBODY'S EVER COVERED FOR ME!
PEOPLE ALWAYS BLAME ME FOR EVERYTHING.
JUST BECAUSE OF THE WAY I LOOK!!
GGGRRWL
I CAN'T WASTE MY TIME DENYING IT ALL, YOU IDIOT!!!
YOU CAN MAKE IT UP TO ME...
BY BEING MY PUNCH-BAG.
KRAK
KRAK
Yeah, that's what I'll do.
EEK
!!!

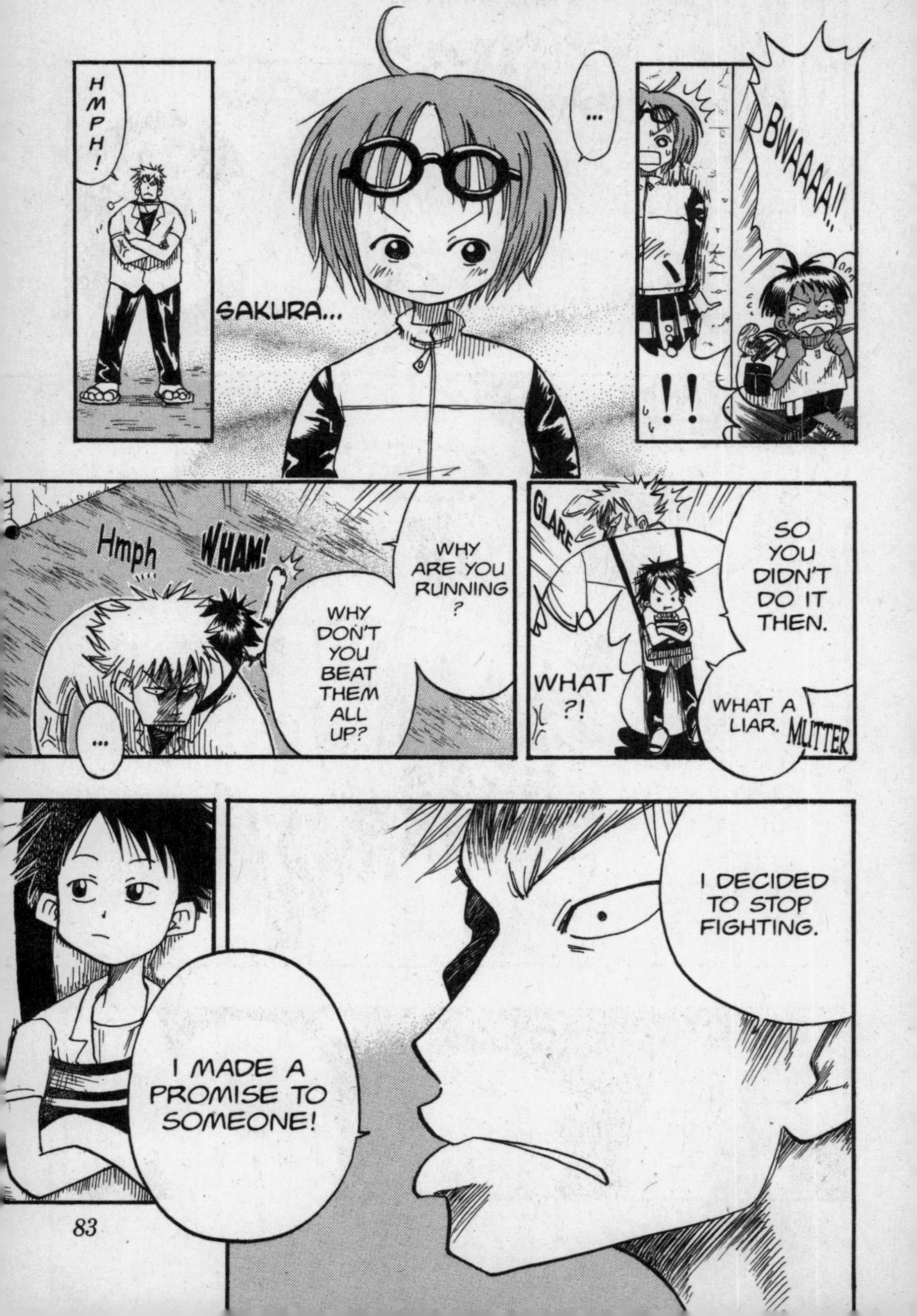
BWAAAA!!
!!
...
SAKURA...
HMPH!
GLARE
SO YOU DIDN'T DO IT THEN.
WHAT A LIAR.
MUTTER
WHAT ?!
WHY ARE YOU RUNNING ?
WHY DON'T YOU BEAT THEM ALL UP?
WHAM!
Hmph
...
I DECIDED TO STOP FIGHTING.
I MADE A PROMISE TO SOMEONE!

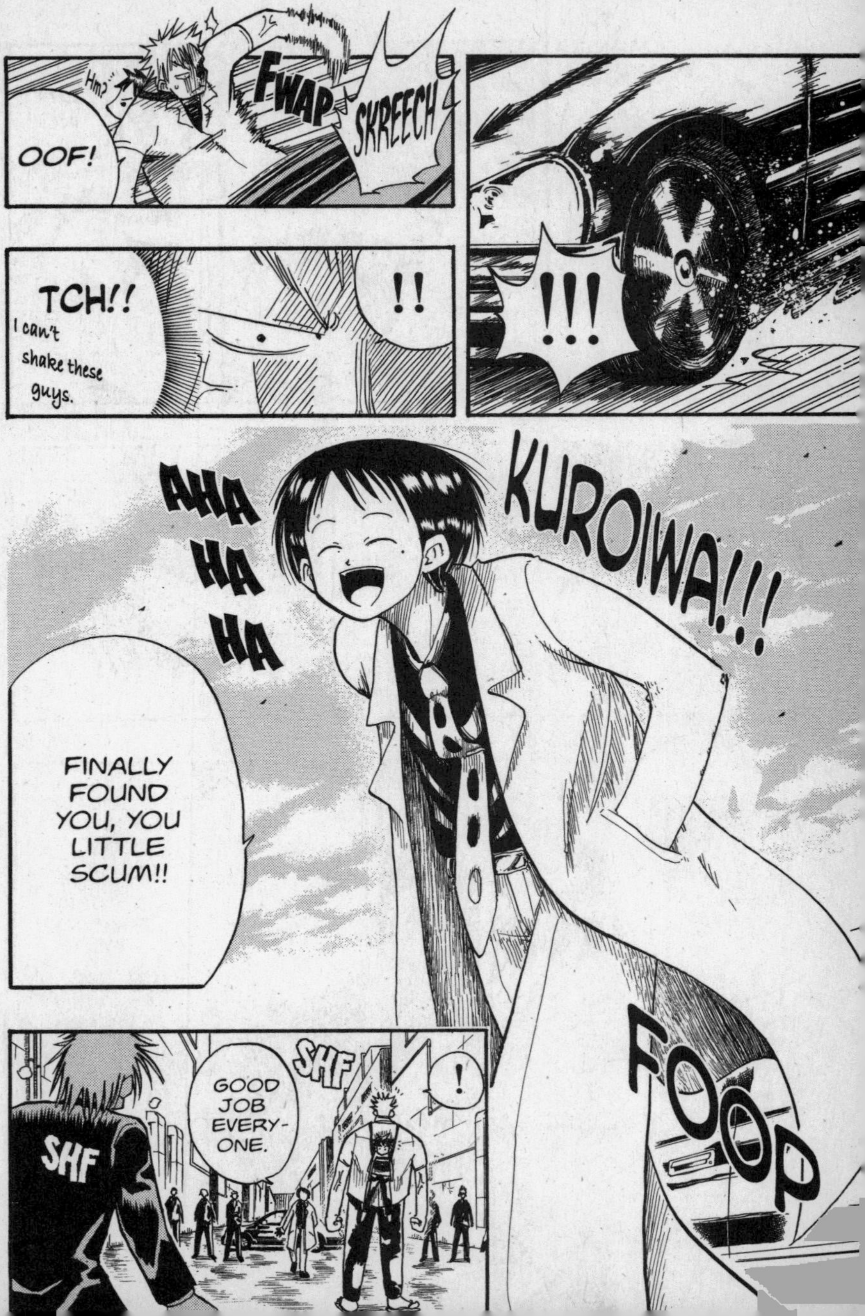
!!!
SKREECH
FWAP
Hm?
OOF!
!!
TCH!!
I can't shake these guys.
KUROIWA!!!
AHA HA HA
FINALLY FOUND YOU, YOU LITTLE SCUM!!
FOOOP
!
SHF
GOOD JOB EVERY-ONE.
SHF

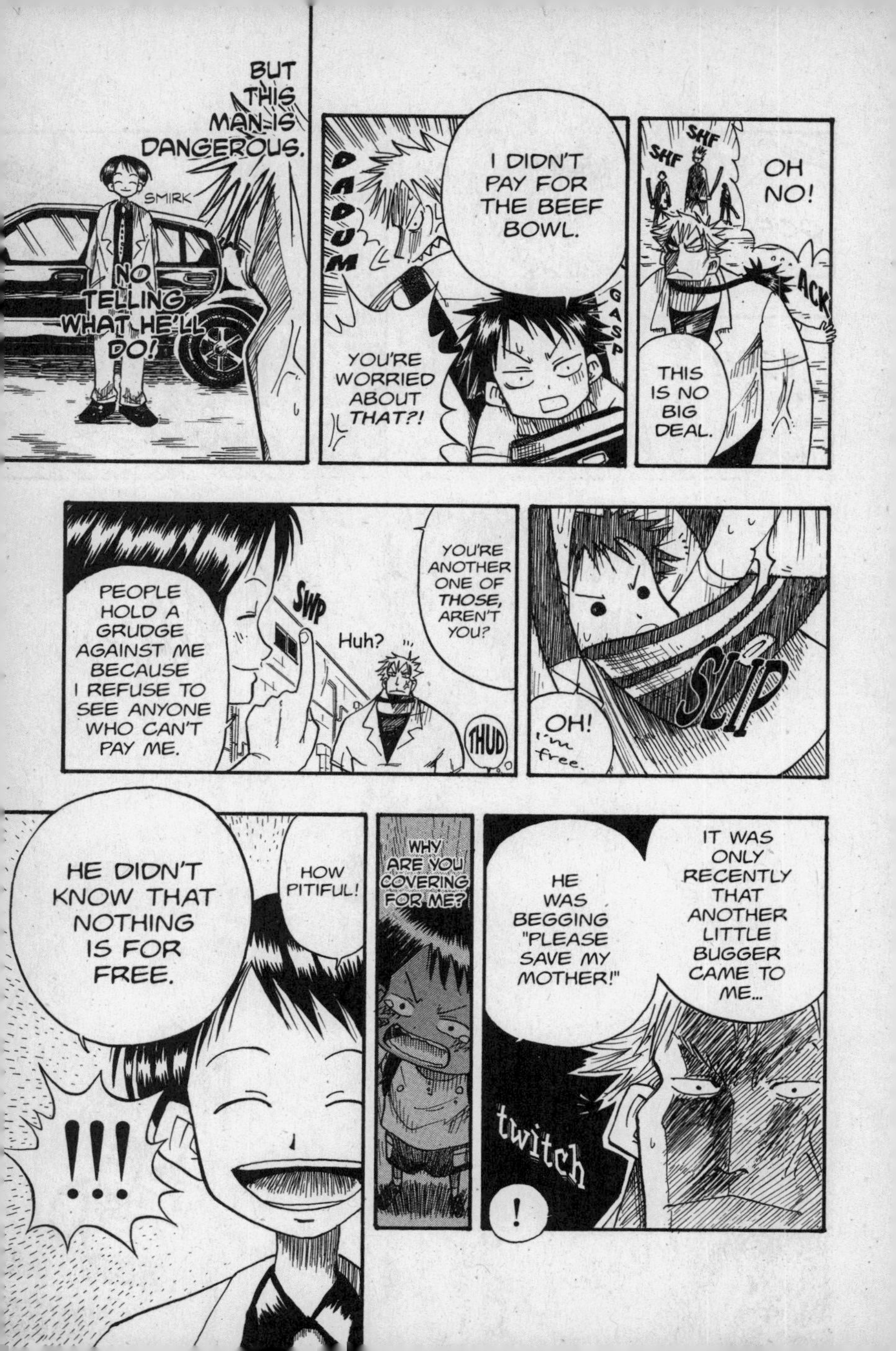

SHF
SHF
OH NO!
ACK
THIS IS NO BIG DEAL.
DADUM
I DIDN'T PAY FOR THE BEEF BOWL.
GASP
YOU'RE WORRIED ABOUT THAT?!
BUT THIS MAN IS DANGEROUS.
SMIRK
NO TELLING WHAT HE'LL DO!
SLIP
OH!
I'm free.
YOU'RE ANOTHER ONE OF THOSE, AREN'T YOU?
Huh?
THUD
SWP
PEOPLE HOLD A GRUDGE AGAINST ME BECAUSE I REFUSE TO SEE ANYONE WHO CAN'T PAY ME.
IT WAS ONLY RECENTLY THAT ANOTHER LITTLE BUGGER CAME TO ME...
HE WAS BEGGING "PLEASE SAVE MY MOTHER!"
twitch
!
WHY ARE YOU COVERING FOR ME?
HOW PITIFUL!
HE DIDN'T KNOW THAT NOTHING IS FOR FREE.
!!!

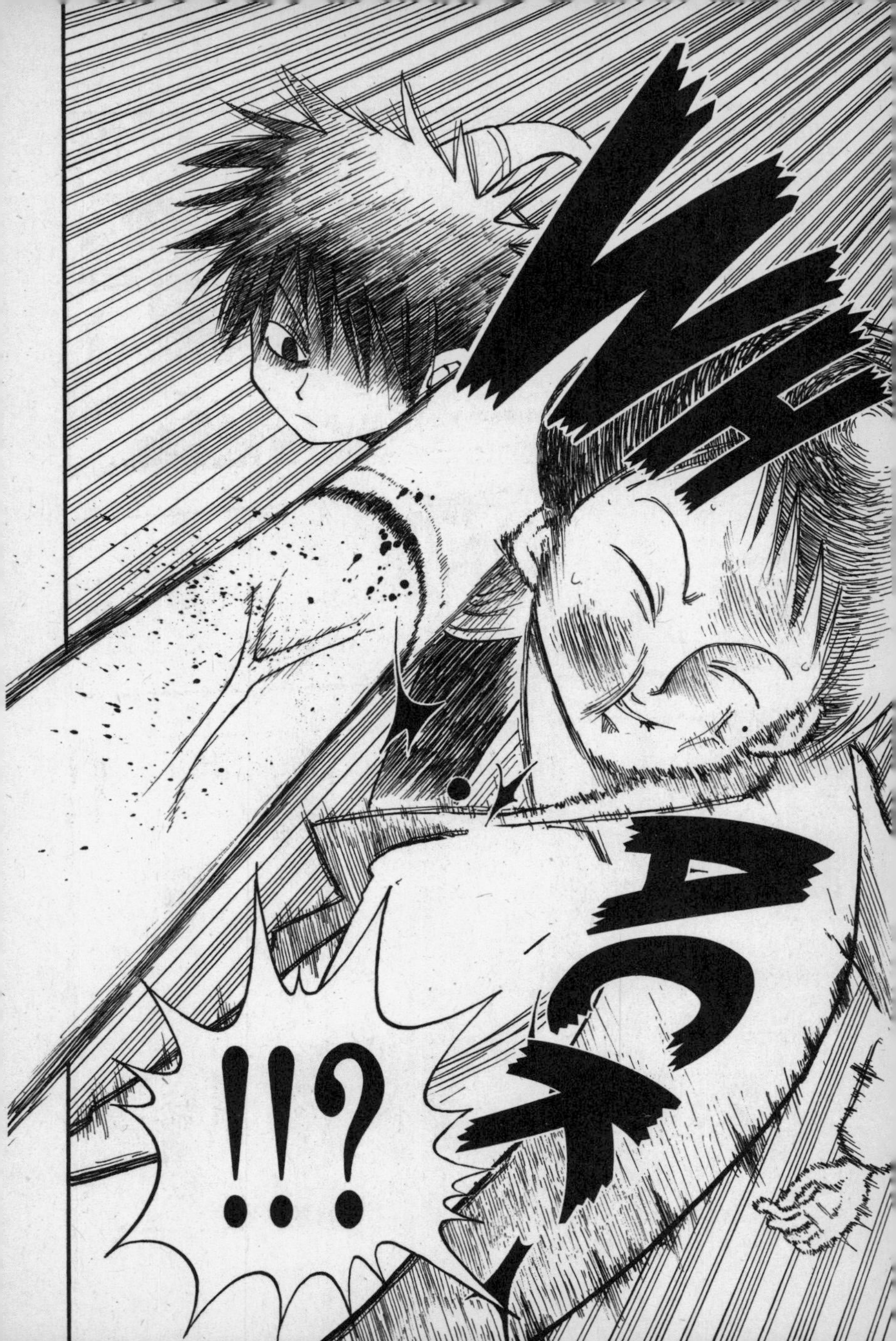
!!?

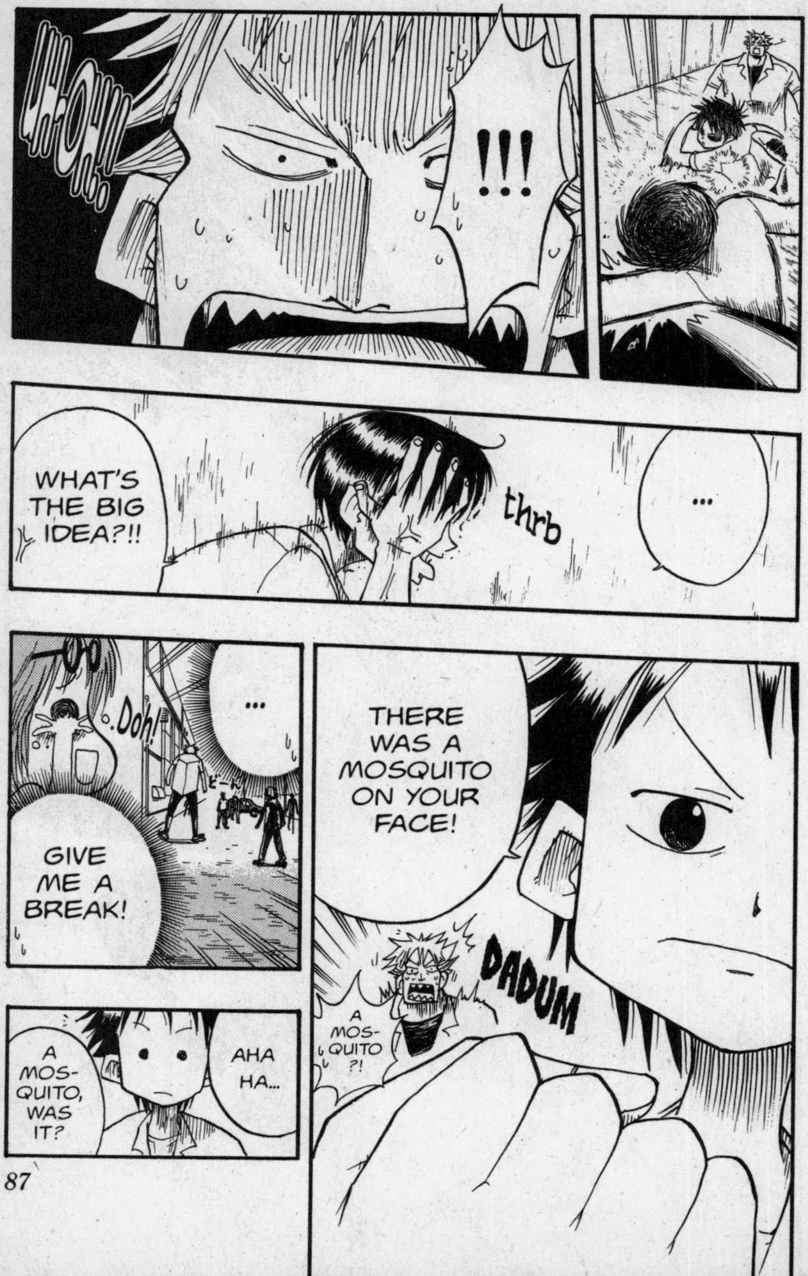
!!!
Uh-Oh!!
...
thrb
WHAT'S THE BIG IDEA?!!
THERE WAS A MOSQUITO ON YOUR FACE!
DADUM
A MOSQUITO ?!
...
Doh!
GIVE ME A BREAK!
AHA HA...
A MOSQUITO, WAS IT?

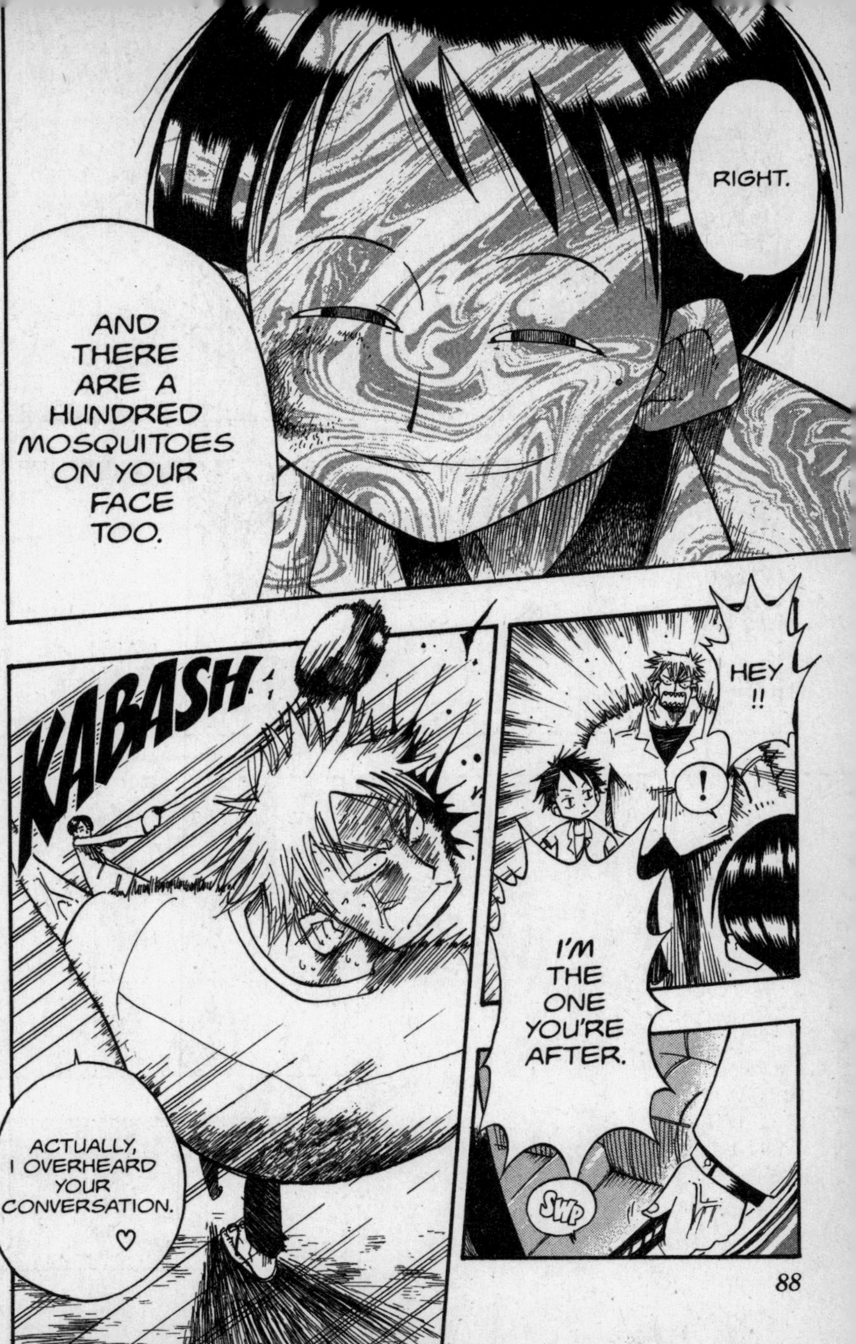
RIGHT.
AND THERE ARE A HUNDRED MOSQUITOES ON YOUR FACE TOO.
HEY !!
!
I'M THE ONE YOU'RE AFTER.
SWP
KABASH
ACTUALLY, I OVERHEARD YOUR CONVERSATION. ♡

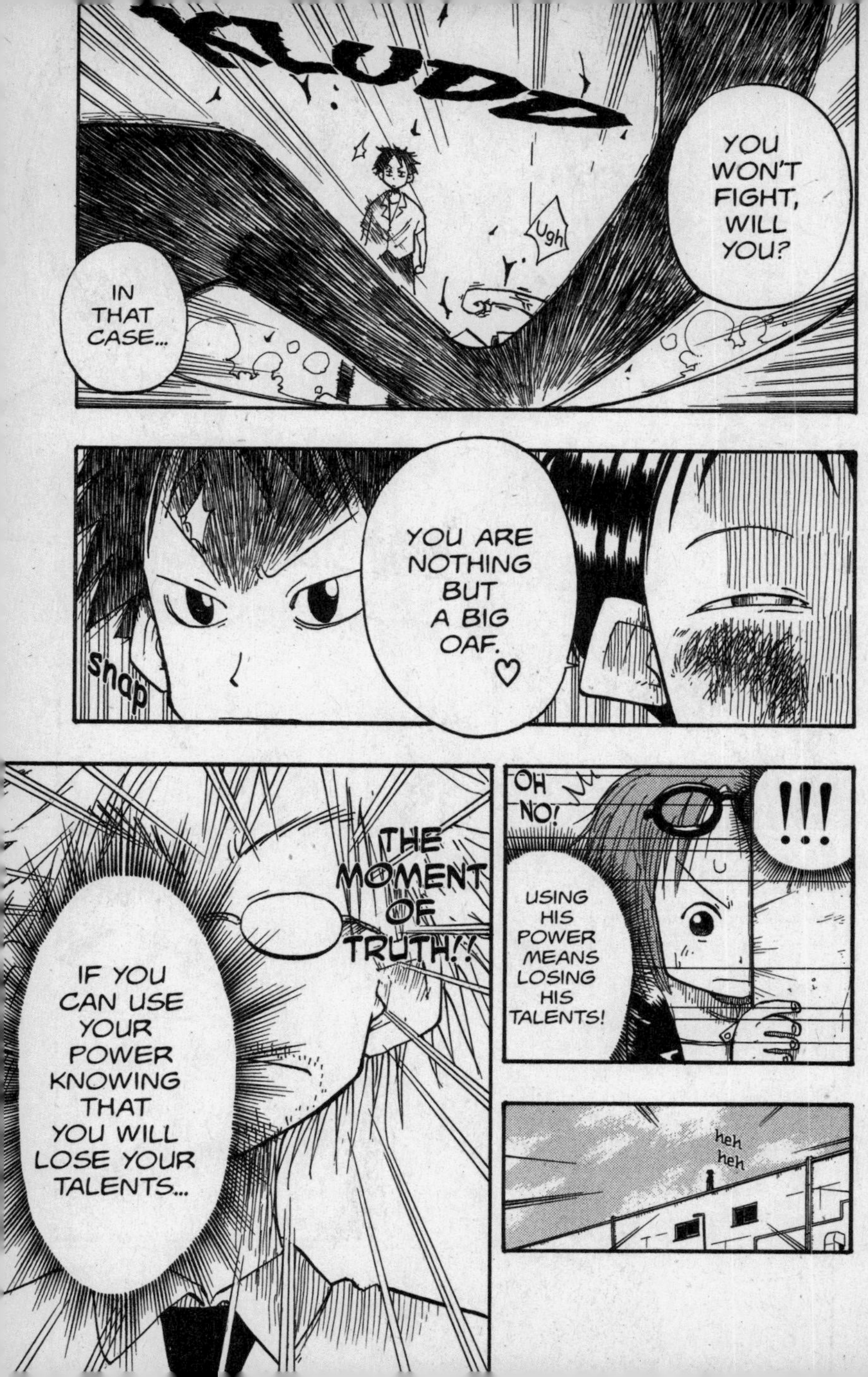
YOU WON'T FIGHT, WILL YOU?
KLUDD
Ugh
IN THAT CASE...
YOU ARE NOTHING BUT A BIG OAF. ♡
snap
!!!
OH NO!
USING HIS POWER MEANS LOSING HIS TALENTS!
heh heh
THE MOMENT OF TRUTH!!
IF YOU CAN USE YOUR POWER KNOWING THAT YOU WILL LOSE YOUR TALENTS...

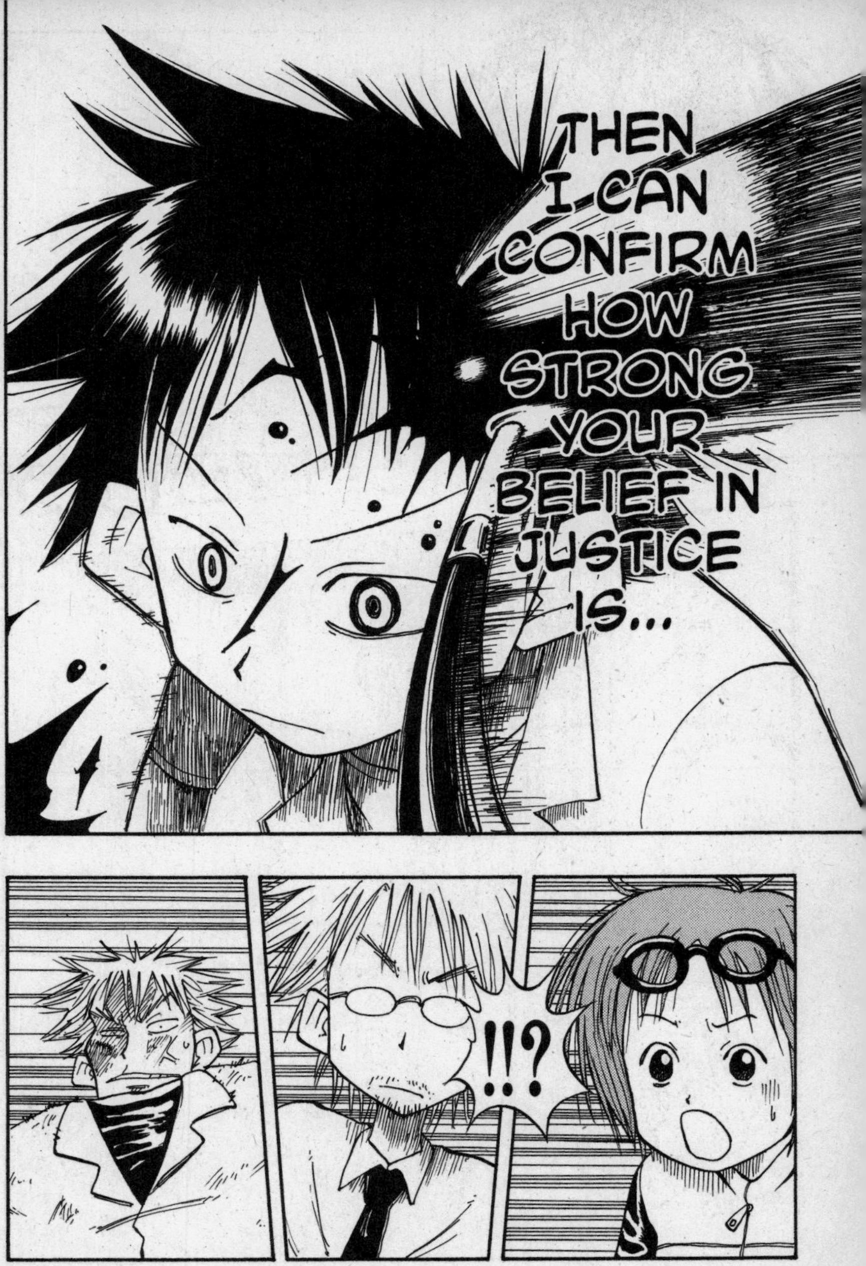
THEN I CAN CONFIRM HOW STRONG YOUR BELIEF IN JUSTICE IS...
!!?

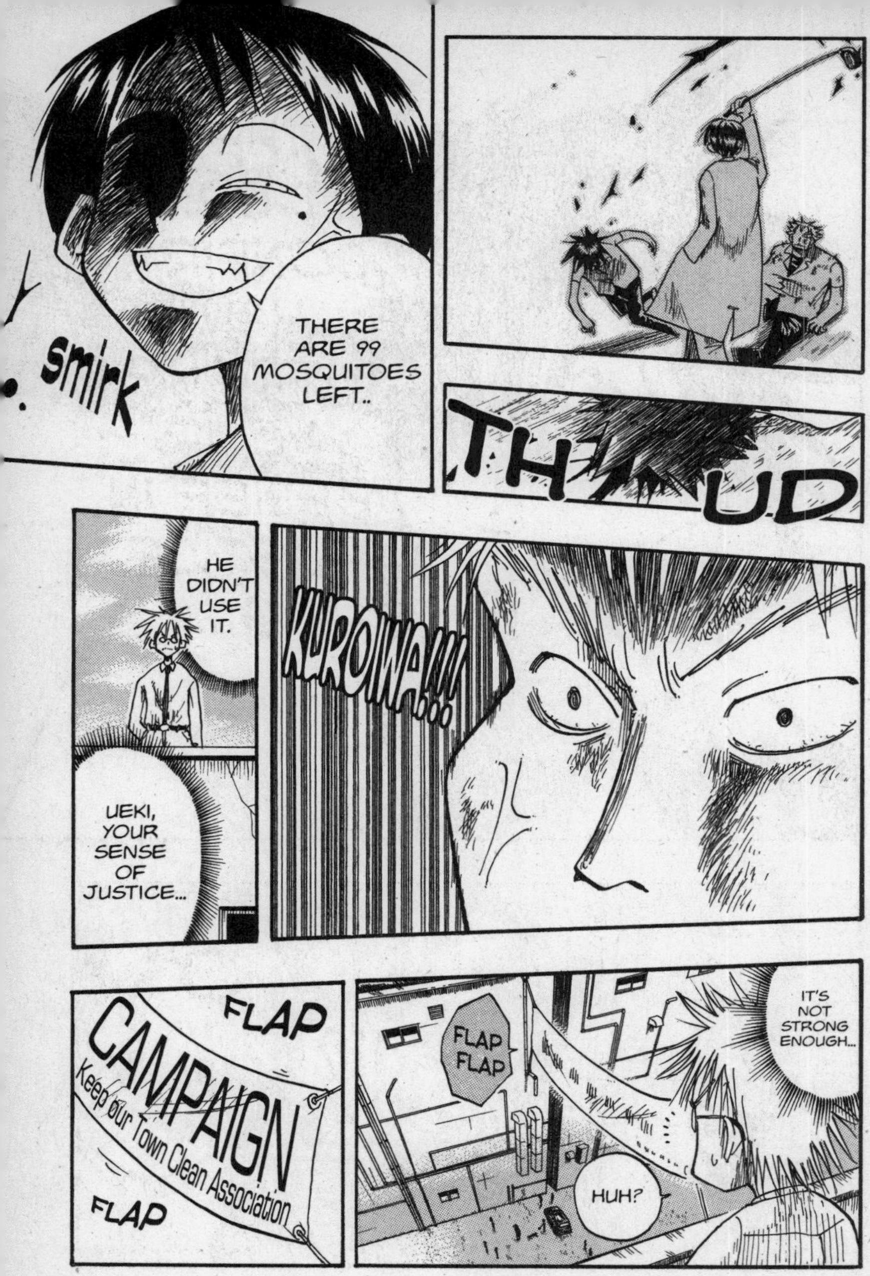
THUD
smirk
THERE ARE 99 MOSQUITOES LEFT..
KUROIWA!!!...
HE DIDN'T USE IT.
UEKI, YOUR SENSE OF JUSTICE...
IT'S NOT STRONG ENOUGH...
FLAP FLAP
HUH?
FLAP
CAMPAIGN
Keep our Town Clean Association
FLAP

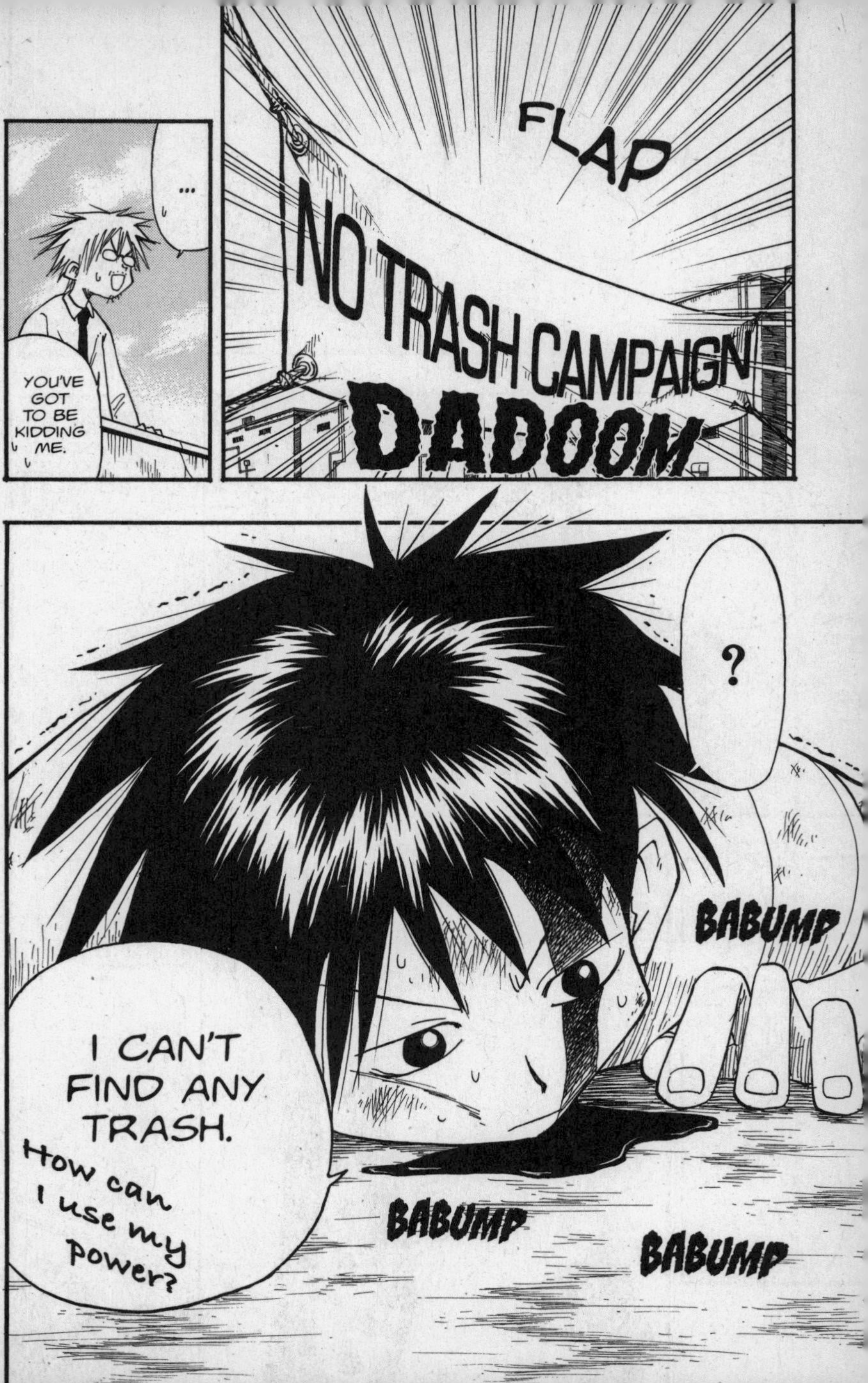
FLAP
NO TRASH CAMPAIGN
DADOOM
...
YOU'VE GOT TO BE KIDDING ME.
?
BABUMP
I CAN'T FIND ANY TRASH. How can I use my power?
BABUMP
BABUMP

Chapter 4
The One Who Won't Fight and the One Who Won't Run Away

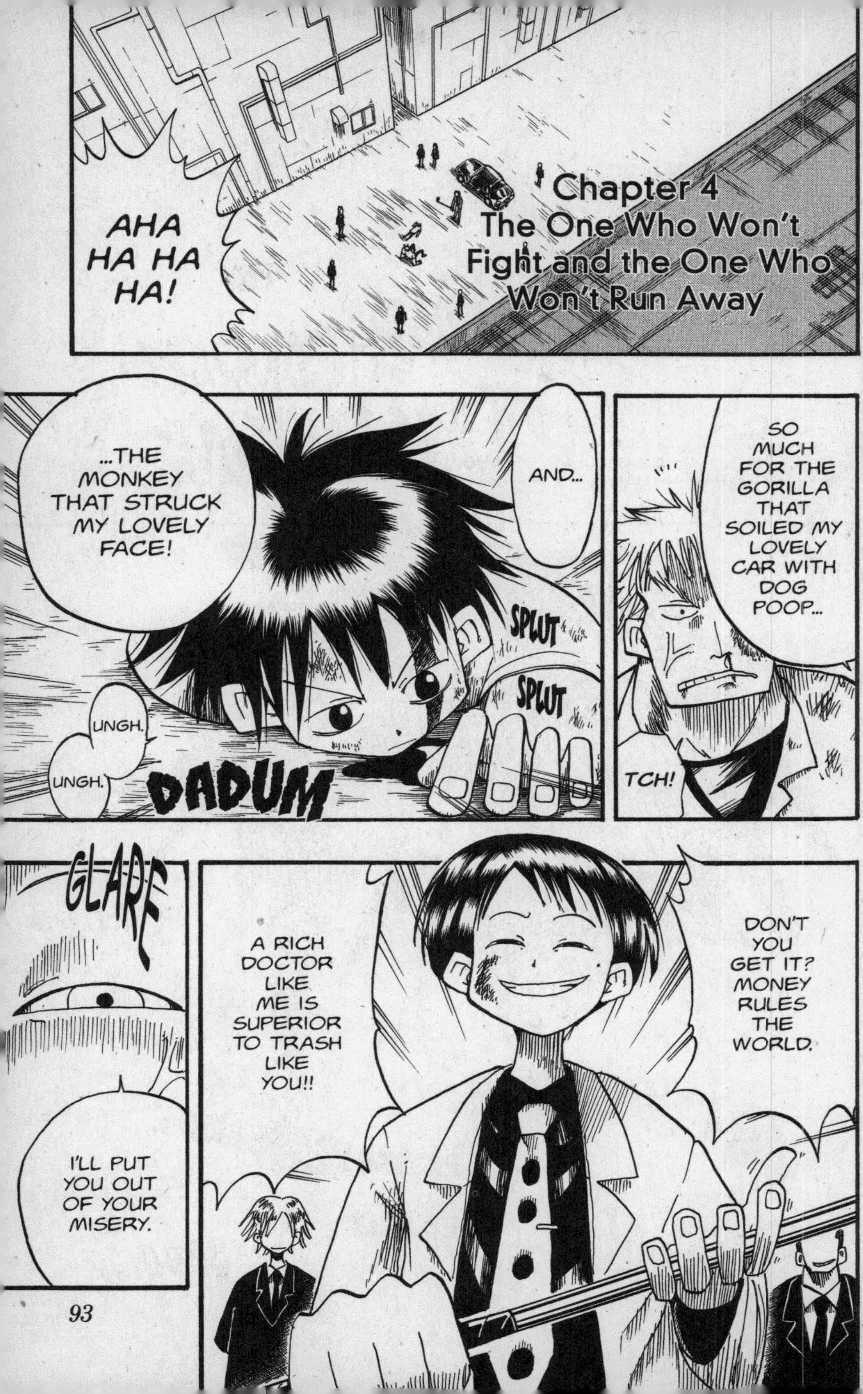
AHA HA HA HA!
SO MUCH FOR THE GORILLA THAT SOILED MY LOVELY CAR WITH DOG POOP...
TCH!
AND...
...THE MONKEY THAT STRUCK MY LOVELY FACE!
SPLUT
SPLUT
UNGH.
UNGH.
DADUM
DON'T YOU GET IT? MONEY RULES THE WORLD.
A RICH DOCTOR LIKE ME IS SUPERIOR TO TRASH LIKE YOU!!
GLARE
I'LL PUT YOU OUT OF YOUR MISERY.

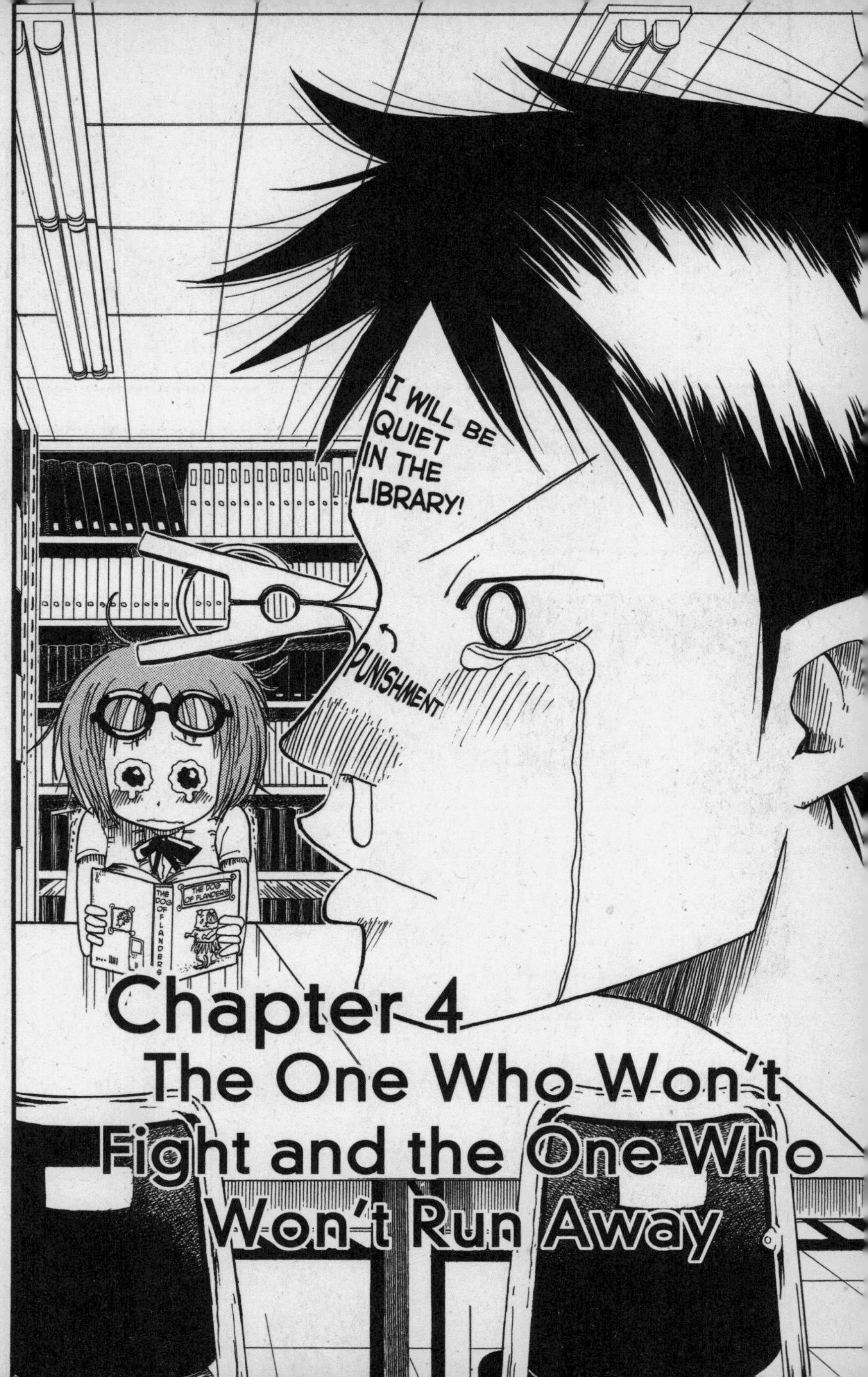
I WILL BE QUIET IN THE LIBRARY!
PUNISHMENT
THE DOG OF FLANDERS
THE DOG OF FLANDERS
Chapter 4
The One Who Won't Fight and the One Who Won't Run Away

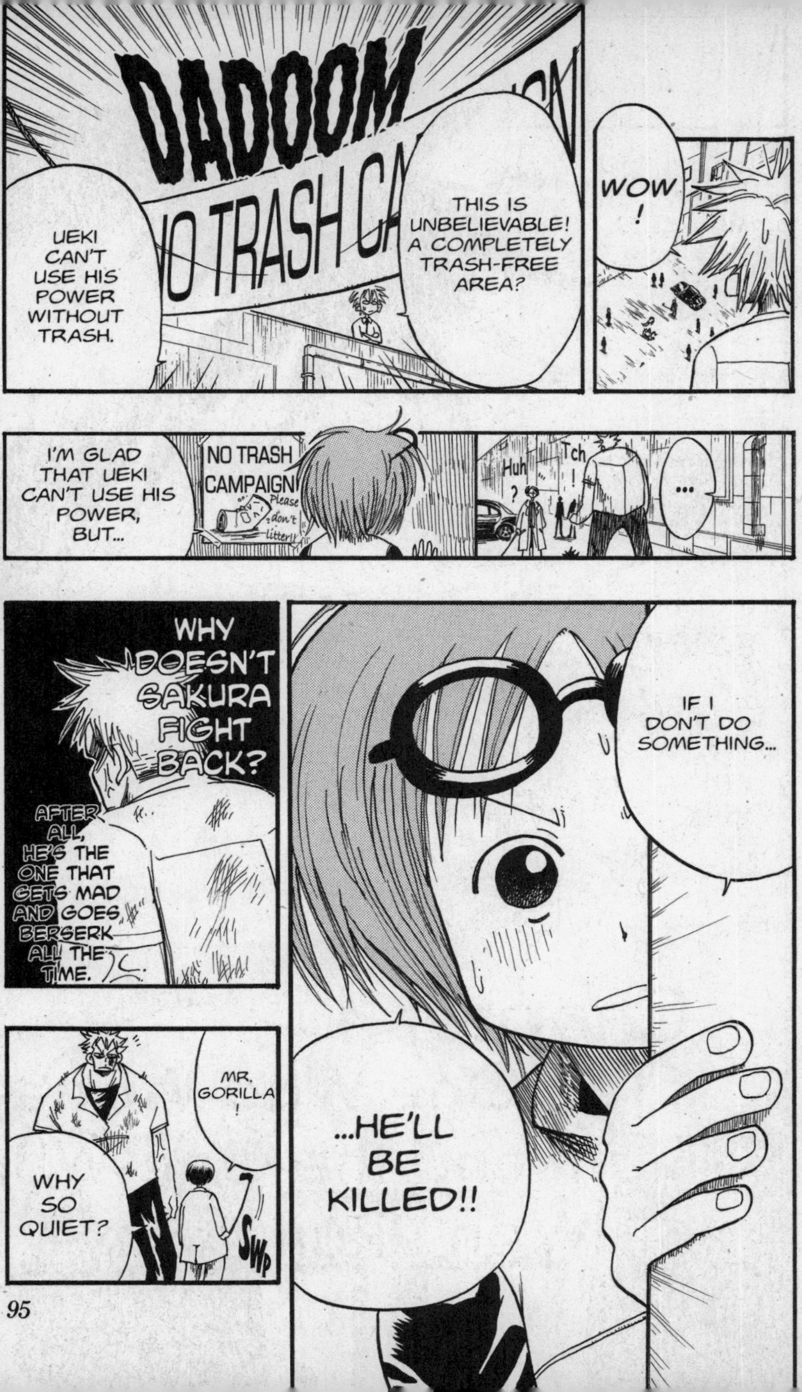
WOW!
DADOOM
NO TRASH CA
THIS IS UNBELIEVABLE! A COMPLETELY TRASH-FREE AREA?
UEKI CAN'T USE HIS POWER WITHOUT TRASH.
...
Tch!
Huh?
NO TRASH CAMPAIGN
Please don't litter!!
I'M GLAD THAT UEKI CAN'T USE HIS POWER, BUT...
IF I DON'T DO SOMETHING...
...HE'LL BE KILLED!!
WHY DOESN'T SAKURA FIGHT BACK?
AFTER ALL, HE'S THE ONE THAT GETS MAD AND GOES BERSERK ALL THE TIME.
MR. GORILLA!
WHY SO QUIET?
SWP

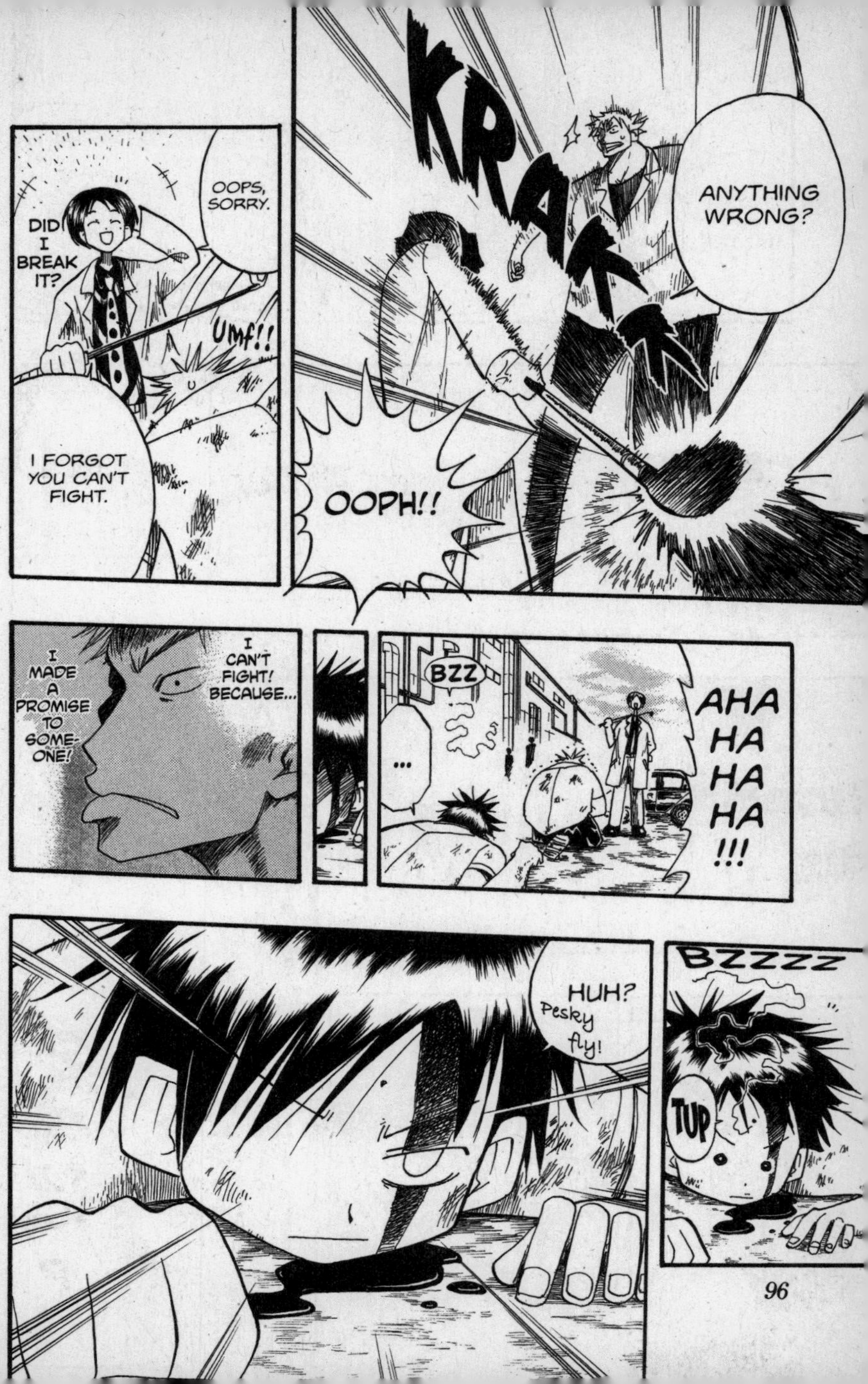
ANYTHING WRONG?
KRAK
OOPH!!
OOPS, SORRY.
DID I BREAK IT?
UMF!!
I FORGOT YOU CAN'T FIGHT.
AHA HA HA HA!!!
BZZ
...
I CAN'T FIGHT! BECAUSE...
I MADE A PROMISE TO SOMEONE!
BZZZZZ
TUP
HUH? Pesky fly!

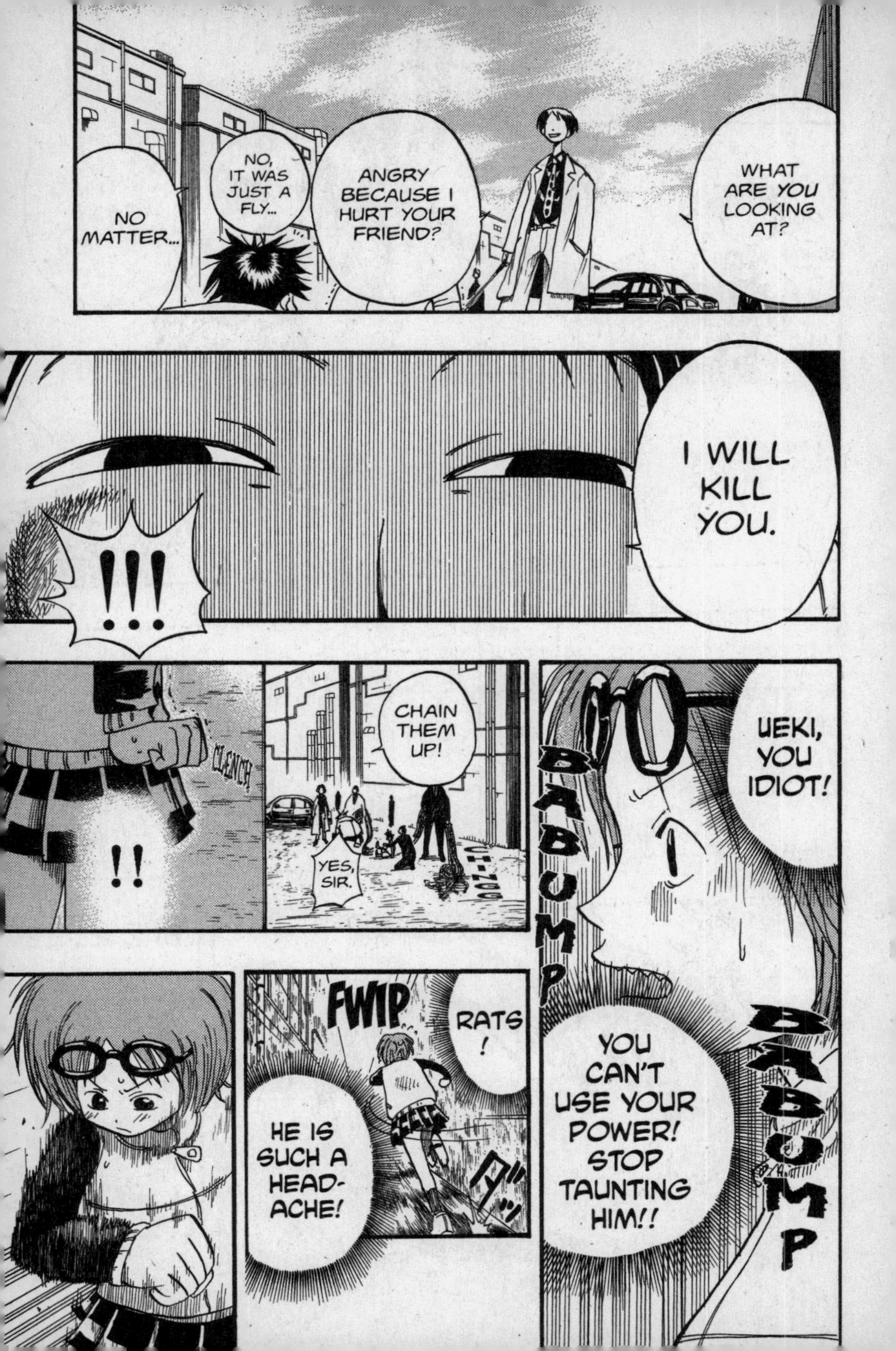
WHAT ARE YOU LOOKING AT?
ANGRY BECAUSE I HURT YOUR FRIEND?
NO, IT WAS JUST A FLY...
NO MATTER...
I WILL KILL YOU.
!!!
UEKI, YOU IDIOT!
BABUMP
YOU CAN'T USE YOUR POWER! STOP TAUNTING HIM!!
BABUMP
CHAIN THEM UP!
YES, SIR.
CH-ZGG
CLENCH
!!
FWIP
RATS!
HE IS SUCH A HEADACHE!

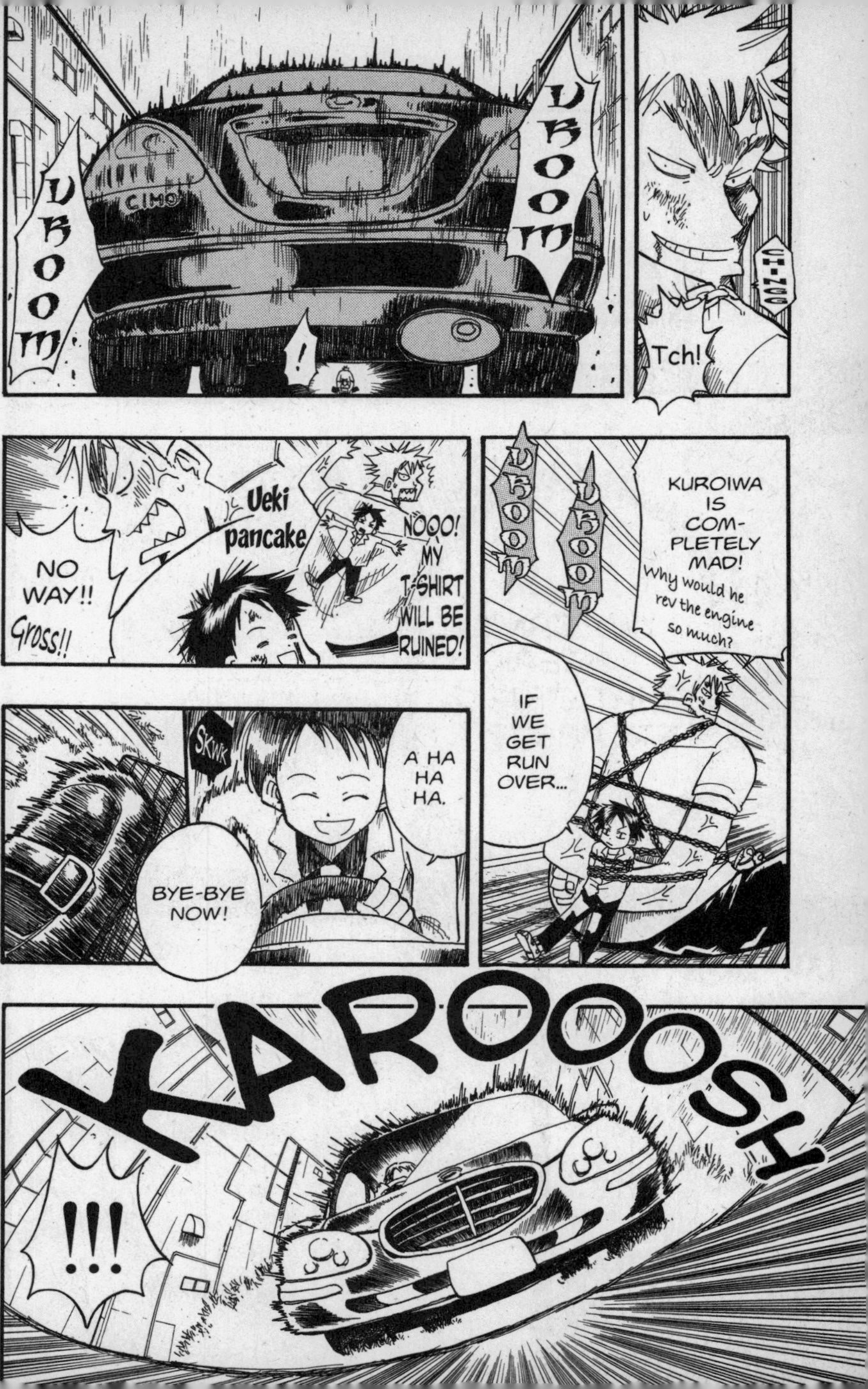
CHINGG
Tch!
VROOM
VROOM
!
VROOM
VROOM
KUROIWA IS COMPLETELY MAD!
Why would he rev the engine so much?
IF WE GET RUN OVER...
NOOO! MY T-SHIRT WILL BE RUINED!
Ueki pancake
NO WAY!!
Gross!!
SKWK
A HA HA HA.
BYE-BYE NOW!
YAROOOSH
!!!

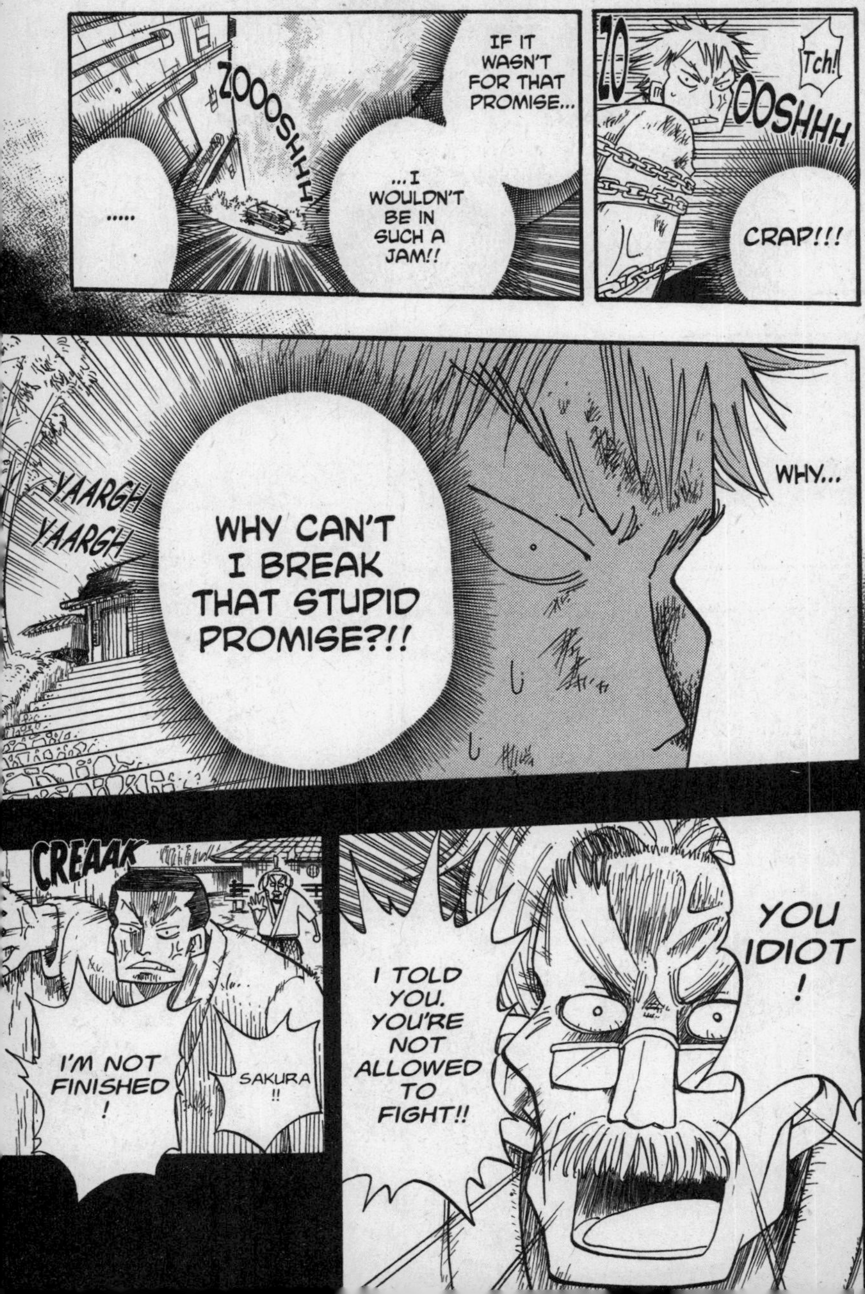
Tch!
ZOOSHHH
CRAP!!!
IF IT WASN'T FOR THAT PROMISE...
...I WOULDN'T BE IN SUCH A JAM!!
ZOOOSHHH
.....
WHY...
WHY CAN'T I BREAK THAT STUPID PROMISE?!!
YAARGH
YAARGH
YOU IDIOT!
I TOLD YOU. YOU'RE NOT ALLOWED TO FIGHT!!
CREAAK
SAKURA!!
I'M NOT FINISHED!

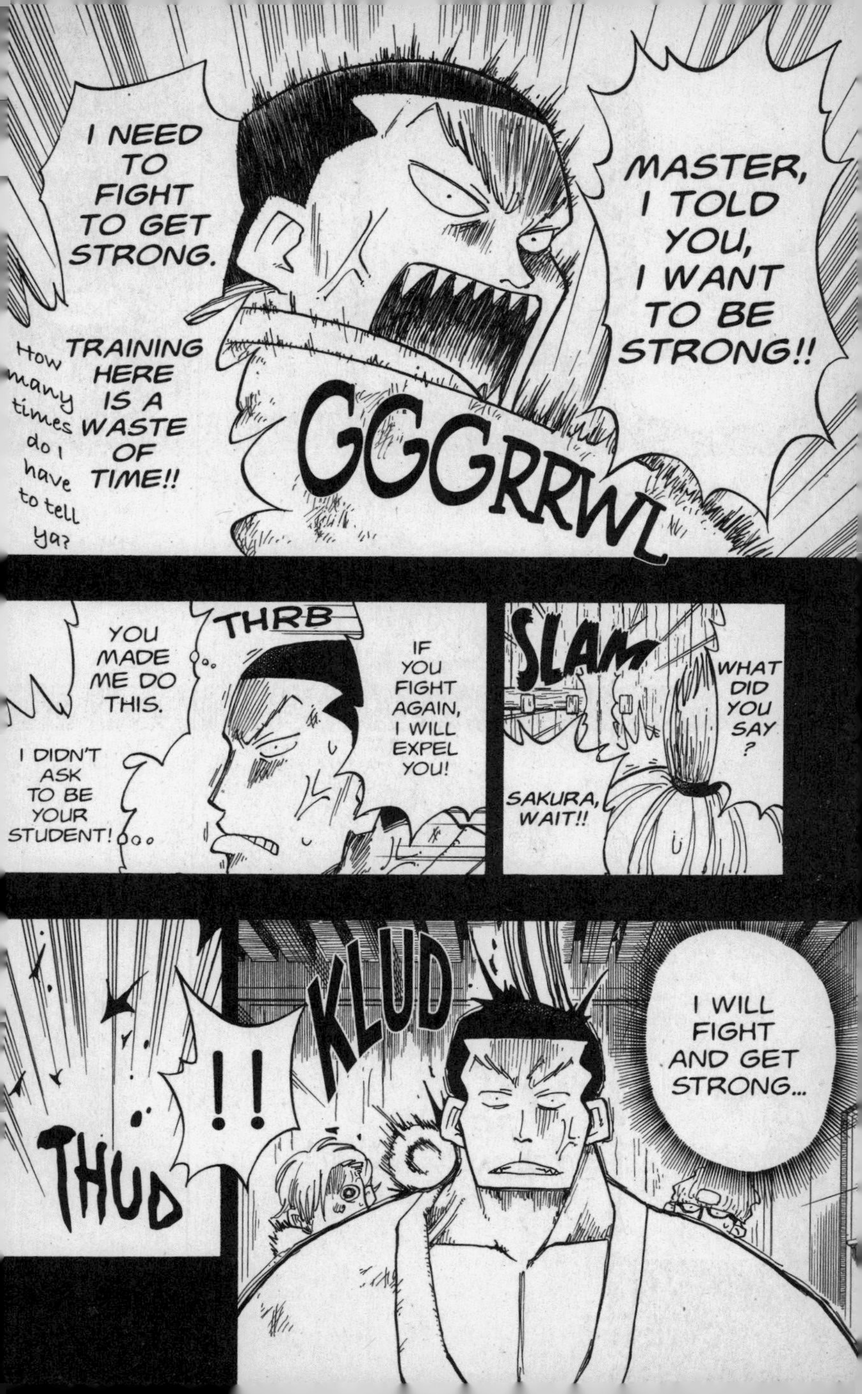
MASTER, I TOLD YOU, I WANT TO BE STRONG!!
GGGRRRWL
I NEED TO FIGHT TO GET STRONG.
TRAINING HERE IS A WASTE OF TIME!!
How many times do I have to tell ya?
SLAM
WHAT DID YOU SAY?
SAKURA, WAIT!!
THRB
IF YOU FIGHT AGAIN, I WILL EXPEL YOU!
YOU MADE ME DO THIS.
I DIDN'T ASK TO BE YOUR STUDENT!
I WILL FIGHT AND GET STRONG...
KLUD
!!
THUD

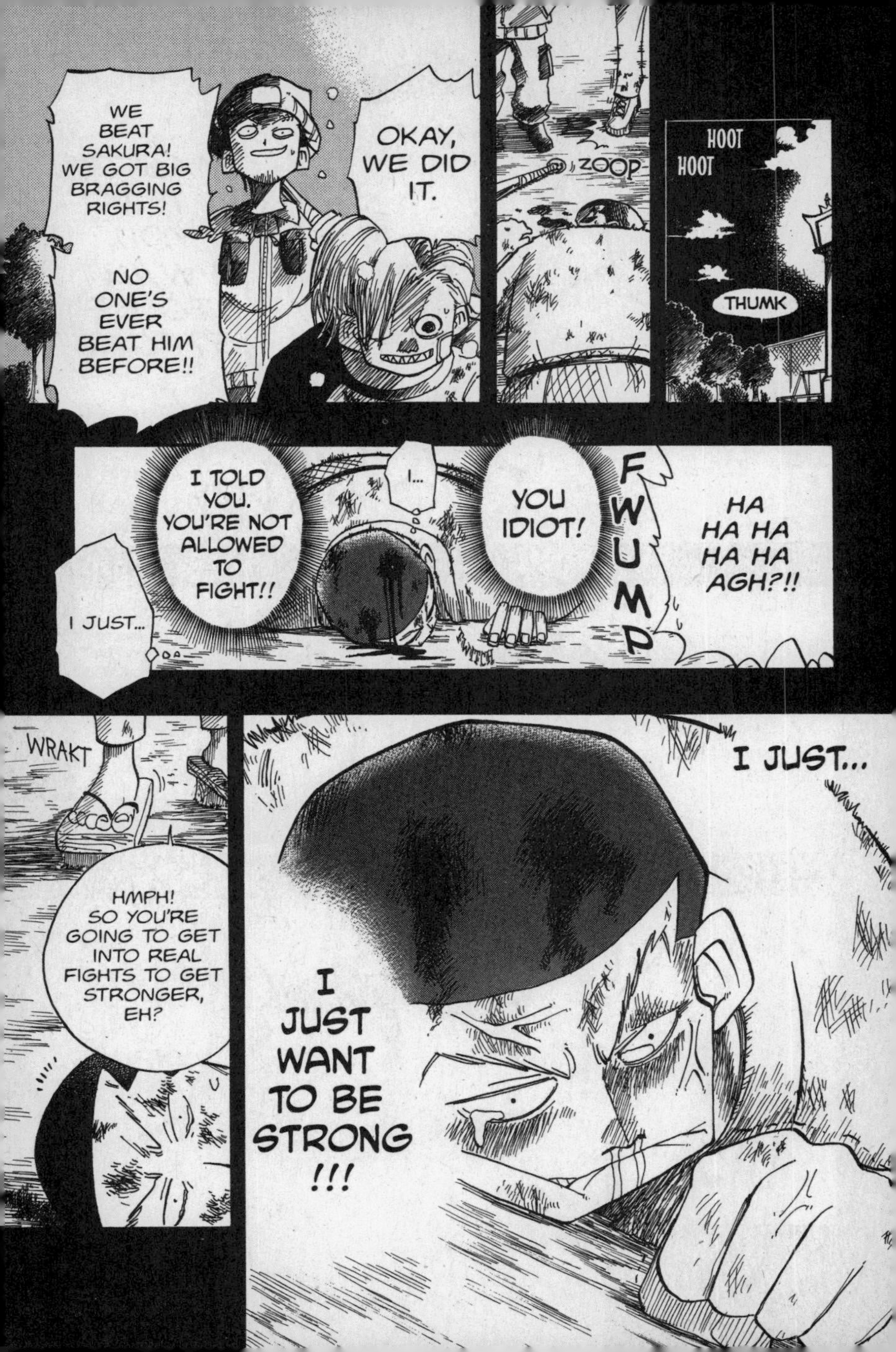
HOOT
HOOT
THUMK
ZOOP
OKAY, WE DID IT.
WE BEAT SAKURA! WE GOT BIG BRAGGING RIGHTS!
NO ONE'S EVER BEAT HIM BEFORE!!
HA HA HA HA HA AGH?!!
FWUMP
YOU IDIOT!
I...
I TOLD YOU. YOU'RE NOT ALLOWED TO FIGHT!!
TWITCH
I JUST...
I JUST...
I JUST WANT TO BE STRONG!!!
WRAKT
HMPH! SO YOU'RE GOING TO GET INTO REAL FIGHTS TO GET STRONGER, EH?

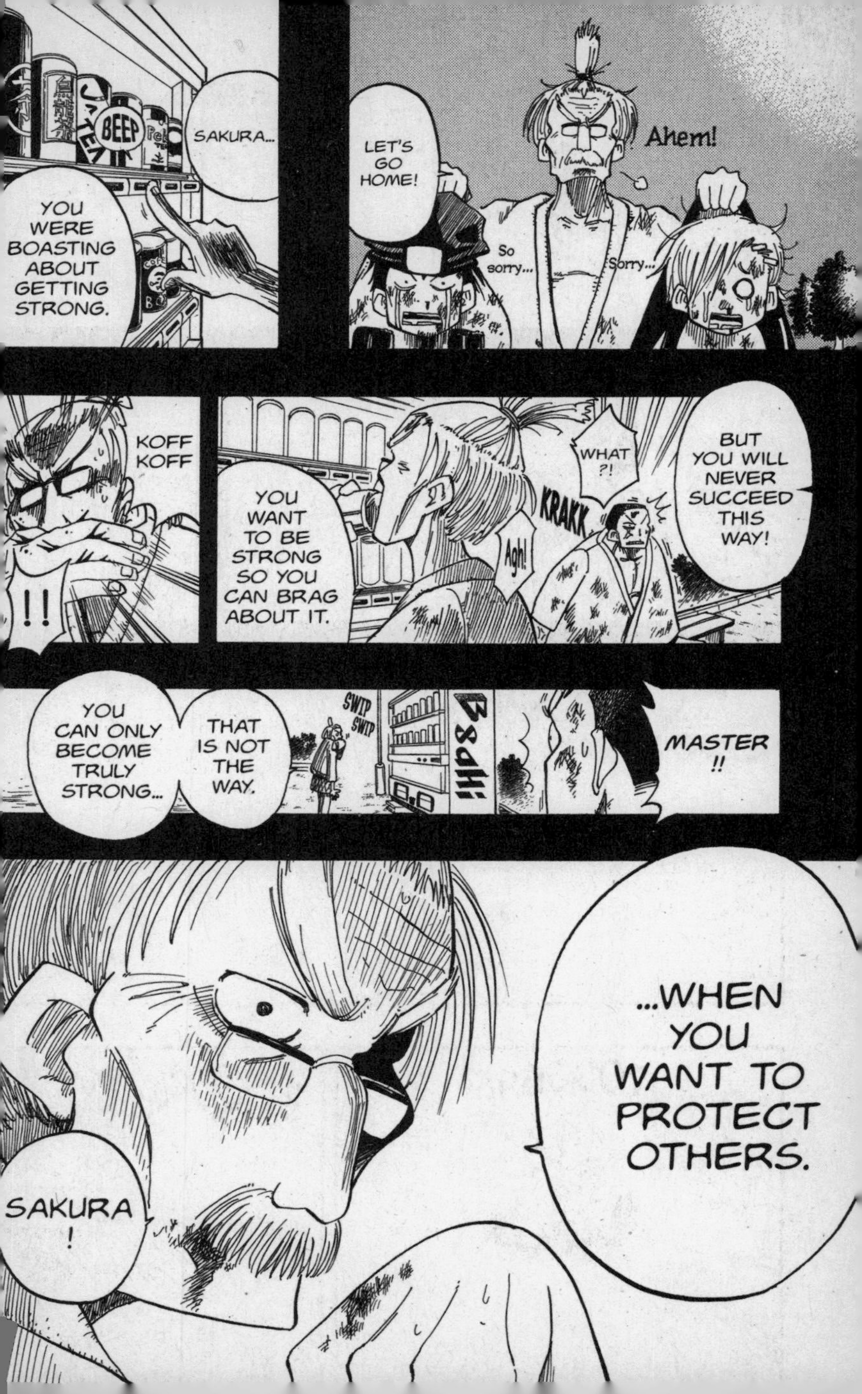
Ahem!
LET'S GO HOME!
Sorry...
So sorry...
SAKURA...
BEEP
YOU WERE BOASTING ABOUT GETTING STRONG.
BUT YOU WILL NEVER SUCCEED THIS WAY!
WHAT ?!
KRAKK
Agh!
YOU WANT TO BE STRONG SO YOU CAN BRAG ABOUT IT.
KOFF KOFF
!!
MASTER !!
SWIP SWIP
THAT IS NOT THE WAY.
YOU CAN ONLY BECOME TRULY STRONG...
...WHEN YOU WANT TO PROTECT OTHERS.
SAKURA !

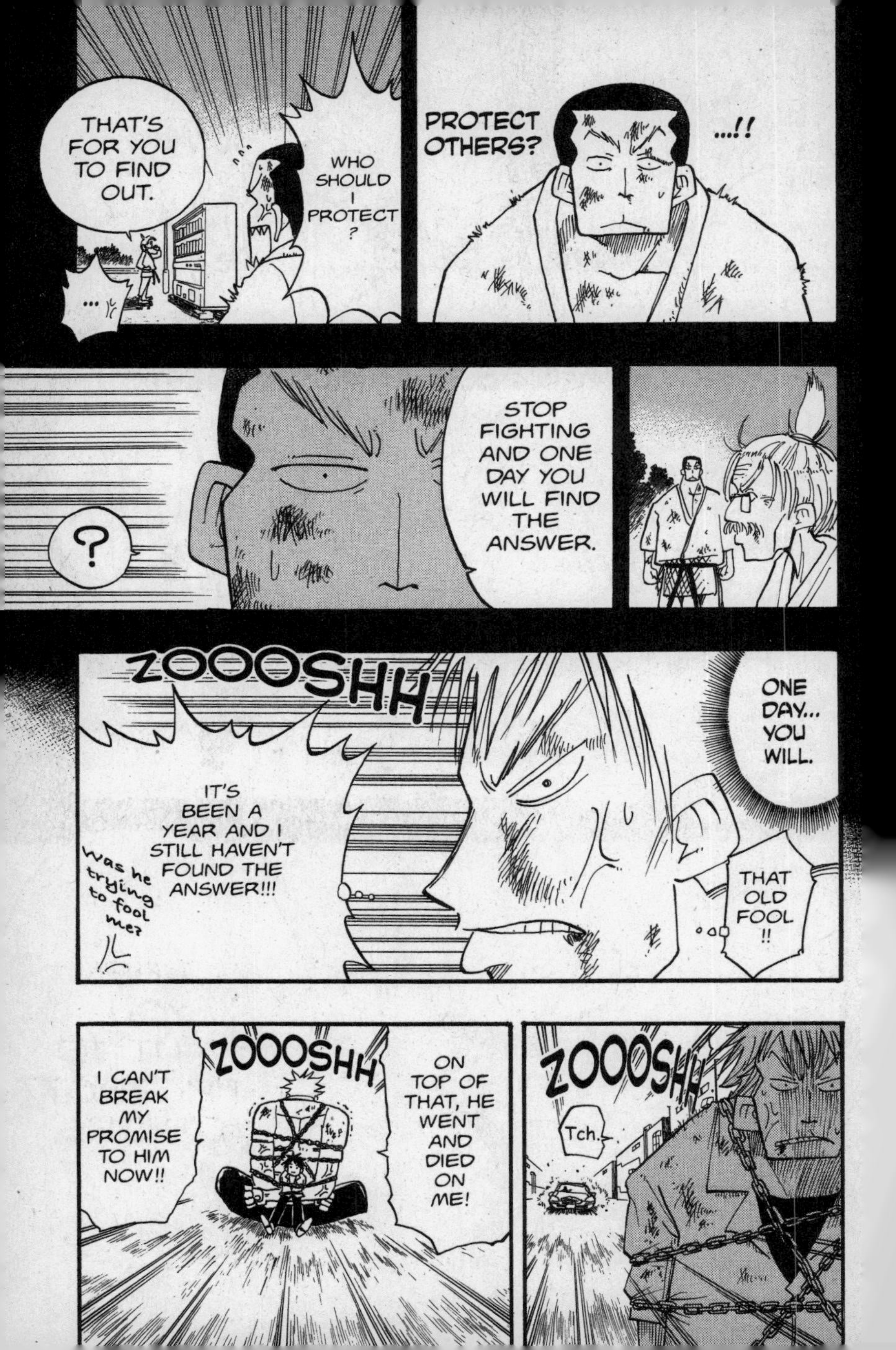
PROTECT OTHERS?
...!!
WHO SHOULD I PROTECT?
THAT'S FOR YOU TO FIND OUT.
...
STOP FIGHTING AND ONE DAY YOU WILL FIND THE ANSWER.
?
ONE DAY... YOU WILL.
THAT OLD FOOL!!
ZOOOSHH
IT'S BEEN A YEAR AND I STILL HAVEN'T FOUND THE ANSWER!!!
Was he trying to fool me?
ZOOOSHH
Tch.
ON TOP OF THAT, HE WENT AND DIED ON ME!
ZOOOSHH
I CAN'T BREAK MY PROMISE TO HIM NOW!!

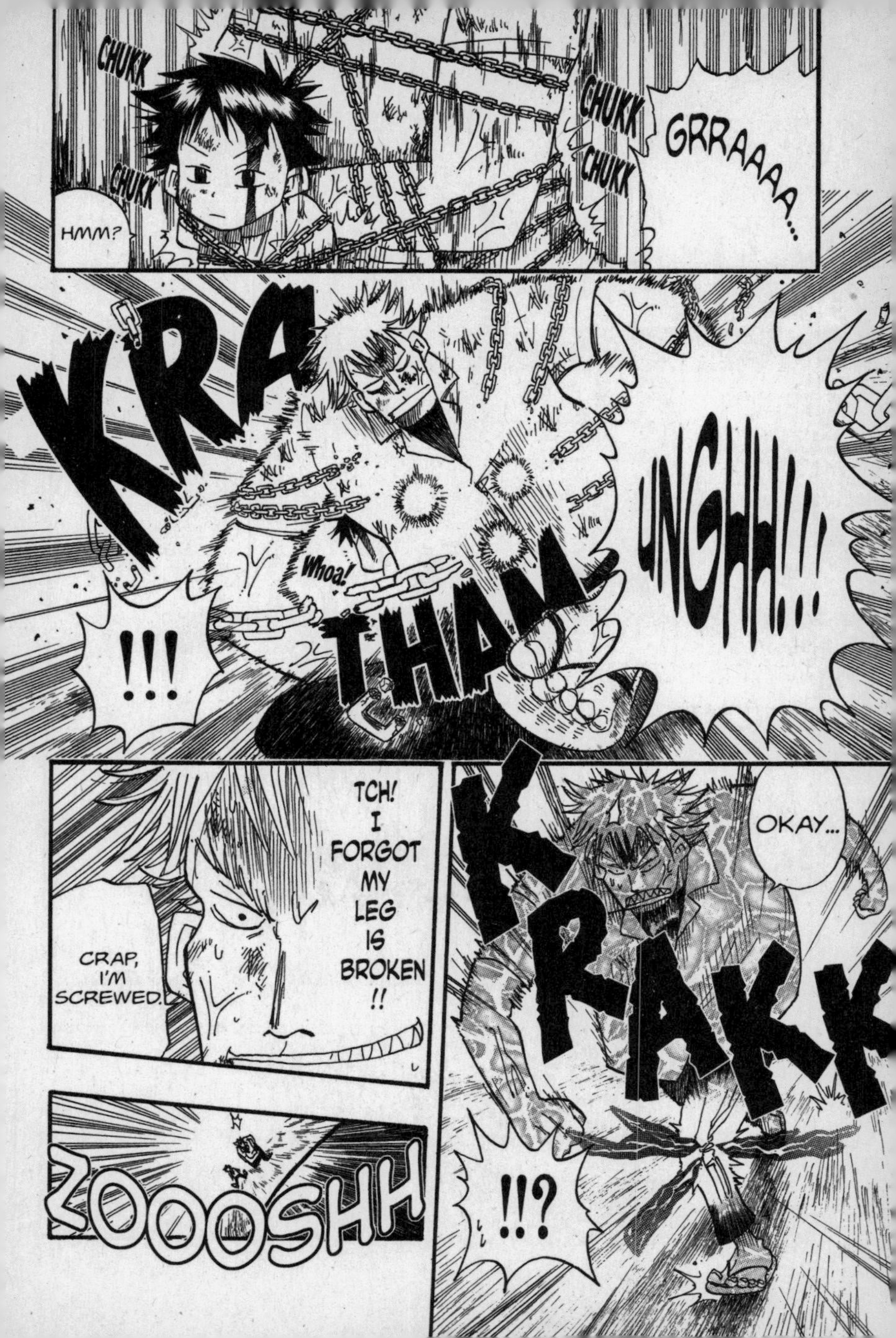
GRRAAAA...
CHUKK
CHUKK
CHUKK
CHUKK
HMM?
UNGHH!!!
KRA
Whoa!
THAM
!!!
OKAY...
KRAKK
!!?
TCH! I FORGOT MY LEG IS BROKEN!!
CRAP, I'M SCREWED.
ZOOOSHH

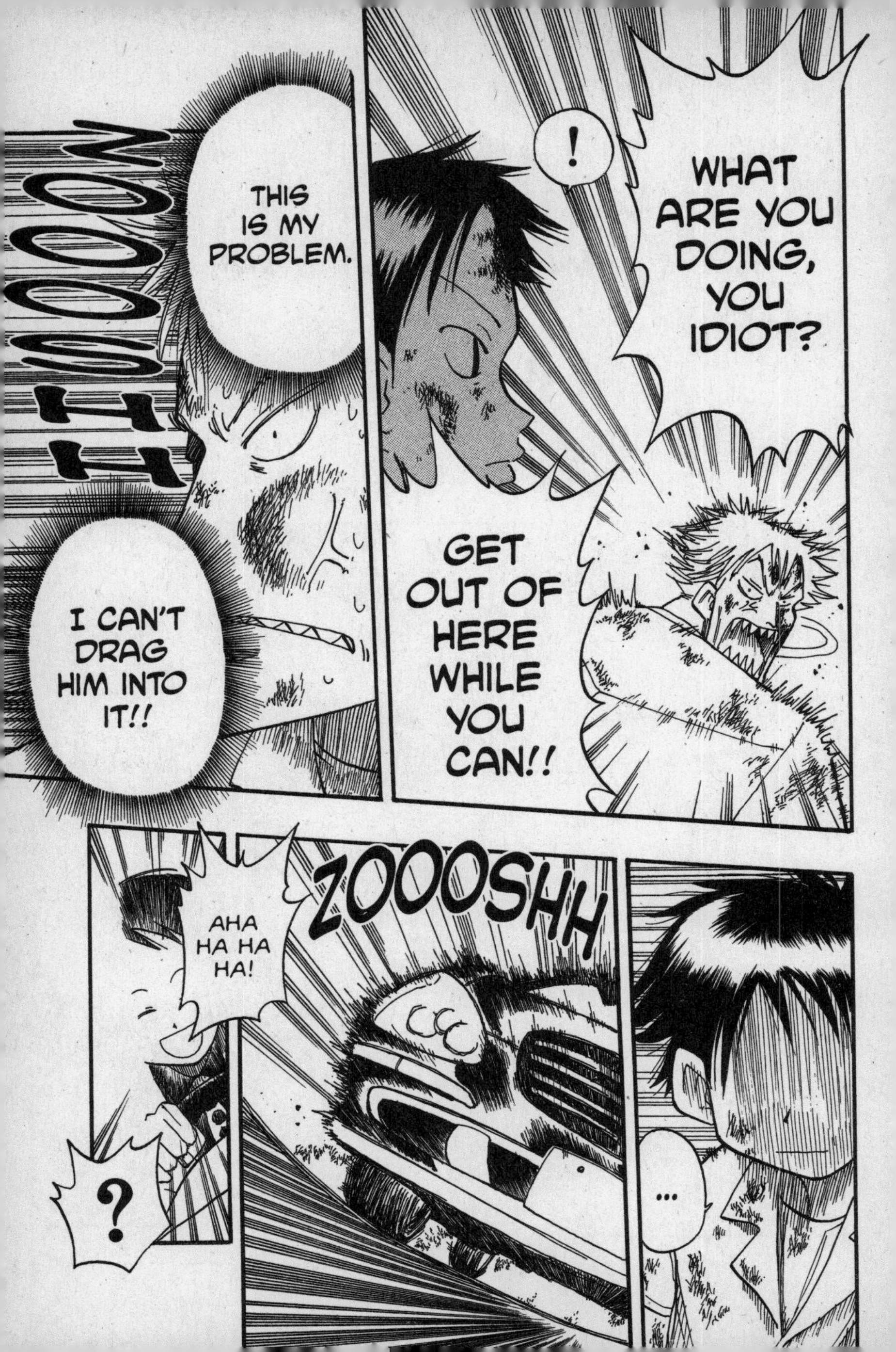
!
WHAT ARE YOU DOING, YOU IDIOT?
GET OUT OF HERE WHILE YOU CAN!!
THIS IS MY PROBLEM.
I CAN'T DRAG HIM INTO IT!!
...
ZOOOSHH
AHA HA HA HA!
?

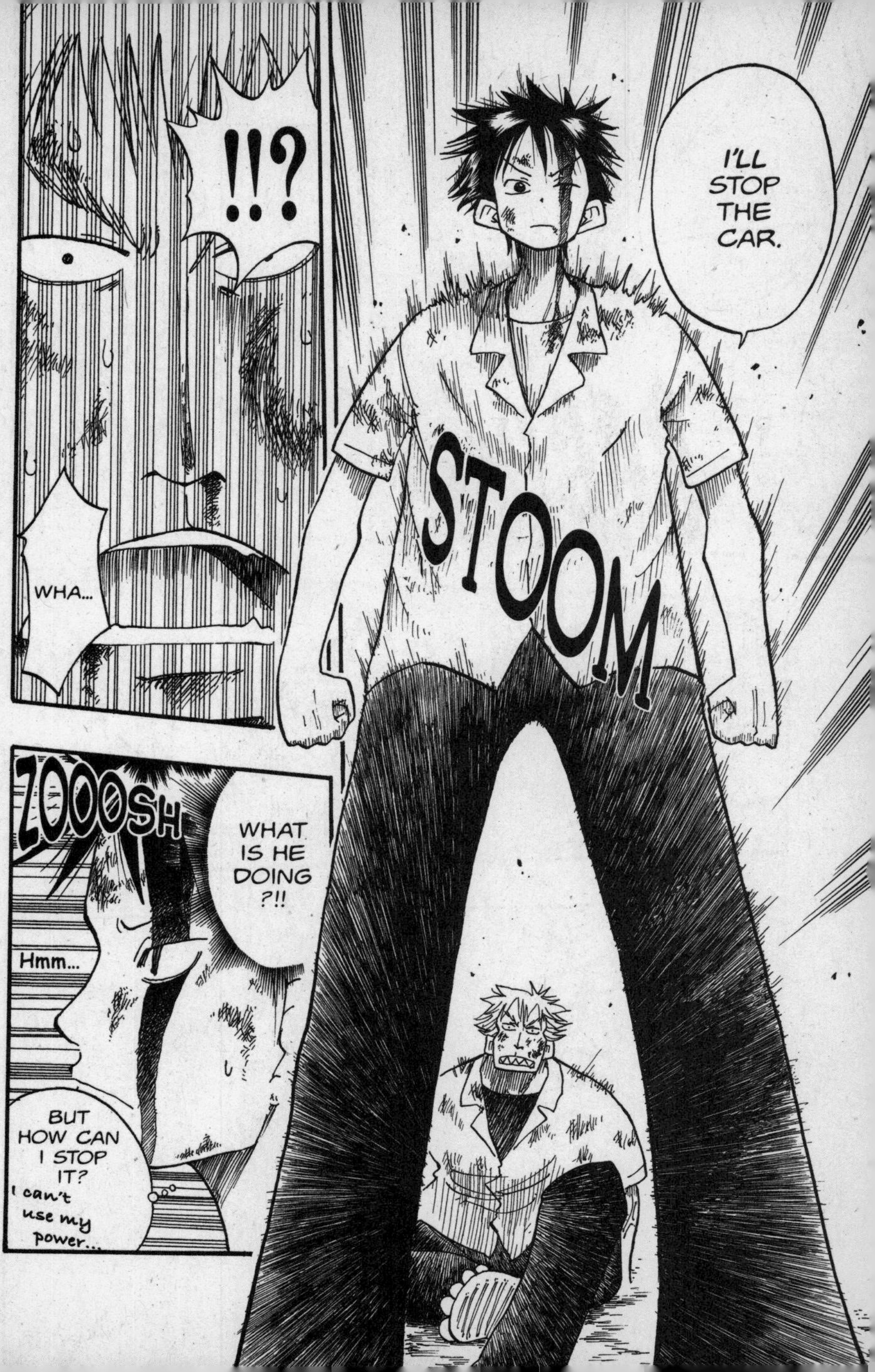
I'LL STOP THE CAR.
STOOM
!!?
WHA...
ZOOOSH
WHAT IS HE DOING ?!!
Hmm...
BUT HOW CAN I STOP IT?
I can't use my power...

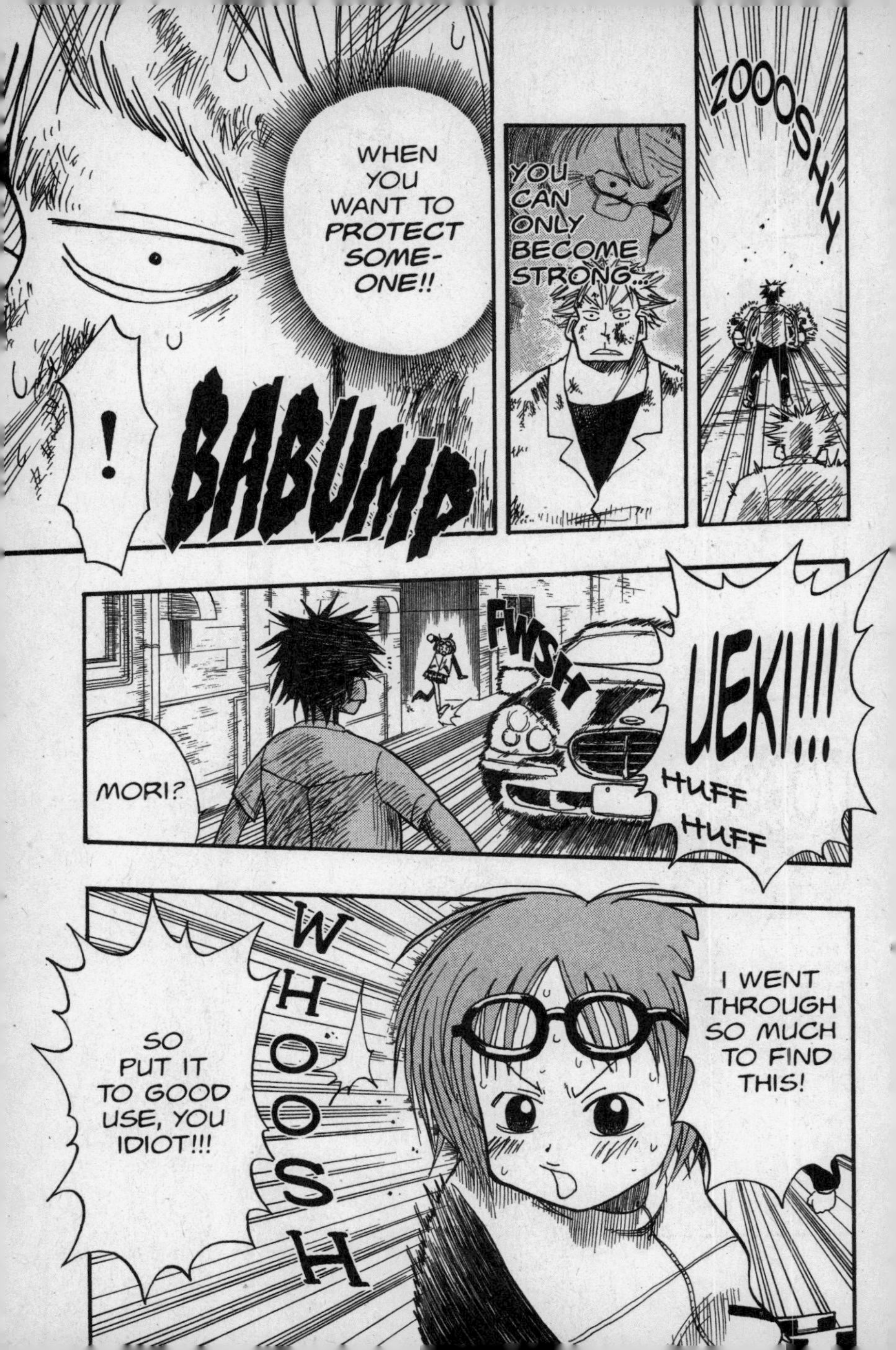
ZOOOSHH
YOU CAN ONLY BECOME STRONG...
WHEN YOU WANT TO PROTECT SOME-ONE!!
!
BABUMP
UEKI!!!
HUFF HUFF
FWSH
MORI?
I WENT THROUGH SO MUCH TO FIND THIS!
WHOOOSH
SO PUT IT TO GOOD USE, YOU IDIOT!!!

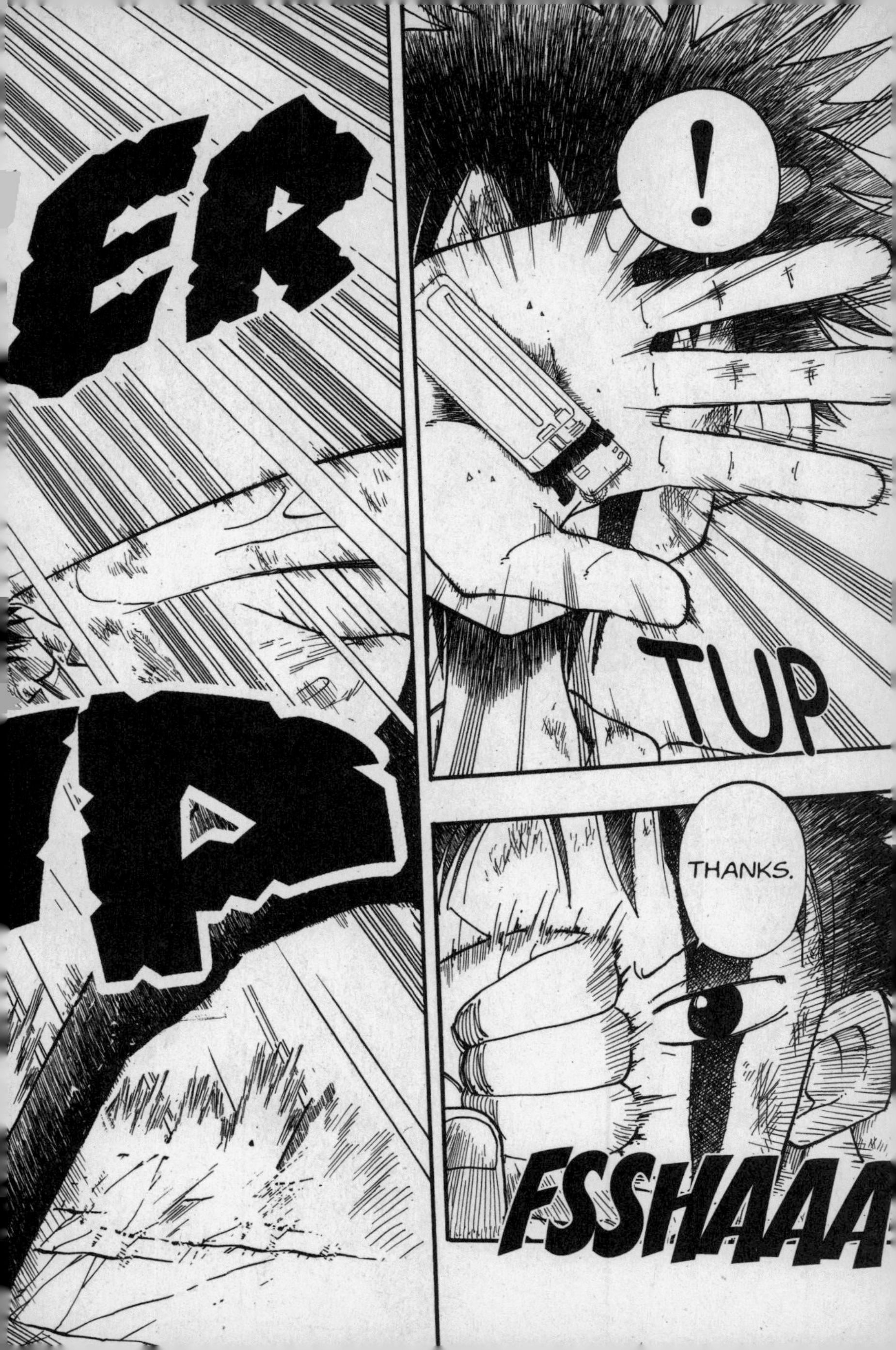
!
TUP
THANKS.
FSSHAAA
ER

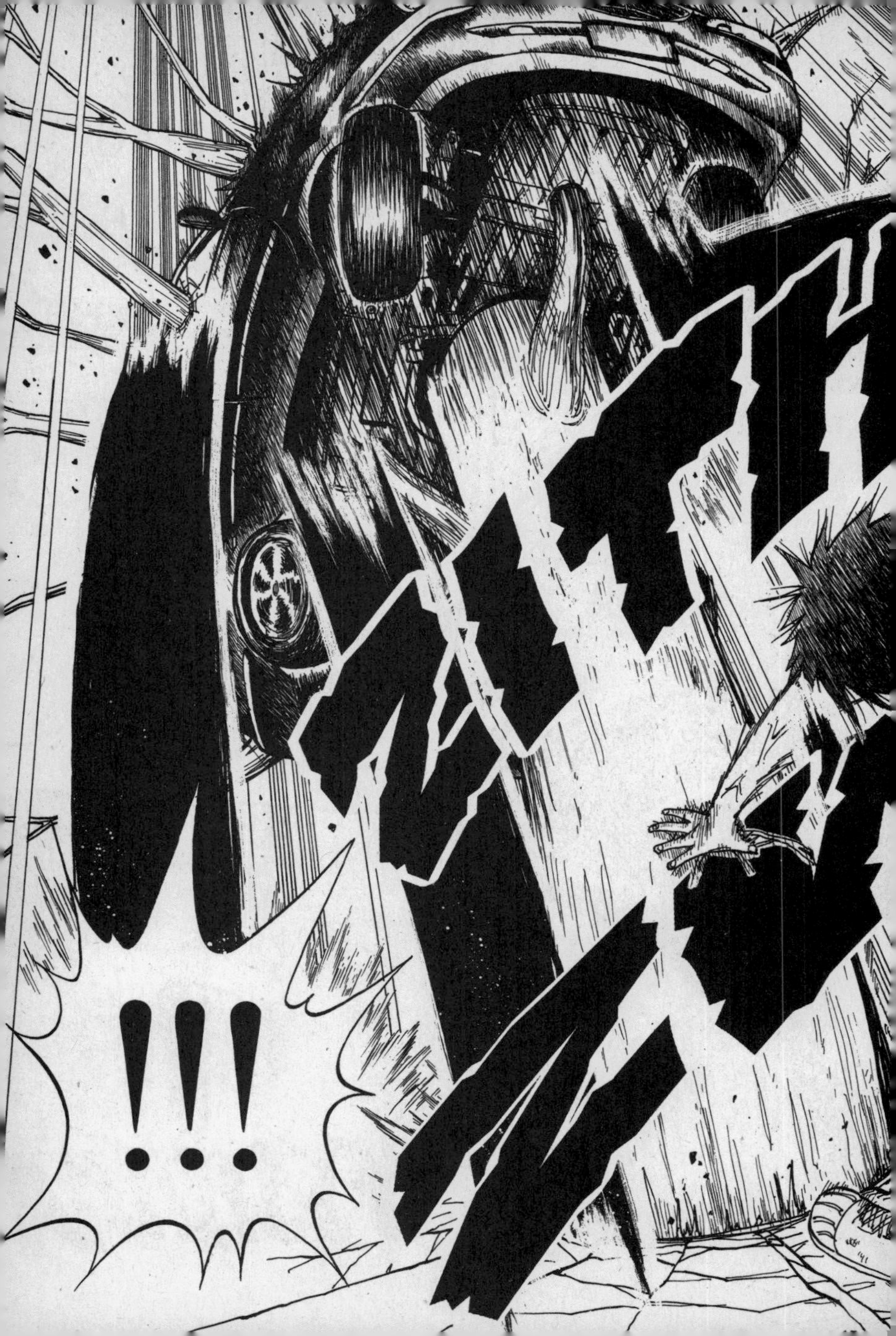
!!!

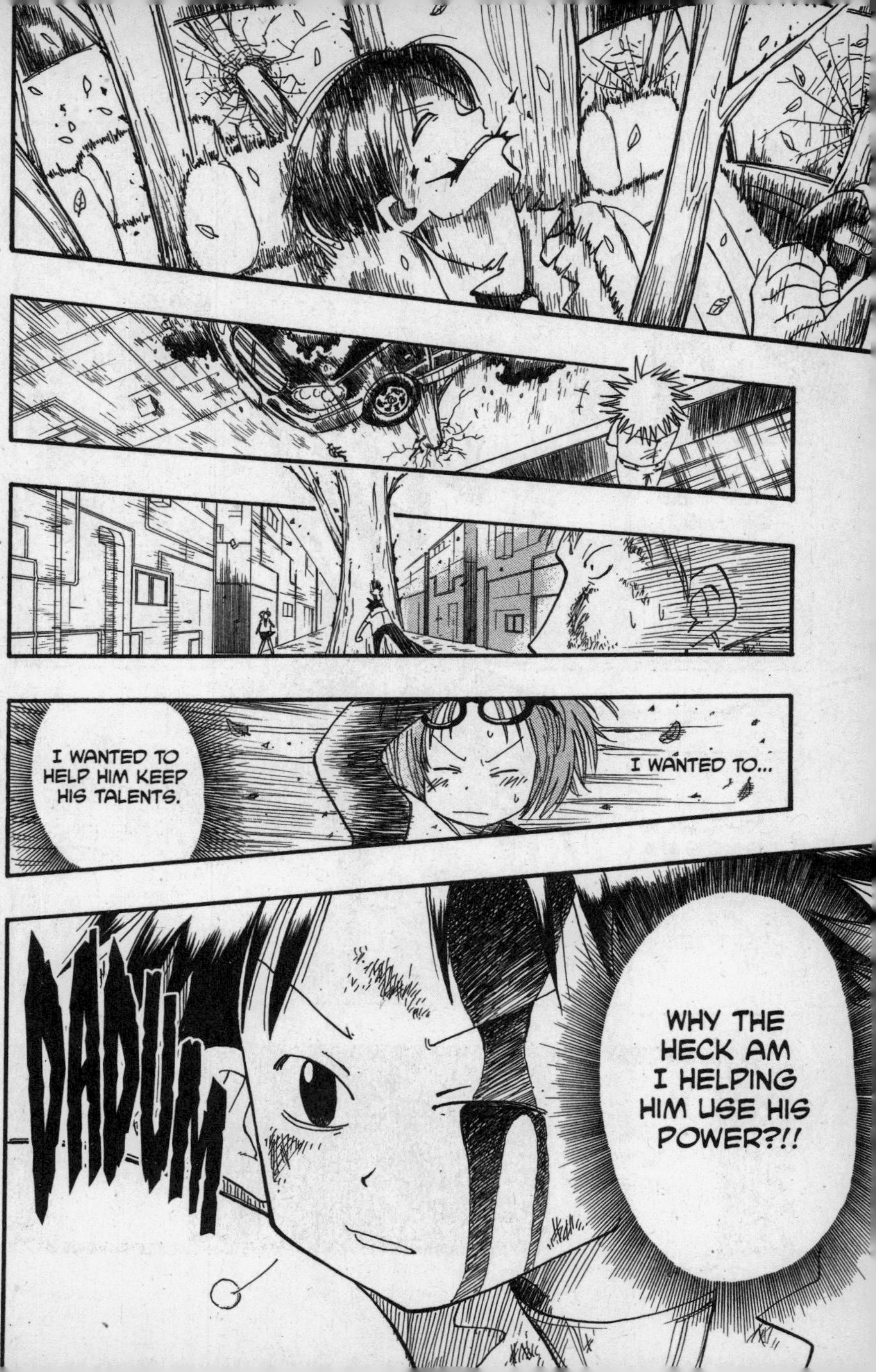
I WANTED TO...
I WANTED TO HELP HIM KEEP HIS TALENTS.
WHY THE HECK AM I HELPING HIM USE HIS POWER?!!
DADUM

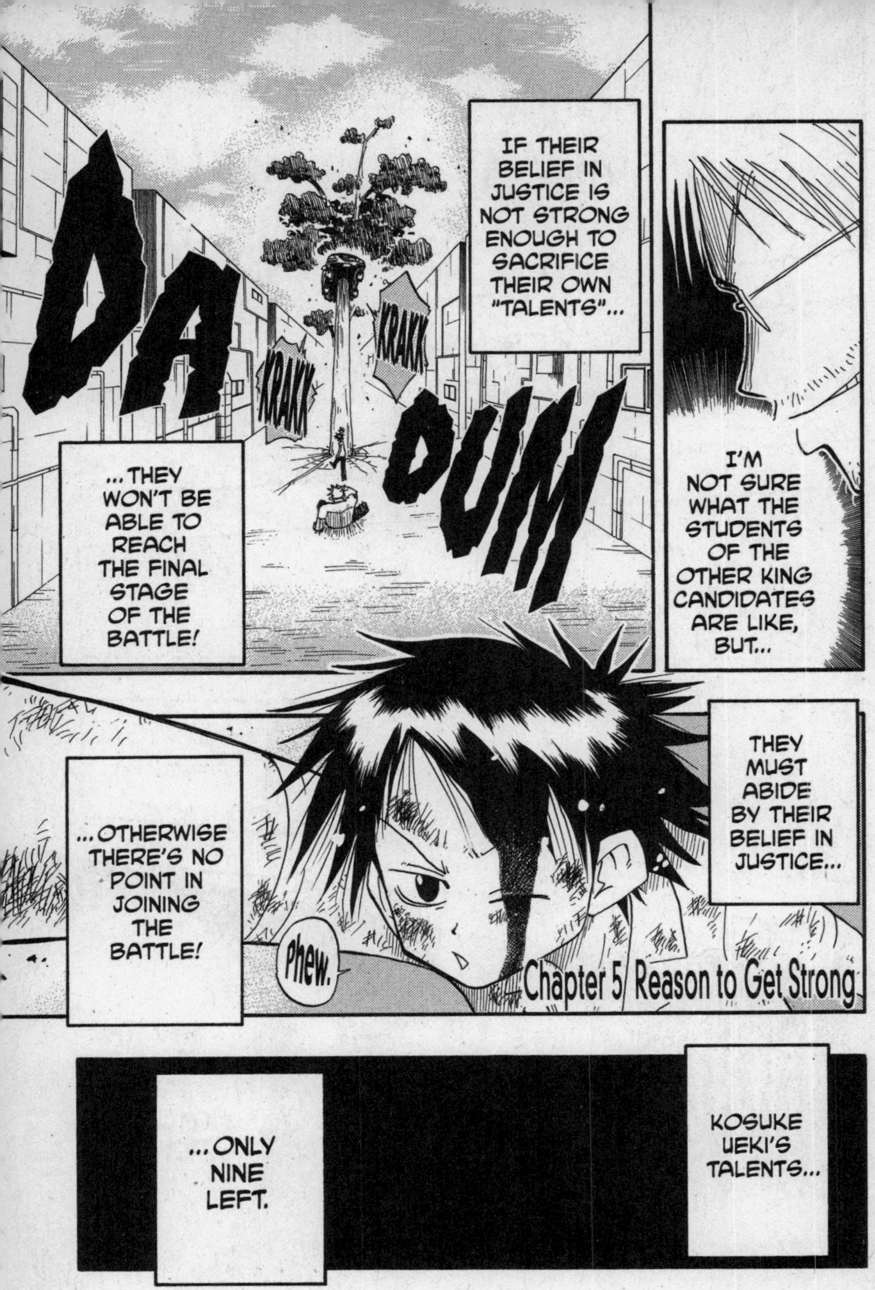
I'M NOT SURE WHAT THE STUDENTS OF THE OTHER KING CANDIDATES ARE LIKE, BUT...
IF THEIR BELIEF IN JUSTICE IS NOT STRONG ENOUGH TO SACRIFICE THEIR OWN "TALENTS"...
KRAKK
KRAKK
DA
OUM
...THEY WON'T BE ABLE TO REACH THE FINAL STAGE OF THE BATTLE!
THEY MUST ABIDE BY THEIR BELIEF IN JUSTICE...
...OTHERWISE THERE'S NO POINT IN JOINING THE BATTLE!
Phew.
Chapter 5 Reason to Get Strong
KOSUKE UEKI'S TALENTS...
...ONLY NINE LEFT.

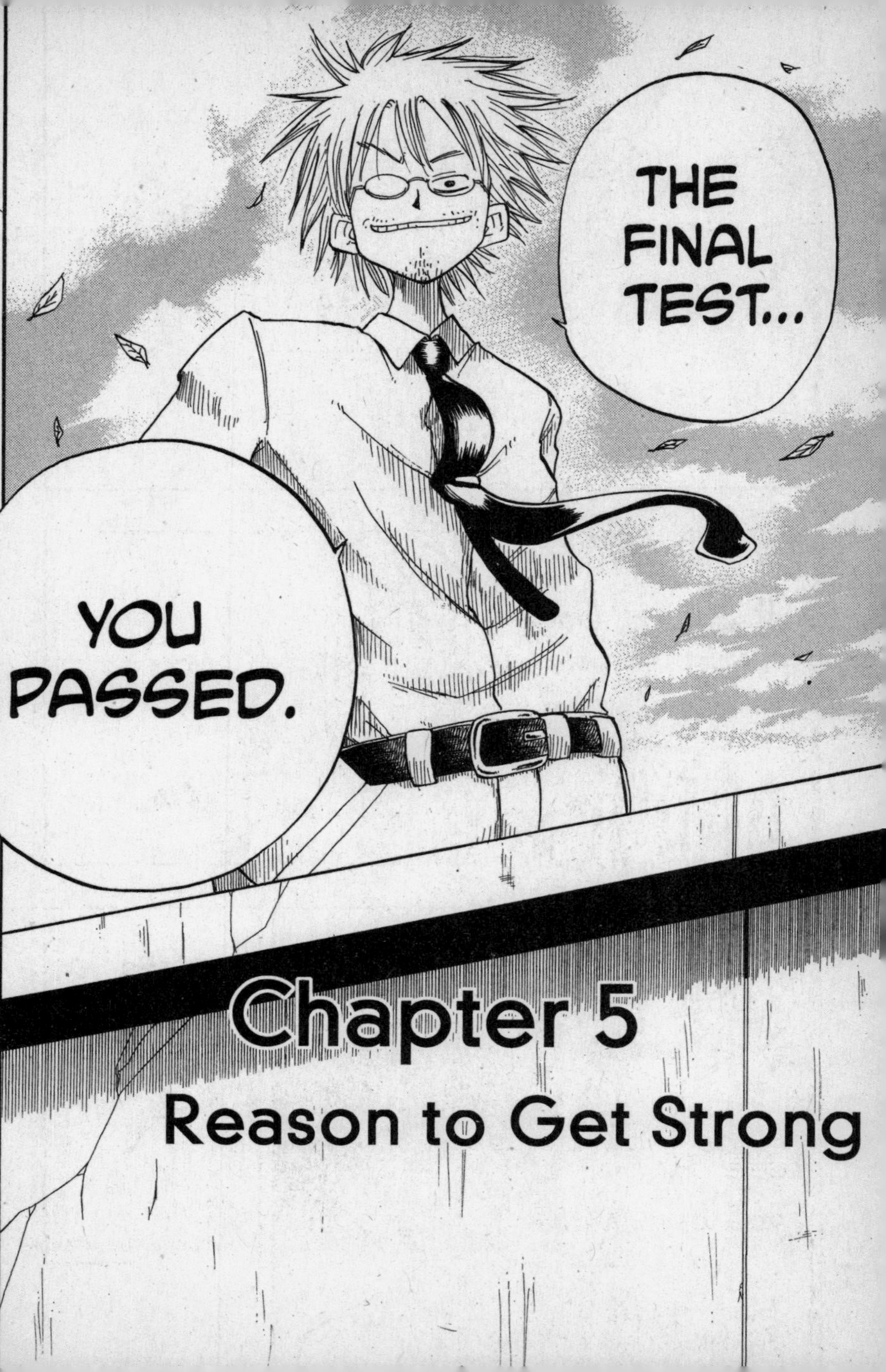
THE FINAL TEST...
YOU PASSED.

Chapter 5
Reason to Get Strong

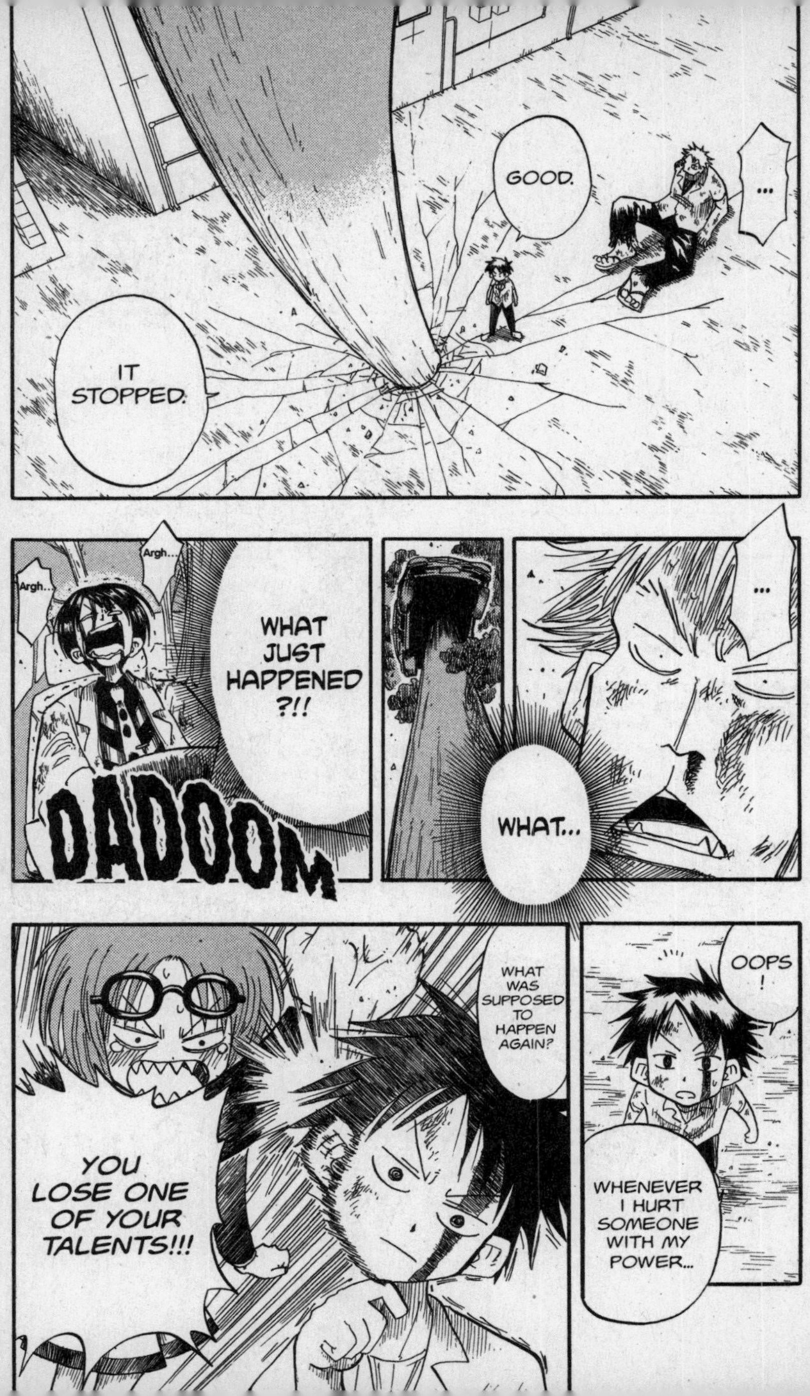
...
GOOD.
IT STOPPED.
...
WHAT...
WHAT JUST HAPPENED ?!!
Argh...
Argh...
DADOOM
OOPS !
WHENEVER I HURT SOMEONE WITH MY POWER...
WHAT WAS SUPPOSED TO HAPPEN AGAIN?
YOU LOSE ONE OF YOUR TALENTS!!!

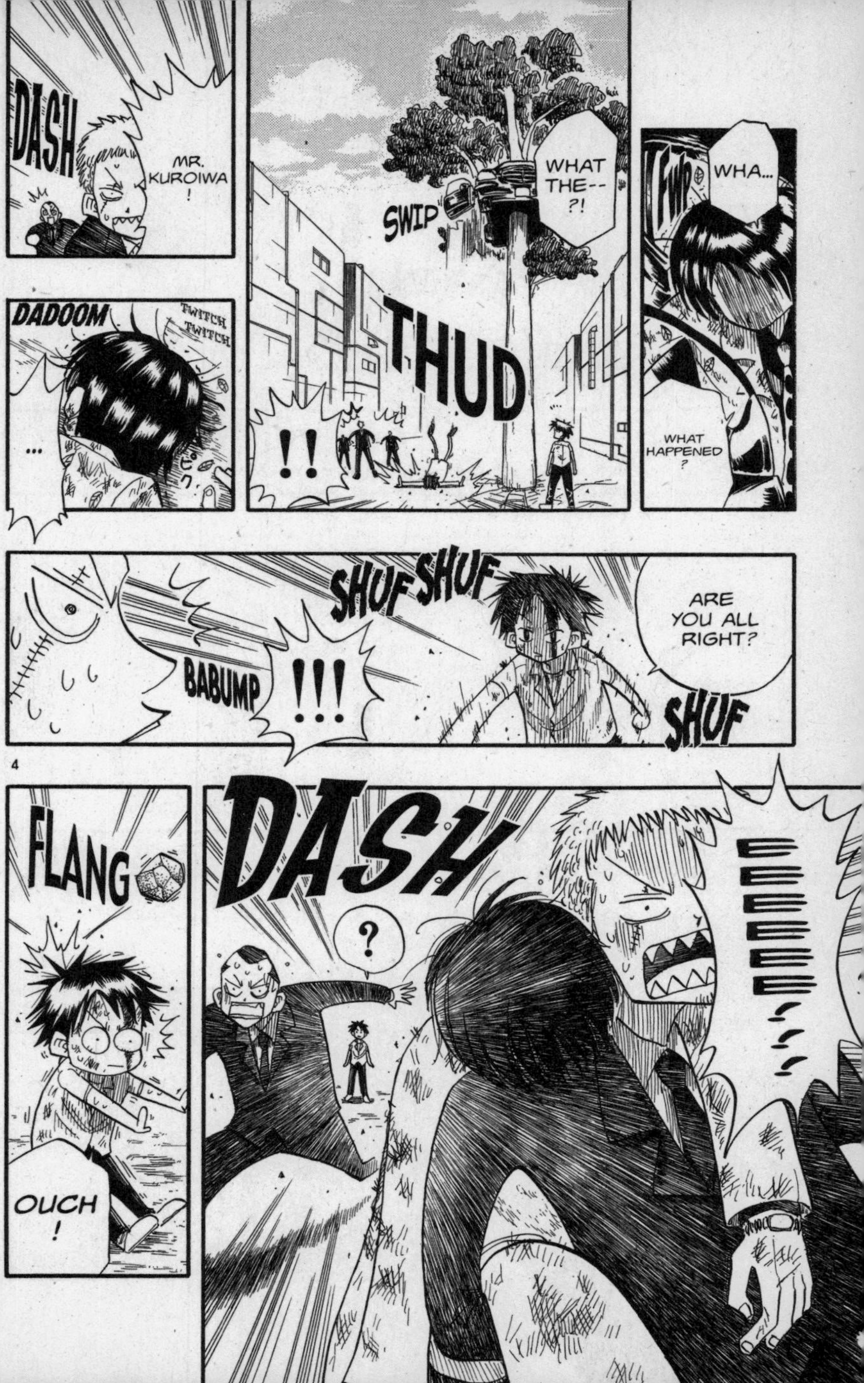
FWIP
WHA...
WHAT HAPPENED?
WHAT THE-- ?!
SWIP
THUD
!!
DASH
MR. KUROIWA!
DADOOM
TWITCH TWITCH
...
ARE YOU ALL RIGHT?
SHUF SHUF
SHUF
!!!
BABUMP
DASH
EEEEEE
?
FLANG
OUCH!

4

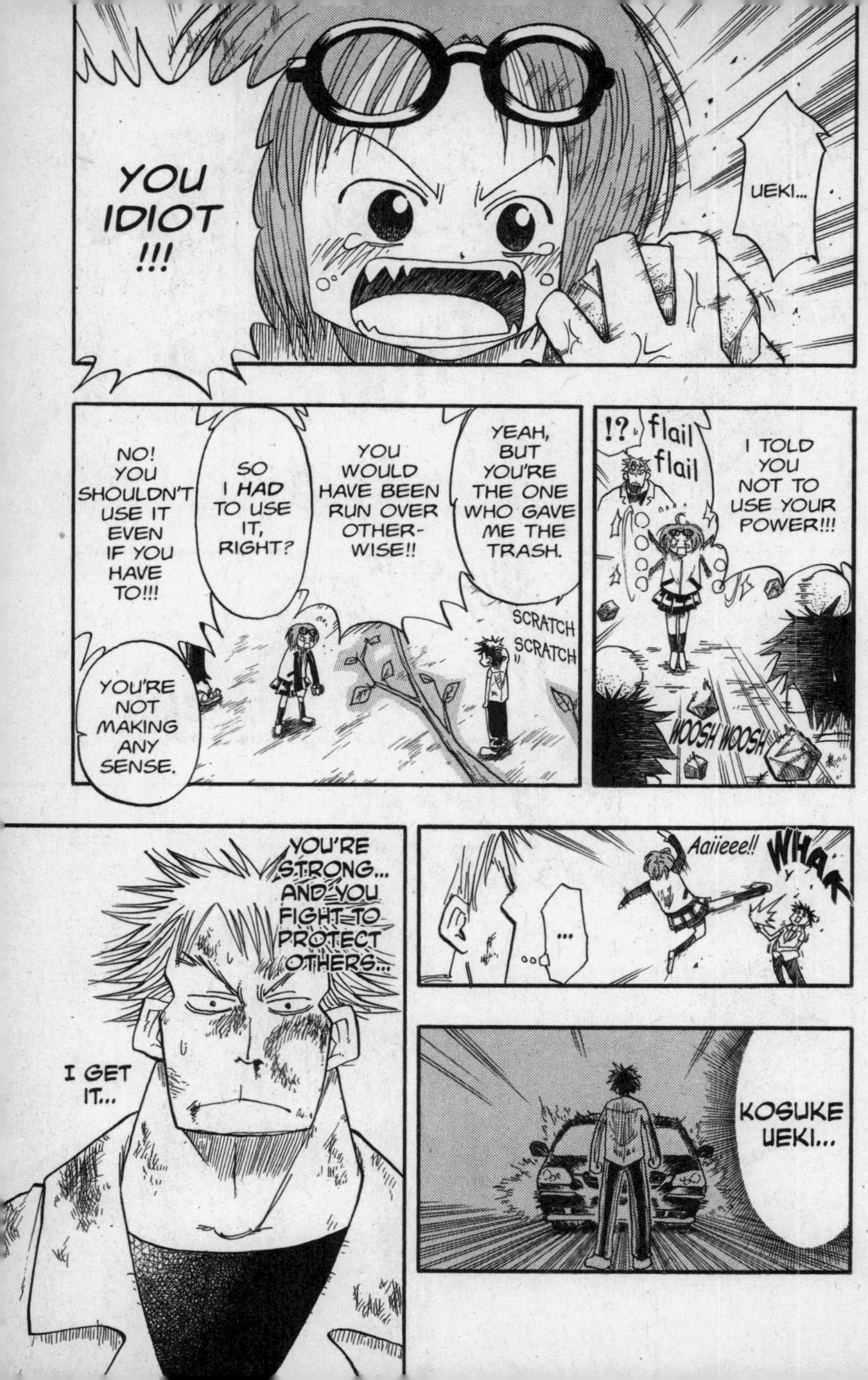
UEKI...
YOU IDIOT !!!
I TOLD YOU NOT TO USE YOUR POWER!!!
flail flail
!?
WOOSH WOOSH
YEAH, BUT YOU'RE THE ONE WHO GAVE ME THE TRASH.
SCRATCH SCRATCH
YOU WOULD HAVE BEEN RUN OVER OTHER-WISE!!
SO I HAD TO USE IT, RIGHT?
NO! YOU SHOULDN'T USE IT EVEN IF YOU HAVE TO!!!
YOU'RE NOT MAKING ANY SENSE.
WHAK
Aaiieee!!
...
KOSUKE UEKI...
YOU'RE STRONG... AND YOU FIGHT TO PROTECT OTHERS...
I GET IT...

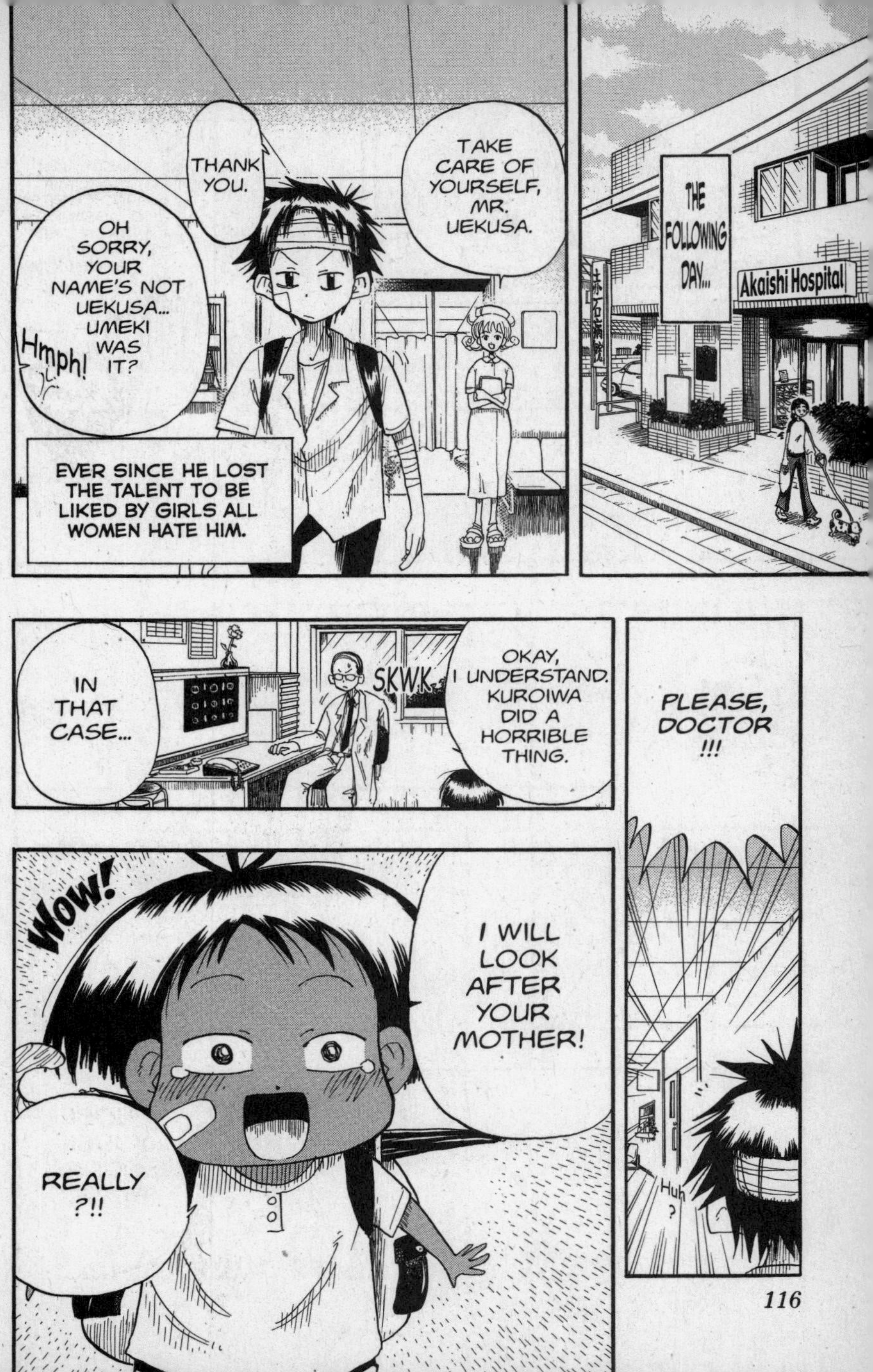
THE FOLLOWING DAY...
Akaishi Hospital
TAKE CARE OF YOURSELF, MR. UEKUSA.
THANK YOU.
OH SORRY, YOUR NAME'S NOT UEKUSA... UMEKI WAS IT?
Hmph!
EVER SINCE HE LOST THE TALENT TO BE LIKED BY GIRLS ALL WOMEN HATE HIM.
PLEASE, DOCTOR !!!
OKAY, I UNDERSTAND. KUROIWA DID A HORRIBLE THING.
SKWK
IN THAT CASE...
Huh ?
I WILL LOOK AFTER YOUR MOTHER!
WOW!
REALLY ?!!

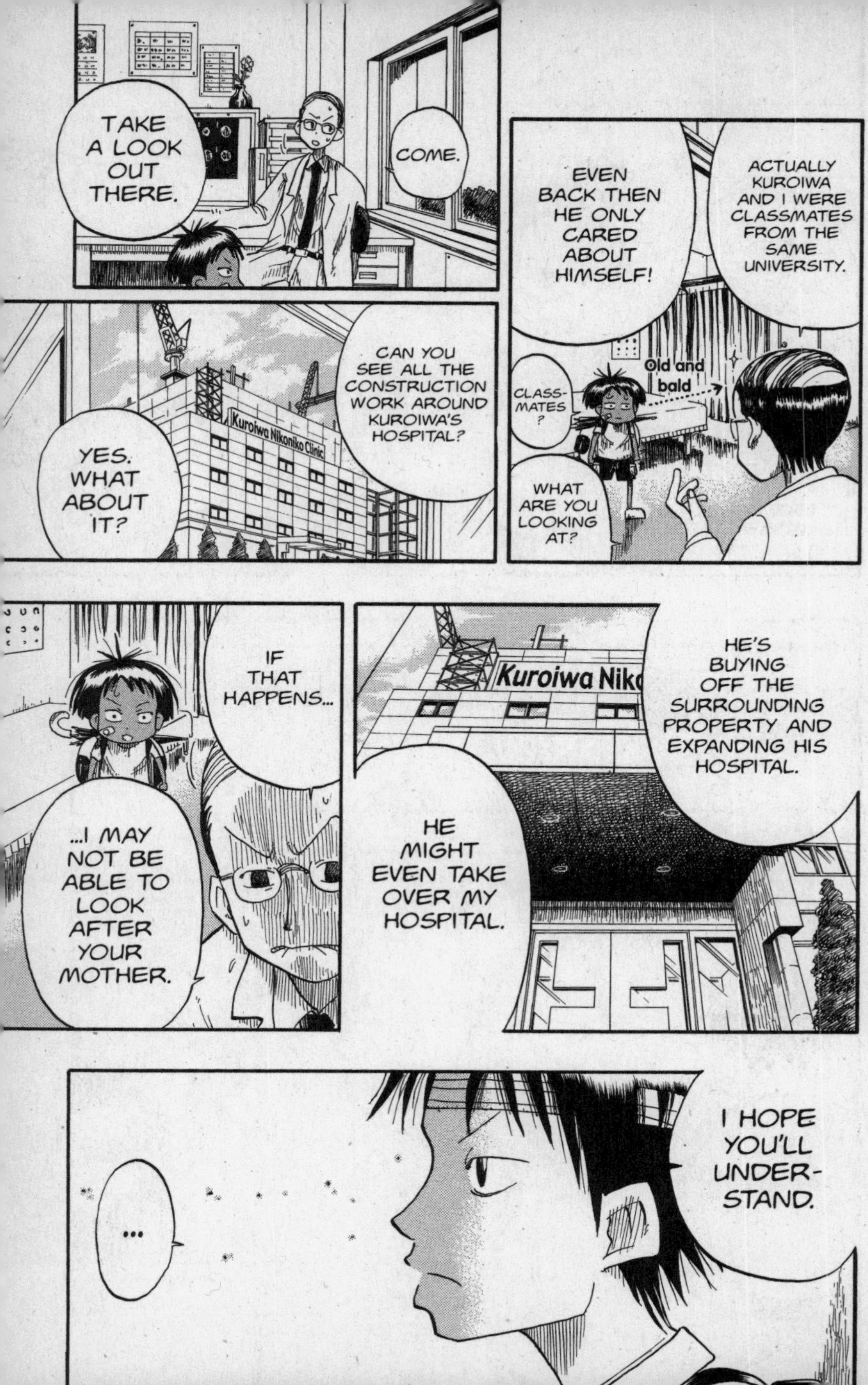
COME.
TAKE A LOOK OUT THERE.
CAN YOU SEE ALL THE CONSTRUCTION WORK AROUND KUROIWA'S HOSPITAL?
Kuroiwa Nikoniko Clinic
YES. WHAT ABOUT IT?
ACTUALLY KUROIWA AND I WERE CLASSMATES FROM THE SAME UNIVERSITY.
EVEN BACK THEN HE ONLY CARED ABOUT HIMSELF!
Old and bald
CLASSMATES?
WHAT ARE YOU LOOKING AT?
HE'S BUYING OFF THE SURROUNDING PROPERTY AND EXPANDING HIS HOSPITAL.
HE MIGHT EVEN TAKE OVER MY HOSPITAL.
IF THAT HAPPENS...
...I MAY NOT BE ABLE TO LOOK AFTER YOUR MOTHER.
I HOPE YOU'LL UNDERSTAND.
...

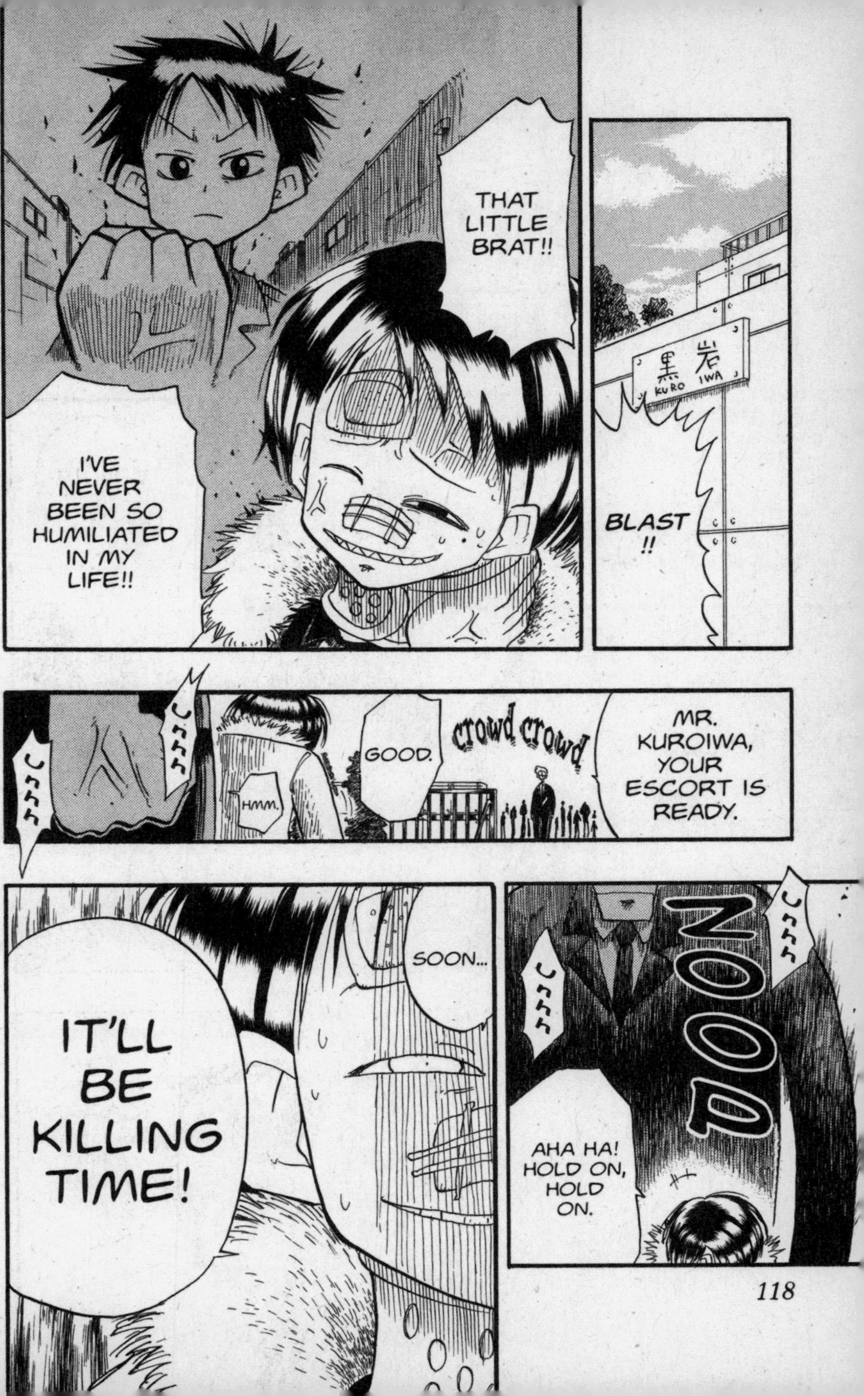

黒岩
KURO IWA
BLAST!!
THAT LITTLE BRAT!!
I'VE NEVER BEEN SO HUMILIATED IN MY LIFE!!
MR. KUROIWA, YOUR ESCORT IS READY.
crowd crowd
GOOD.
HMM.
DOON
AHA HA! HOLD ON, HOLD ON.
SOON...
IT'LL BE KILLING TIME!

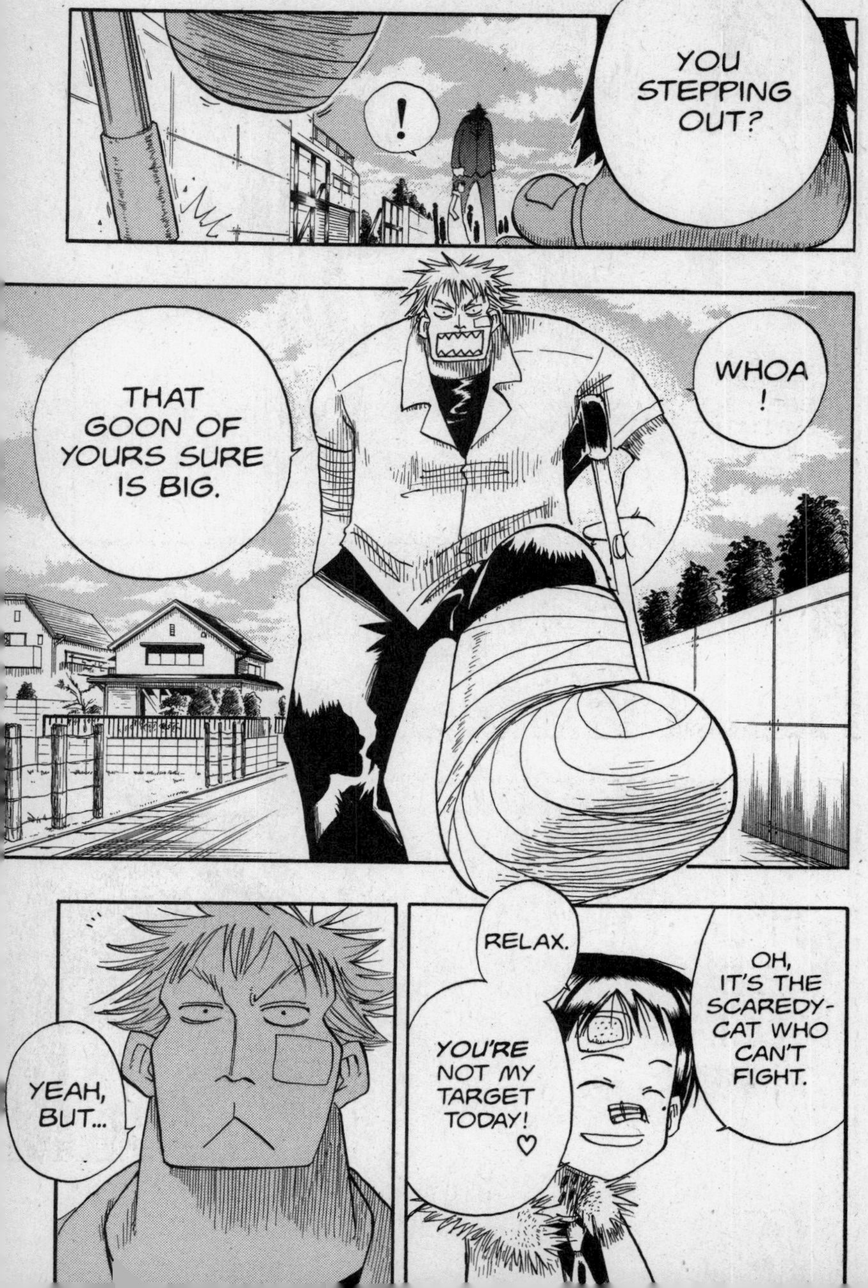
YOU STEPPING OUT?
!
WHOA!
THAT GOON OF YOURS SURE IS BIG.
OH, IT'S THE SCAREDY-CAT WHO CAN'T FIGHT.
RELAX.
YOU'RE NOT MY TARGET TODAY! ♡
YEAH, BUT...

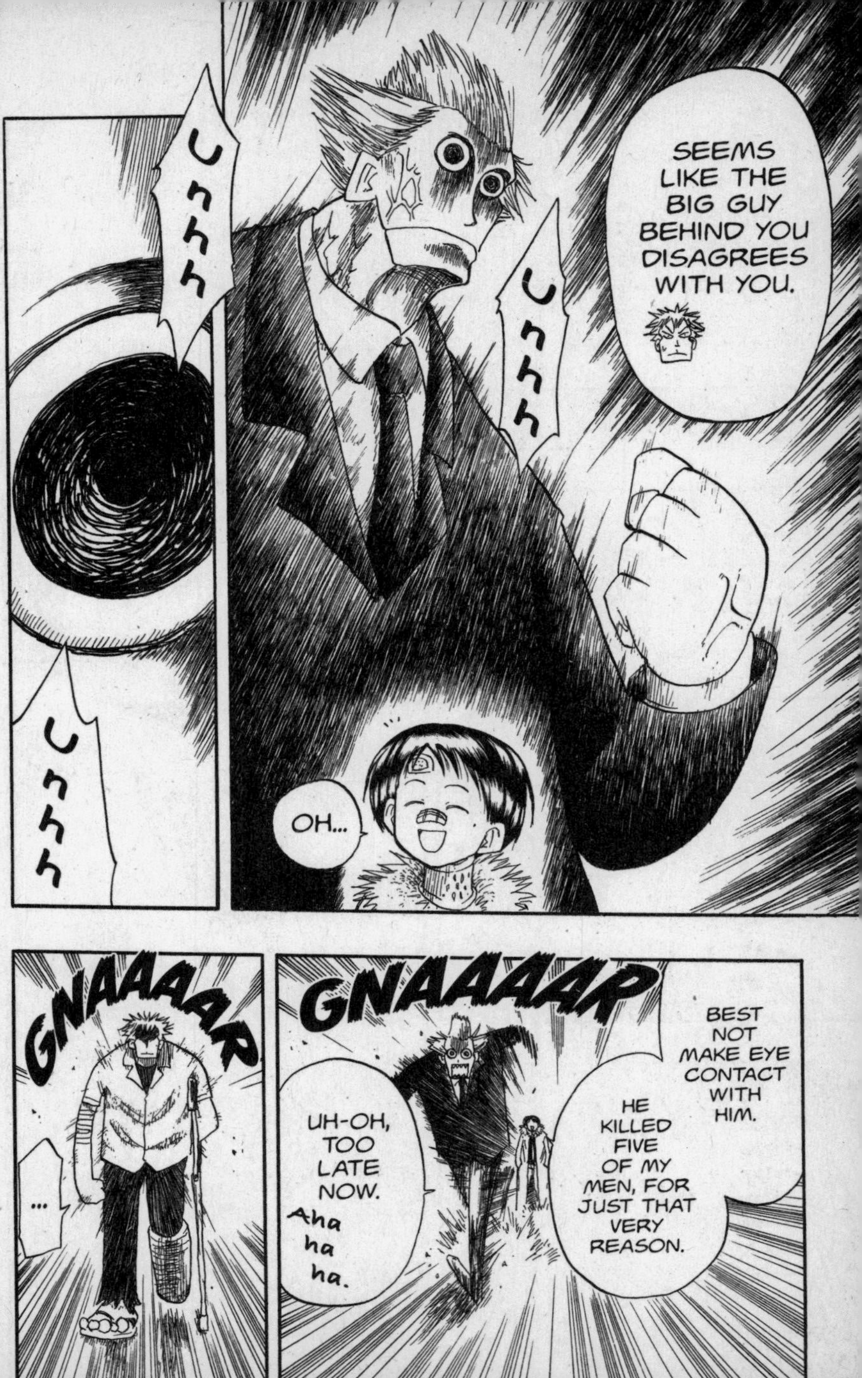

SEEMS LIKE THE BIG GUY BEHIND YOU DISAGREES WITH YOU.
Unnnh
OH...
Unnnh
Unnnh
BEST NOT MAKE EYE CONTACT WITH HIM.
HE KILLED FIVE OF MY MEN, FOR JUST THAT VERY REASON.
UH-OH, TOO LATE NOW. Aha ha ha.
GNAAAAR
GNAAAAR
...

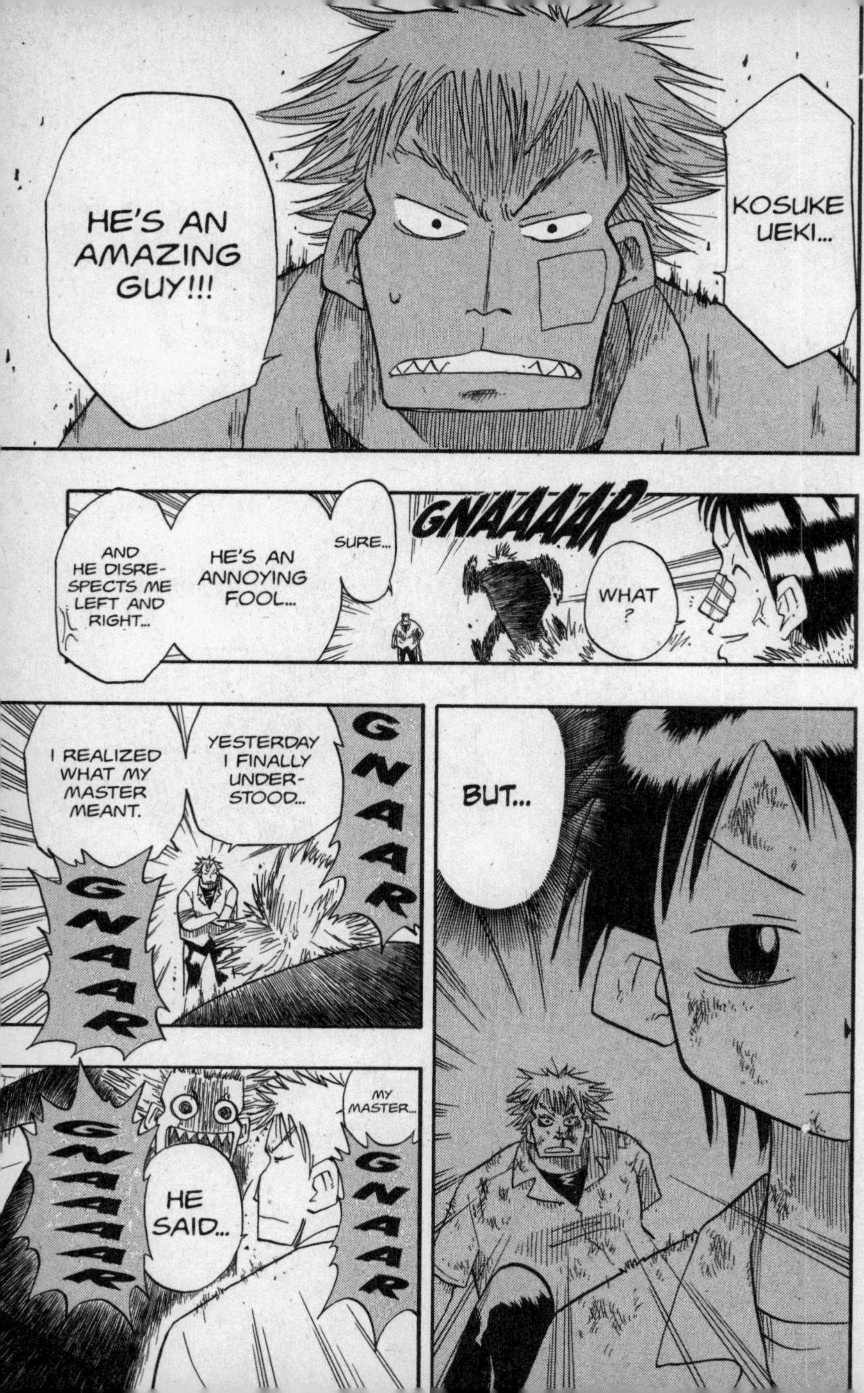
KOSUKE UEKI...
HE'S AN AMAZING GUY!!!
WHAT?
GNAAAAP
SURE...
HE'S AN ANNOYING FOOL...
AND HE DISRE-SPECTS ME LEFT AND RIGHT...
BUT...
GNAAR
YESTERDAY I FINALLY UNDER-STOOD...
I REALIZED WHAT MY MASTER MEANT.
GNAAR
MY MASTER...
GNAAR
HE SAID...
GNAAAAAR

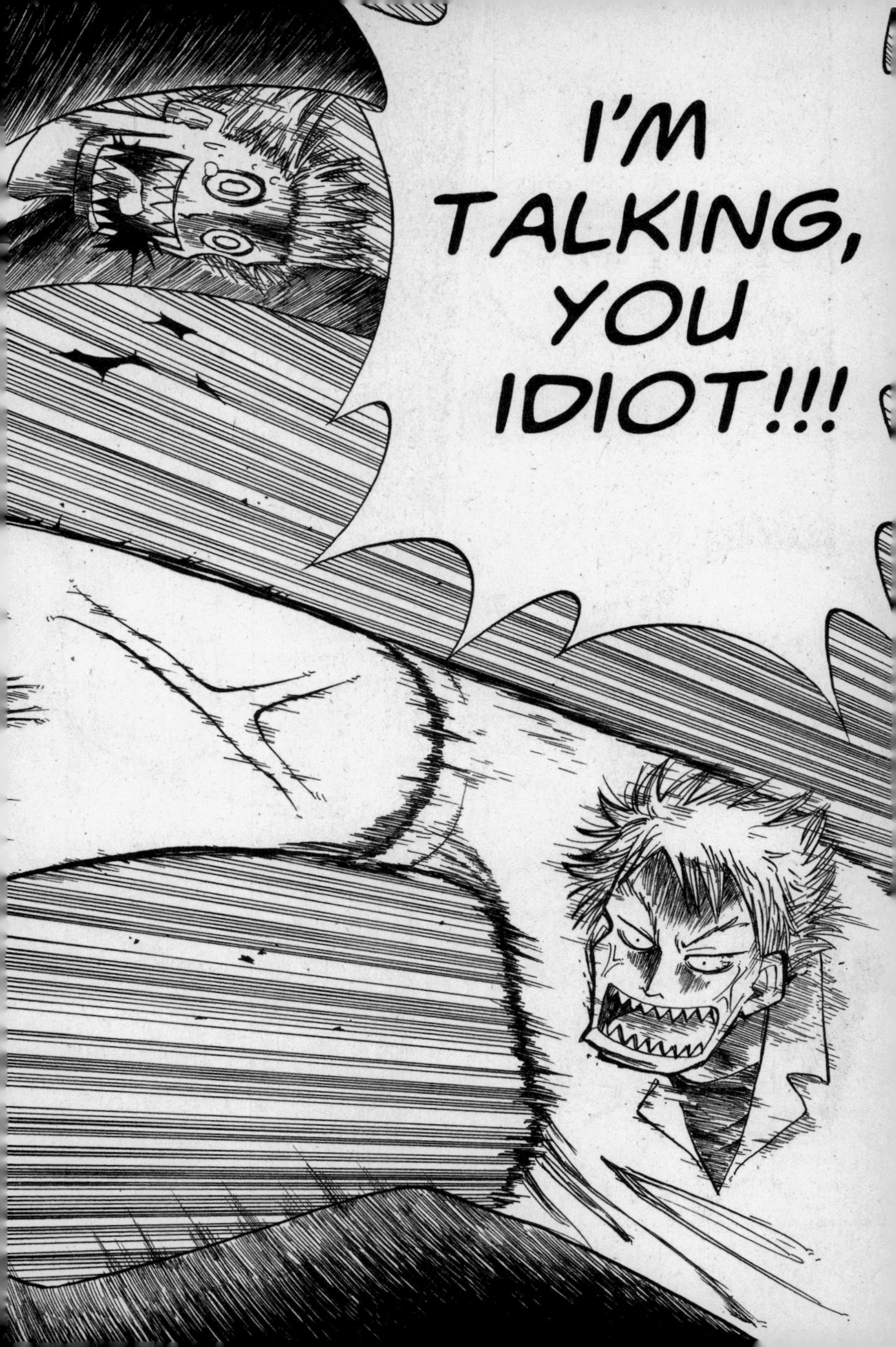
I'M TALKING, YOU IDIOT!!!

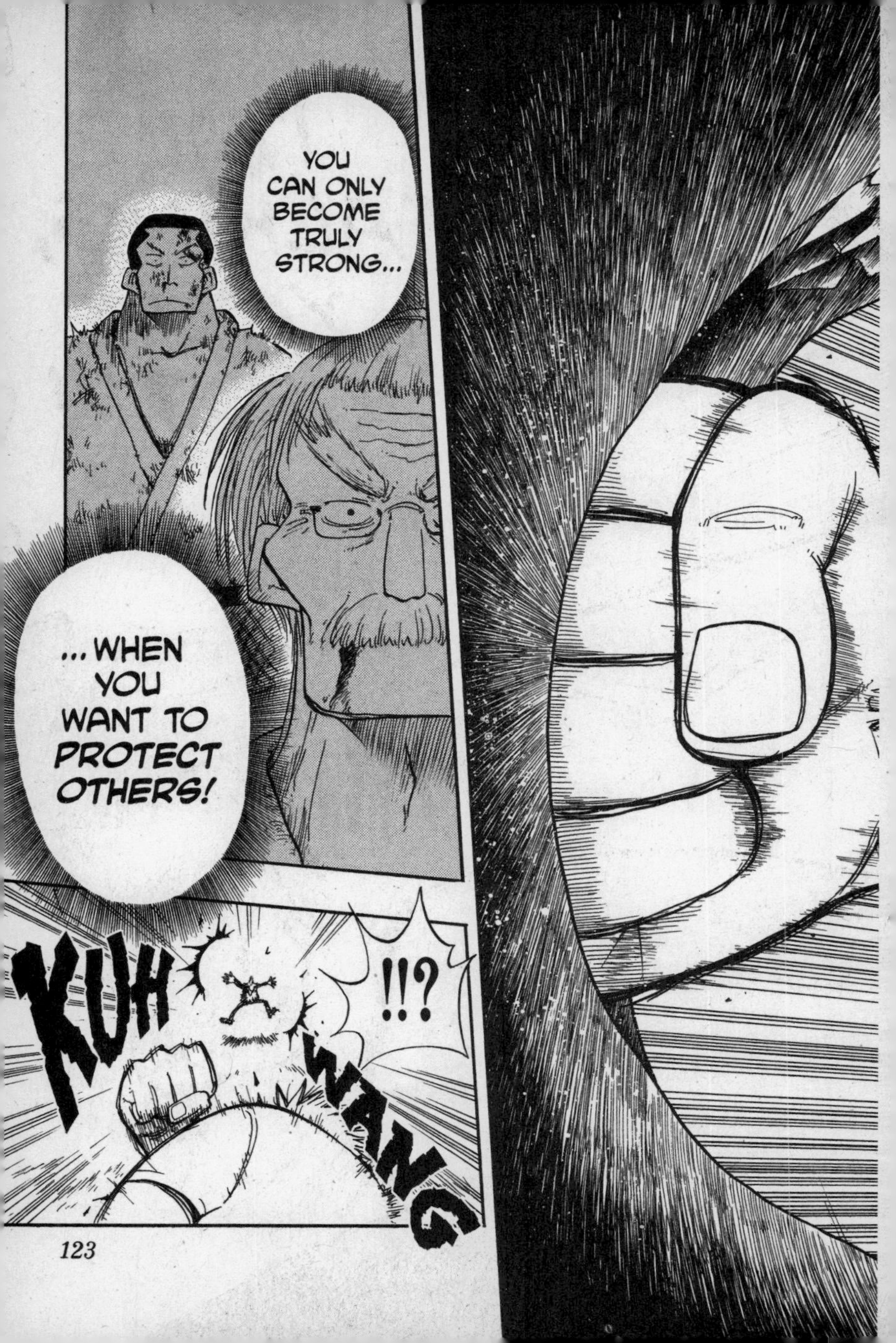
YOU CAN ONLY BECOME TRULY STRONG...
...WHEN YOU WANT TO PROTECT OTHERS!
KUH
WANG
!!?

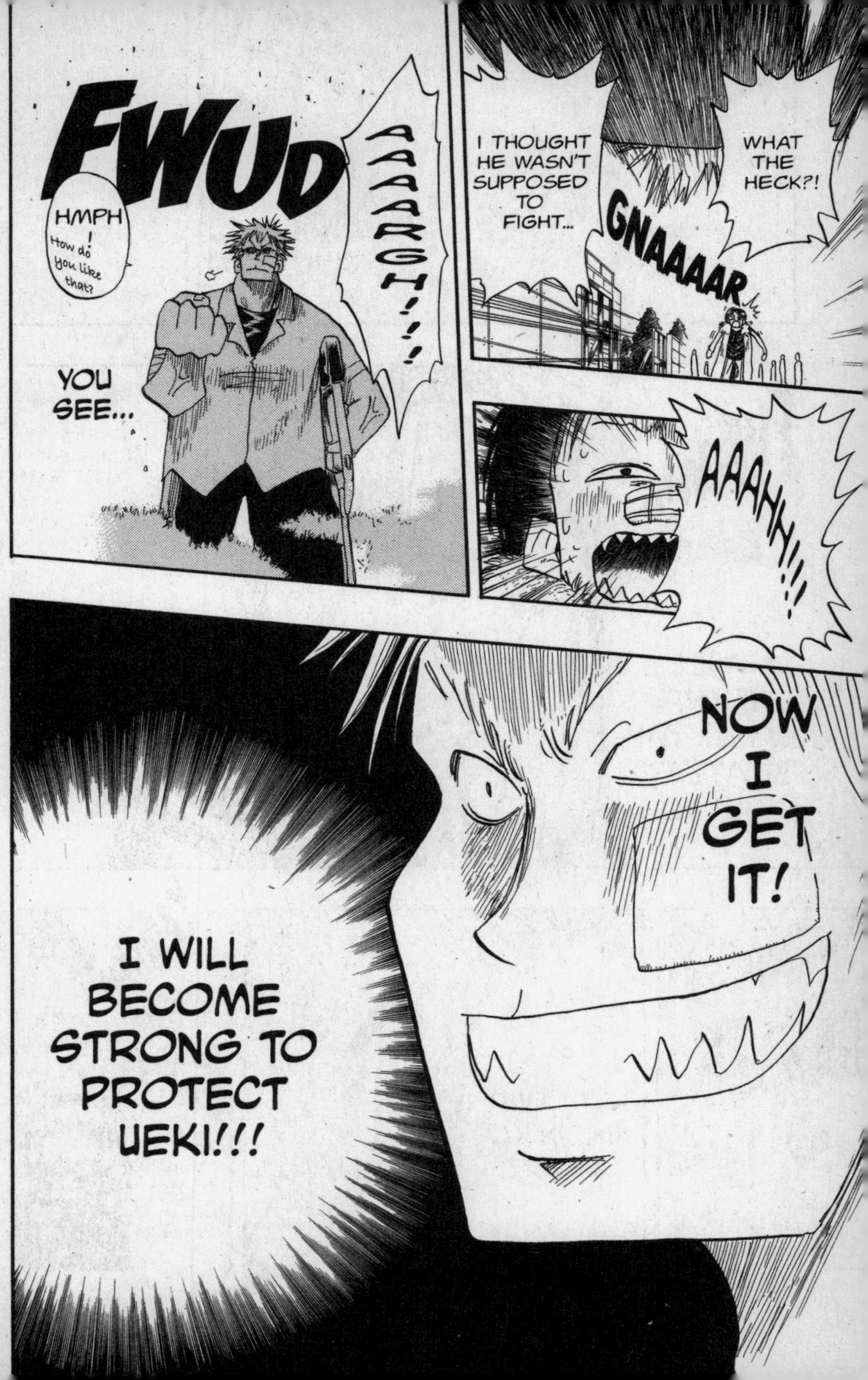
WHAT THE HECK?!
I THOUGHT HE WASN'T SUPPOSED TO FIGHT...
GNAAAAR
AAAHH!!!
AAAARGH!!!
FWUD
HMPH! How do you like that?
YOU SEE...
NOW I GET IT!
I WILL BECOME STRONG TO PROTECT UEKI!!!

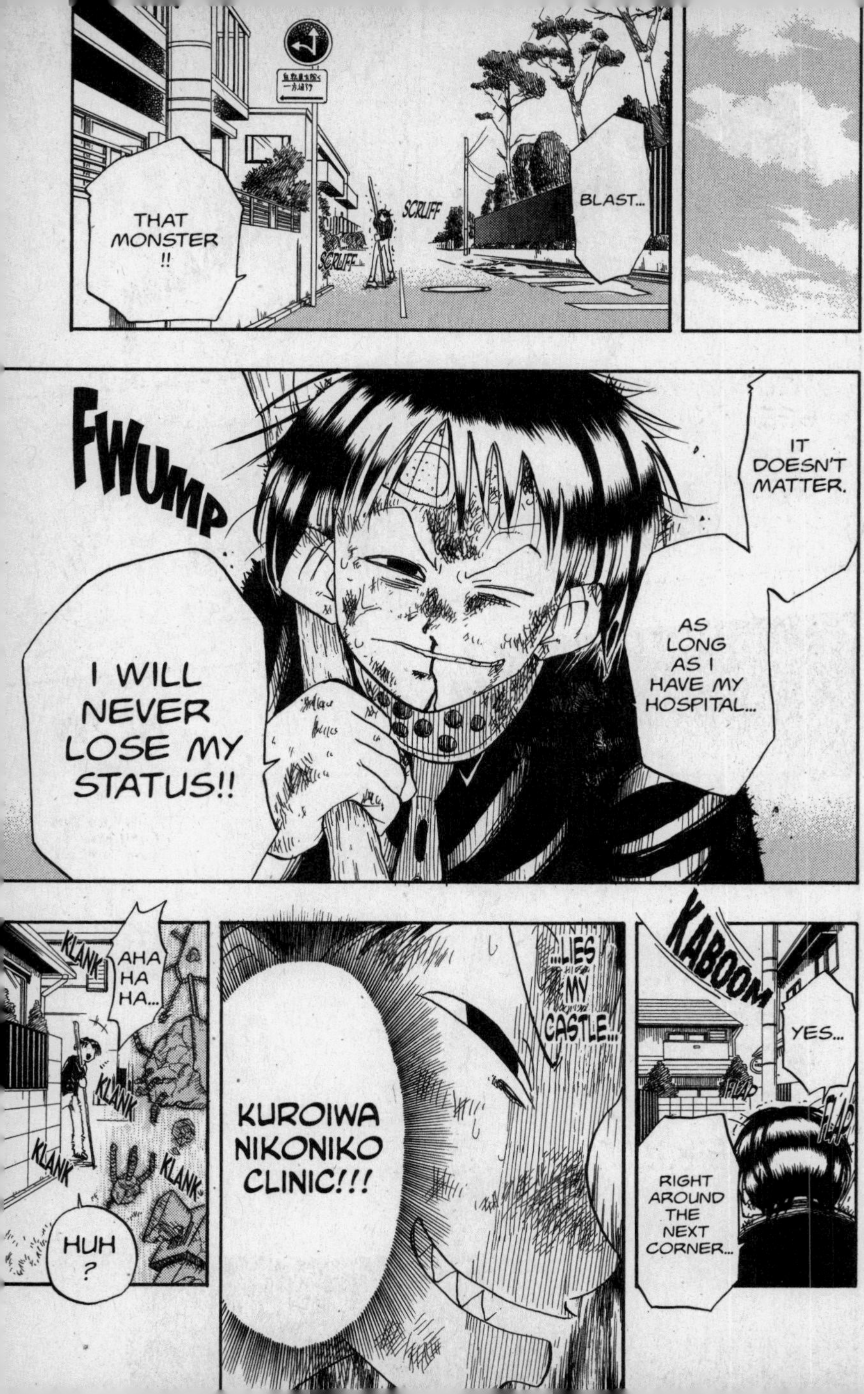
BLAST...
SCRUFF
SCRUFF
THAT MONSTER !!
IT DOESN'T MATTER.
AS LONG AS I HAVE MY HOSPITAL...
FWUMP
I WILL NEVER LOSE MY STATUS!!
KABOOM
YES...
FLAP
FLAP
RIGHT AROUND THE NEXT CORNER...
...LIES MY CASTLE...
KUROIWA NIKONIKO CLINIC!!!
AHA HA HA...
KLANK
KLANK
KLANK
KLANK
HUH ?

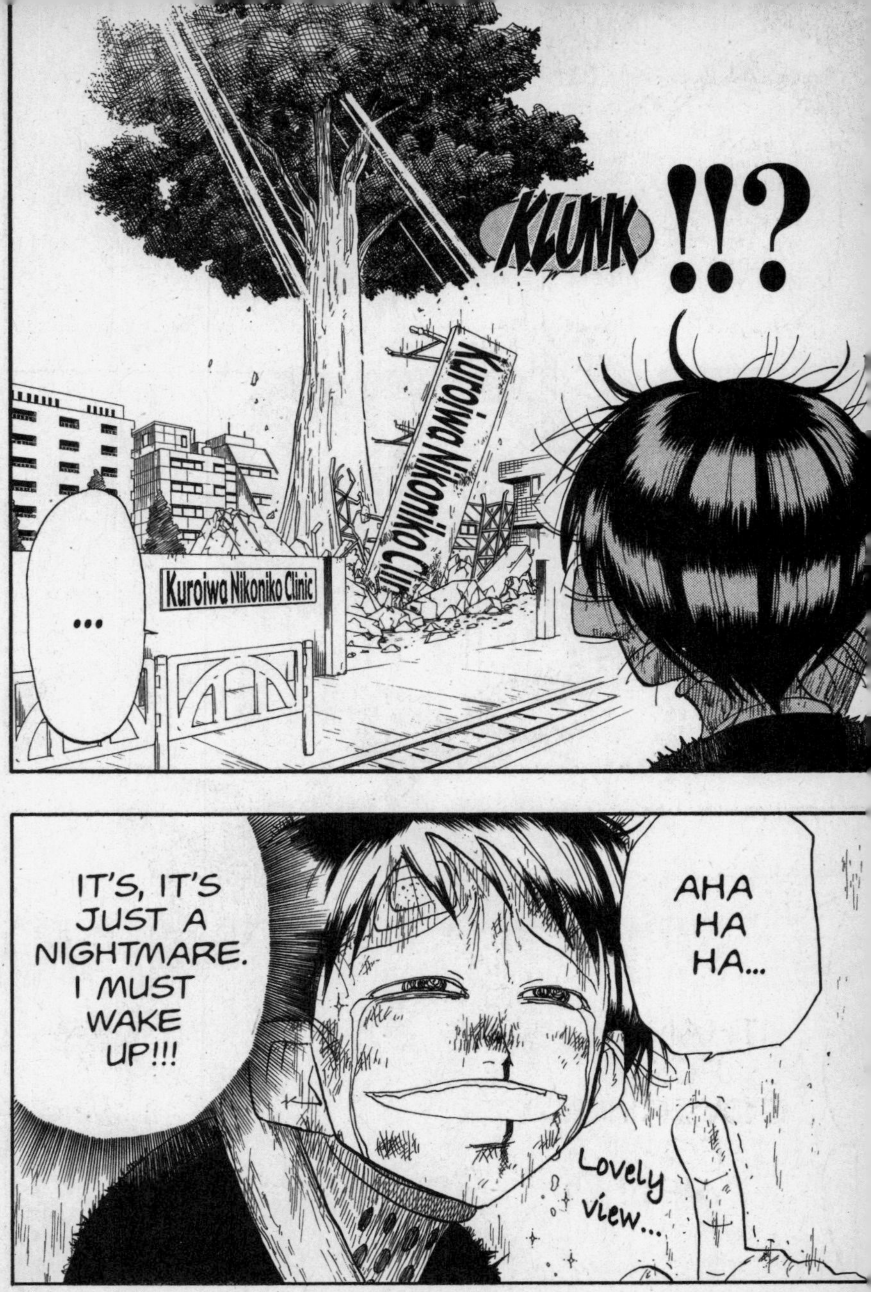
KLUNK
!!?
Kuroiwa Nikoniko Clinic
Kuroiwa Nikoniko Clinic
...
AHA HA HA...
IT'S, IT'S JUST A NIGHTMARE. I MUST WAKE UP!!!
Lovely view...

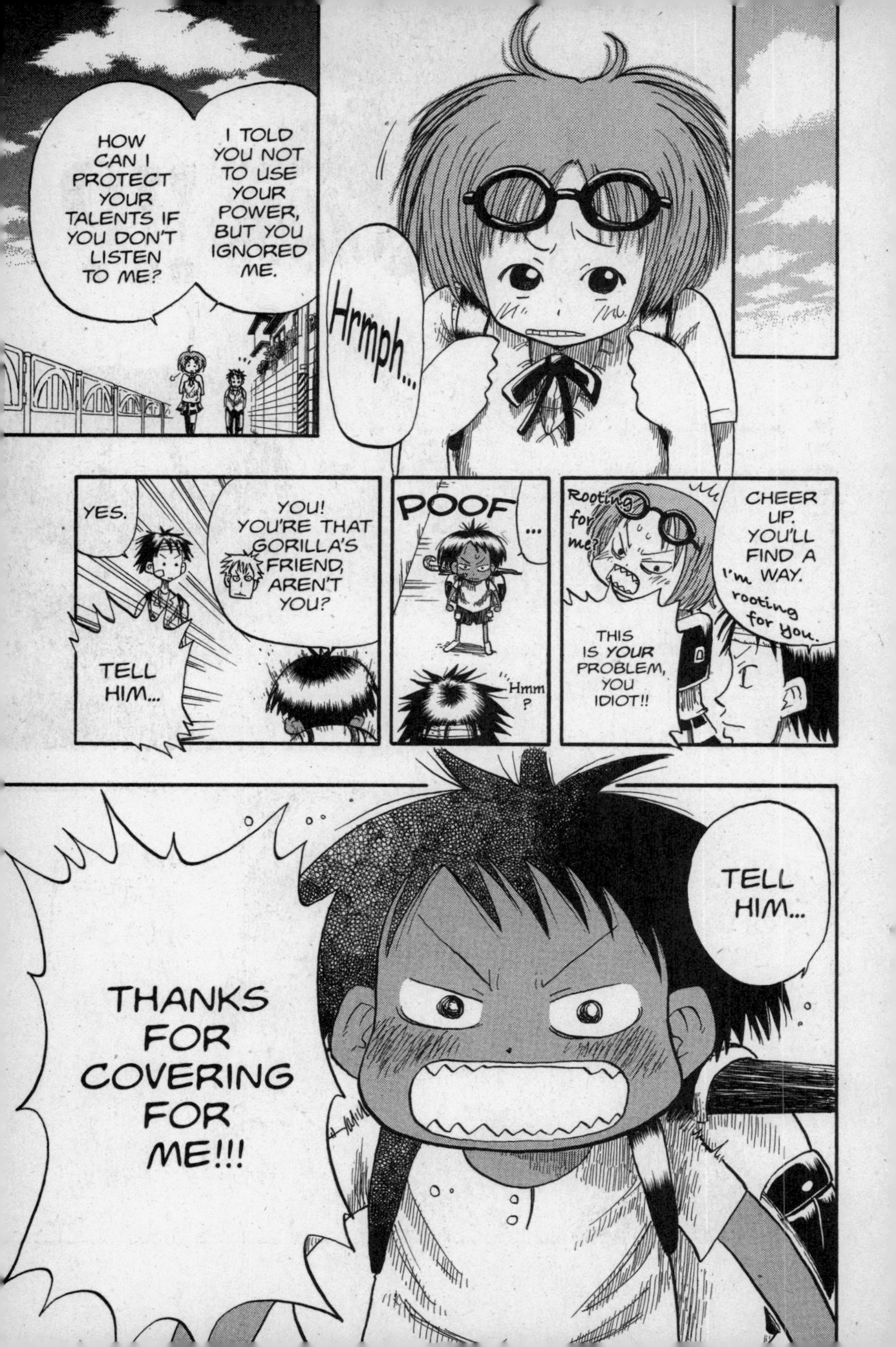
Hrmph...
I TOLD YOU NOT TO USE YOUR POWER, BUT YOU IGNORED ME.
HOW CAN I PROTECT YOUR TALENTS IF YOU DON'T LISTEN TO ME?
CHEER UP. YOU'LL FIND A WAY.
I'm rooting for you.
Rooting for me?
THIS IS YOUR PROBLEM, YOU IDIOT!!
POOF
...
Hmm?
YOU! YOU'RE THAT GORILLA'S FRIEND, AREN'T YOU?
YES.
TELL HIM...
TELL HIM...
THANKS FOR COVERING FOR ME!!!

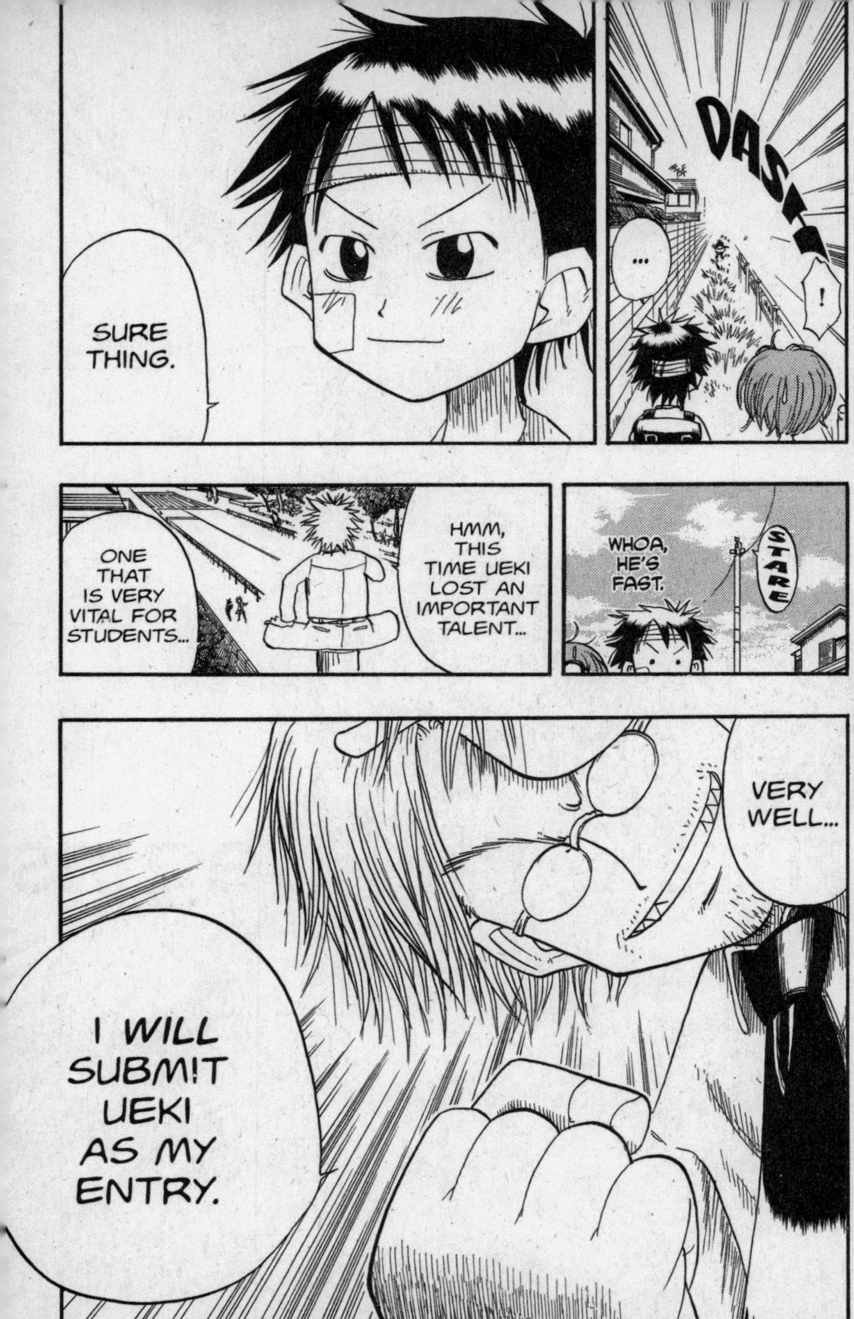
DASH
...
!
SURE THING.
STARE
WHOA, HE'S FAST.
HMM, THIS TIME UEKI LOST AN IMPORTANT TALENT...
ONE THAT IS VERY VITAL FOR STUDENTS...
VERY WELL...
I WILL SUBMIT UEKI AS MY ENTRY.

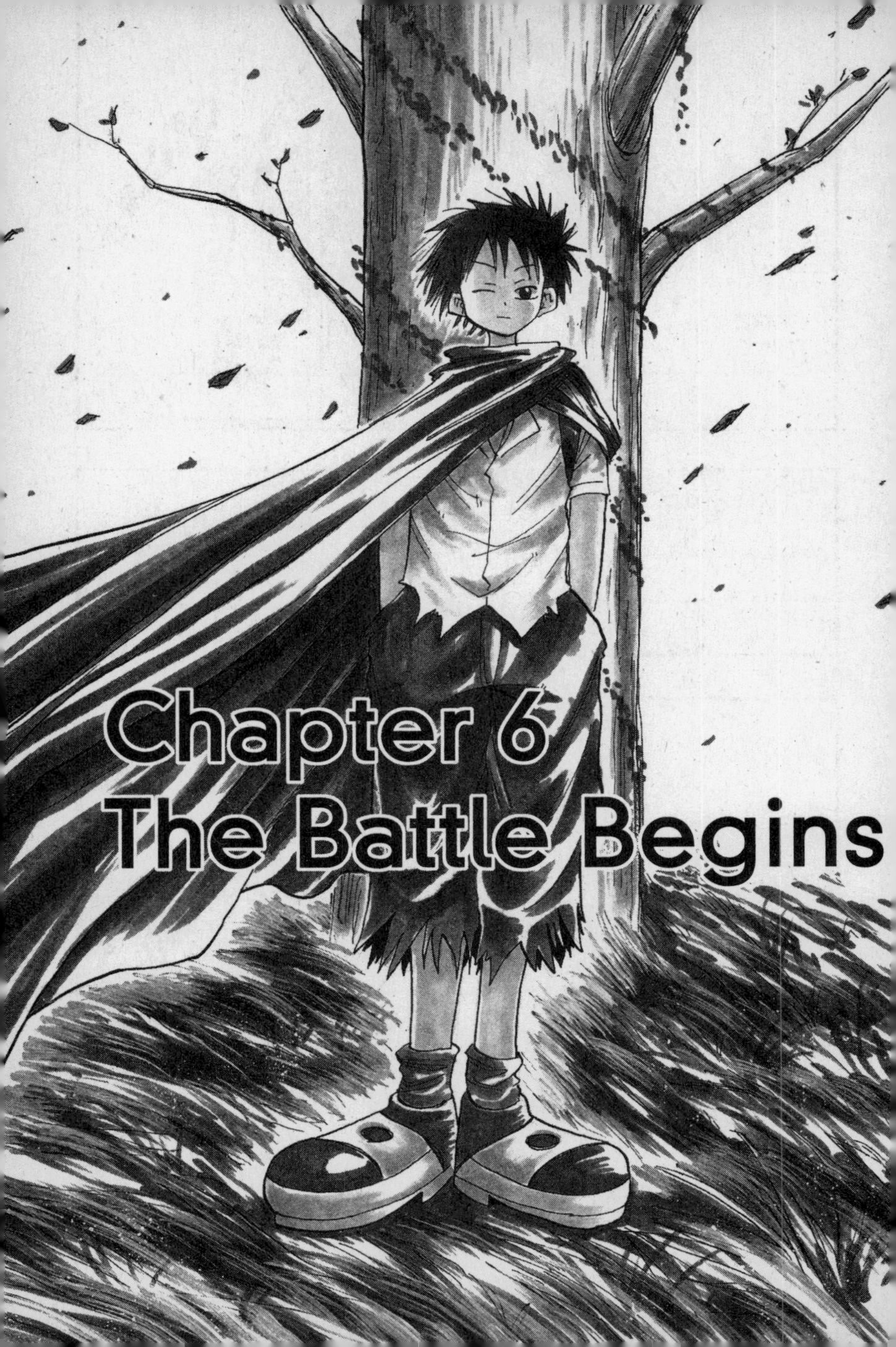
Chapter 6
The Battle Begins

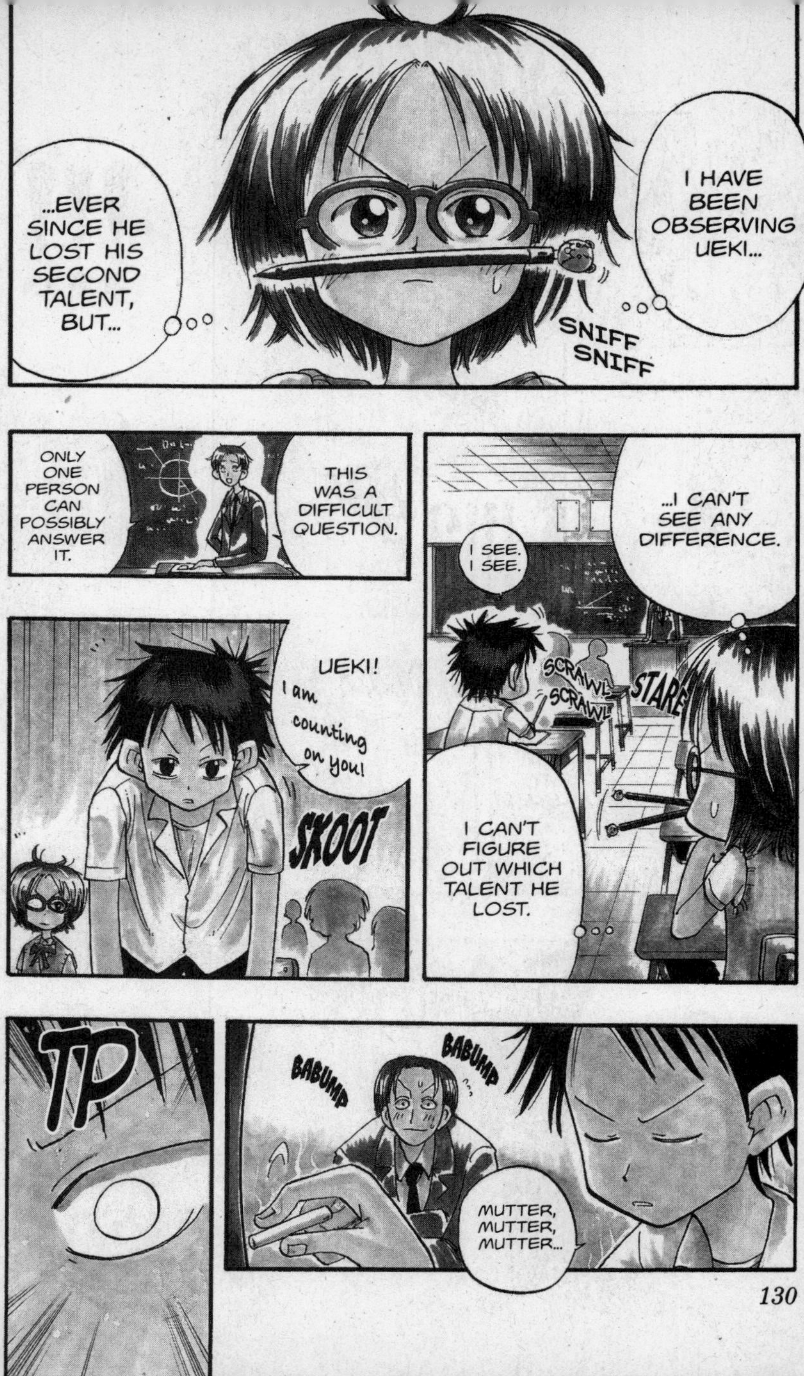
I HAVE BEEN OBSERVING UEKI...
...EVER SINCE HE LOST HIS SECOND TALENT, BUT...
SNIFF SNIFF
...I CAN'T SEE ANY DIFFERENCE.
I SEE. I SEE.
SCRAWL SCRAWL
STARE
I CAN'T FIGURE OUT WHICH TALENT HE LOST.
THIS WAS A DIFFICULT QUESTION.
ONLY ONE PERSON CAN POSSIBLY ANSWER IT.
UEKI! I am counting on you!
SKOOT
BABUMP
BABUMP
MUTTER, MUTTER, MUTTER...
TP

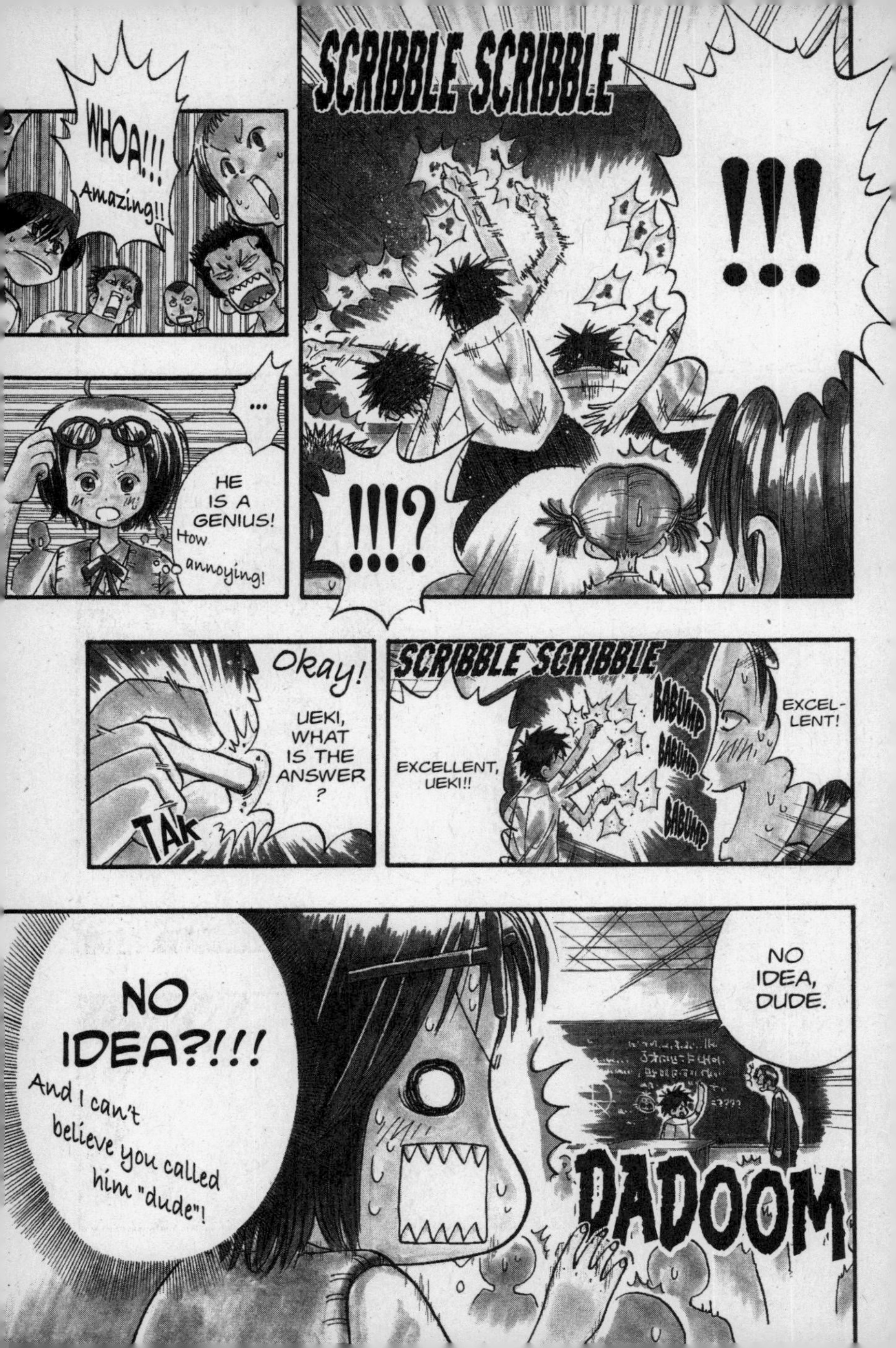

SCRIBBLE SCRIBBLE
!!!
!!!?
WHOA!!! Amazing!!
...
HE IS A GENIUS!
How annoying!
EXCEL-LENT!
SCRIBBLE SCRIBBLE
BABUMP
BABUMP
BABUMP
EXCELLENT, UEKI!!
Okay!
UEKI, WHAT IS THE ANSWER?
TAK
NO IDEA, DUDE.
DADOOM
NO IDEA?!!!
And I can't believe you called him "dude"!

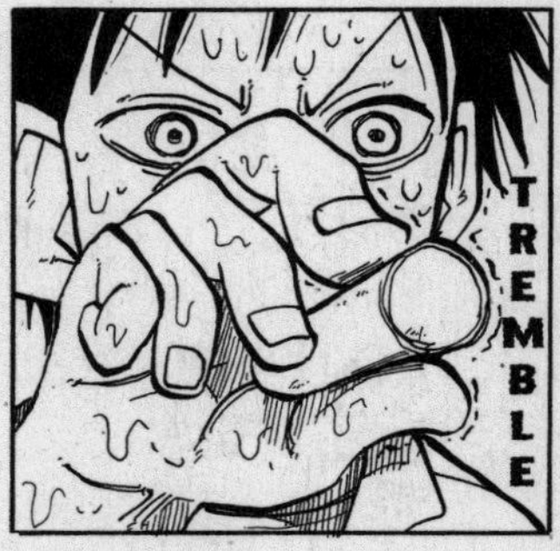
TREMBLE

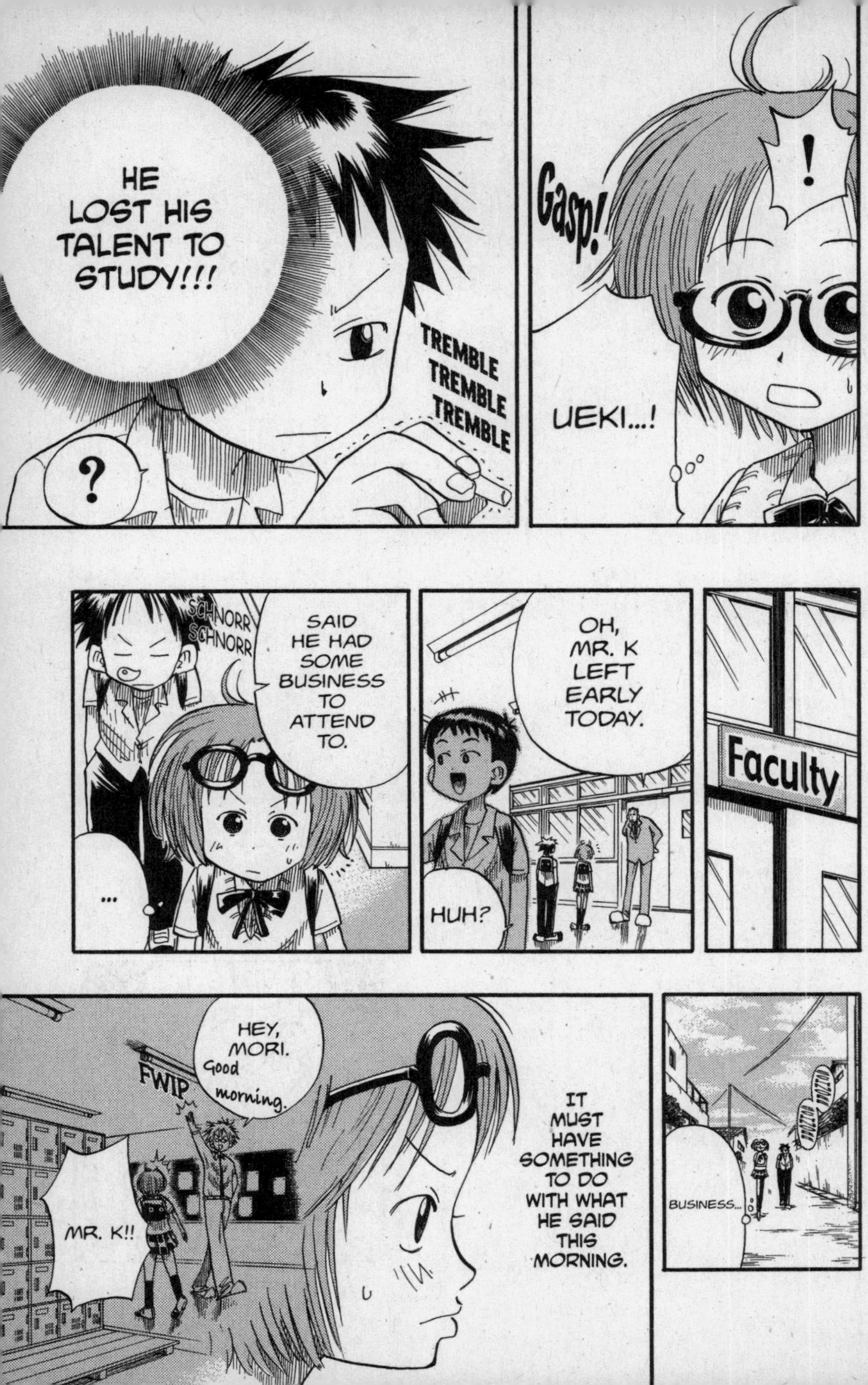

Gasp!
!
UEKI...!
HE LOST HIS TALENT TO STUDY!!!
TREMBLE TREMBLE TREMBLE
?
Faculty
OH, MR. K LEFT EARLY TODAY.
HUH?
SAID HE HAD SOME BUSINESS TO ATTEND TO.
SCHNORR SCHNORR
...
BUSINESS...
HEY, MORI. Good morning.
FWIP
IT MUST HAVE SOMETHING TO DO WITH WHAT HE SAID THIS MORNING.
MR. K!!

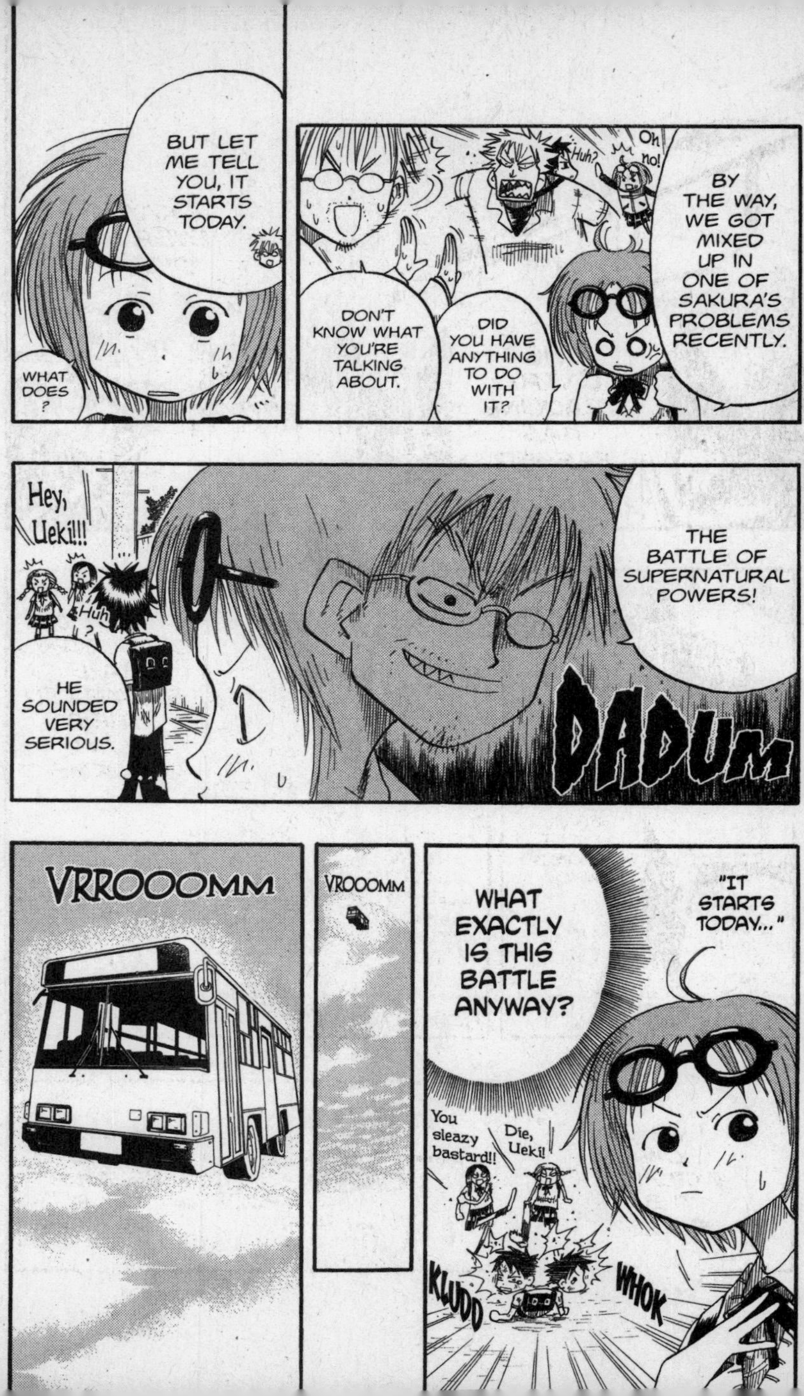
Oh no!
Huh?
BY THE WAY, WE GOT MIXED UP IN ONE OF SAKURA'S PROBLEMS RECENTLY.
DID YOU HAVE ANYTHING TO DO WITH IT?
DON'T KNOW WHAT YOU'RE TALKING ABOUT.
BUT LET ME TELL YOU, IT STARTS TODAY.
WHAT DOES ?
THE BATTLE OF SUPERNATURAL POWERS!
DADUM
Hey, Ueki!!!
Huh?
HE SOUNDED VERY SERIOUS.
"IT STARTS TODAY..."
WHAT EXACTLY IS THIS BATTLE ANYWAY?
Die, Ueki!
You sleazy bastard!!
WHOK
KLUDD
VROOOMM
VRROOOMM

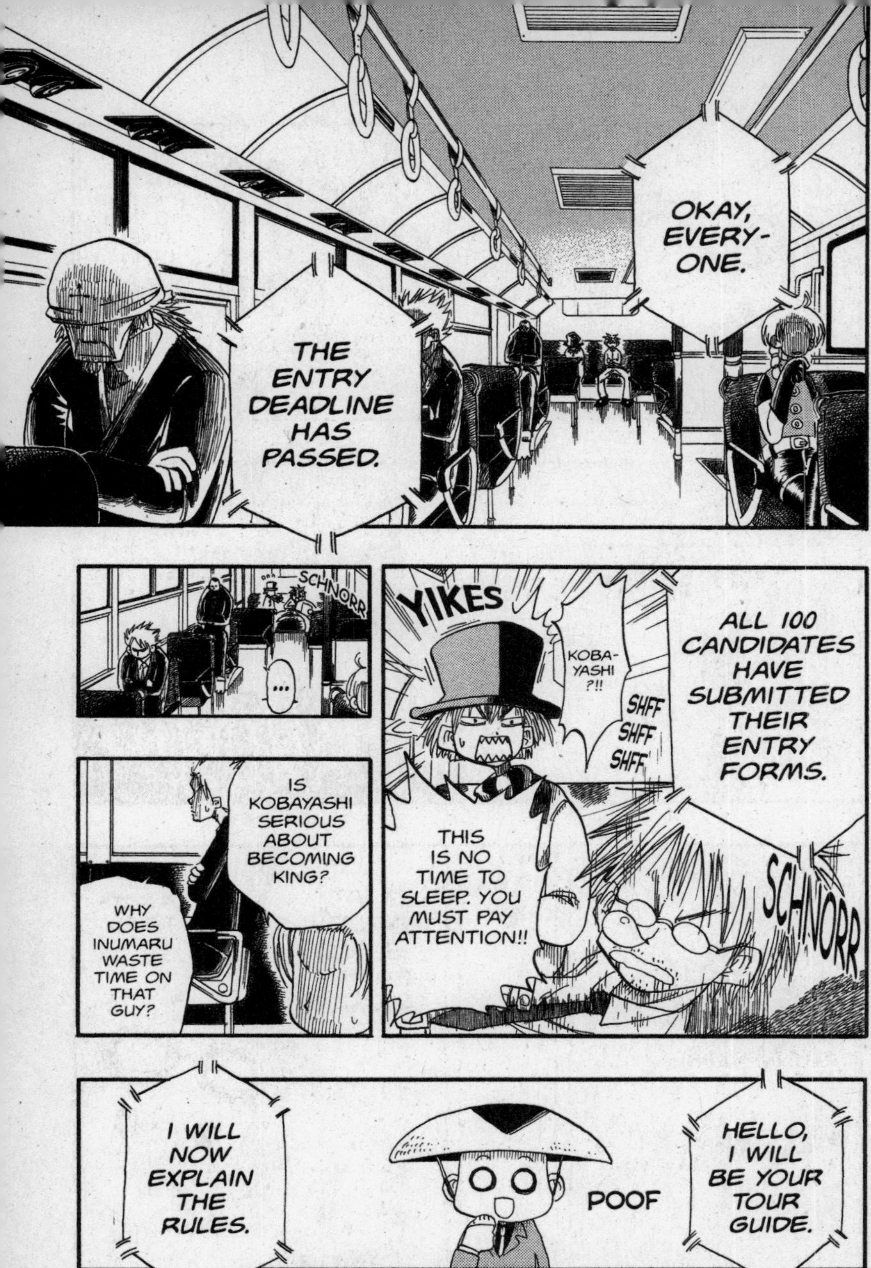

OKAY, EVERYONE.
THE ENTRY DEADLINE HAS PASSED.
ALL 100 CANDIDATES HAVE SUBMITTED THEIR ENTRY FORMS.
SCHNORR
KOBAYASHI?!!
YIKES
SHFF SHFF SHFF
THIS IS NO TIME TO SLEEP. YOU MUST PAY ATTENTION!!
SCHNORR
...
IS KOBAYASHI SERIOUS ABOUT BECOMING KING?
WHY DOES INUMARU WASTE TIME ON THAT GUY?
HELLO, I WILL BE YOUR TOUR GUIDE.
POOF
I WILL NOW EXPLAIN THE RULES.

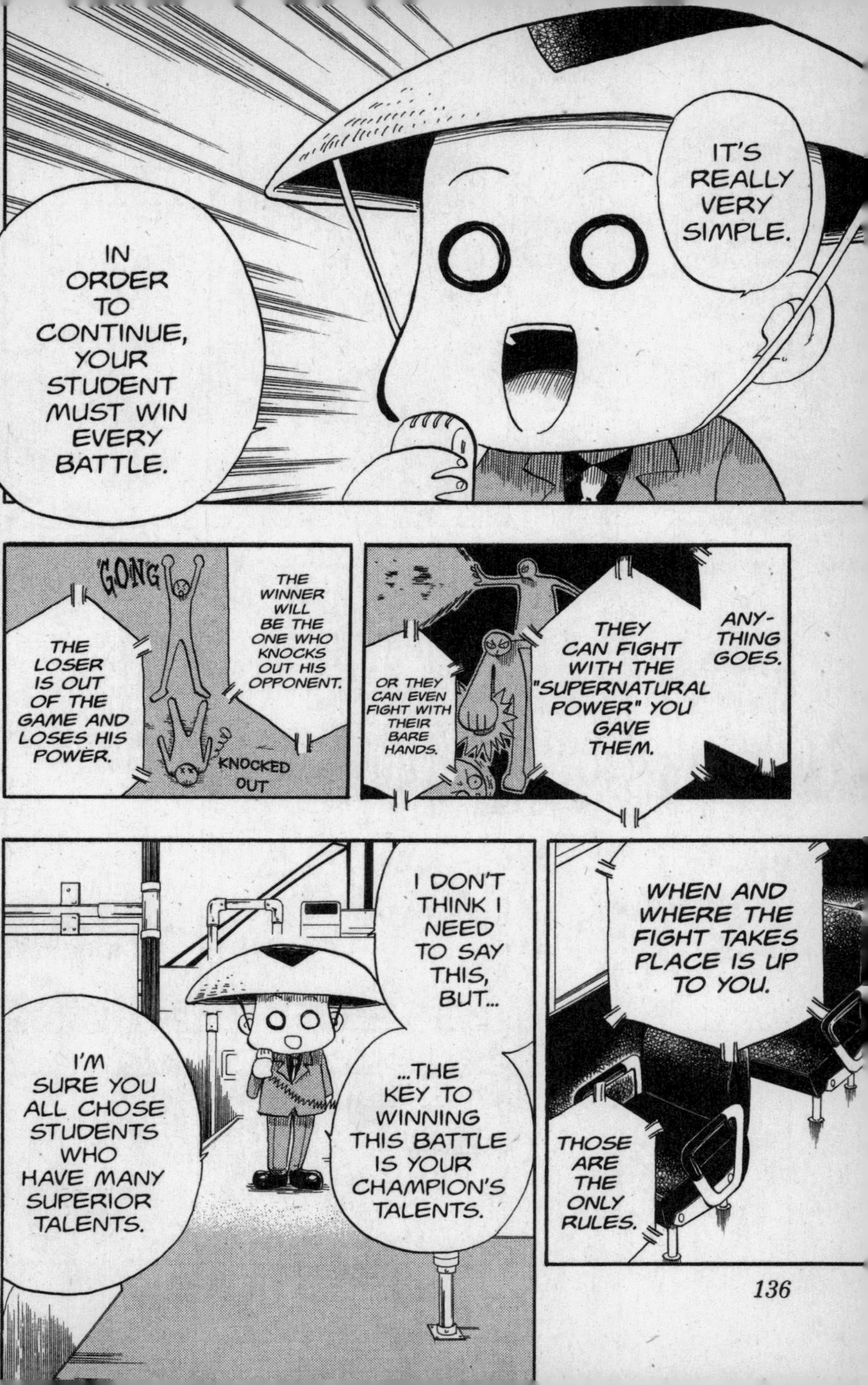

IT'S REALLY VERY SIMPLE.
IN ORDER TO CONTINUE, YOUR STUDENT MUST WIN EVERY BATTLE.
ANY-THING GOES.
THEY CAN FIGHT WITH THE "SUPERNATURAL POWER" YOU GAVE THEM.
OR THEY CAN EVEN FIGHT WITH THEIR BARE HANDS.
THE WINNER WILL BE THE ONE WHO KNOCKS OUT HIS OPPONENT.
GONG
THE LOSER IS OUT OF THE GAME AND LOSES HIS POWER.
KNOCKED OUT
WHEN AND WHERE THE FIGHT TAKES PLACE IS UP TO YOU.
THOSE ARE THE ONLY RULES.
I DON'T THINK I NEED TO SAY THIS, BUT...
...THE KEY TO WINNING THIS BATTLE IS YOUR CHAMPION'S TALENTS.
I'M SURE YOU ALL CHOSE STUDENTS WHO HAVE MANY SUPERIOR TALENTS.

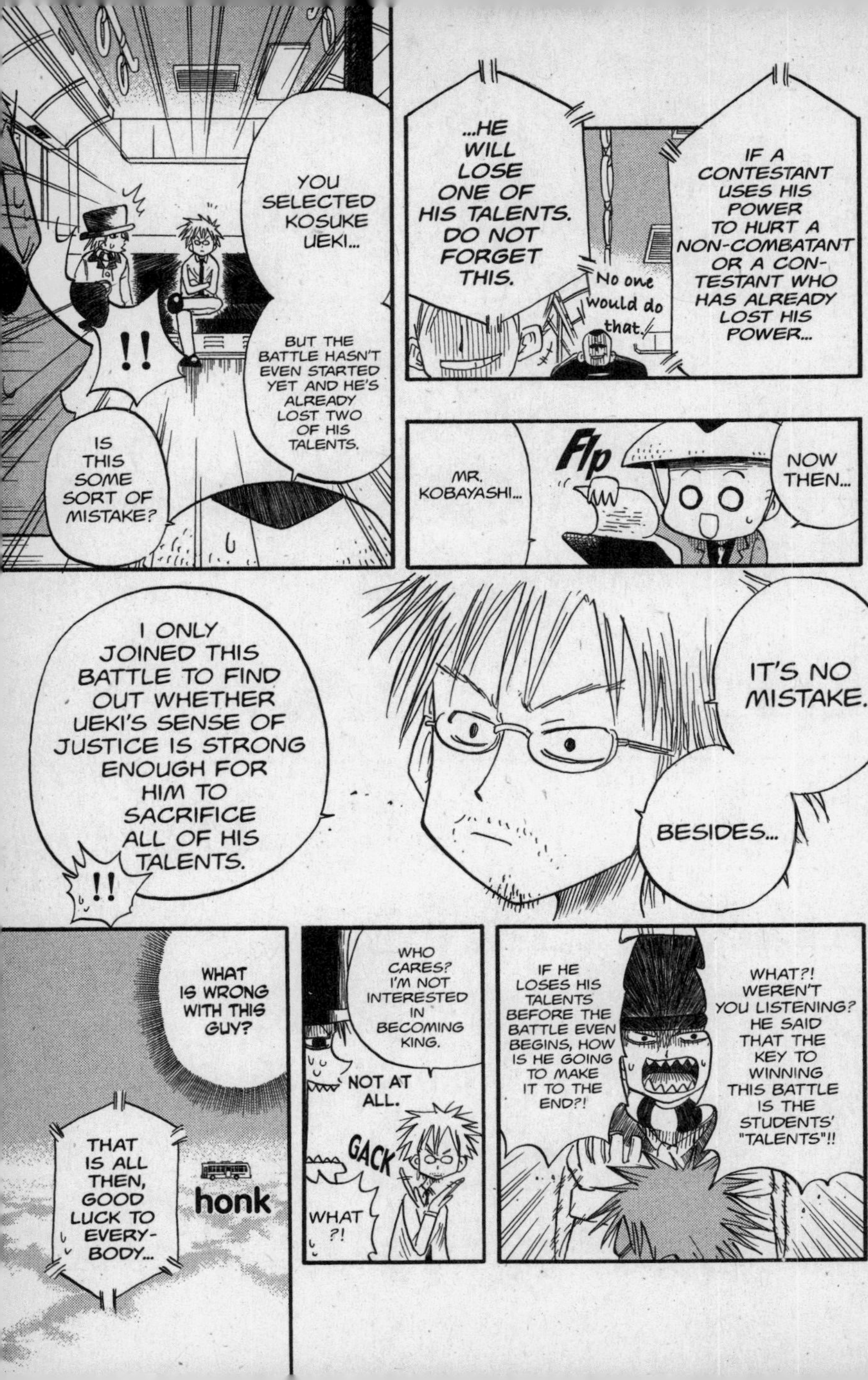
IF A CONTESTANT USES HIS POWER TO HURT A NON-COMBATANT OR A CON-TESTANT WHO HAS ALREADY LOST HIS POWER...
No one would do that.
...HE WILL LOSE ONE OF HIS TALENTS. DO NOT FORGET THIS.
NOW THEN...
Flp
MR. KOBAYASHI...
YOU SELECTED KOSUKE UEKI...
BUT THE BATTLE HASN'T EVEN STARTED YET AND HE'S ALREADY LOST TWO OF HIS TALENTS.
!!
IS THIS SOME SORT OF MISTAKE?
IT'S NO MISTAKE.
BESIDES...
I ONLY JOINED THIS BATTLE TO FIND OUT WHETHER UEKI'S SENSE OF JUSTICE IS STRONG ENOUGH FOR HIM TO SACRIFICE ALL OF HIS TALENTS.
!!
WHAT?! WEREN'T YOU LISTENING? HE SAID THAT THE KEY TO WINNING THIS BATTLE IS THE STUDENTS' "TALENTS"!!
IF HE LOSES HIS TALENTS BEFORE THE BATTLE EVEN BEGINS, HOW IS HE GOING TO MAKE IT TO THE END?!
WHO CARES? I'M NOT INTERESTED IN BECOMING KING.
NOT AT ALL.
GACK
WHAT ?!
WHAT IS WRONG WITH THIS GUY?
honk
THAT IS ALL THEN, GOOD LUCK TO EVERY-BODY...

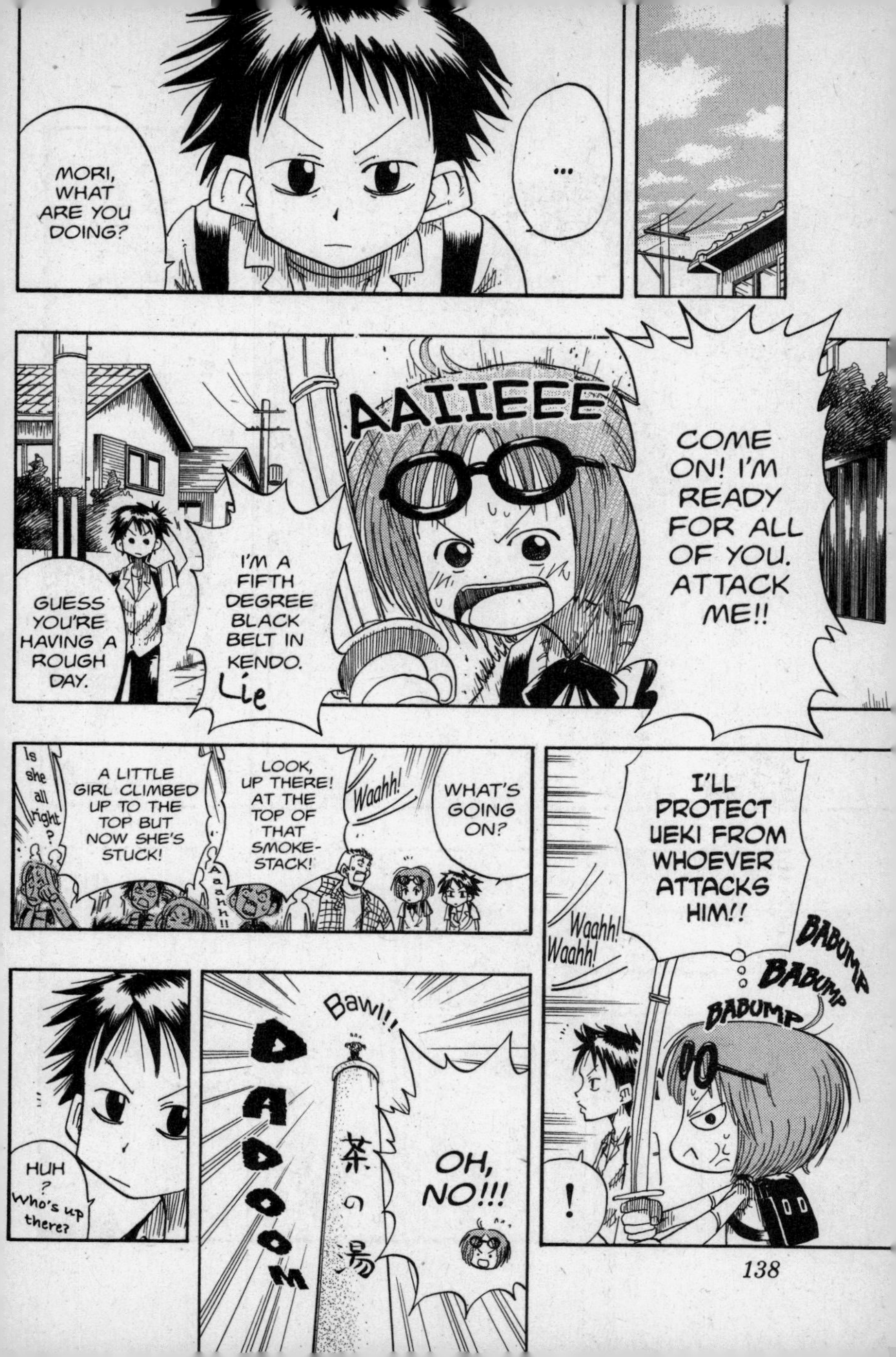
...
MORI, WHAT ARE YOU DOING?
AAIIEEE
COME ON! I'M READY FOR ALL OF YOU. ATTACK ME!!
I'M A FIFTH DEGREE BLACK BELT IN KENDO.
Lie
GUESS YOU'RE HAVING A ROUGH DAY.
I'LL PROTECT UEKI FROM WHOEVER ATTACKS HIM!!
Waahh!
Waahh!
BABUMP
BABUMP
BABUMP
!
WHAT'S GOING ON?
Waahh!
LOOK, UP THERE! AT THE TOP OF THAT SMOKE-STACK!
Aaahh!!
A LITTLE GIRL CLIMBED UP TO THE TOP BUT NOW SHE'S STUCK!
Is she all right?
Bawl!!
OH, NO!!!
茶の湯
DADOOOM
HUH?
Who's up there?

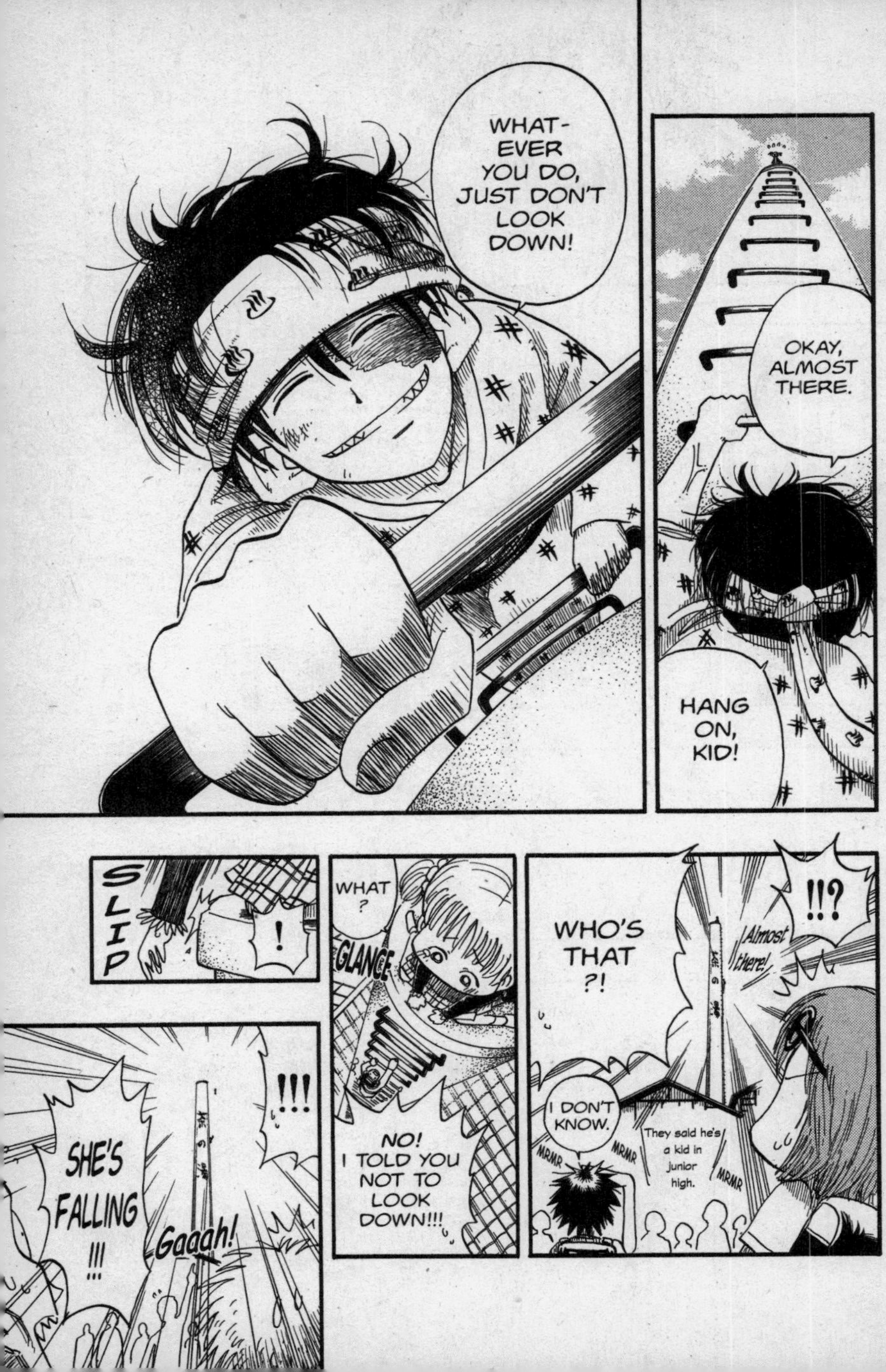
OKAY, ALMOST THERE.
HANG ON, KID!
WHAT-EVER YOU DO, JUST DON'T LOOK DOWN!
!!?
Almost there!
WHO'S THAT ?!
I DON'T KNOW.
They said he's a kid in junior high.
MRMR
MRMR
MRMR
WHAT ?
GLANCE
NO! I TOLD YOU NOT TO LOOK DOWN!!!
SLIP
!
!!!
SHE'S FALLING !!!
Gaaah!

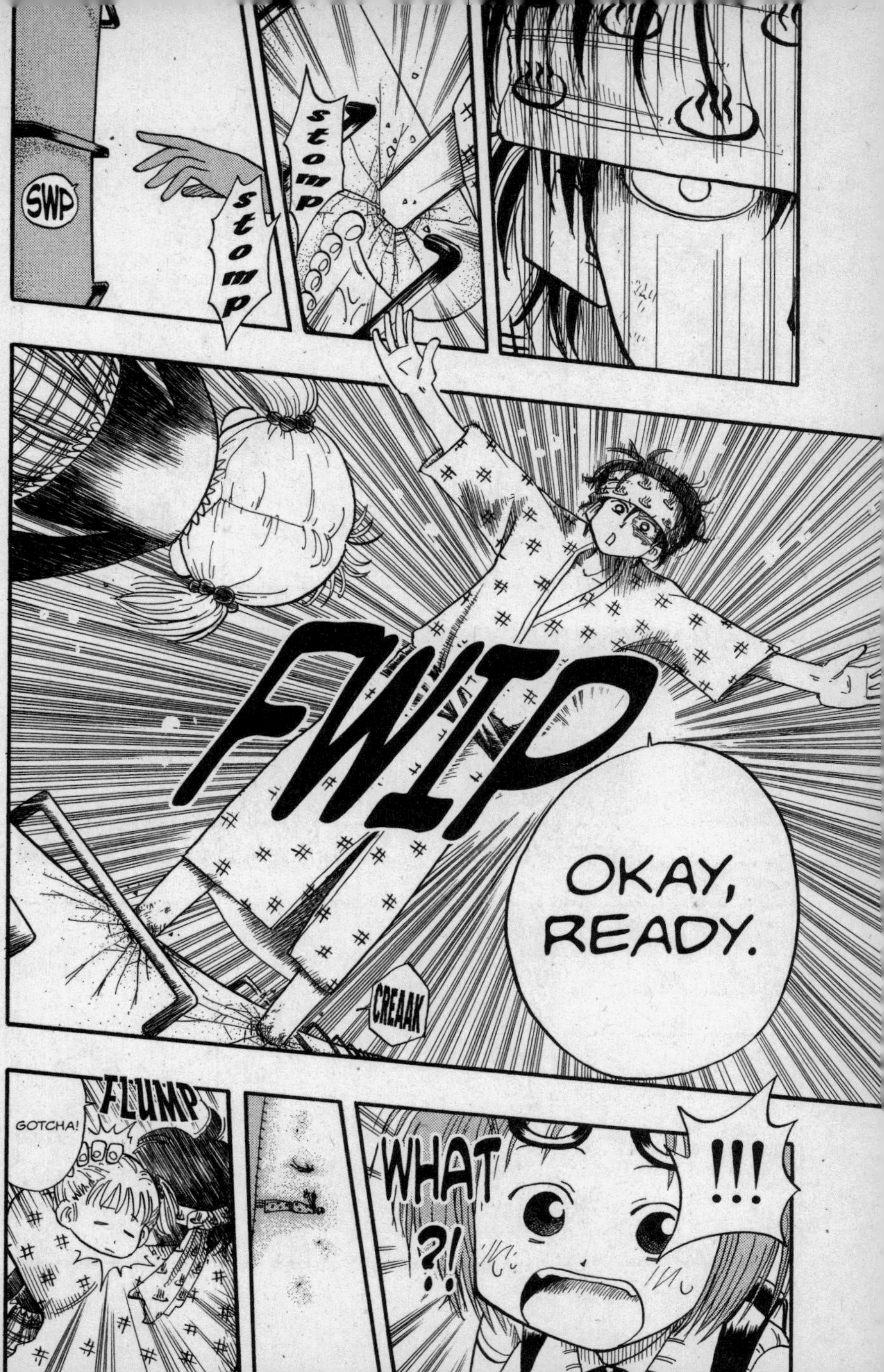
stomp
stomp
SWP
OKAY, READY.
FWIP
CREAAK
!!!
WHAT ?!
FLUMP
GOTCHA!

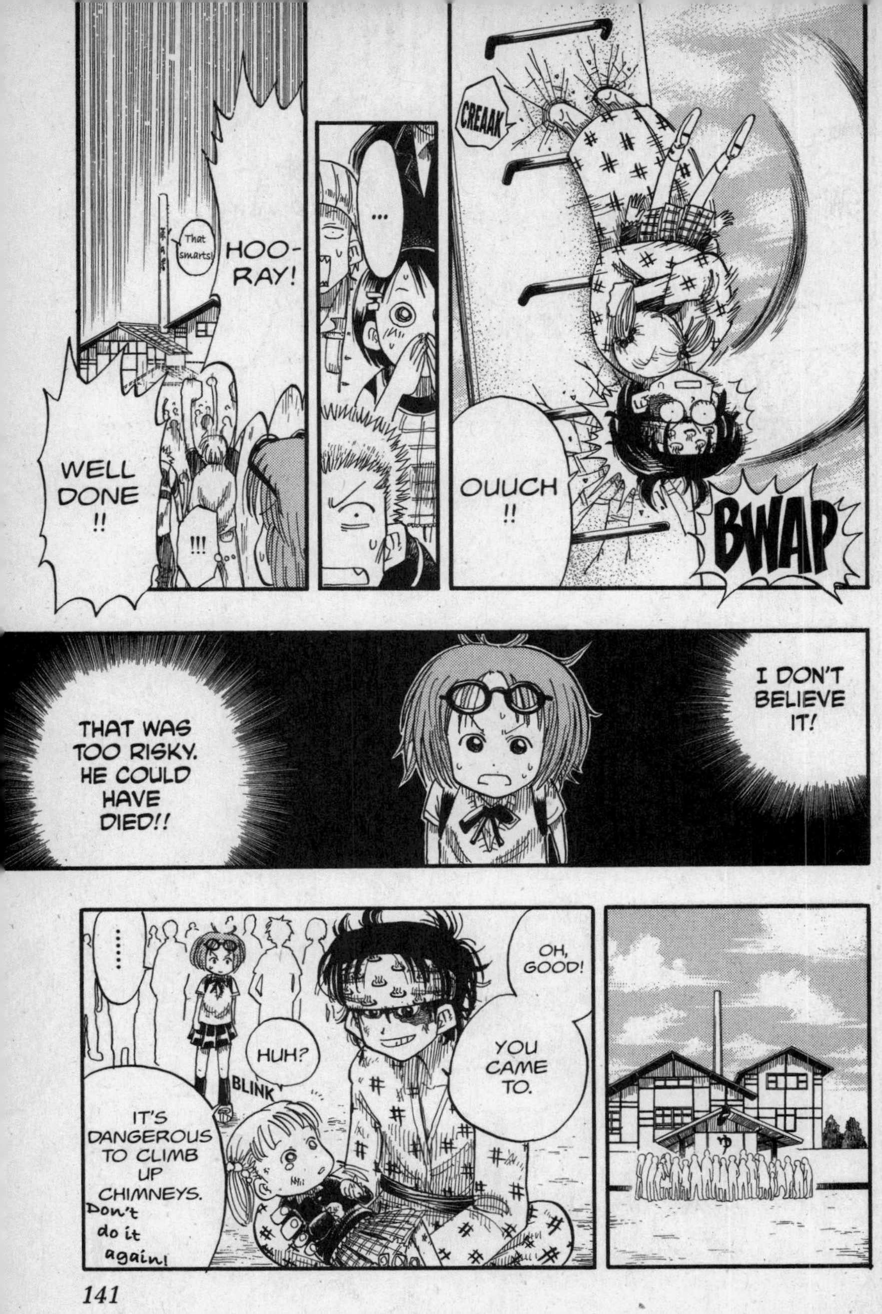
CREAAK
BWAP
OUUCH !!
...
HOO-RAY!
That smarts!
WELL DONE !!
!!!
I DON'T BELIEVE IT!
THAT WAS TOO RISKY. HE COULD HAVE DIED!!
OH, GOOD!
YOU CAME TO.
HUH?
BLINK
......
IT'S DANGEROUS TO CLIMB UP CHIMNEYS.
Don't do it again!

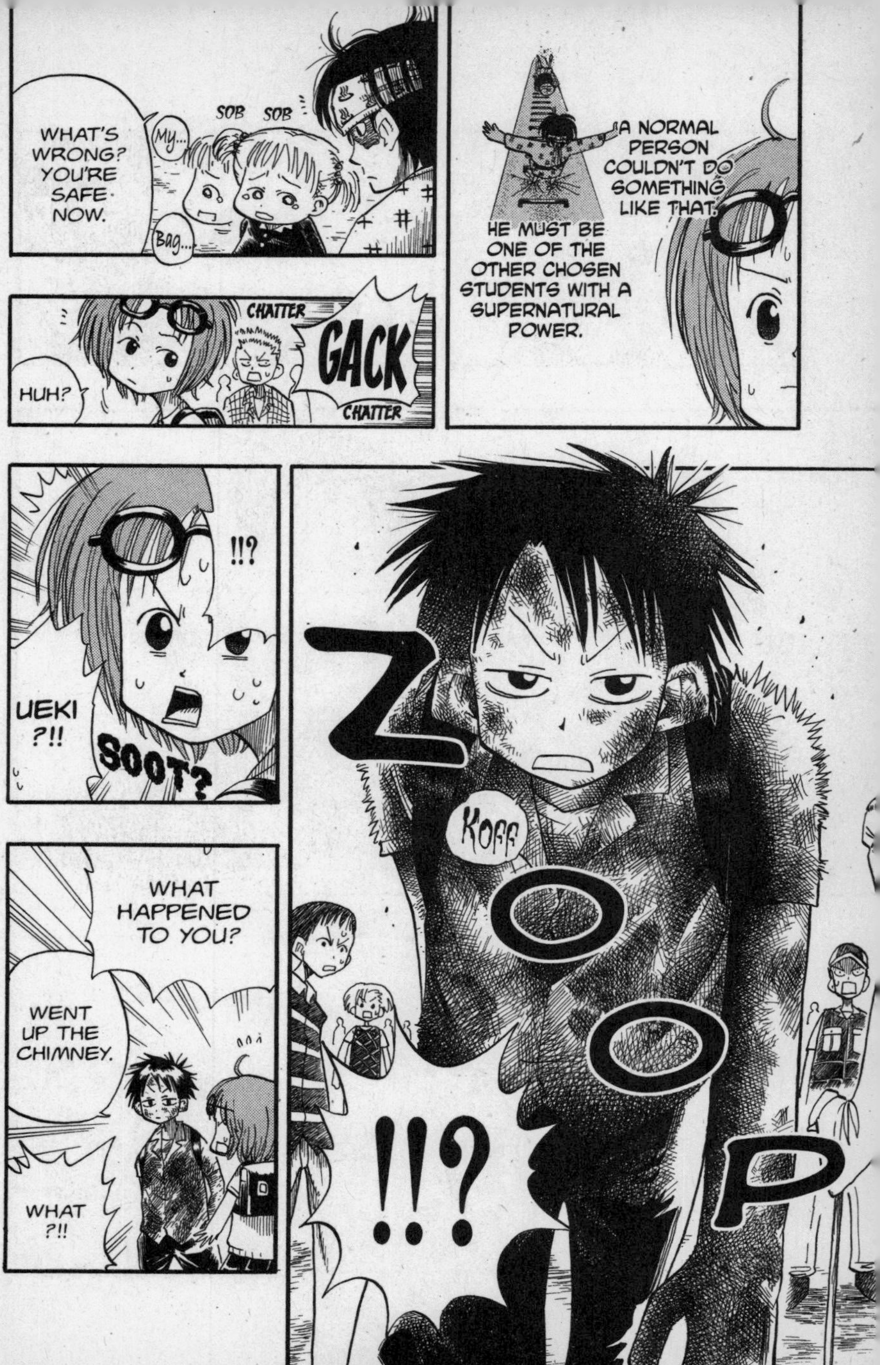
A NORMAL PERSON COULDN'T DO SOMETHING LIKE THAT.
HE MUST BE ONE OF THE OTHER CHOSEN STUDENTS WITH A SUPERNATURAL POWER.
SOB SOB
WHAT'S WRONG? YOU'RE SAFE NOW.
My...
Bag...
CHATTER
GACK
CHATTER
HUH?
ZOOOP
!!?
KOFF
!!?
UEKI ?!!
SOOT?
WHAT HAPPENED TO YOU?
WENT UP THE CHIMNEY.
WHAT ?!!

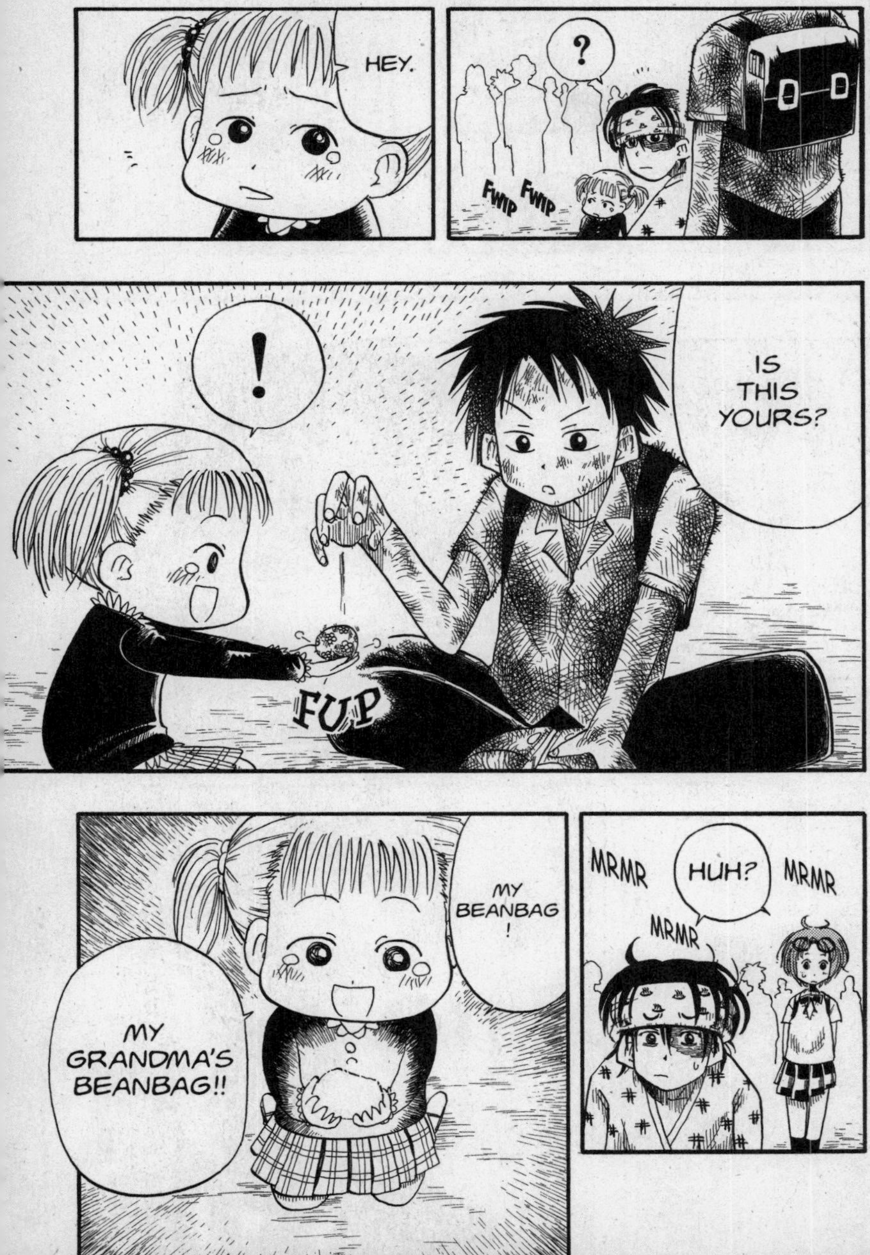
?
FWIP
FWIP
HEY.
IS THIS YOURS?
!
FUP
MRMR
HUH?
MRMR
MRMR
MY BEANBAG!
MY GRANDMA'S BEANBAG!!

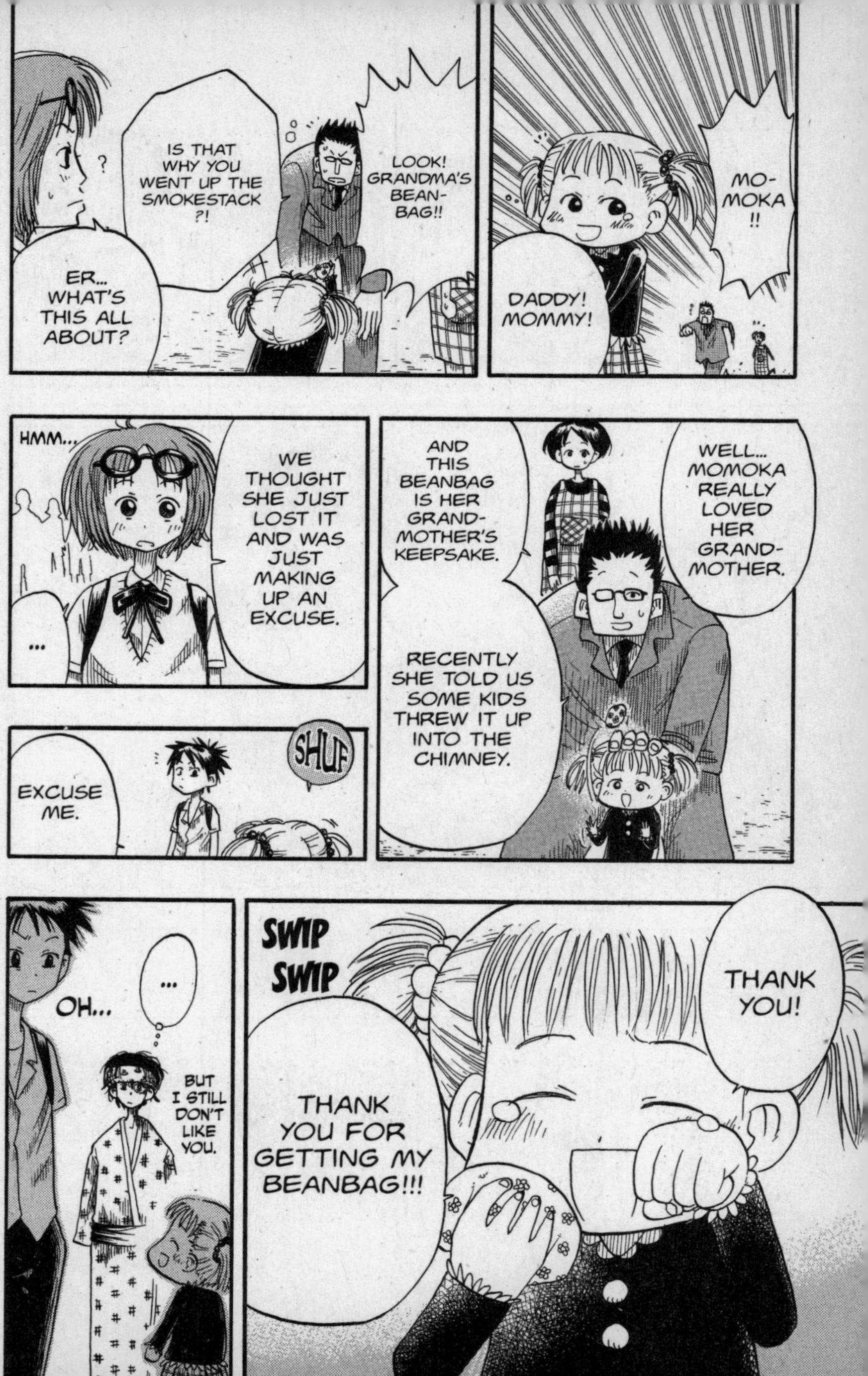
MO-MOKA!!
DADDY! MOMMY!
LOOK! GRANDMA'S BEAN-BAG!!
IS THAT WHY YOU WENT UP THE SMOKESTACK?!
ER... WHAT'S THIS ALL ABOUT?
WELL... MOMOKA REALLY LOVED HER GRAND-MOTHER.
AND THIS BEANBAG IS HER GRAND-MOTHER'S KEEPSAKE.
RECENTLY SHE TOLD US SOME KIDS THREW IT UP INTO THE CHIMNEY.
HMM...
WE THOUGHT SHE JUST LOST IT AND WAS JUST MAKING UP AN EXCUSE.
...
SHUF
EXCUSE ME.
THANK YOU!
SWIP SWIP
THANK YOU FOR GETTING MY BEANBAG!!!
...
OH...
BUT I STILL DON'T LIKE YOU.

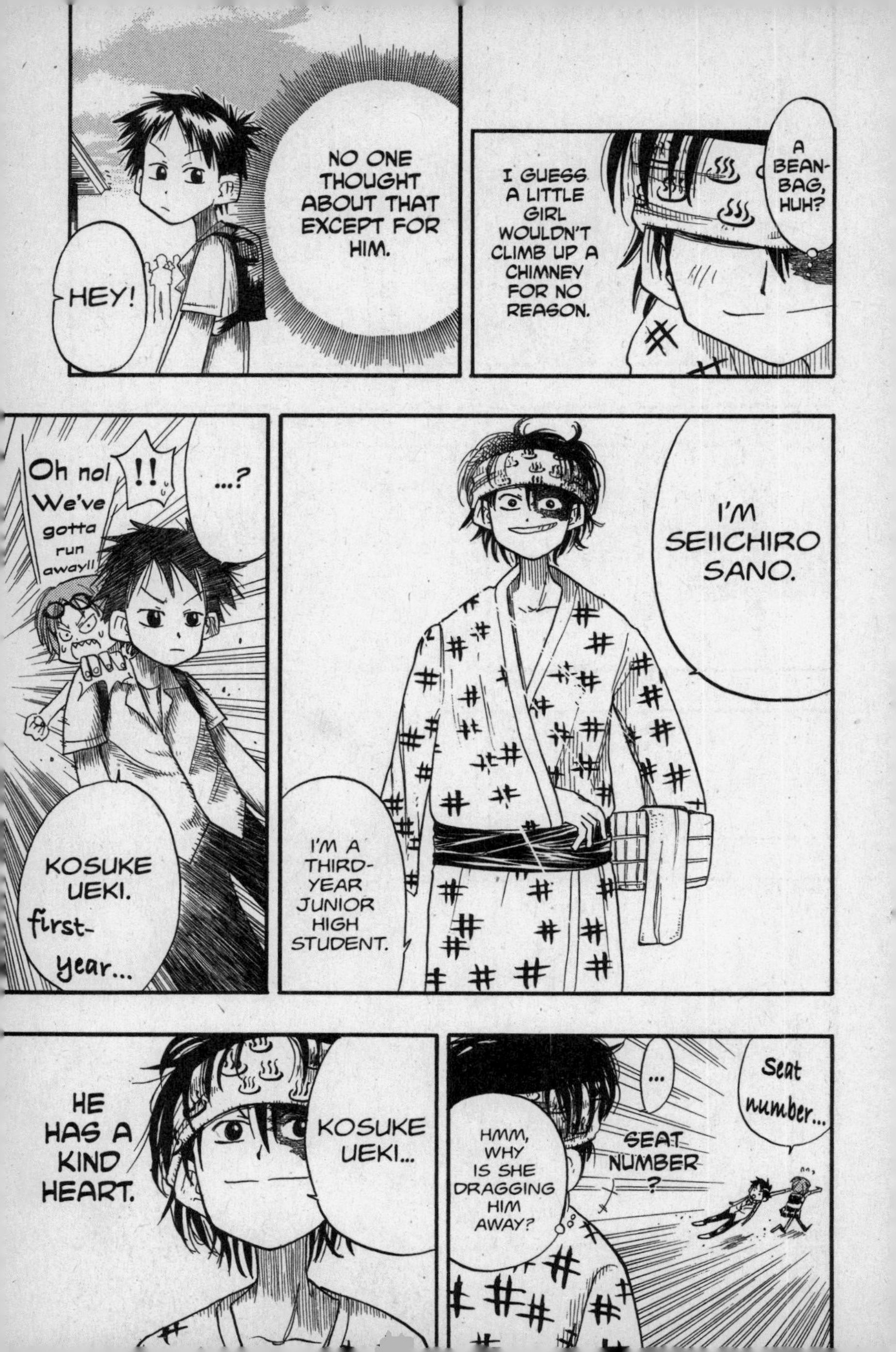
A BEAN-BAG, HUH?
I GUESS A LITTLE GIRL WOULDN'T CLIMB UP A CHIMNEY FOR NO REASON.
NO ONE THOUGHT ABOUT THAT EXCEPT FOR HIM.
HEY!
I'M SEIICHIRO SANO.
I'M A THIRD-YEAR JUNIOR HIGH STUDENT.
...?
!!
Oh no! We've gotta run away!!
KOSUKE UEKI. first-year...
Seat number...
...
SEAT NUMBER?
HMM, WHY IS SHE DRAGGING HIM AWAY?
KOSUKE UEKI...
HE HAS A KIND HEART.

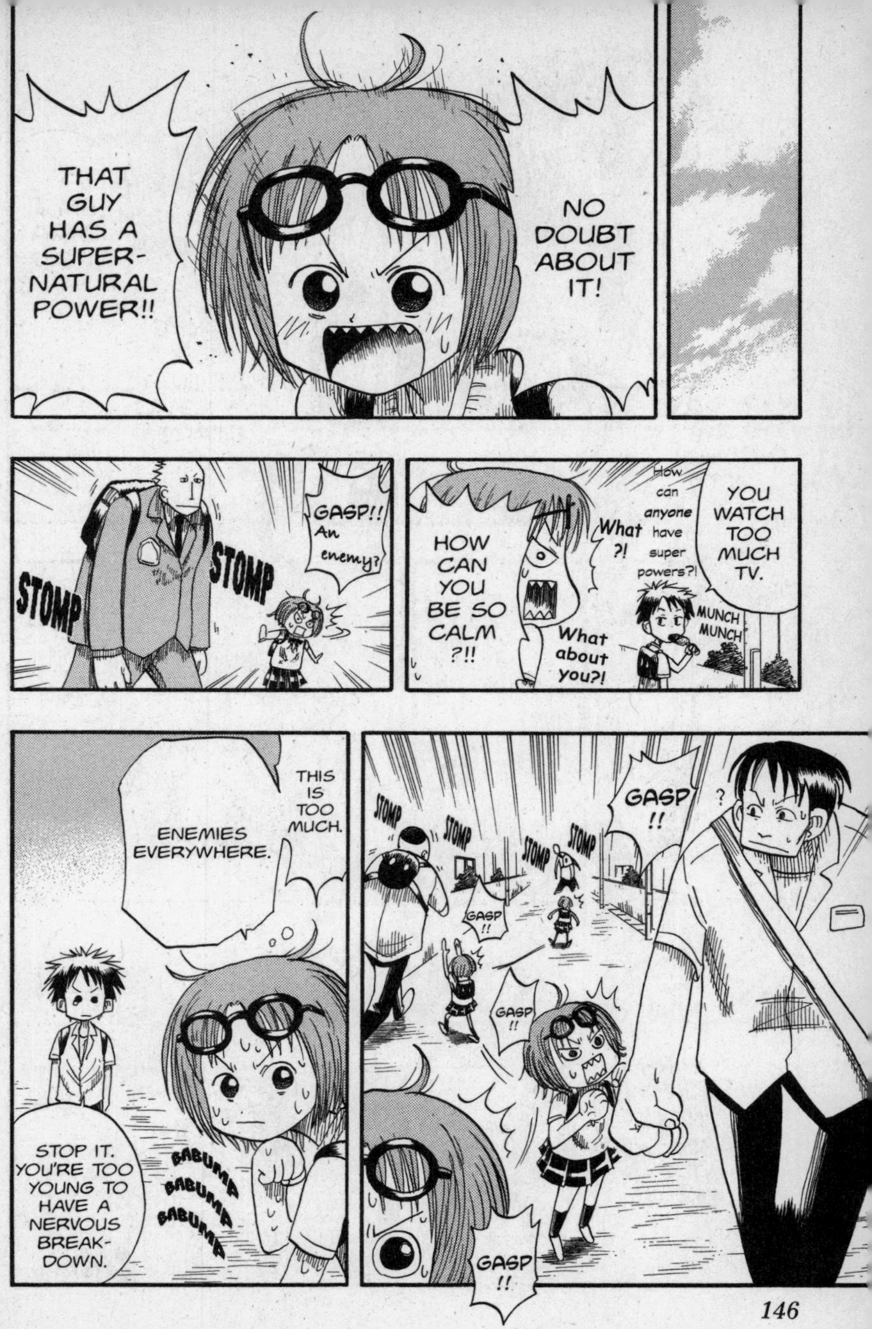
NO DOUBT ABOUT IT!
THAT GUY HAS A SUPER-NATURAL POWER!!
YOU WATCH TOO MUCH TV.
How can anyone have super powers?!
What ?!
HOW CAN YOU BE SO CALM ?!!
MUNCH MUNCH
What about you?!
GASP!! An enemy?
STOMP
STOMP
GASP !!
STOMP
STOMP
STOMP
STOMP
GASP !!
GASP !!
GASP !!
THIS IS TOO MUCH.
ENEMIES EVERYWHERE.
BABUMP
BABUMP
BABUMP
STOP IT. YOU'RE TOO YOUNG TO HAVE A NERVOUS BREAK-DOWN.

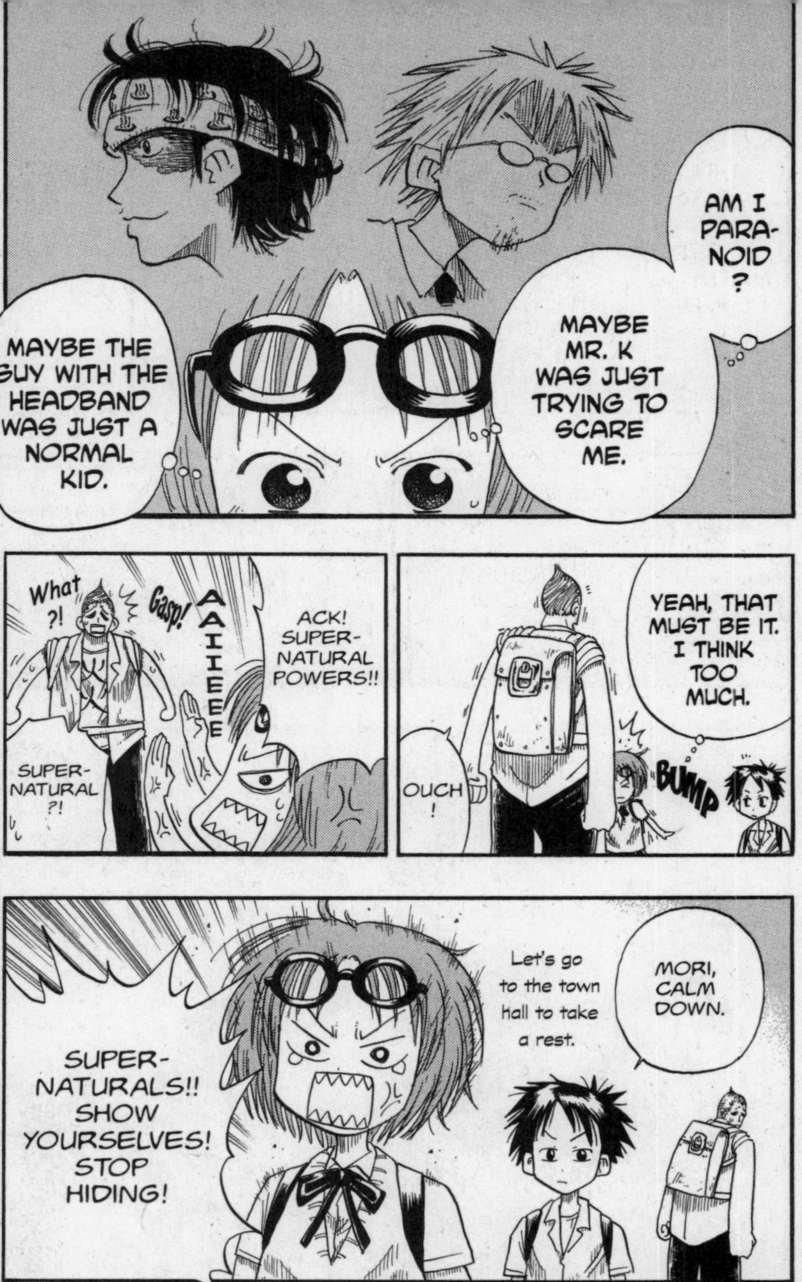
AM I PARA-NOID?
MAYBE MR. K WAS JUST TRYING TO SCARE ME.
MAYBE THE GUY WITH THE HEADBAND WAS JUST A NORMAL KID.
YEAH, THAT MUST BE IT. I THINK TOO MUCH.
BUMP
OUCH!
ACK! SUPER-NATURAL POWERS!!
AAIIEEE
Gasp!
What?!
SUPER-NATURAL?!
MORI, CALM DOWN.
Let's go to the town hall to take a rest.
SUPER-NATURALS!! SHOW YOURSELVES! STOP HIDING!

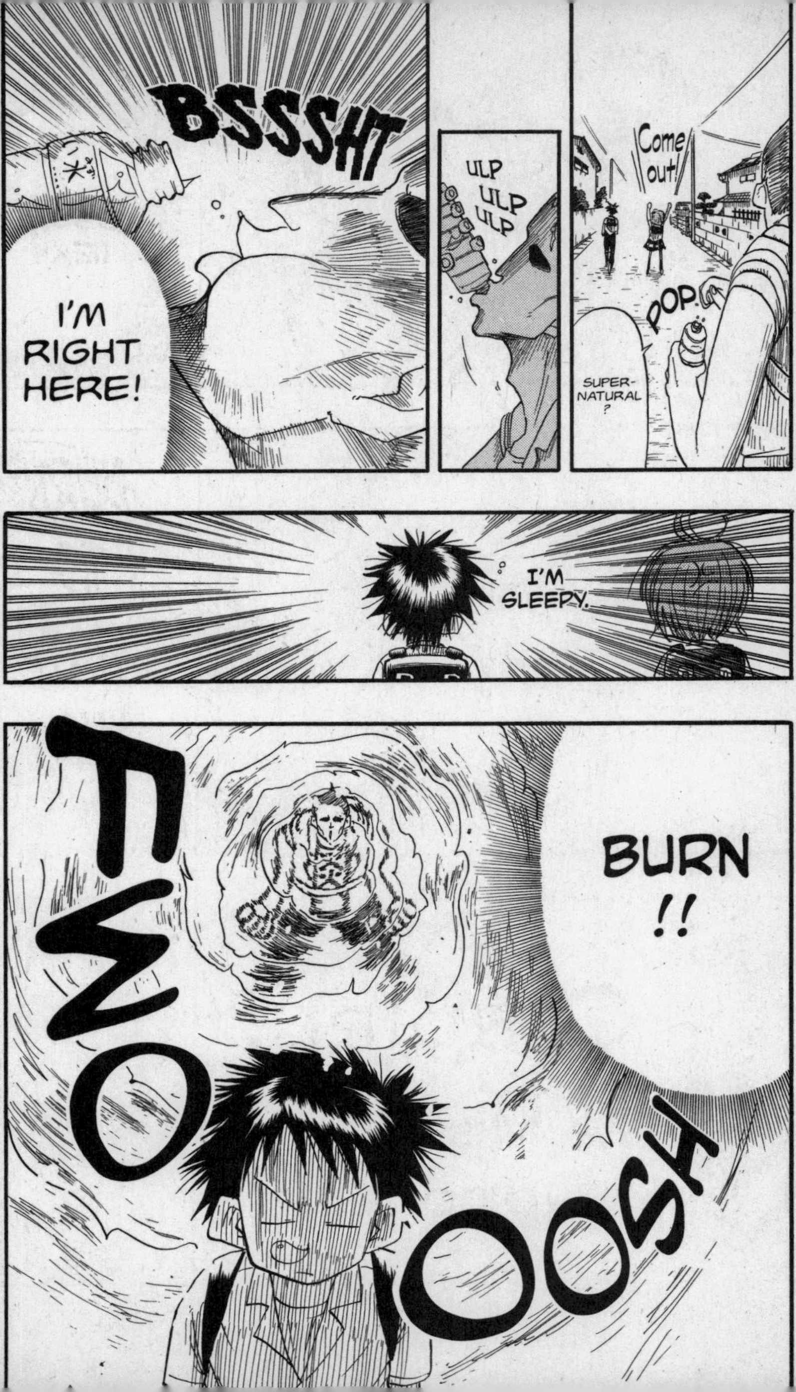
Come out!
POP
SUPER-NATURAL?
ULP ULP ULP
BSSSHT
I'M RIGHT HERE!
I'M SLEEPY.
BURN !!
FWOOOSH

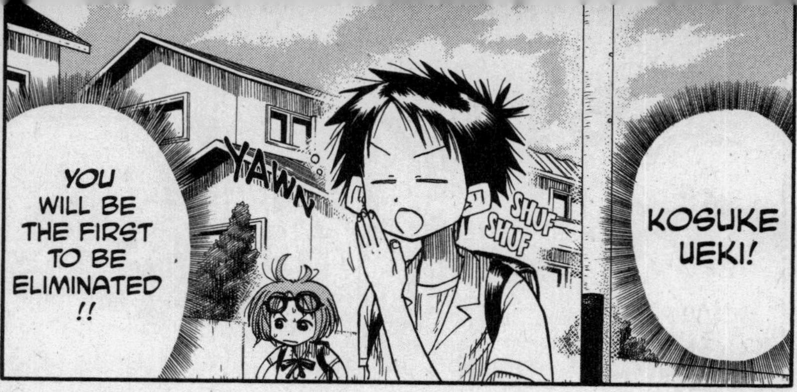
KOSUKE UEKI!
SHUF SHUF
YAWN
YOU WILL BE THE FIRST TO BE ELIMINATED !!

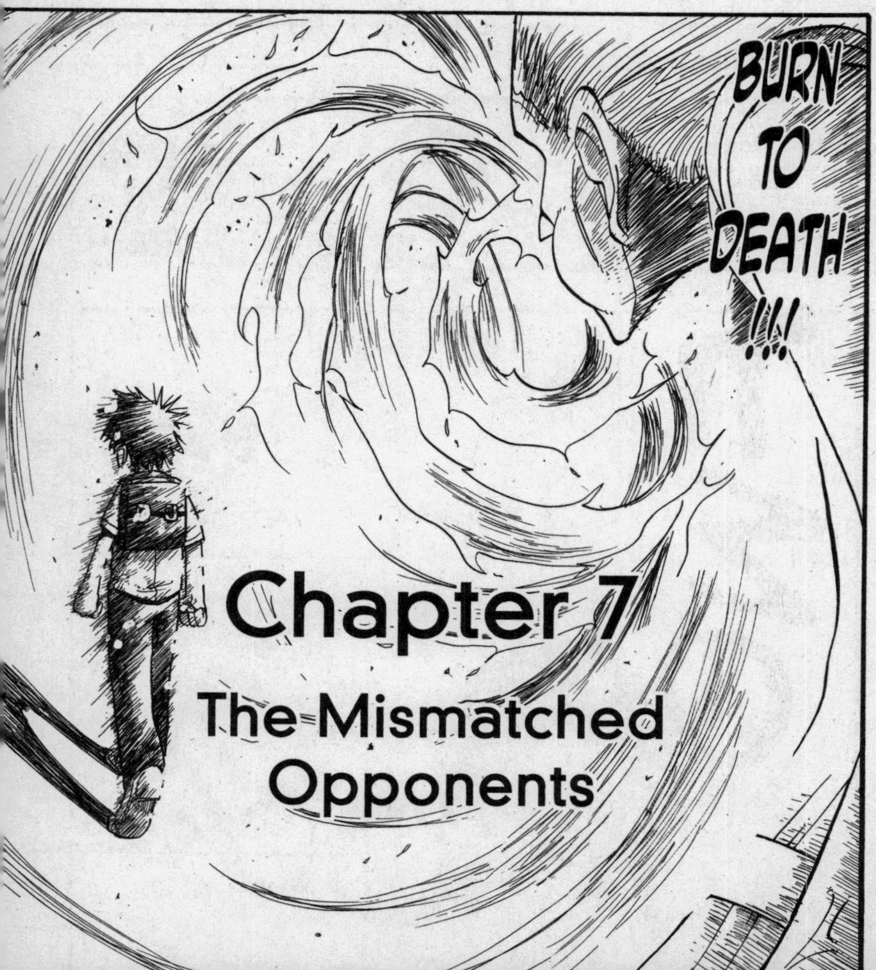
BURN TO DEATH !!!
Chapter 7
The Mismatched Opponents

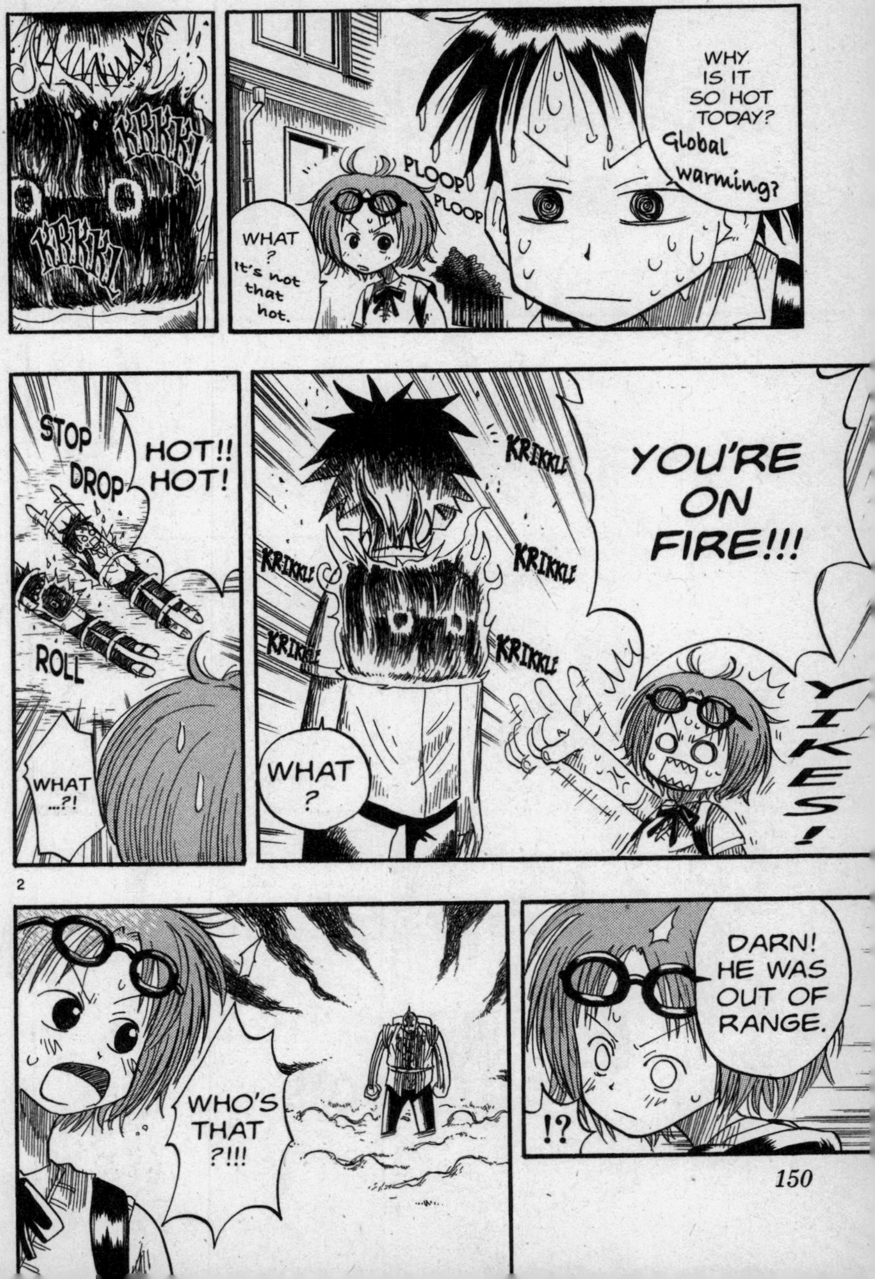
WHY IS IT SO HOT TODAY?
Global warming?
PLOOP PLOOP
WHAT? It's not that hot.
KRKKL
KRKKL
YOU'RE ON FIRE!!!
YIKES!
KRIKKLE
KRIKKLE
KRIKKLE
KRIKKLE
KRIKKLE
WHAT?
HOT!! HOT!
STOP DROP
ROLL
WHAT...?!
DARN! HE WAS OUT OF RANGE.
!?
WHO'S THAT?!!!

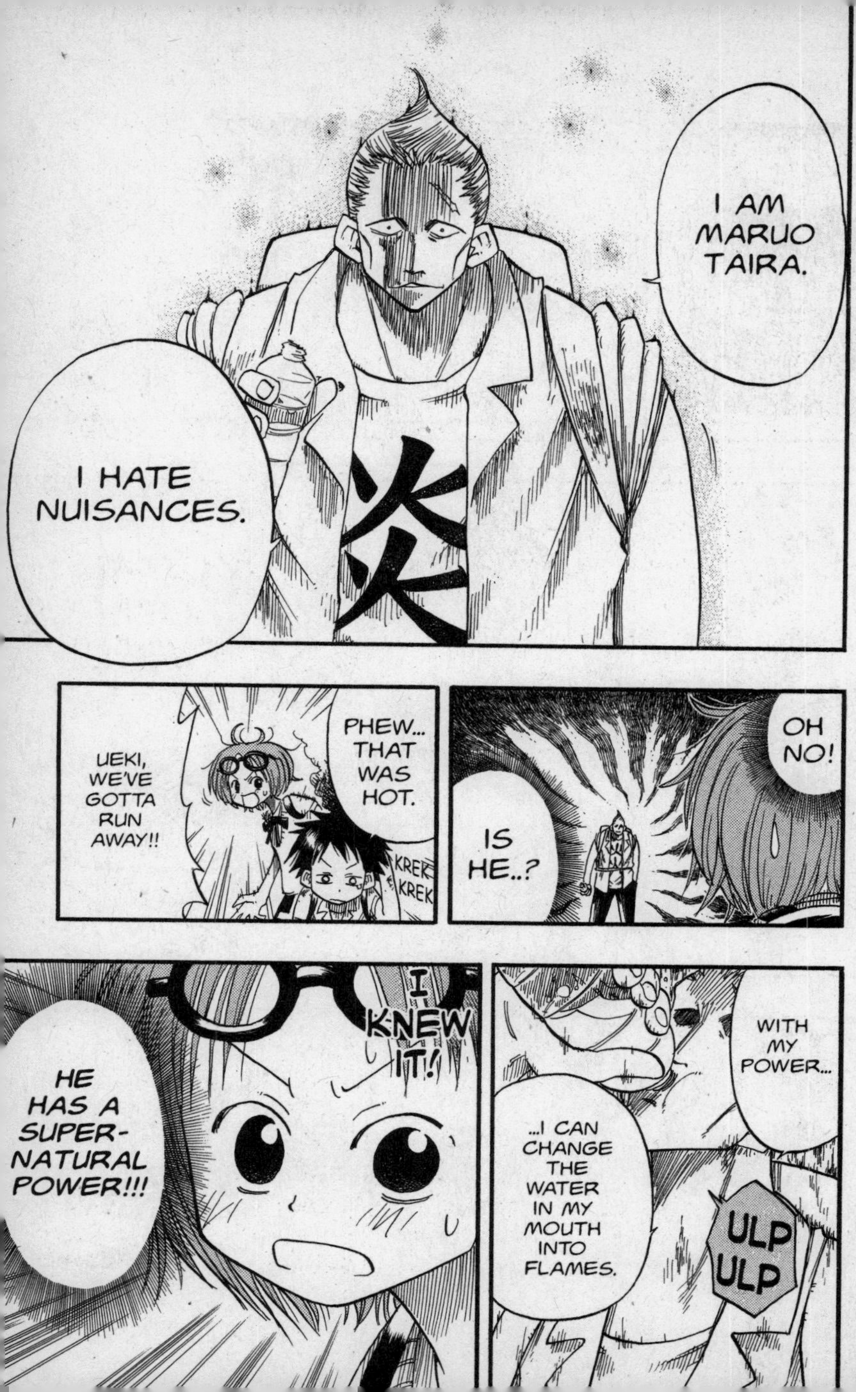
I AM MARUO TAIRA.
I HATE NUISANCES.
炎
OH NO!
IS HE..?
PHEW... THAT WAS HOT.
KREK KREK
UEKI, WE'VE GOTTA RUN AWAY!!
WITH MY POWER...
...I CAN CHANGE THE WATER IN MY MOUTH INTO FLAMES.
ULP ULP
I KNEW IT!
HE HAS A SUPER-NATURAL POWER!!!

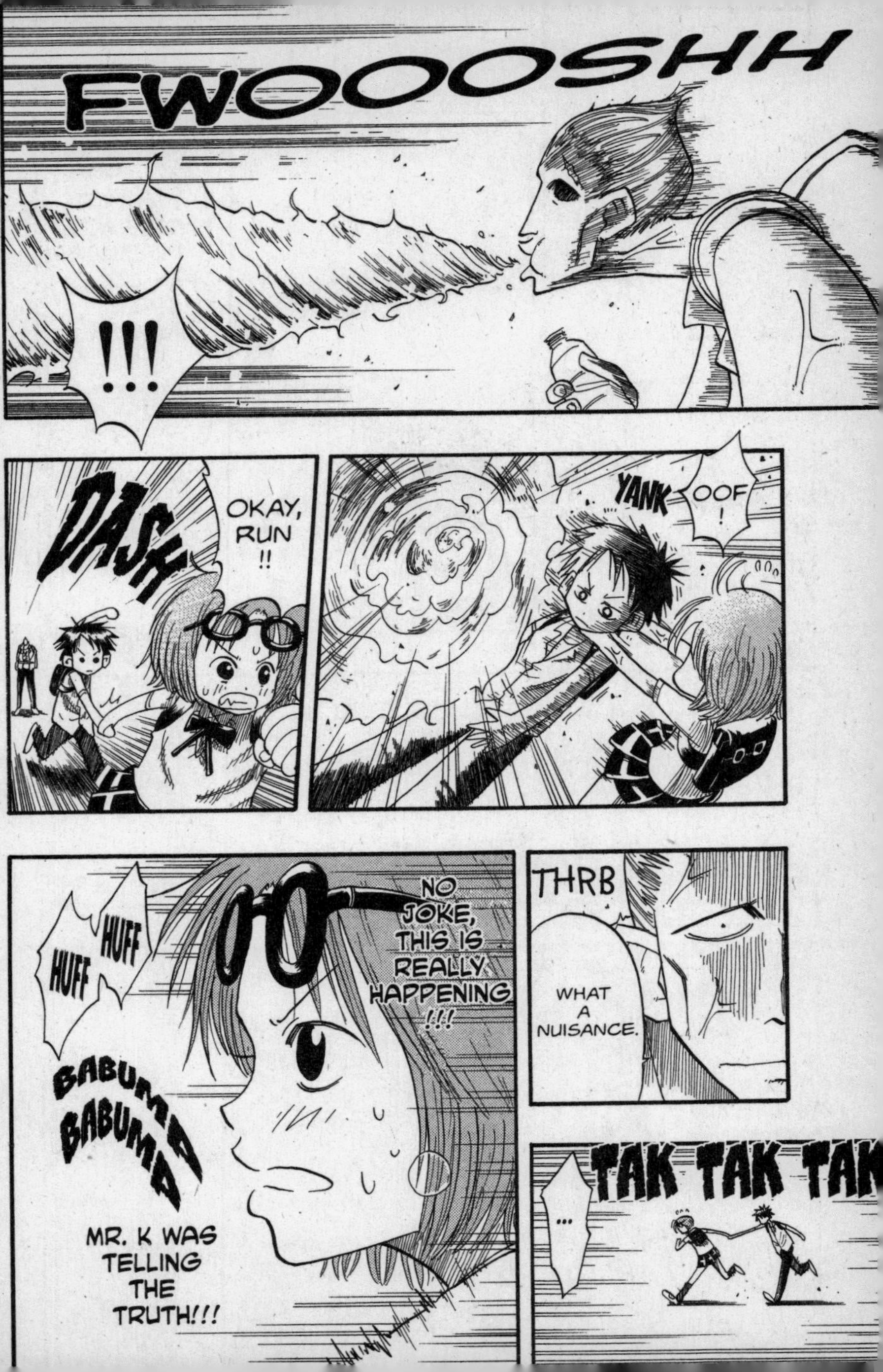

FWOOOSHH
!!!
YANK
OOF !
DASH
OKAY, RUN !!
THRB
WHAT A NUISANCE.
TAK TAK TAK
...
NO JOKE, THIS IS REALLY HAPPENING !!!
HUFF HUFF
BABUMP BABUMP
MR. K WAS TELLING THE TRUTH!!!

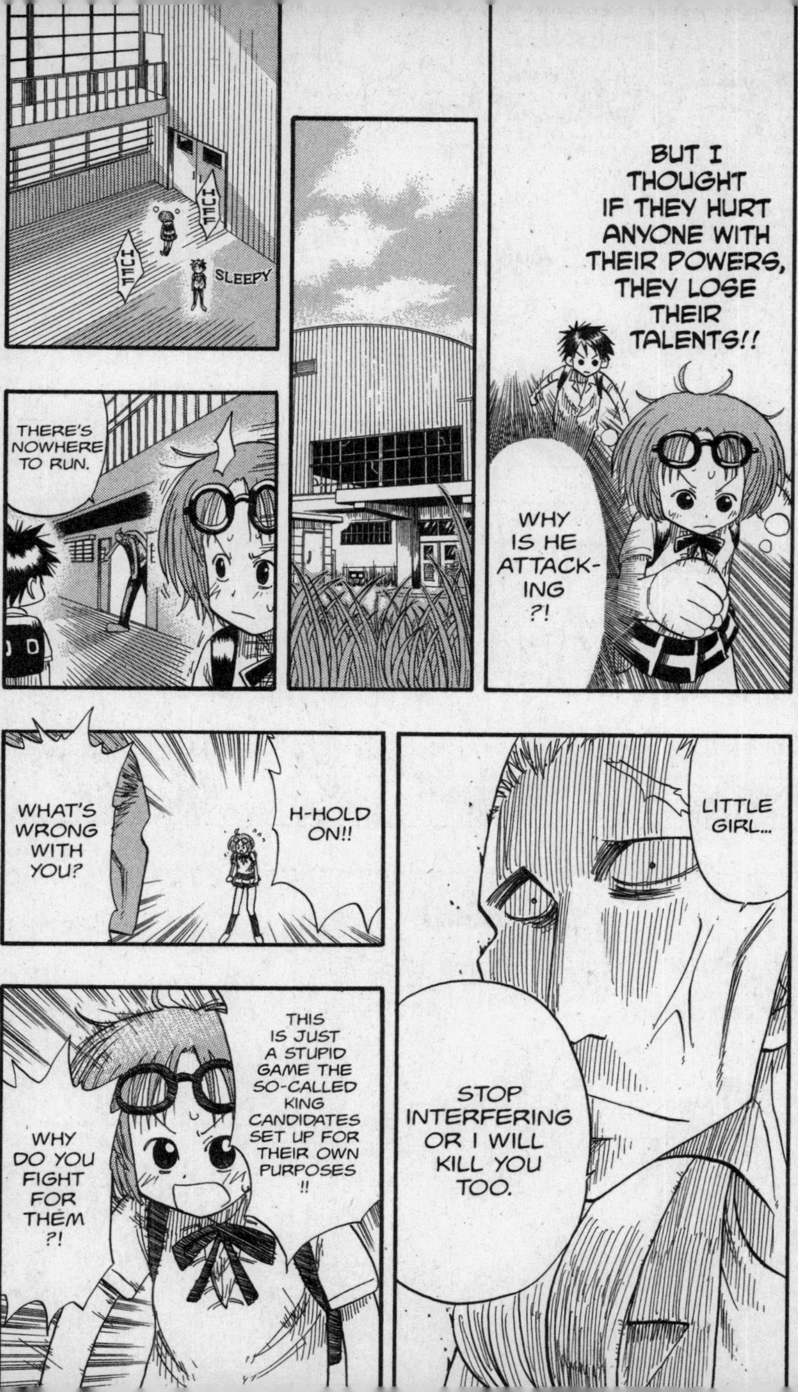
BUT I THOUGHT IF THEY HURT ANYONE WITH THEIR POWERS, THEY LOSE THEIR TALENTS!!
WHY IS HE ATTACKING ?!
HUFF
HUFF
SLEEPY
THERE'S NOWHERE TO RUN.
LITTLE GIRL...
STOP INTERFERING OR I WILL KILL YOU TOO.
H-HOLD ON!!
WHAT'S WRONG WITH YOU?
THIS IS JUST A STUPID GAME THE SO-CALLED KING CANDIDATES SET UP FOR THEIR OWN PURPOSES !!
WHY DO YOU FIGHT FOR THEM ?!

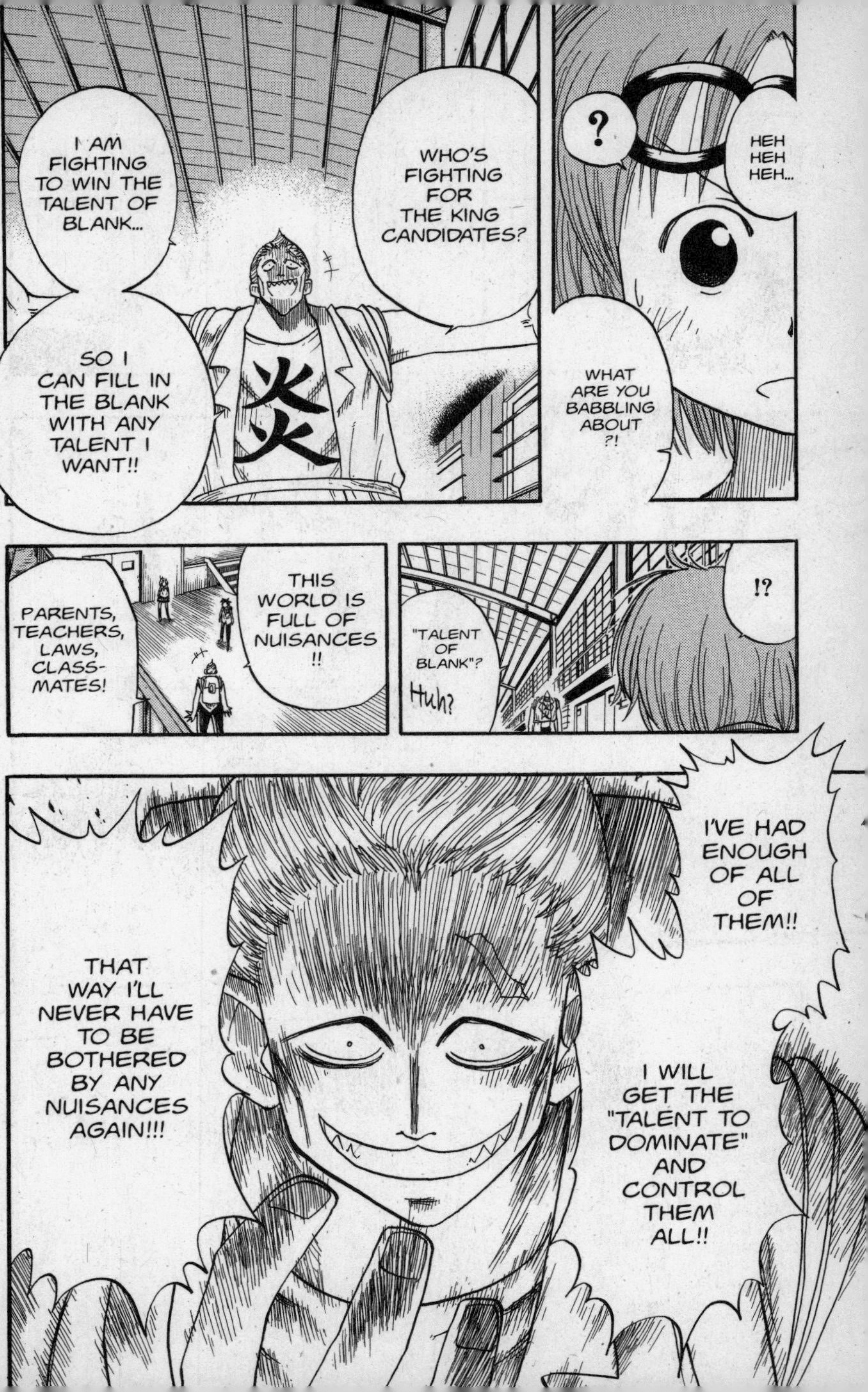
HEH HEH HEH...
?
WHAT ARE YOU BABBLING ABOUT ?!
WHO'S FIGHTING FOR THE KING CANDIDATES?
I AM FIGHTING TO WIN THE TALENT OF BLANK...
SO I CAN FILL IN THE BLANK WITH ANY TALENT I WANT!!
!?
"TALENT OF BLANK"?
Huh?
THIS WORLD IS FULL OF NUISANCES !!
PARENTS, TEACHERS, LAWS, CLASS-MATES!
I'VE HAD ENOUGH OF ALL OF THEM!!
I WILL GET THE "TALENT TO DOMINATE" AND CONTROL THEM ALL!!
THAT WAY I'LL NEVER HAVE TO BE BOTHERED BY ANY NUISANCES AGAIN!!!

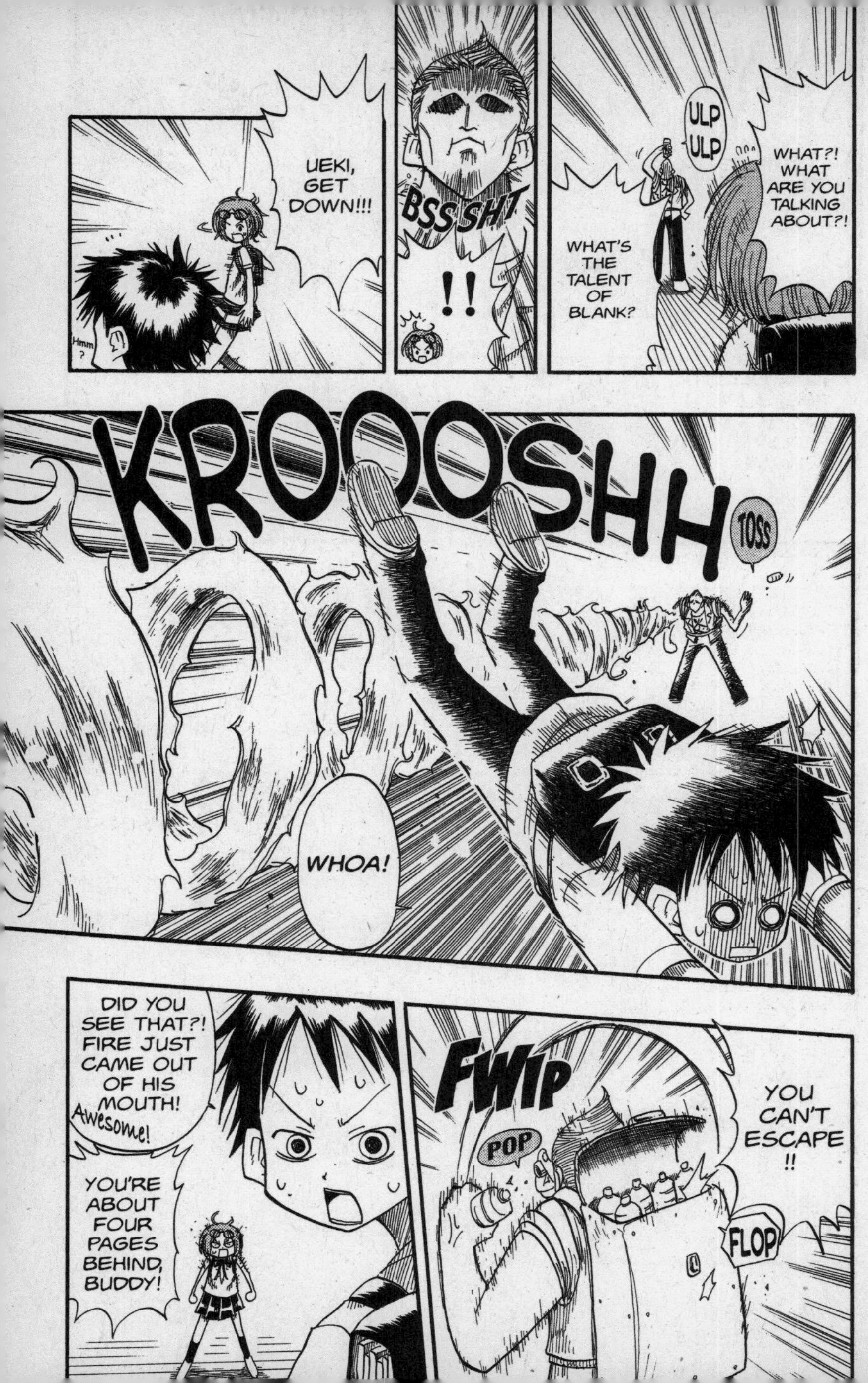
WHAT?! WHAT ARE YOU TALKING ABOUT?!
ULP ULP
WHAT'S THE TALENT OF BLANK?
BSS SHT
!!
UEKI, GET DOWN!!!
Hmm?
KROOOSHH
TOSS
WHOA!
YOU CAN'T ESCAPE !!
FWIP
POP
FLOP
DID YOU SEE THAT?! FIRE JUST CAME OUT OF HIS MOUTH!
Awesome!
YOU'RE ABOUT FOUR PAGES BEHIND, BUDDY!

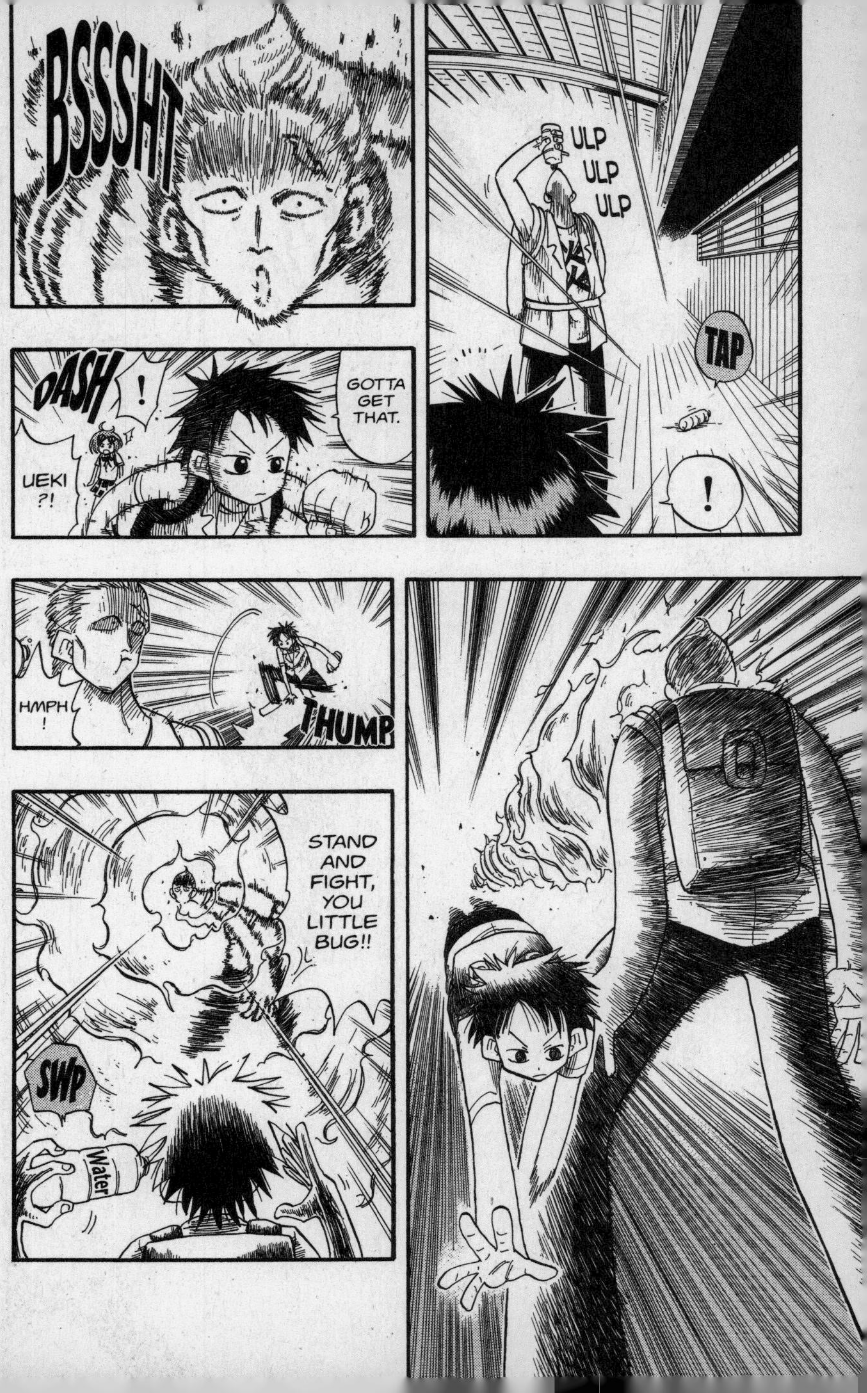
ULP
ULP
ULP
TAP
!
BSSHT
GOTTA GET THAT.
!
DASH
UEKI ?!
THUMP
HMPH !
STAND AND FIGHT, YOU LITTLE BUG!!
SWP
Water

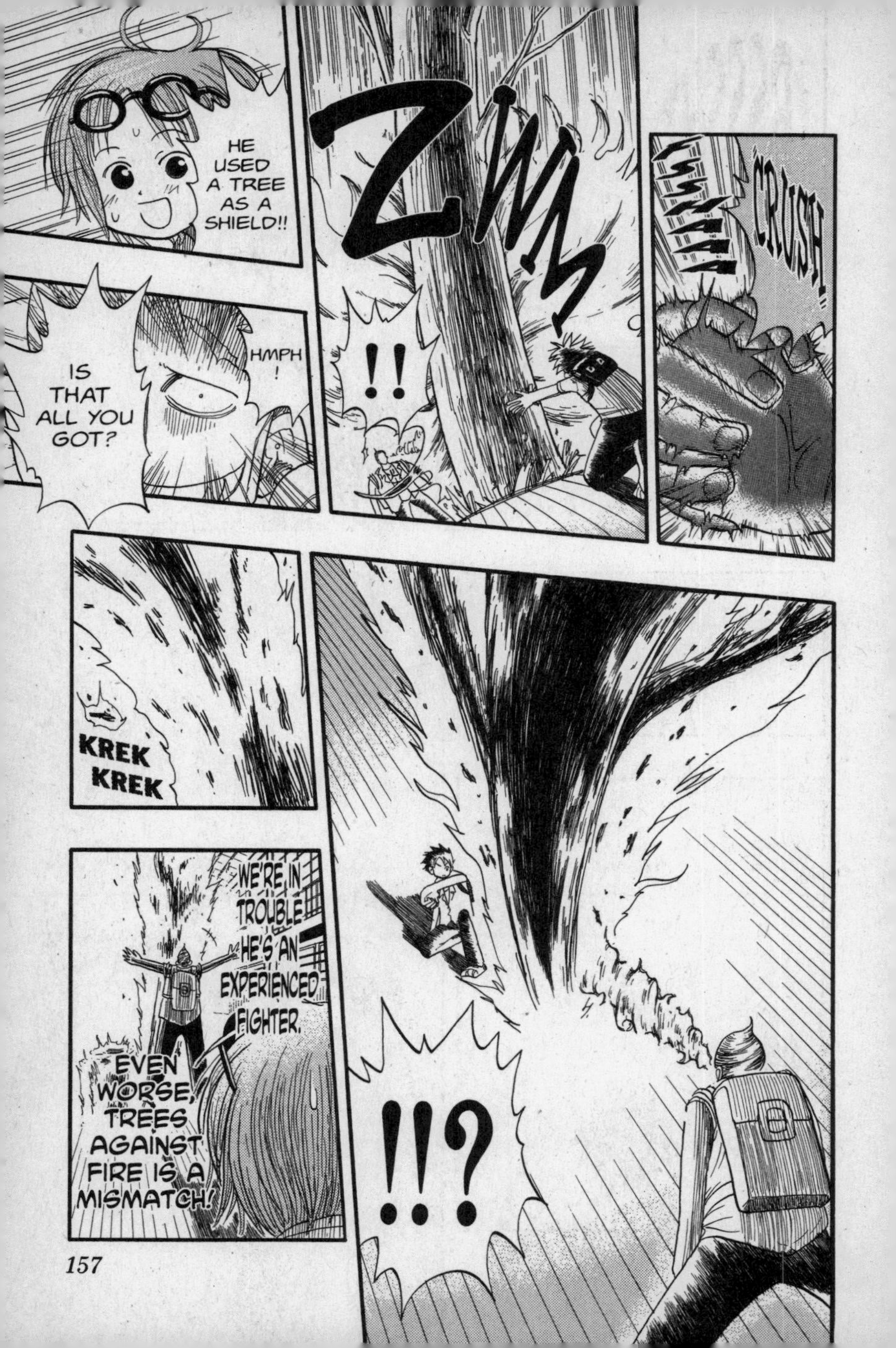
FSSHAAA
CRUSH
ZWM
!!
HE USED A TREE AS A SHIELD!!
HMPH!
IS THAT ALL YOU GOT?
!!?
KREK KREK
WE'RE IN TROUBLE. HE'S AN EXPERIENCED FIGHTER.
EVEN WORSE, TREES AGAINST FIRE IS A MISMATCH!

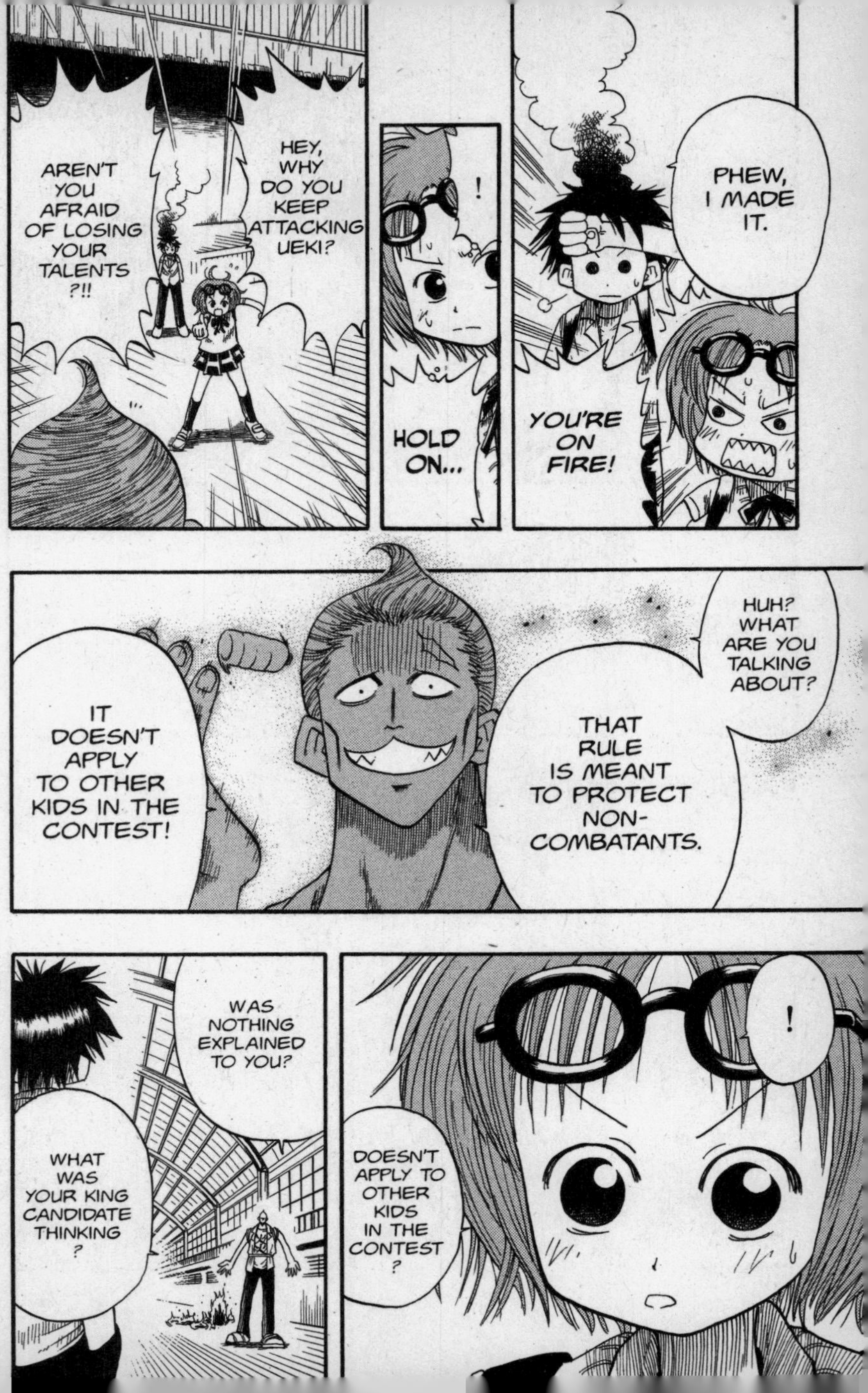
PHEW, I MADE IT.
YOU'RE ON FIRE!
!
HOLD ON...
HEY, WHY DO YOU KEEP ATTACKING UEKI?
AREN'T YOU AFRAID OF LOSING YOUR TALENTS?!!
HUH? WHAT ARE YOU TALKING ABOUT?
THAT RULE IS MEANT TO PROTECT NON-COMBATANTS.
IT DOESN'T APPLY TO OTHER KIDS IN THE CONTEST!
!
DOESN'T APPLY TO OTHER KIDS IN THE CONTEST?
WAS NOTHING EXPLAINED TO YOU?
WHAT WAS YOUR KING CANDIDATE THINKING?

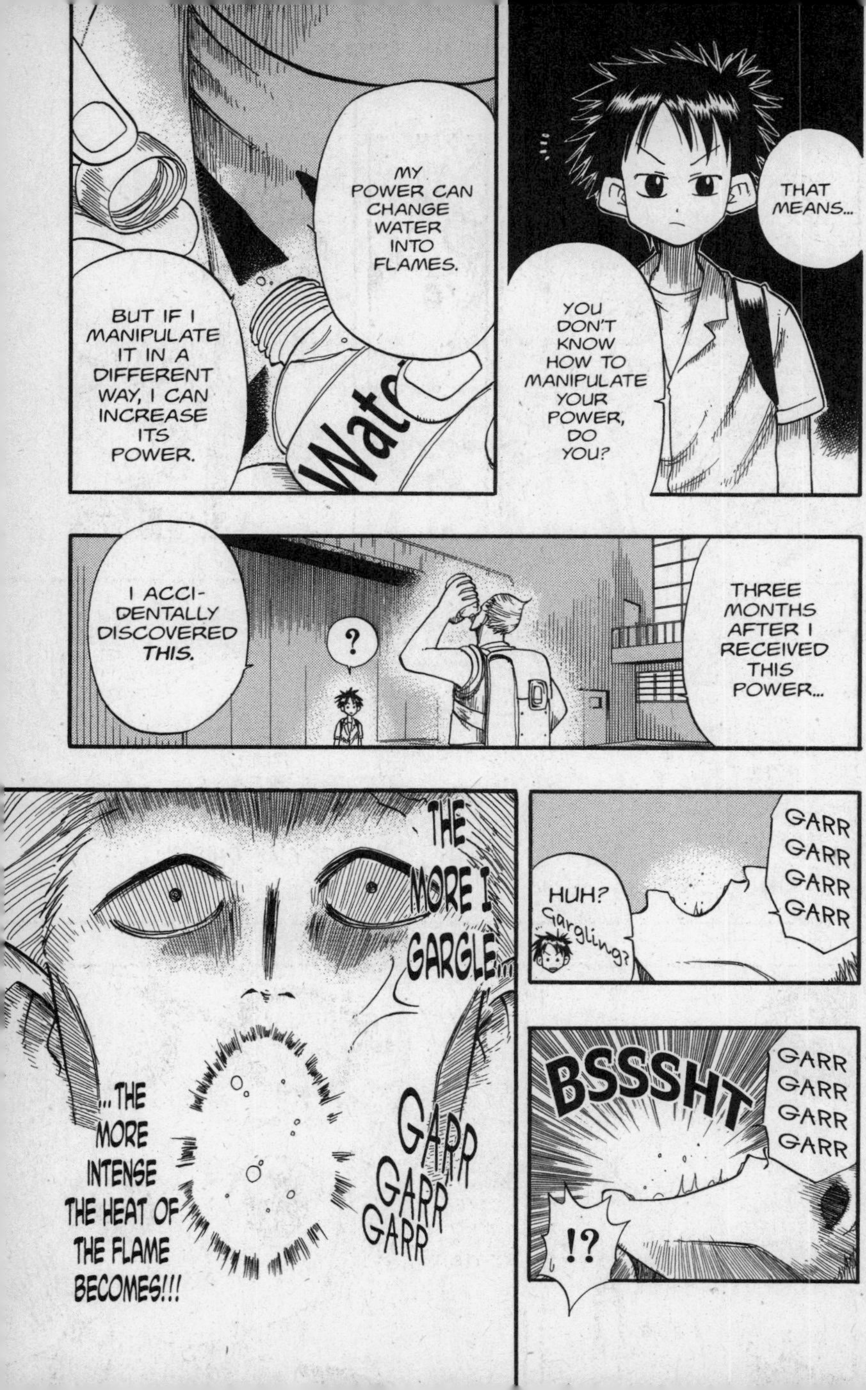
THAT MEANS...
YOU DON'T KNOW HOW TO MANIPULATE YOUR POWER, DO YOU?
MY POWER CAN CHANGE WATER INTO FLAMES.
BUT IF I MANIPULATE IT IN A DIFFERENT WAY, I CAN INCREASE ITS POWER.
Wate
THREE MONTHS AFTER I RECEIVED THIS POWER...
?
I ACCI-DENTALLY DISCOVERED THIS.
GARR GARR GARR GARR
HUH? Gargling?
GARR GARR GARR GARR
BSSSHT
!?
THE MORE I GARGLE...
GARR GARR GARR
...THE MORE INTENSE THE HEAT OF THE FLAME BECOMES!!!

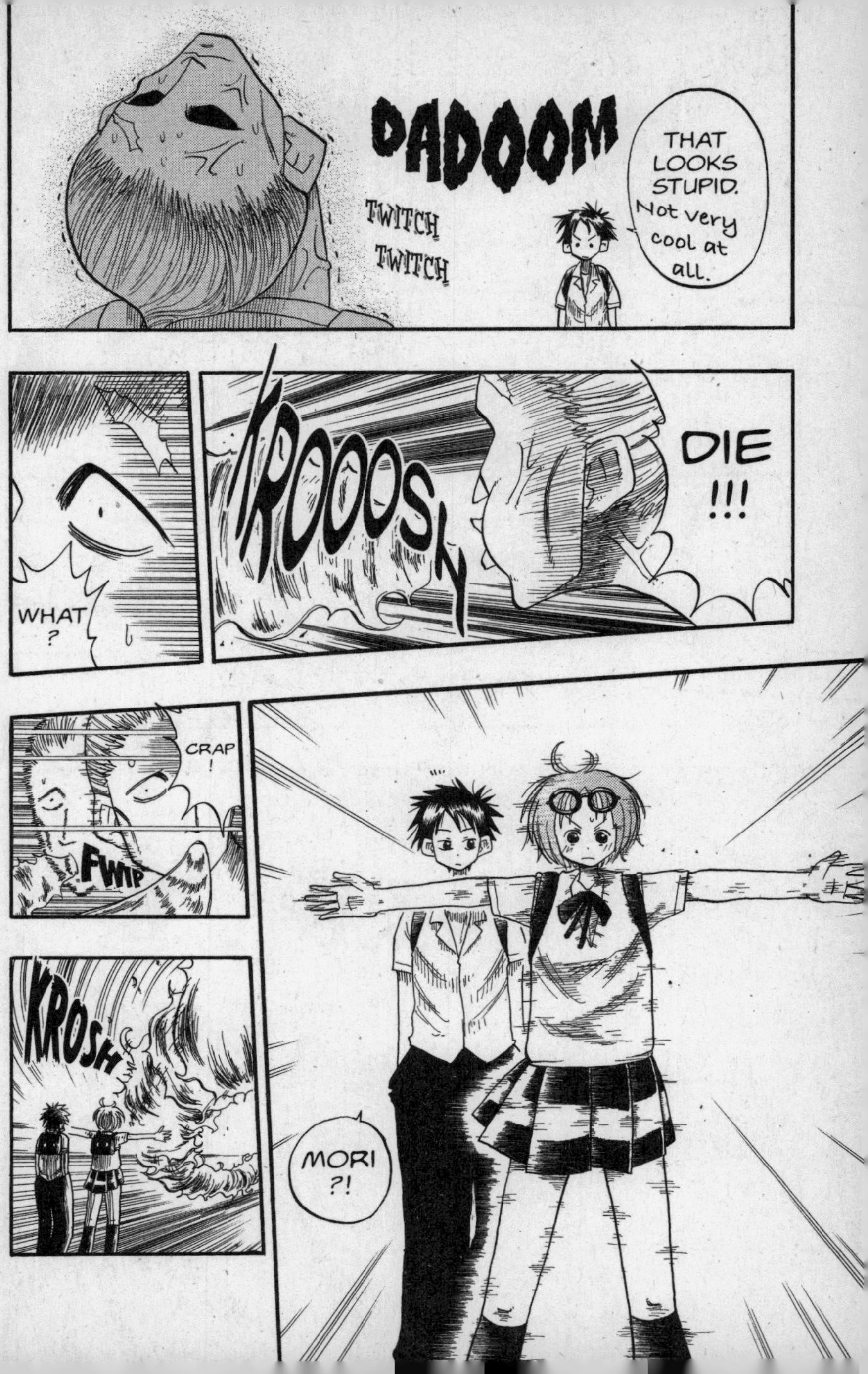
THAT LOOKS STUPID. Not very cool at all.
DADOOM
TWITCH
TWITCH
DIE !!!
KROOOSH
WHAT ?
MORI ?!
CRAP !
FWIP
KROSH

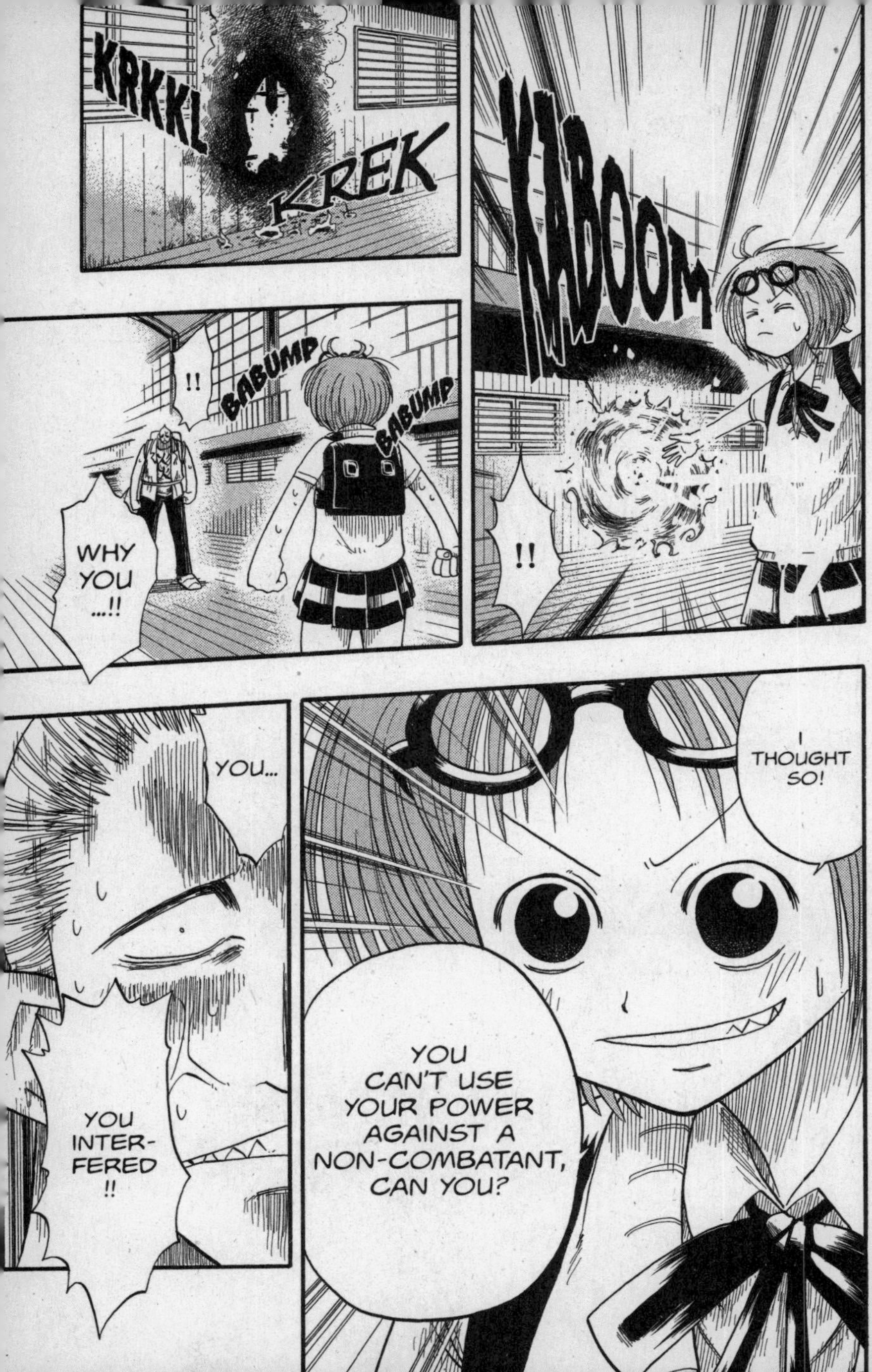
KABOOM
!!
KRKKL
KREK
!!
BABUMP
BABUMP
WHY YOU ...!!
I THOUGHT SO!
YOU CAN'T USE YOUR POWER AGAINST A NON-COMBATANT, CAN YOU?
YOU...
YOU INTER-FERED !!

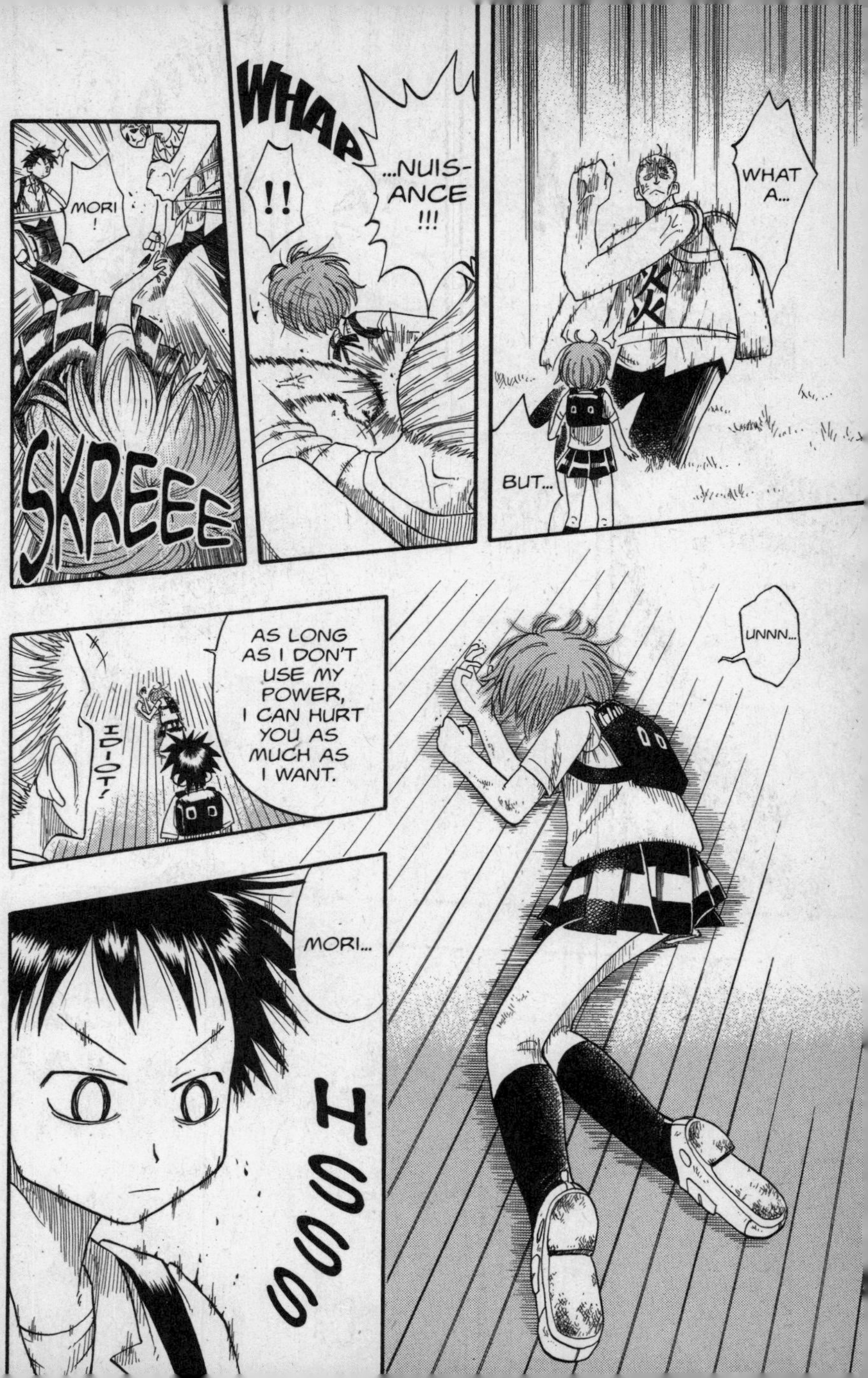
WHAT A...
BUT...
...NUISANCE!!!
WHAP
!!
MORI!
SKREEE
UNNN...
AS LONG AS I DON'T USE MY POWER, I CAN HURT YOU AS MUCH AS I WANT.
IDIOT!
MORI...
HSSS

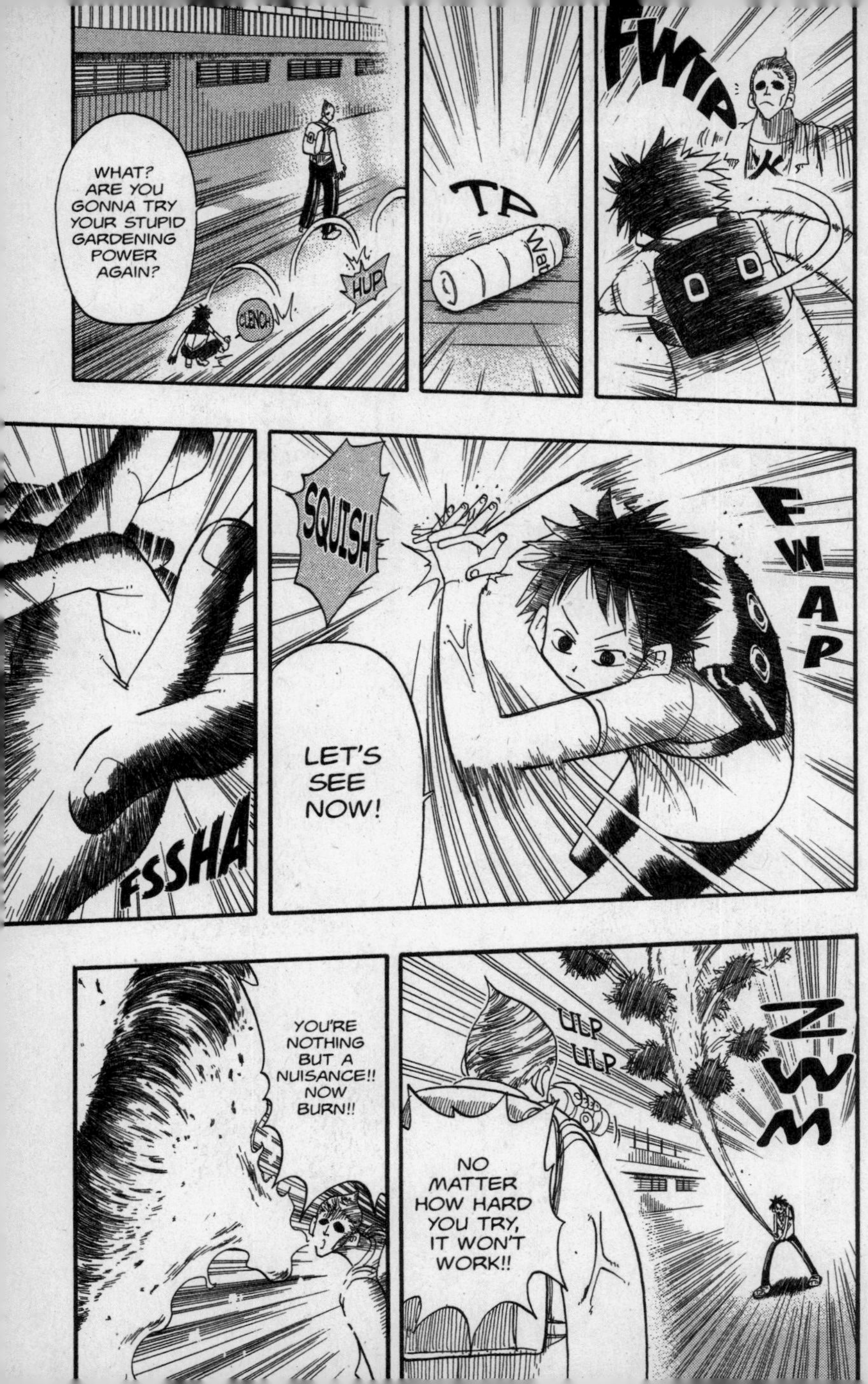
FWIP
TP
WHAT? ARE YOU GONNA TRY YOUR STUPID GARDENING POWER AGAIN?
HUP
CLENCH
FWAP
SQUISH
LET'S SEE NOW!
FSSHA
ZWM
ULP ULP
NO MATTER HOW HARD YOU TRY, IT WON'T WORK!!
YOU'RE NOTHING BUT A NUISANCE!! NOW BURN!!

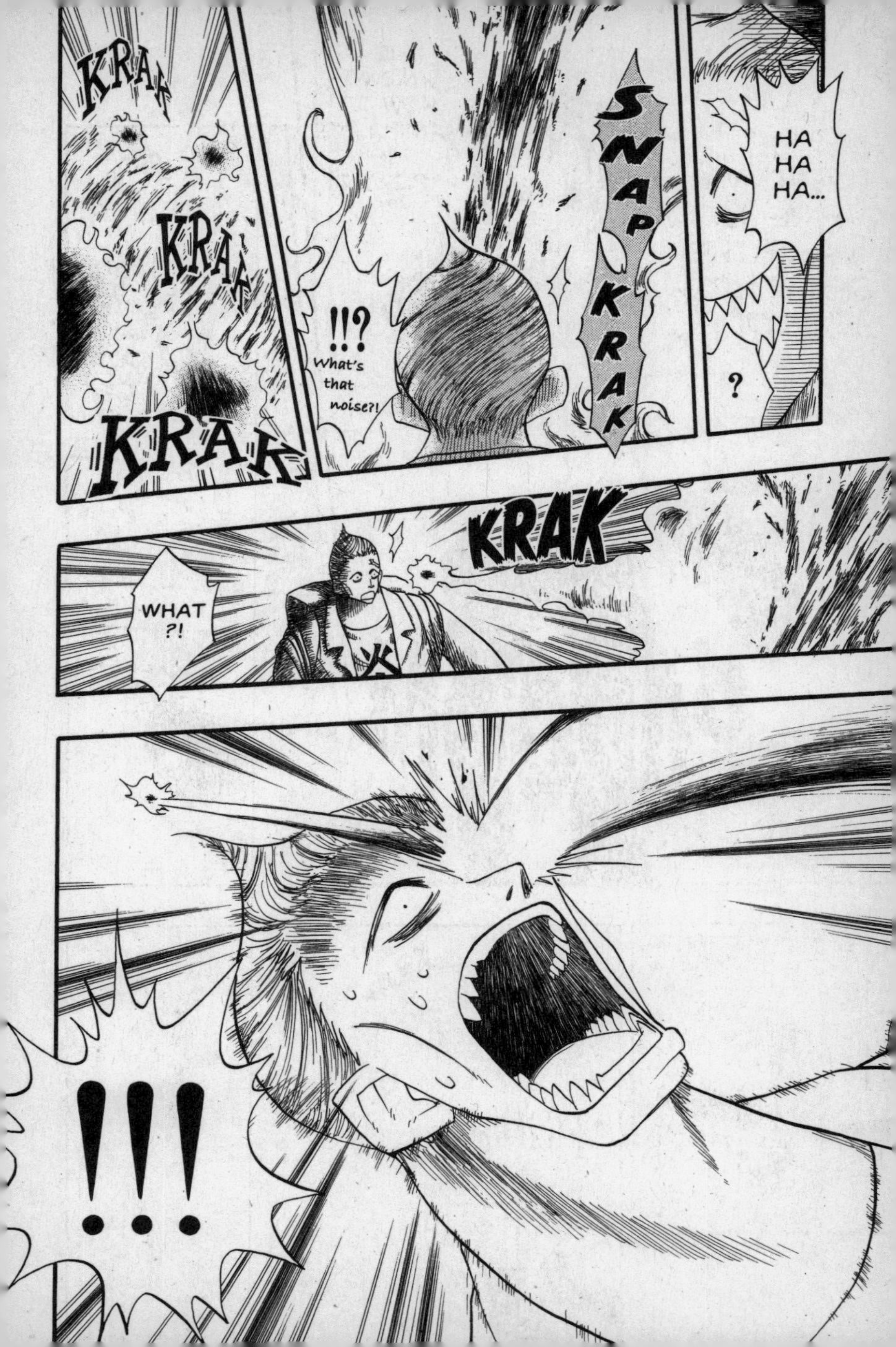
HA HA HA...
?
SNAP
KRAK
KRAK
!!? What's that noise?!
KRAK
KRAK
KRAK
KRAK
WHAT ?!
!!!

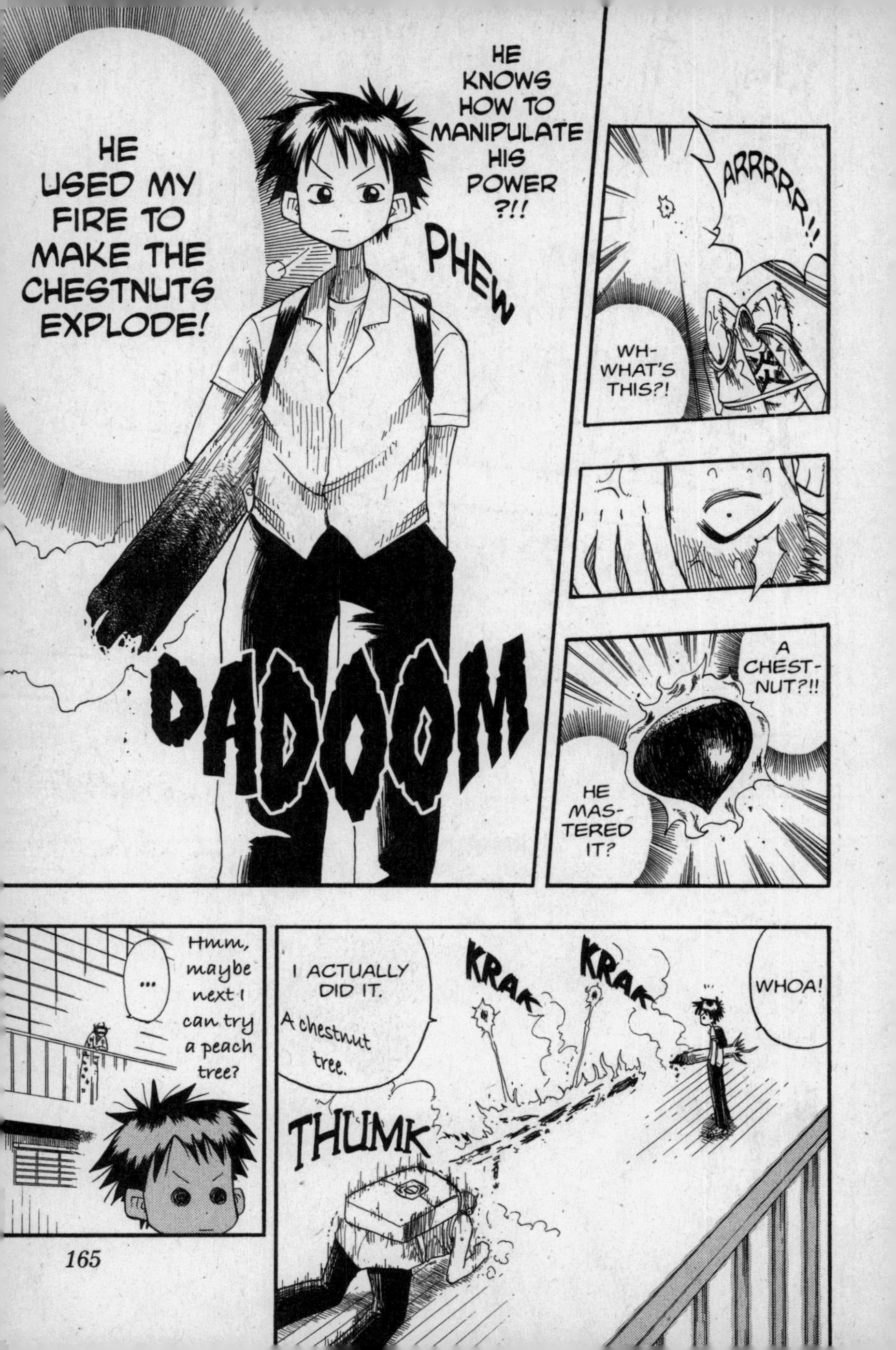
ARRRRR!!
WH-WHAT'S THIS?!
A CHEST-NUT?!!
HE MASTERED IT?
HE KNOWS HOW TO MANIPULATE HIS POWER ?!!
HE USED MY FIRE TO MAKE THE CHESTNUTS EXPLODE!
PHEW
DADOOM
WHOA!
KRAK
KRAK
I ACTUALLY DID IT.
A chestnut tree.
THUMK
Hmm, maybe next I can try a peach tree?
...

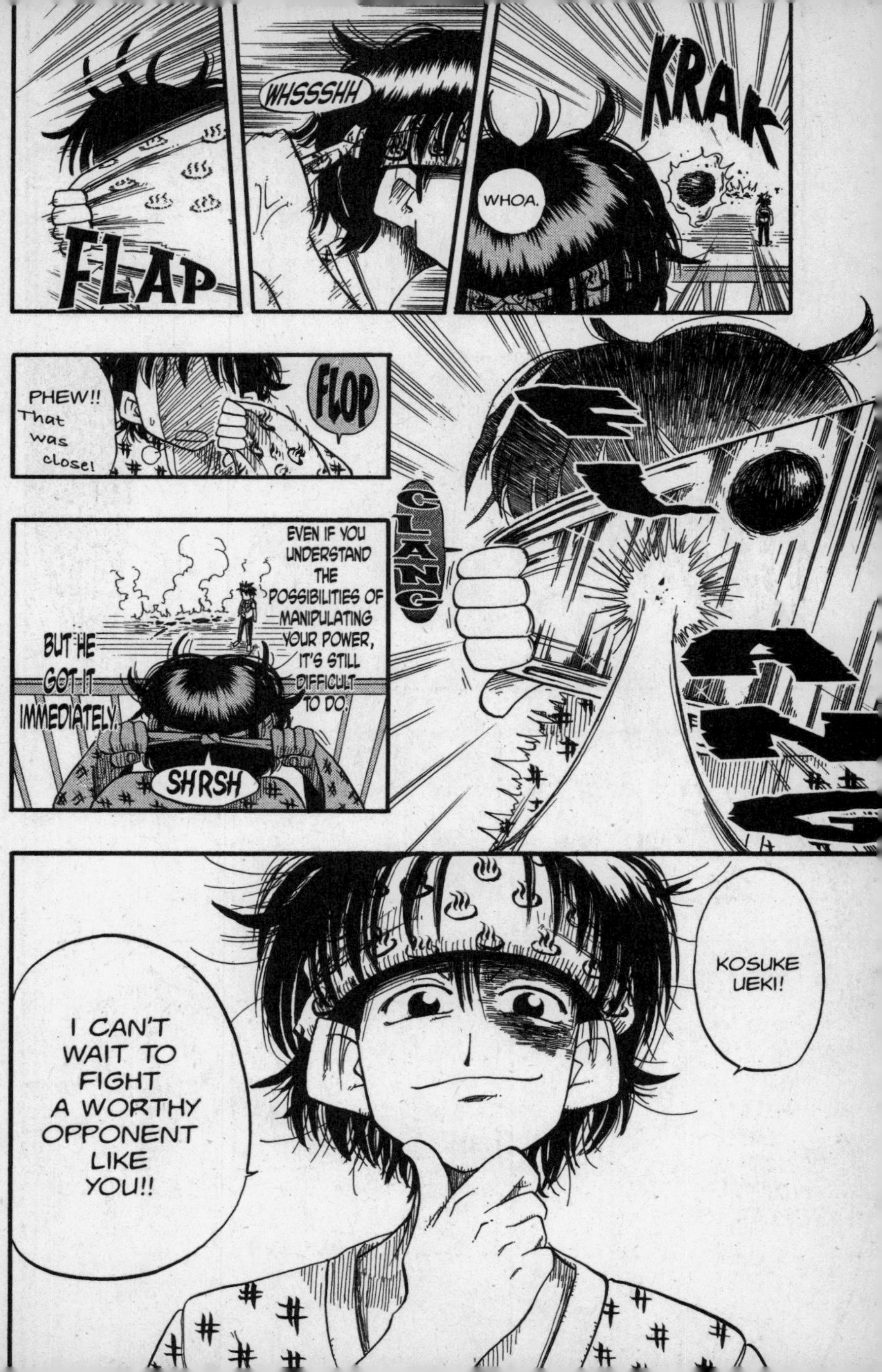
KRAK
WHOA.
WHSSSHH
FLAP
CLANG
FLOP
PHEW!! That was close!
EVEN IF YOU UNDERSTAND THE POSSIBILITIES OF MANIPULATING YOUR POWER, IT'S STILL DIFFICULT TO DO.
BUT HE GOT IT IMMEDIATELY.
SHRSH
KOSUKE UEKI!
I CAN'T WAIT TO FIGHT A WORTHY OPPONENT LIKE YOU!!

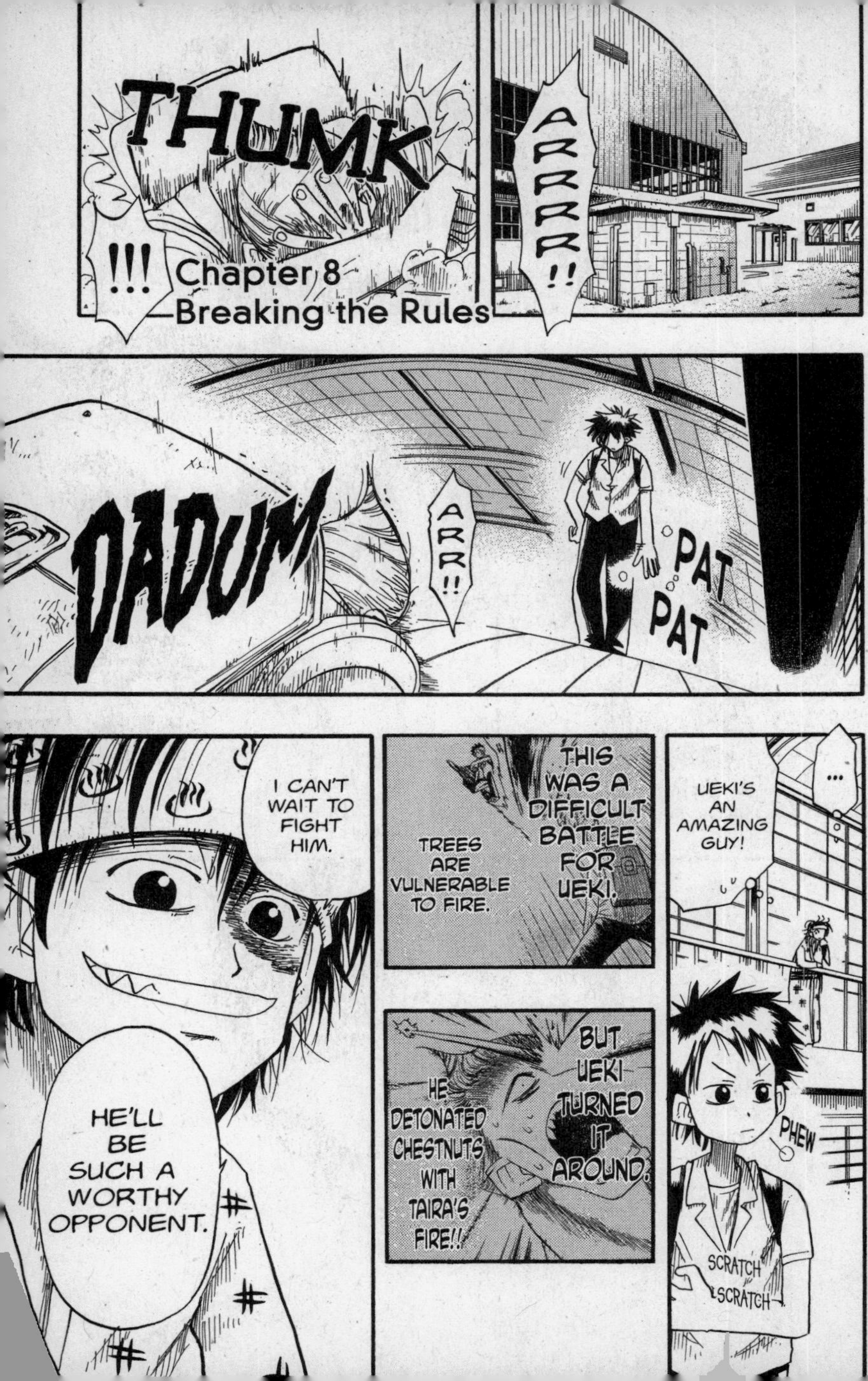
ARRRRR!!
THUMK
!!!
Chapter 8
Breaking the Rules
PAT PAT
ARR!!
DADUM
...
UEKI'S AN AMAZING GUY!
PHEW
SCRATCH SCRATCH
THIS WAS A DIFFICULT BATTLE FOR UEKI.
TREES ARE VULNERABLE TO FIRE.
BUT UEKI TURNED IT AROUND.
HE DETONATED CHESTNUTS WITH TAIRA'S FIRE!!
I CAN'T WAIT TO FIGHT HIM.
HE'LL BE SUCH A WORTHY OPPONENT.

Chapter 8
Breaking the Rules

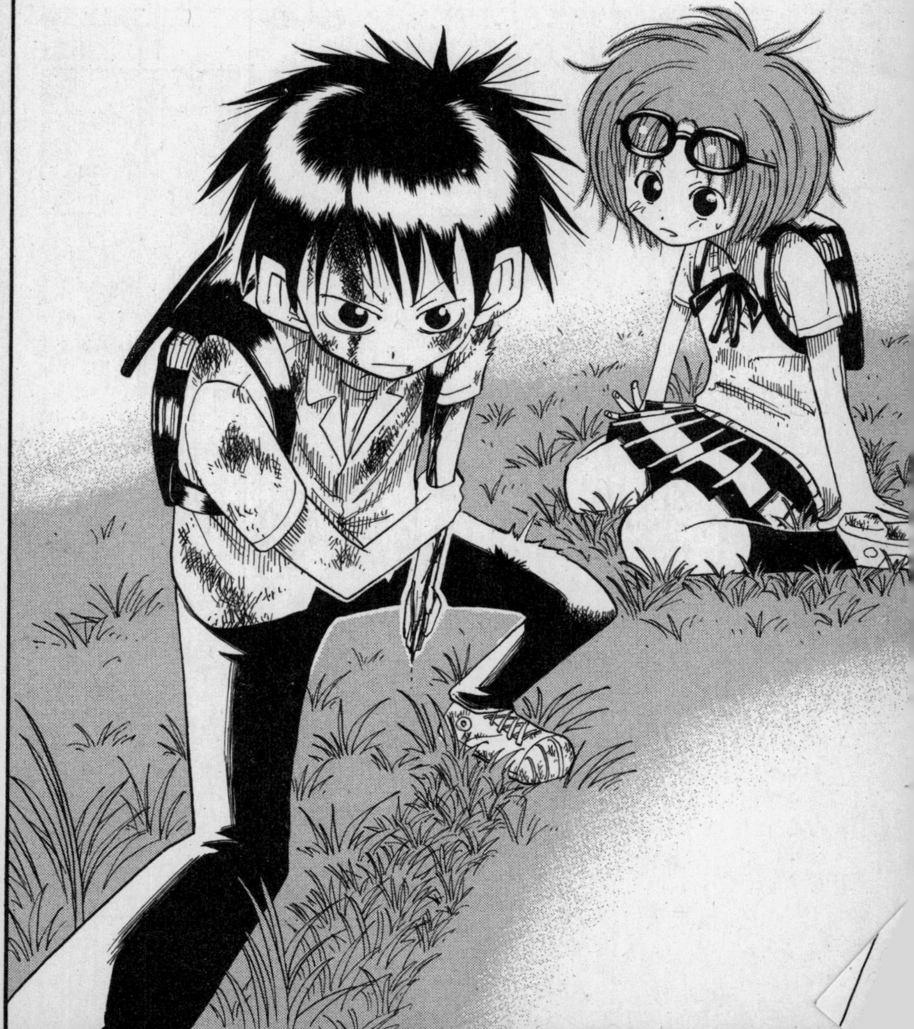

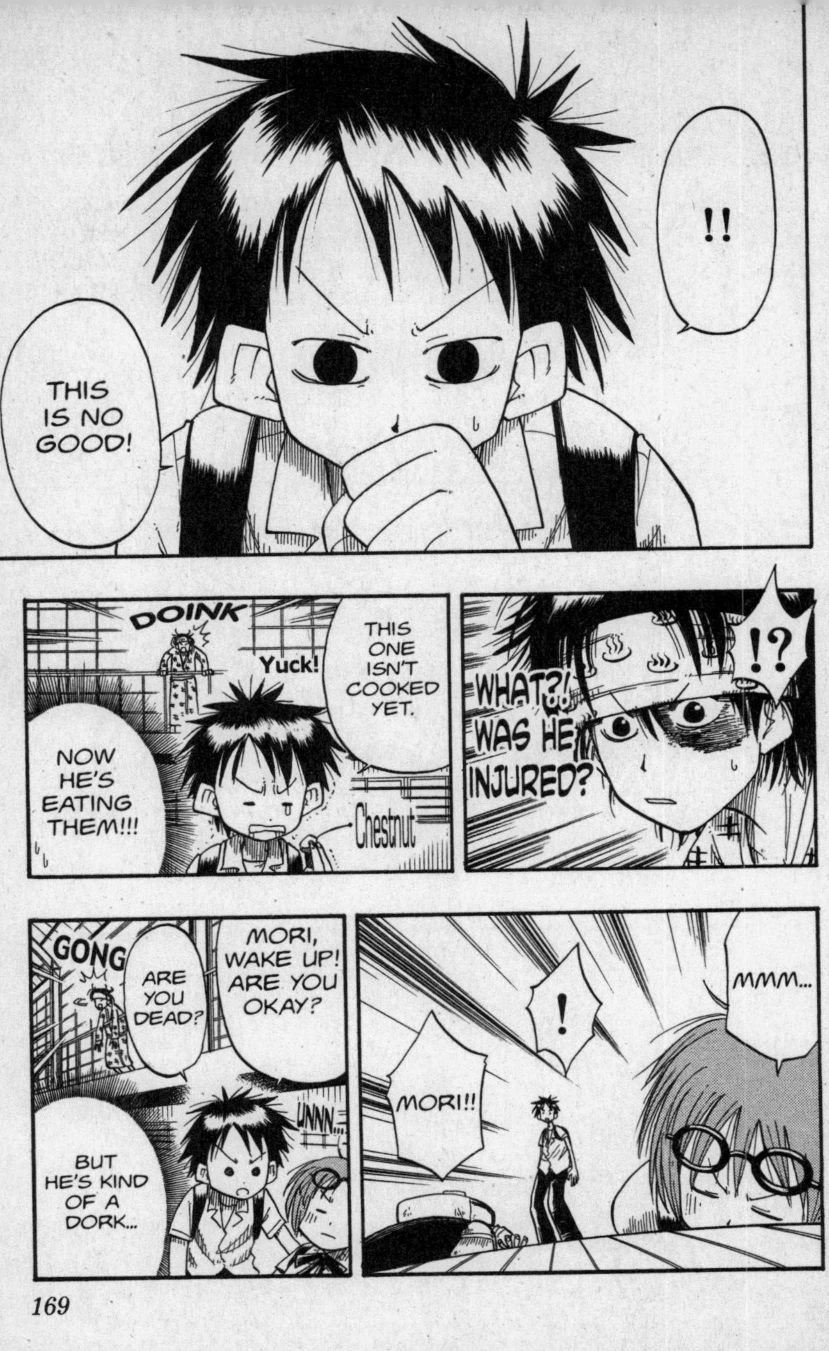
!!
THIS IS NO GOOD!
!?
WHAT?! WAS HE INJURED?
THIS ONE ISN'T COOKED YET.
Yuck!
DOINK
NOW HE'S EATING THEM!!!
Chestnut
MMM...
!
MORI!!
MORI, WAKE UP! ARE YOU OKAY?
ARE YOU DEAD?
GONG
UNNN...
BUT HE'S KIND OF A DORK...

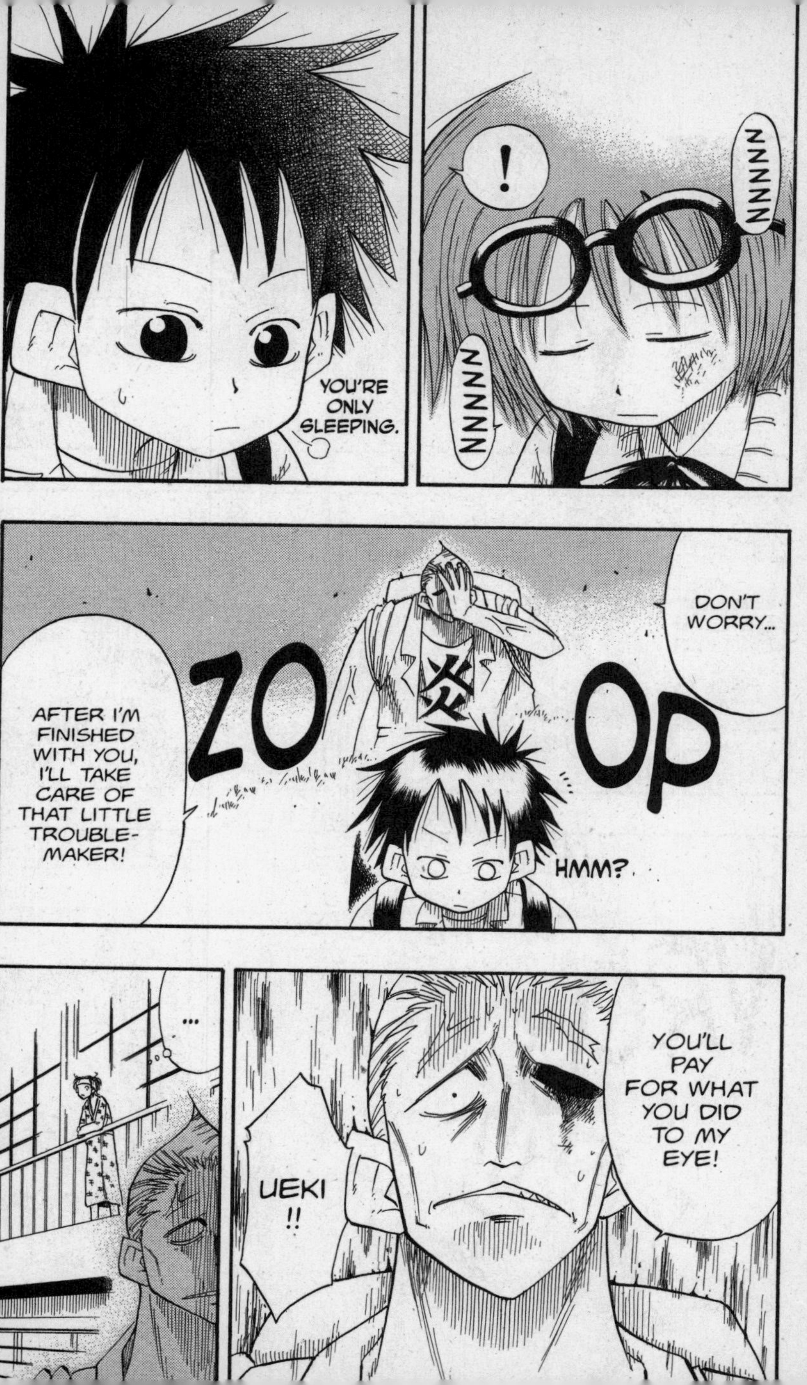
!
NNNNN
NNNNN
YOU'RE ONLY SLEEPING.
DON'T WORRY...
AFTER I'M FINISHED WITH YOU, I'LL TAKE CARE OF THAT LITTLE TROUBLE-MAKER!
ZOOP
HMM?
YOU'LL PAY FOR WHAT YOU DID TO MY EYE!
UEKI !!
...

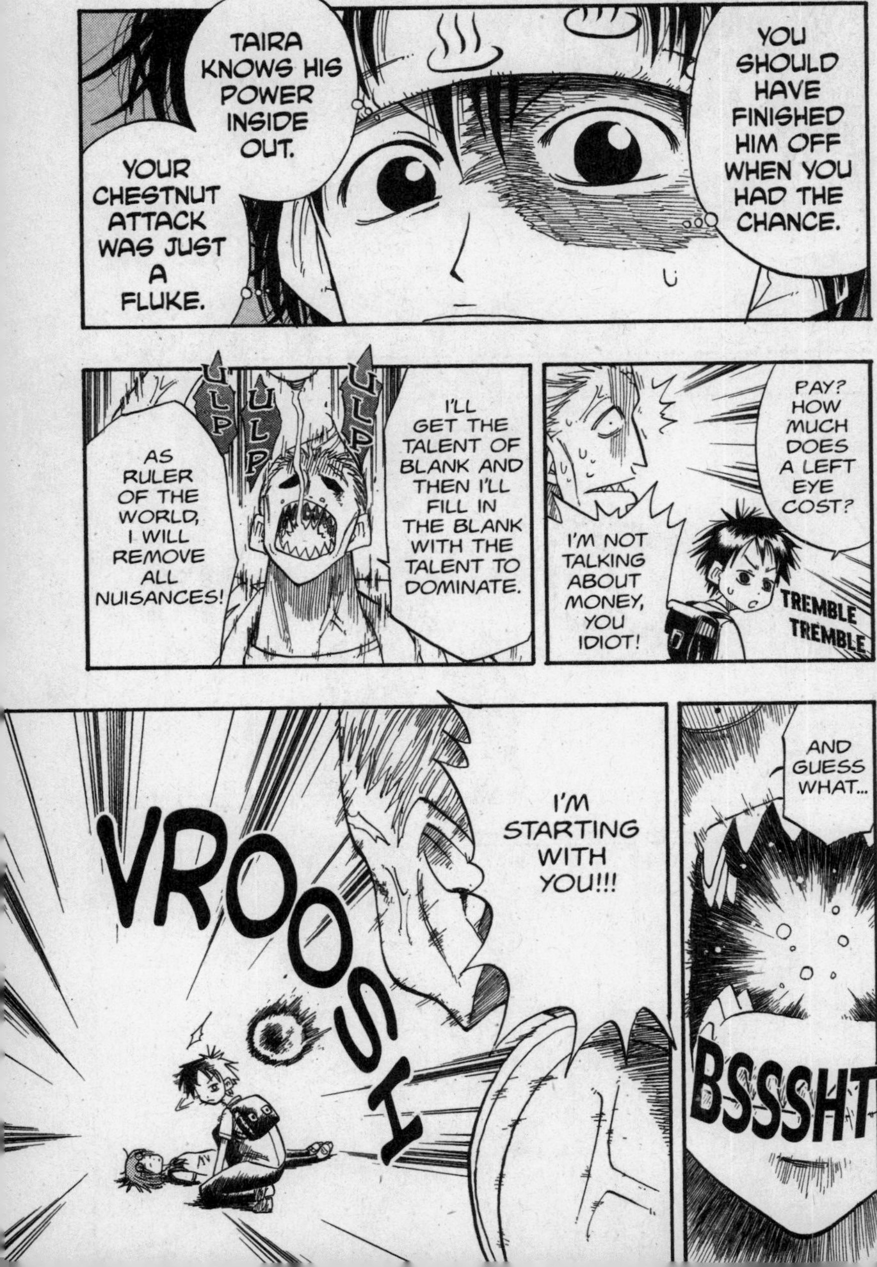
YOU SHOULD HAVE FINISHED HIM OFF WHEN YOU HAD THE CHANCE.
TAIRA KNOWS HIS POWER INSIDE OUT.
YOUR CHESTNUT ATTACK WAS JUST A FLUKE.
PAY? HOW MUCH DOES A LEFT EYE COST?
TREMBLE TREMBLE
I'M NOT TALKING ABOUT MONEY, YOU IDIOT!
ULP ULP ULP
I'LL GET THE TALENT OF BLANK AND THEN I'LL FILL IN THE BLANK WITH THE TALENT TO DOMINATE.
AS RULER OF THE WORLD, I WILL REMOVE ALL NUISANCES!
AND GUESS WHAT...
BSSSHT
I'M STARTING WITH YOU!!!
VROOSH

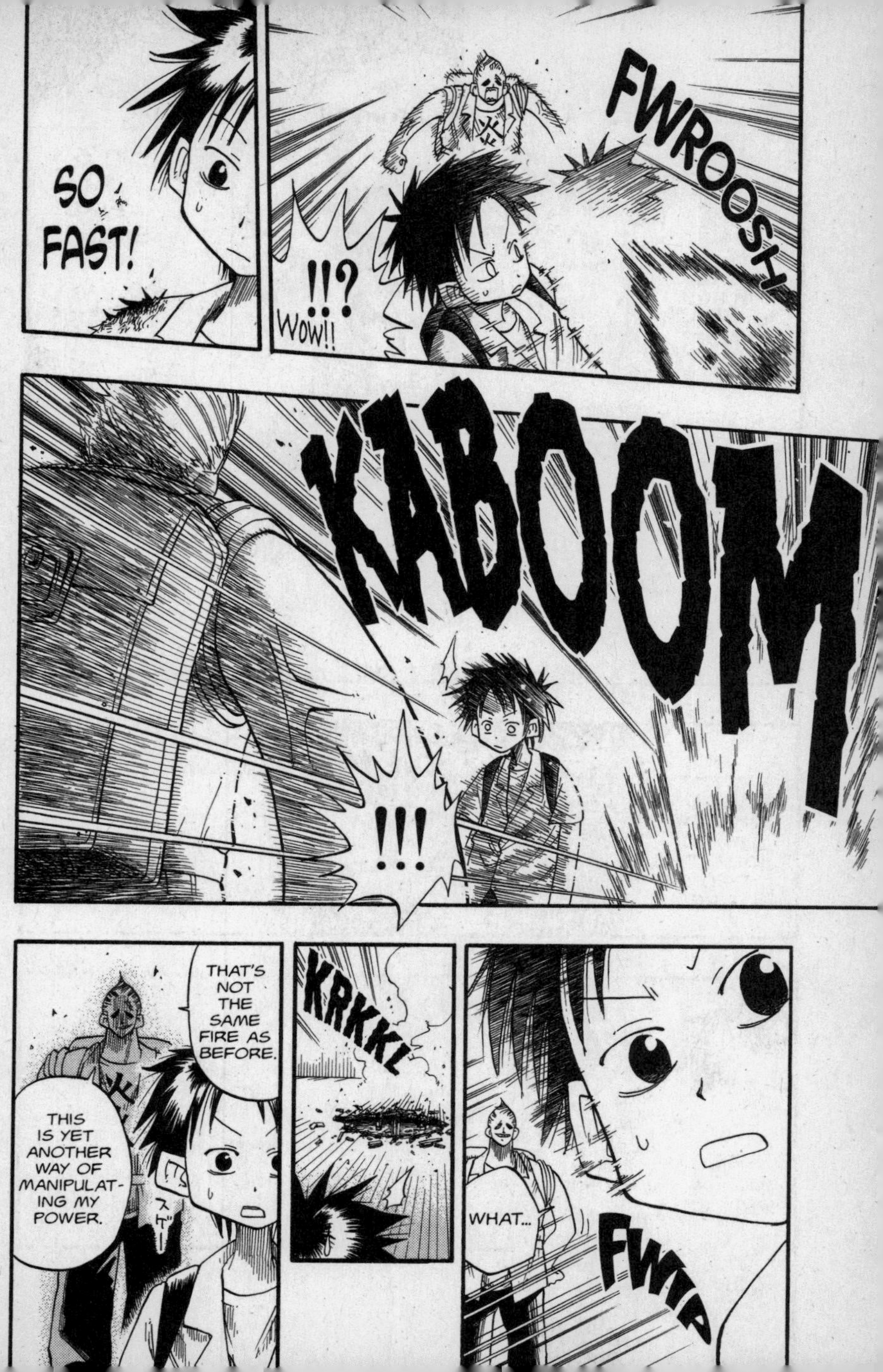
FWROOSH
!!?
WOW!!
SO FAST!
KABOOM
!!!
WHAT...
FWTP
KRKKL
THAT'S NOT THE SAME FIRE AS BEFORE.
THIS IS YET ANOTHER WAY OF MANIPULATING MY POWER.

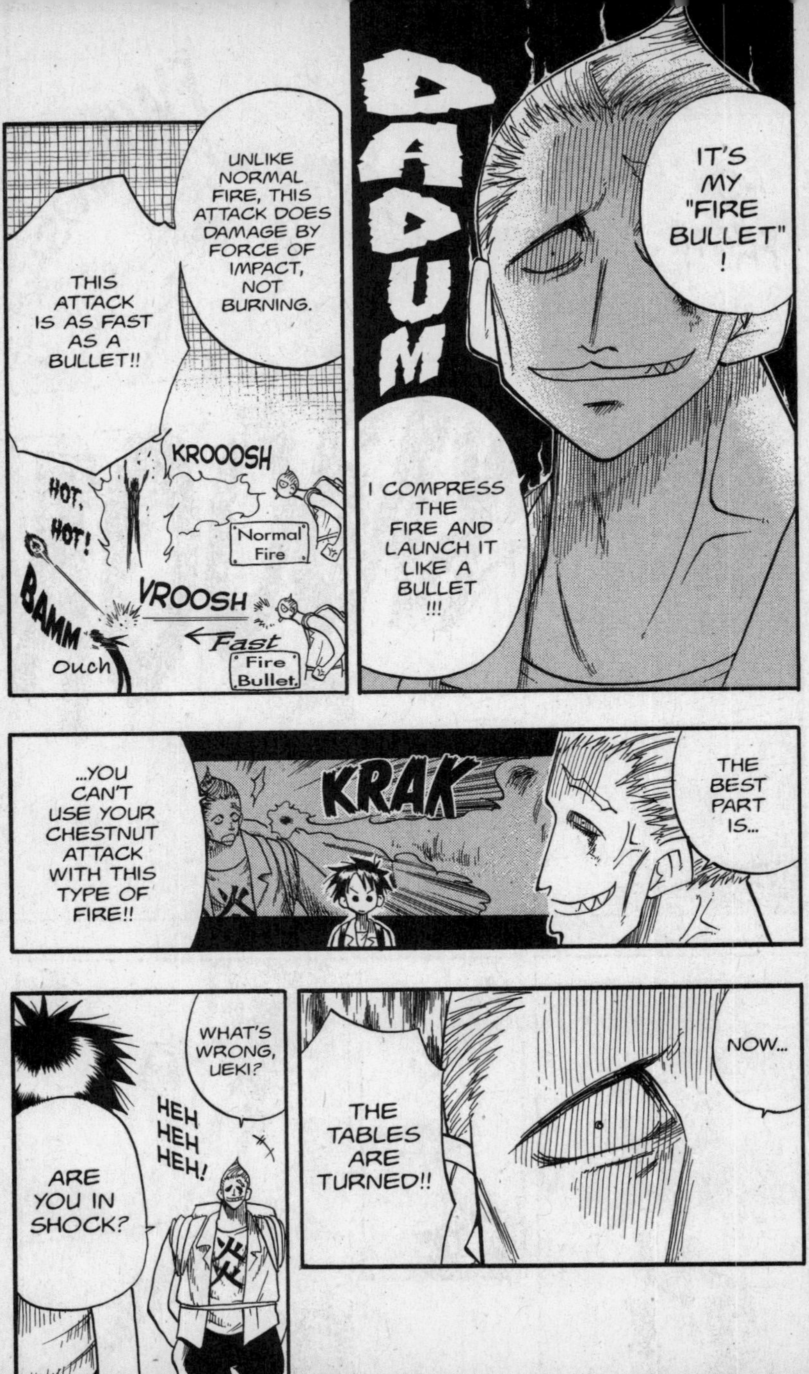
DADUM
IT'S MY "FIRE BULLET"!
I COMPRESS THE FIRE AND LAUNCH IT LIKE A BULLET!!!
UNLIKE NORMAL FIRE, THIS ATTACK DOES DAMAGE BY FORCE OF IMPACT, NOT BURNING.
THIS ATTACK IS AS FAST AS A BULLET!!
KROOOSH
HOT, HOT!
Normal Fire
VROOSH
BAMM
Fast
Fire Bullet
Ouch
THE BEST PART IS...
KRAK
...YOU CAN'T USE YOUR CHESTNUT ATTACK WITH THIS TYPE OF FIRE!!
NOW...
THE TABLES ARE TURNED!!
WHAT'S WRONG, UEKI?
HEH HEH HEH!
ARE YOU IN SHOCK?

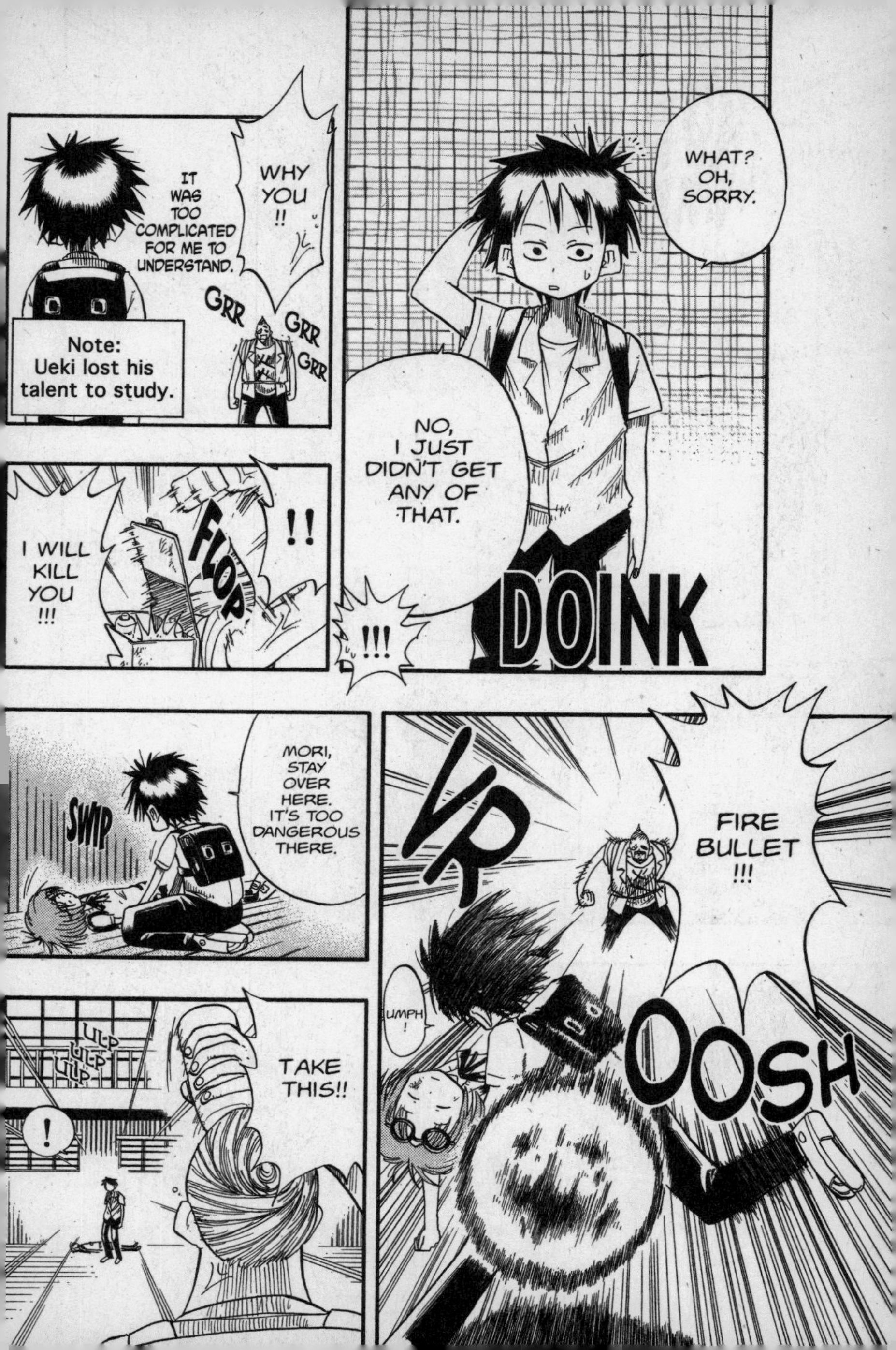
WHAT? OH, SORRY.
NO, I JUST DIDN'T GET ANY OF THAT.
DOINK
!!!
WHY YOU !!
IT WAS TOO COMPLICATED FOR ME TO UNDERSTAND.
GRR
GRR
GRR
Note: Ueki lost his talent to study.
!!
FLOP
I WILL KILL YOU !!!
FIRE BULLET !!!
VR
UMPH !
OOSH
MORI, STAY OVER HERE. IT'S TOO DANGEROUS THERE.
SWIP
TAKE THIS!!
ULP ULP ULP
!

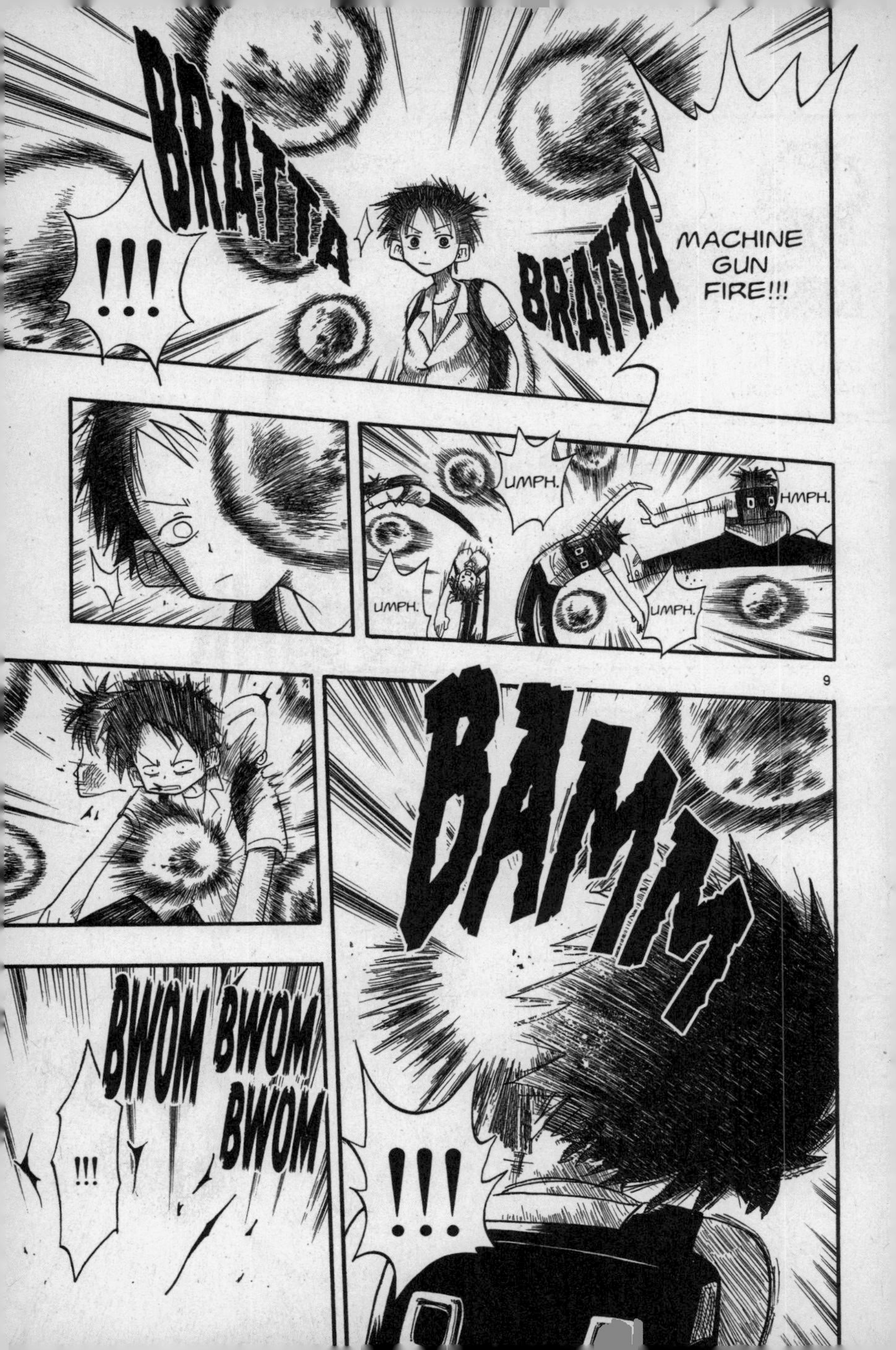
MACHINE GUN FIRE!!!
BRATTA
BRATTA
!!!
HMPH.
UMPH.
UMPH.
UMPH.
BAMM
!!!
BWOM BWOM BWOM
!!!

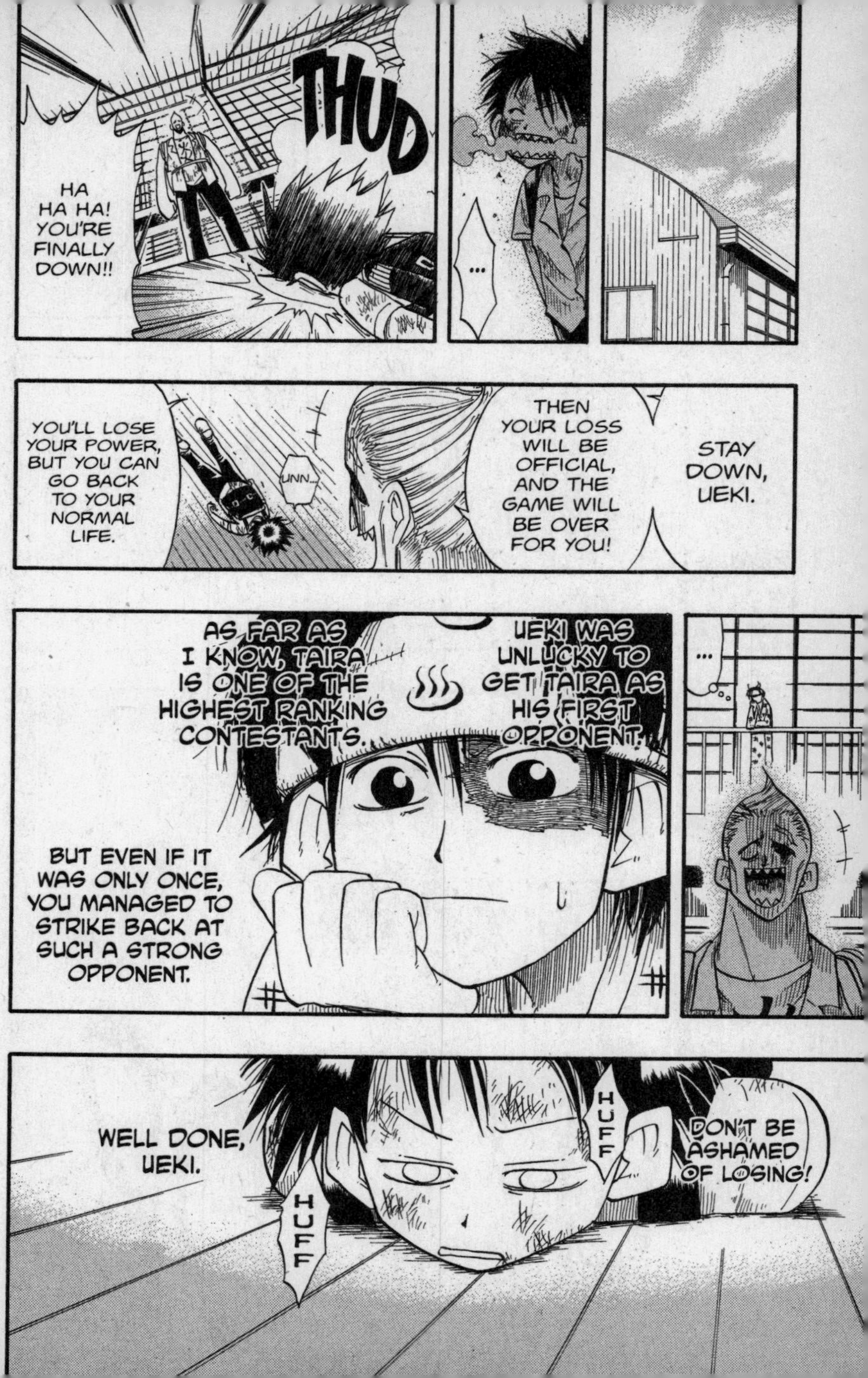
...
THUD
HA HA HA! YOU'RE FINALLY DOWN!!
STAY DOWN, UEKI.
THEN YOUR LOSS WILL BE OFFICIAL, AND THE GAME WILL BE OVER FOR YOU!
UNN...
YOU'LL LOSE YOUR POWER, BUT YOU CAN GO BACK TO YOUR NORMAL LIFE.
...
UEKI WAS UNLUCKY TO GET TAIRA AS HIS FIRST OPPONENT.
AS FAR AS I KNOW, TAIRA IS ONE OF THE HIGHEST RANKING CONTESTANTS.
BUT EVEN IF IT WAS ONLY ONCE, YOU MANAGED TO STRIKE BACK AT SUCH A STRONG OPPONENT.
DON'T BE ASHAMED OF LOSING!
HUFF
HUFF
WELL DONE, UEKI.

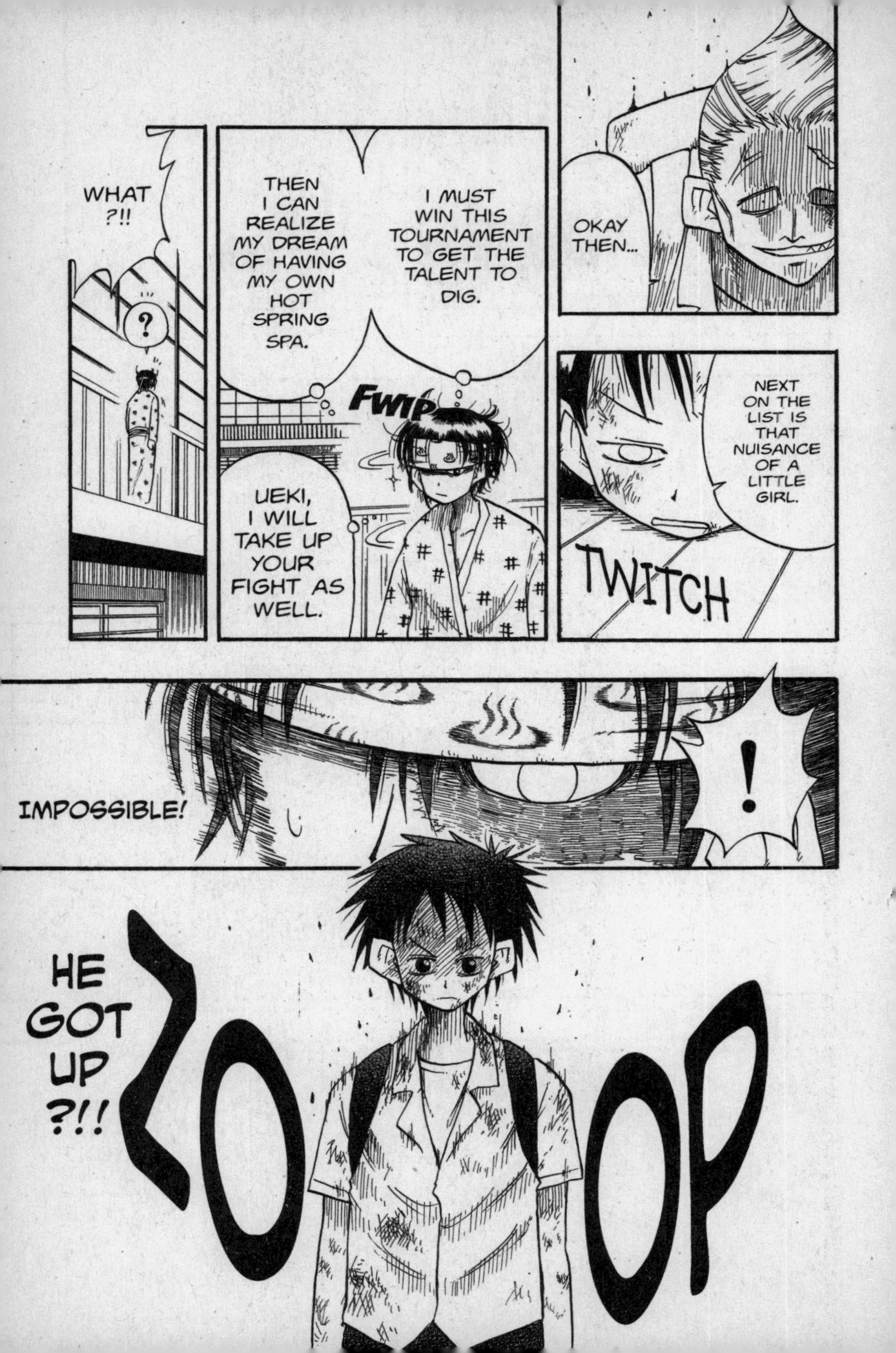
OKAY THEN...
NEXT ON THE LIST IS THAT NUISANCE OF A LITTLE GIRL.
TWITCH
I MUST WIN THIS TOURNAMENT TO GET THE TALENT TO DIG.
THEN I CAN REALIZE MY DREAM OF HAVING MY OWN HOT SPRING SPA.
FWIP
UEKI, I WILL TAKE UP YOUR FIGHT AS WELL.
WHAT ?!!
?
!
IMPOSSIBLE!
HE GOT UP ?!!
ZOOP

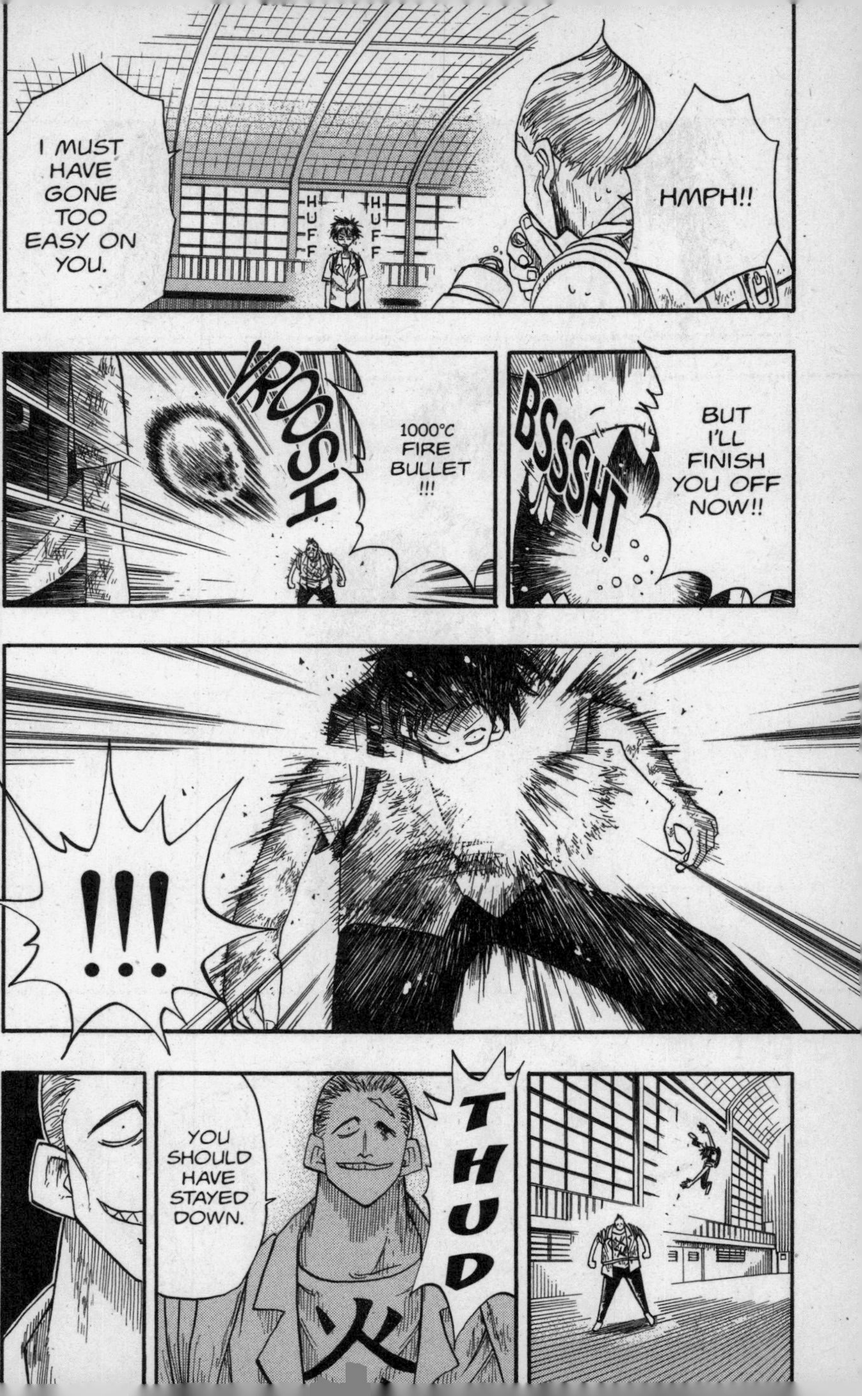
HMPH!!
HUFF
HUFF
I MUST HAVE GONE TOO EASY ON YOU.
BSSSHT
BUT I'LL FINISH YOU OFF NOW!!
VROOSH
1000°C FIRE BULLET !!!
!!!
THUD
YOU SHOULD HAVE STAYED DOWN.

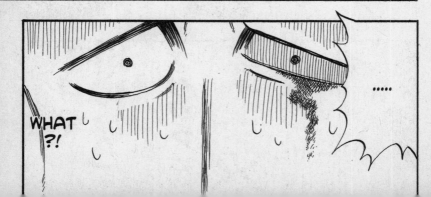

WHAT
?!

.....

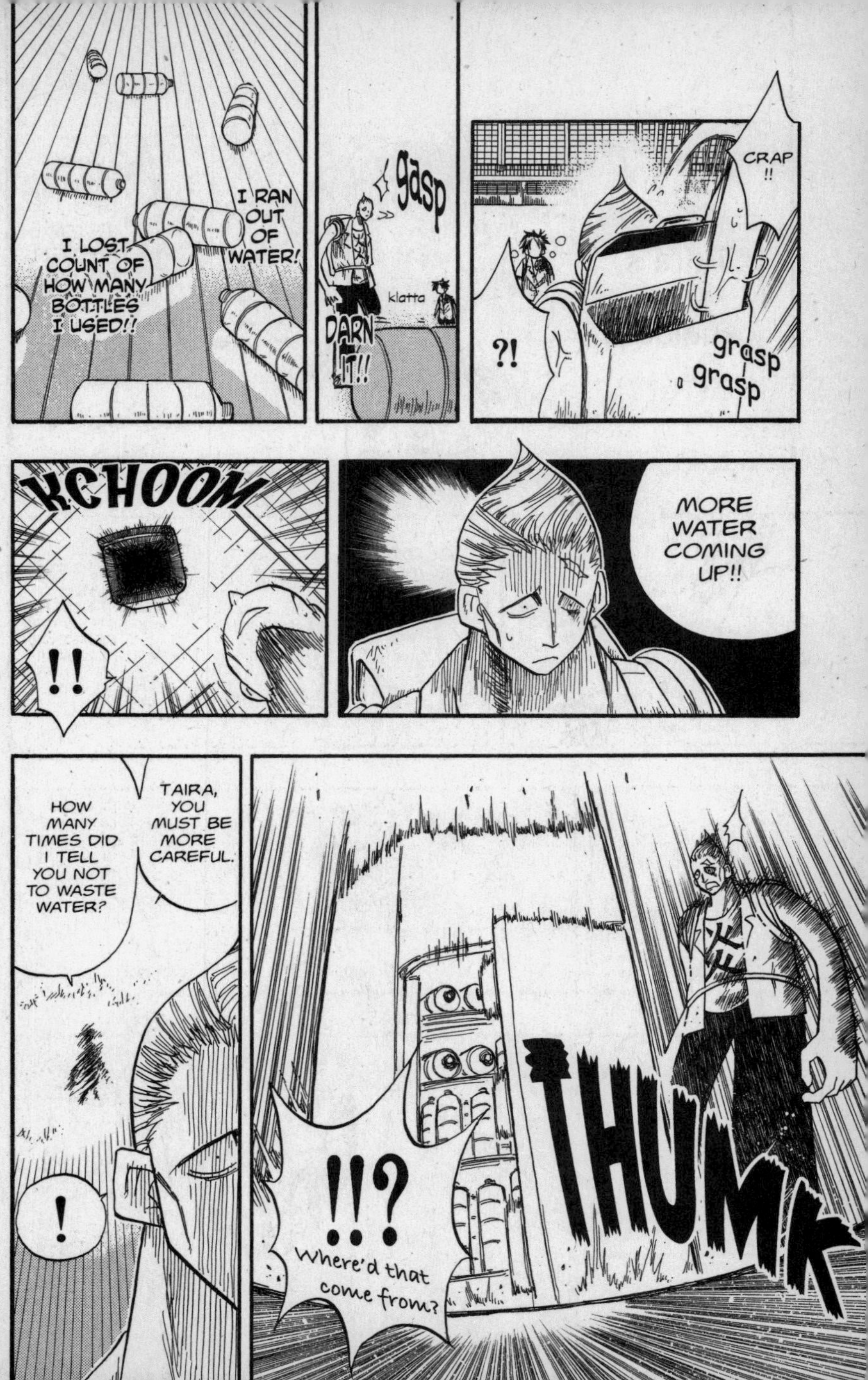
CRAP!!
?!
grasp grasp
gasp
DARN IT!!
klatta
I RAN OUT OF WATER!
I LOST COUNT OF HOW MANY BOTTLES I USED!!
MORE WATER COMING UP!!
KCHOOM
!!
THUMK
!!?
Where'd that come from?
TAIRA, YOU MUST BE MORE CAREFUL.
HOW MANY TIMES DID I TELL YOU NOT TO WASTE WATER?
!

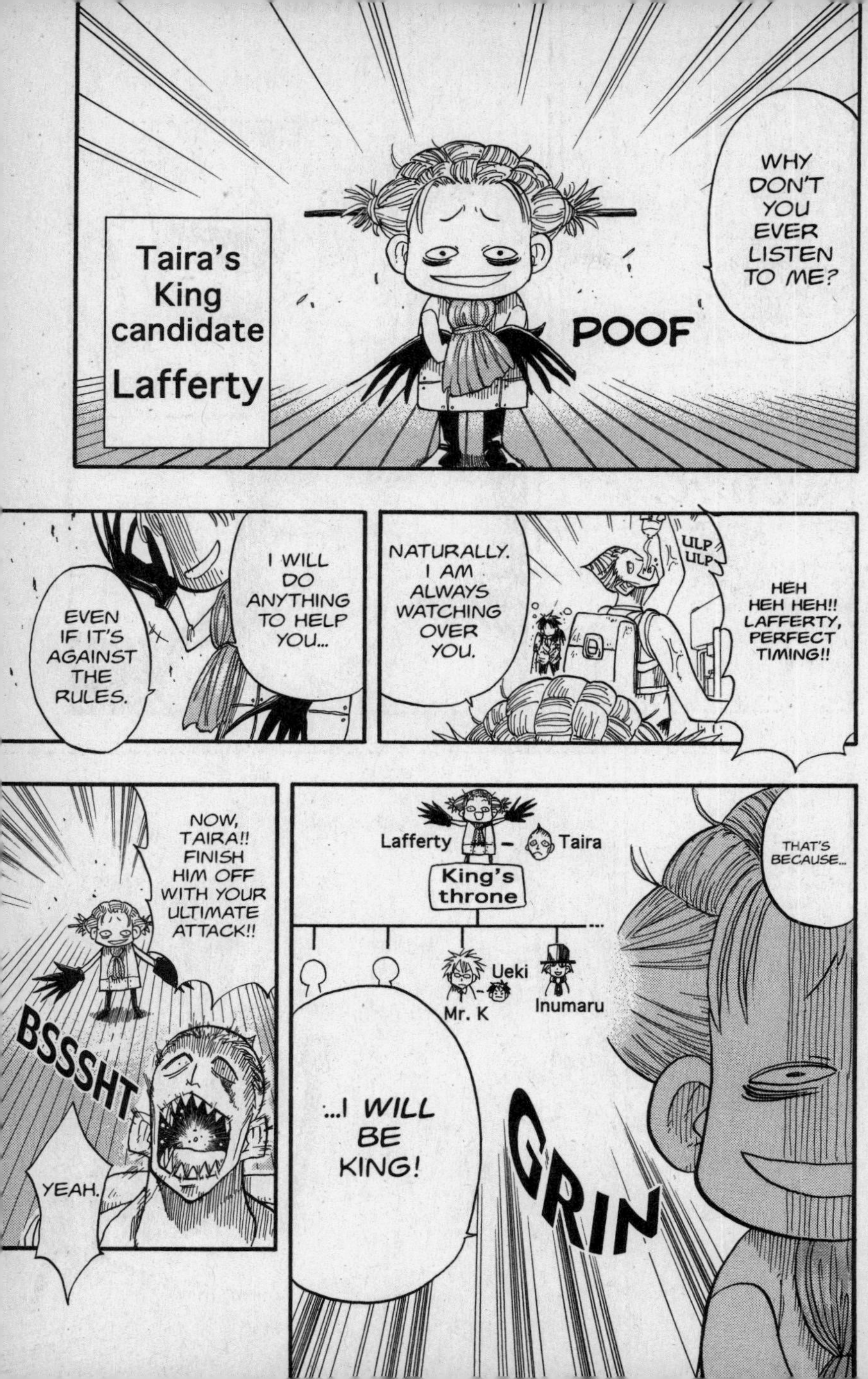
WHY DON'T YOU EVER LISTEN TO ME?
POOF
Taira's King candidate Lafferty
ULP ULP
HEH HEH HEH!! LAFFERTY, PERFECT TIMING!!
NATURALLY. I AM ALWAYS WATCHING OVER YOU.
I WILL DO ANYTHING TO HELP YOU...
EVEN IF IT'S AGAINST THE RULES.
THAT'S BECAUSE...
Lafferty
Taira
King's throne
Ueki
Inumaru
Mr. K
GRIN
...I WILL BE KING!
NOW, TAIRA!! FINISH HIM OFF WITH YOUR ULTIMATE ATTACK!!
BSSSHT
YEAH.

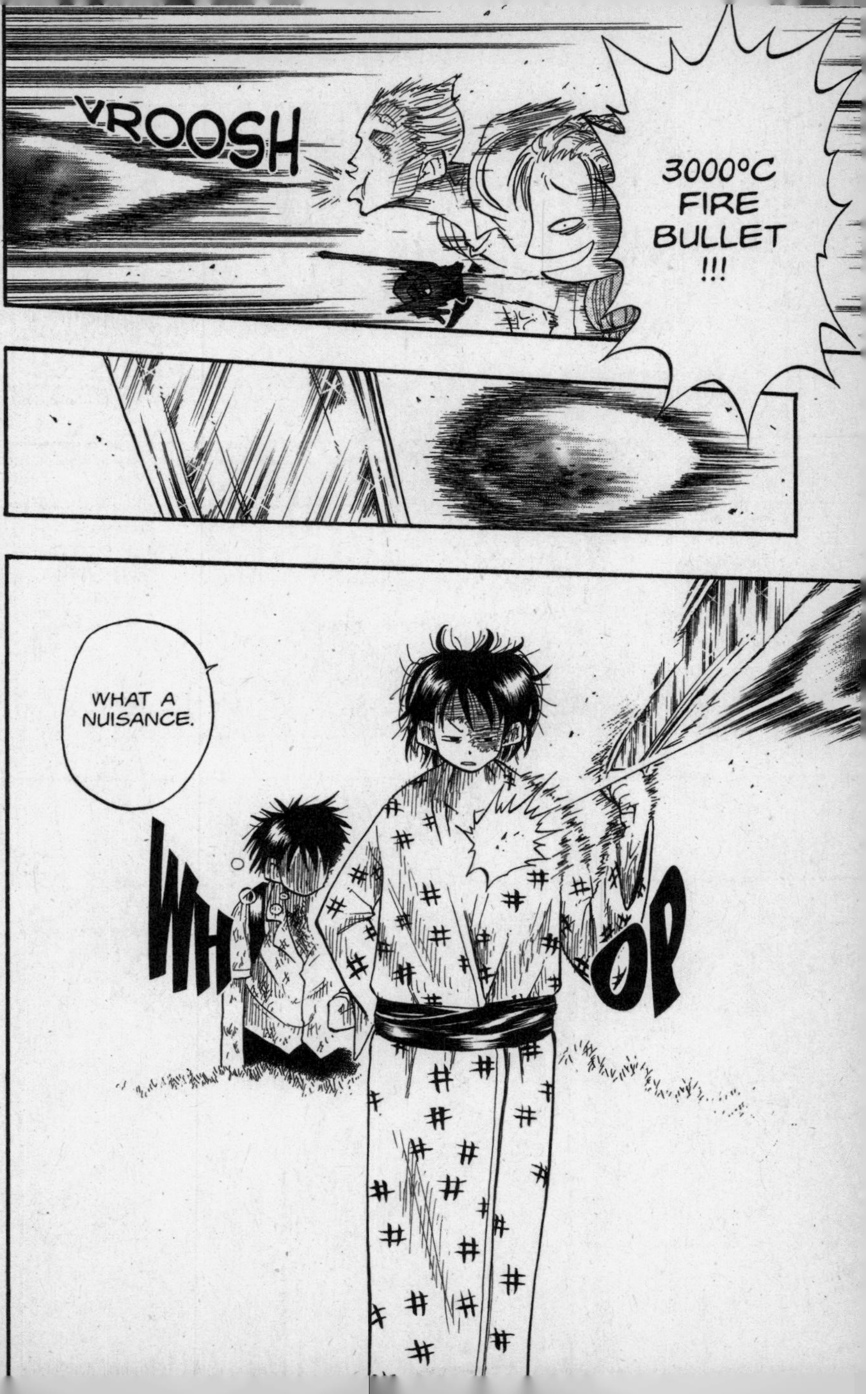
3000°C FIRE BULLET !!!
VROOSH
WHAT A NUISANCE.
WH OP

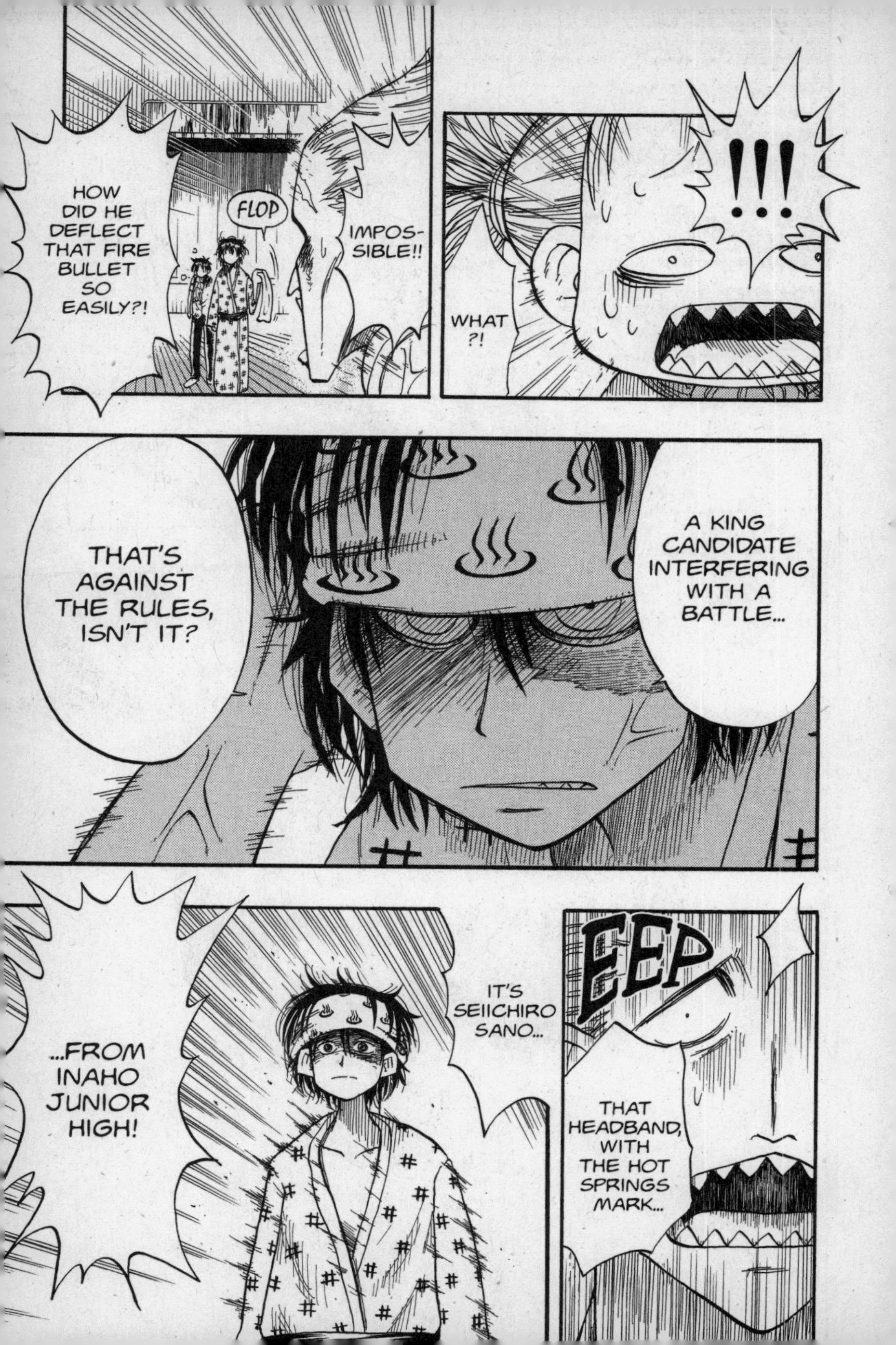
!!!
WHAT ?!
IMPOS-SIBLE!!
FLOP
HOW DID HE DEFLECT THAT FIRE BULLET SO EASILY?!
A KING CANDIDATE INTERFERING WITH A BATTLE...
THAT'S AGAINST THE RULES, ISN'T IT?
EEP
THAT HEADBAND, WITH THE HOT SPRINGS MARK...
IT'S SEIICHIRO SANO...
...FROM INAHO JUNIOR HIGH!

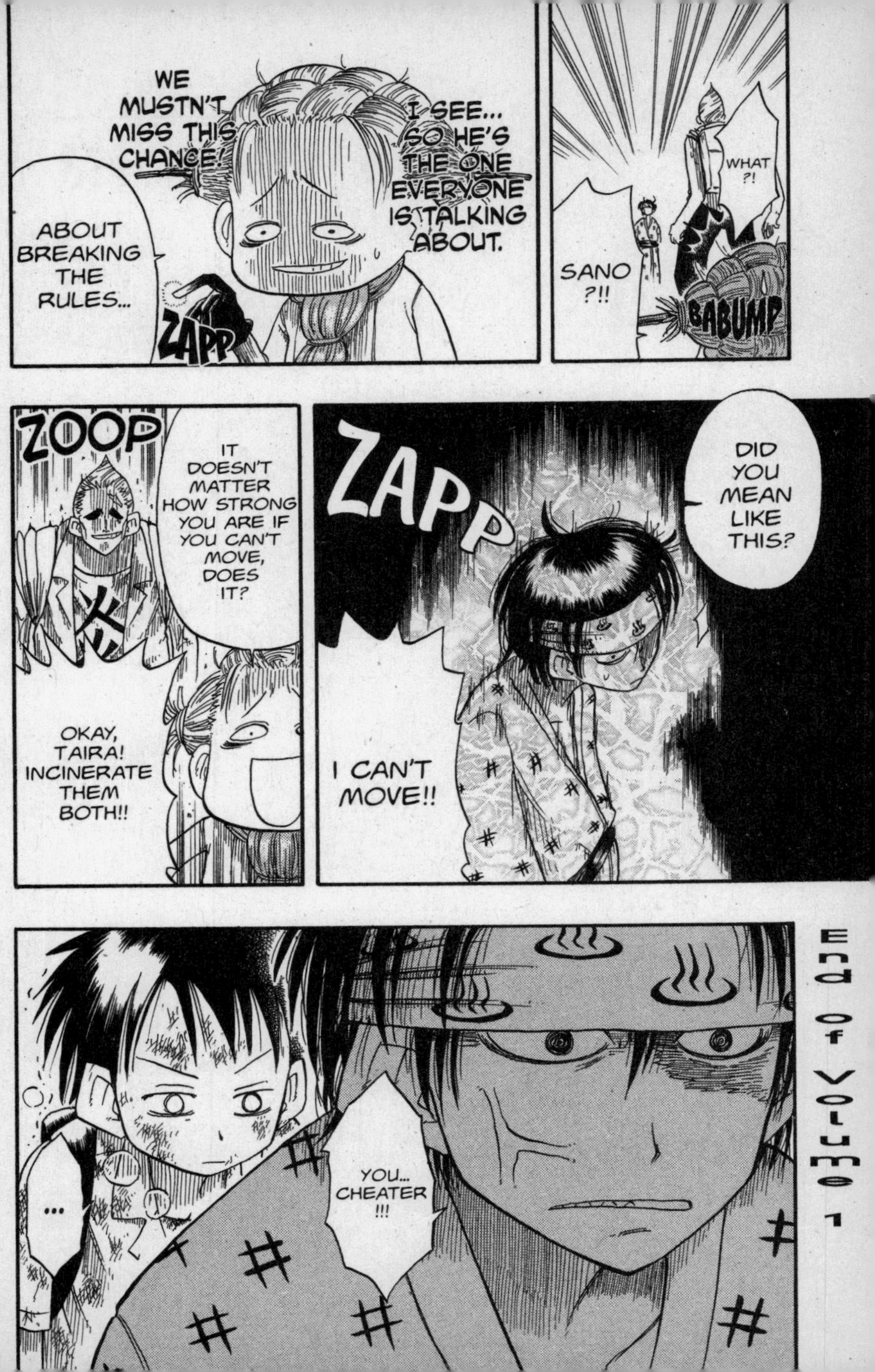
WHAT ?!
SANO ?!!
BABUMP
I SEE... SO HE'S THE ONE EVERYONE IS TALKING ABOUT.
WE MUSTN'T MISS THIS CHANCE!
ABOUT BREAKING THE RULES...
ZAPP
DID YOU MEAN LIKE THIS?
ZAPP
I CAN'T MOVE!!
ZOOP
IT DOESN'T MATTER HOW STRONG YOU ARE IF YOU CAN'T MOVE, DOES IT?
OKAY, TAIRA! INCINERATE THEM BOTH!!
YOU... CHEATER !!!
...
End of Volume 1

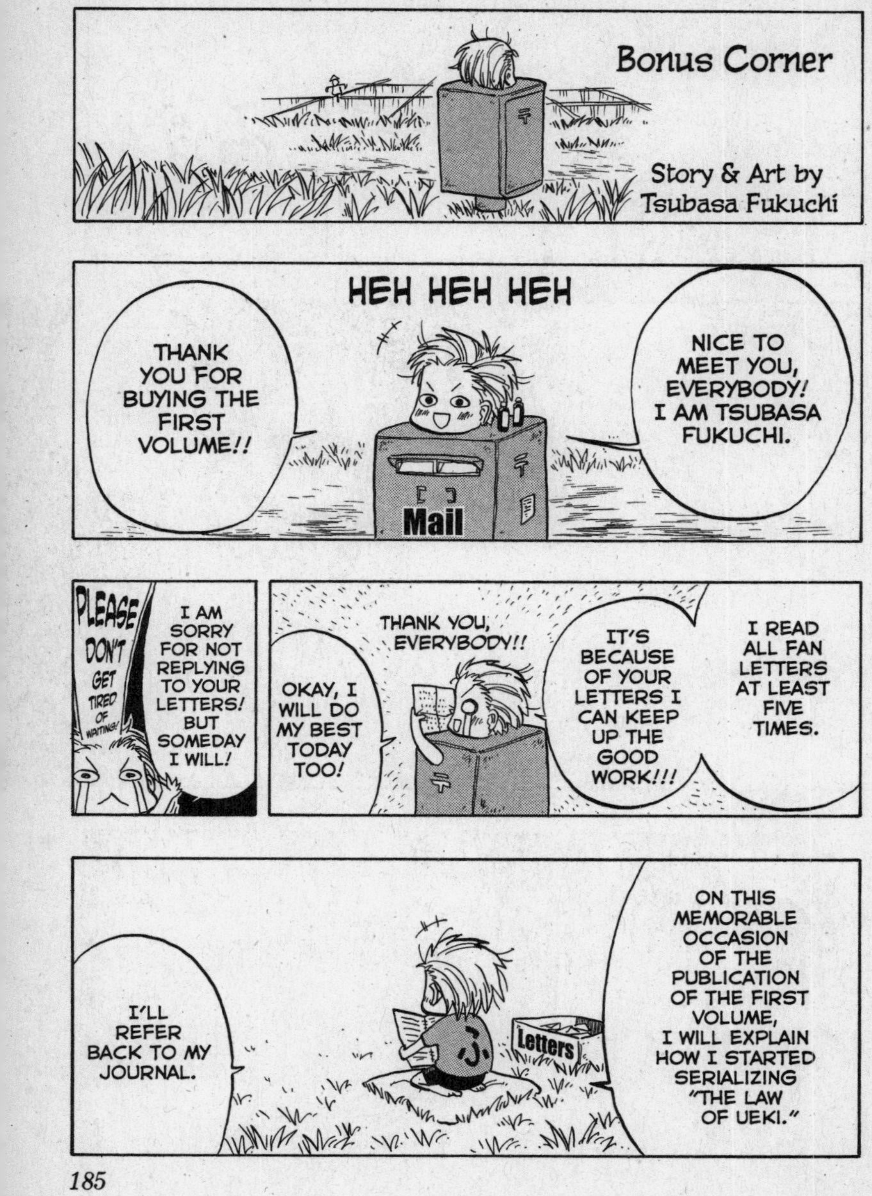
Bonus Corner
Story & Art by Tsubasa Fukuchi
NICE TO MEET YOU, EVERYBODY! I AM TSUBASA FUKUCHI.
HEH HEH HEH
Mail
THANK YOU FOR BUYING THE FIRST VOLUME!!
I READ ALL FAN LETTERS AT LEAST FIVE TIMES.
IT'S BECAUSE OF YOUR LETTERS I CAN KEEP UP THE GOOD WORK!!!
THANK YOU, EVERYBODY!!
OKAY, I WILL DO MY BEST TODAY TOO!
I AM SORRY FOR NOT REPLYING TO YOUR LETTERS! BUT SOMEDAY I WILL!
PLEASE DON'T GET TIRED OF WAITING!
ON THIS MEMORABLE OCCASION OF THE PUBLICATION OF THE FIRST VOLUME, I WILL EXPLAIN HOW I STARTED SERIALIZING "THE LAW OF UEKI."
Letters
I'LL REFER BACK TO MY JOURNAL.

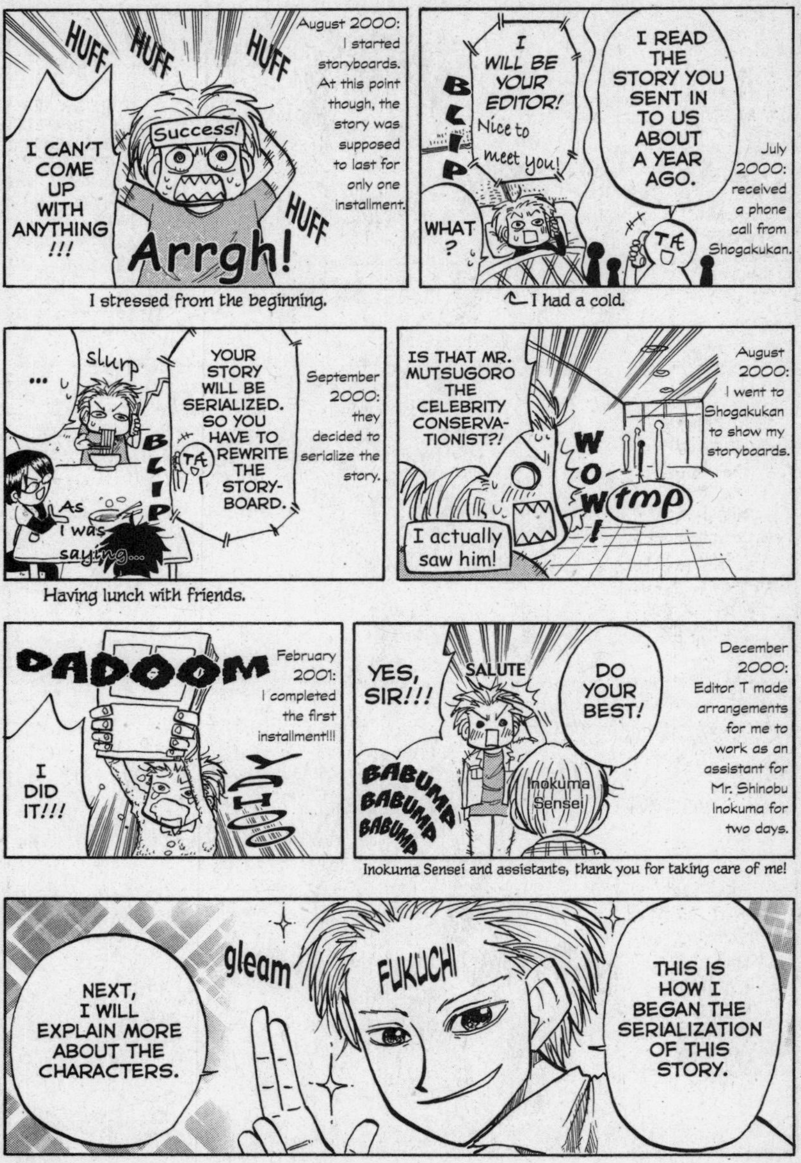
July 2000: received a phone call from Shogakukan.
I READ THE STORY YOU SENT IN TO US ABOUT A YEAR AGO.
I WILL BE YOUR EDITOR! Nice to meet you!
BLIP
WHAT?
TÆ
I had a cold.
August 2000: I started storyboards. At this point though, the story was supposed to last for only one installment.
HUFF HUFF HUFF
HUFF
Success!
I CAN'T COME UP WITH ANYTHING!!!
Arrgh!
I stressed from the beginning.
August 2000: I went to Shogakukan to show my storyboards.
IS THAT MR. MUTSUGORO THE CELEBRITY CONSERVATIONIST?!
WOW!
tmp
I actually saw him!
September 2000: they decided to serialize the story.
YOUR STORY WILL BE SERIALIZED. SO YOU HAVE TO REWRITE THE STORYBOARD.
slurp
...
BLIP
TÆ
As I was saying...
Having lunch with friends.
December 2000: Editor T made arrangements for me to work as an assistant for Mr. Shinobu Inokuma for two days.
DO YOUR BEST!
SALUTE
YES, SIR!!!
BABUMP BABUMP BABUMP
Inokuma Sensei
Inokuma Sensei and assistants, thank you for taking care of me!
February 2001: I completed the first installment!!!
DADOOM
YAHOO
I DID IT!!!
THIS IS HOW I BEGAN THE SERIALIZATION OF THIS STORY.
FUKUCHI
gleam
NEXT, I WILL EXPLAIN MORE ABOUT THE CHARACTERS.

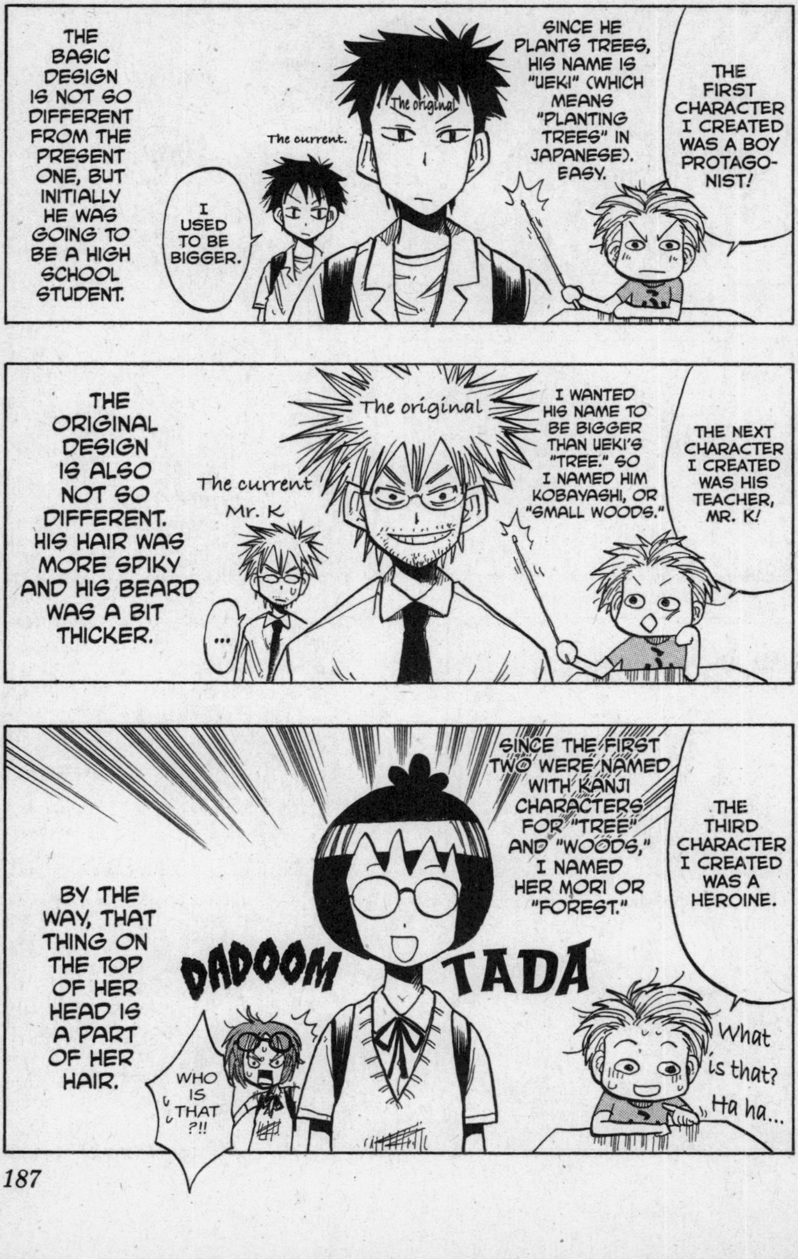

THE FIRST CHARACTER I CREATED WAS A BOY PROTAGONIST!
SINCE HE PLANTS TREES, HIS NAME IS "UEKI" (WHICH MEANS "PLANTING TREES" IN JAPANESE). EASY.
The original
The current.
I USED TO BE BIGGER.
THE BASIC DESIGN IS NOT SO DIFFERENT FROM THE PRESENT ONE, BUT INITIALLY HE WAS GOING TO BE A HIGH SCHOOL STUDENT.
THE NEXT CHARACTER I CREATED WAS HIS TEACHER, MR. K!
I WANTED HIS NAME TO BE BIGGER THAN UEKI'S "TREE." SO I NAMED HIM KOBAYASHI, OR "SMALL WOODS."
The original
The current Mr. K
...
THE ORIGINAL DESIGN IS ALSO NOT SO DIFFERENT. HIS HAIR WAS MORE SPIKY AND HIS BEARD WAS A BIT THICKER.
THE THIRD CHARACTER I CREATED WAS A HEROINE.
SINCE THE FIRST TWO WERE NAMED WITH KANJI CHARACTERS FOR "TREE" AND "WOODS," I NAMED HER MORI OR "FOREST."
What is that? Ha ha...
TADA
DADOOM
WHO IS THAT ?!!
BY THE WAY, THAT THING ON THE TOP OF HER HEAD IS A PART OF HER HAIR.

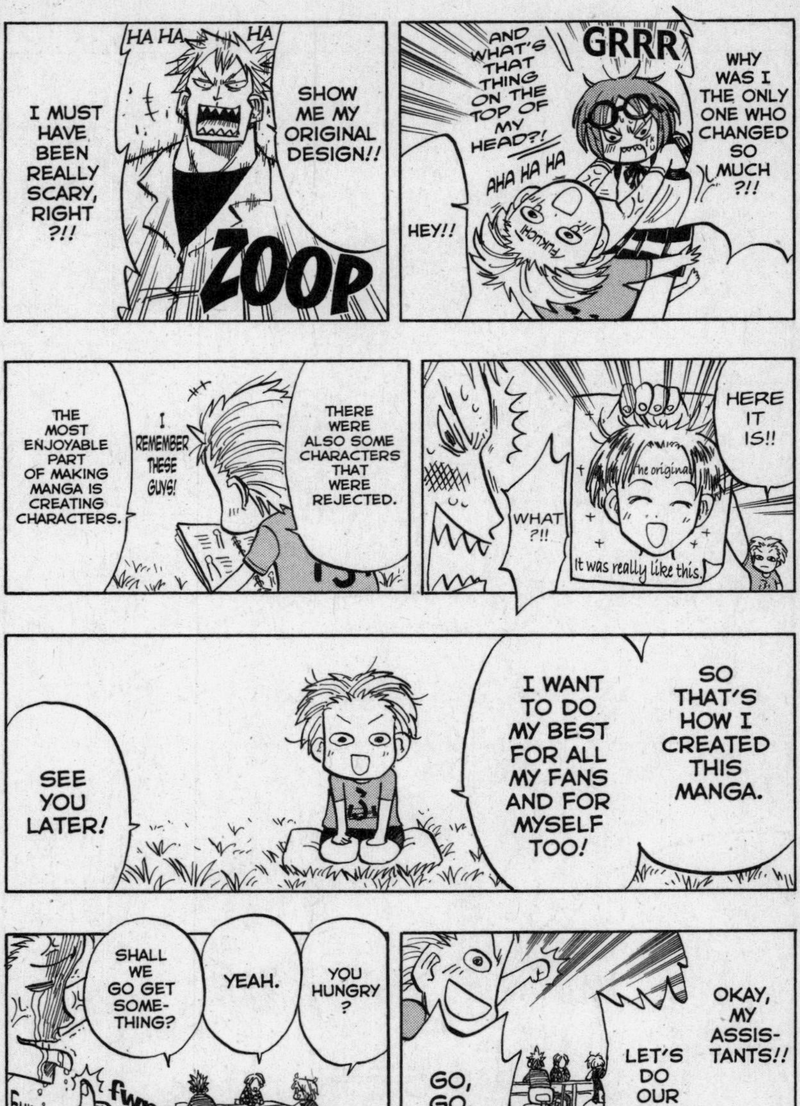
WHY WAS I THE ONLY ONE WHO CHANGED SO MUCH ?!!
GRRR
AND WHAT'S THAT THING ON THE TOP OF MY HEAD?!
AHA HA HA
FUKUCHI
HEY!!
SHOW ME MY ORIGINAL DESIGN!!
HA HA HA
ZOOP
I MUST HAVE BEEN REALLY SCARY, RIGHT ?!!
HERE IT IS!!
The original
It was really like this.
WHAT ?!!
THERE WERE ALSO SOME CHARACTERS THAT WERE REJECTED.
I REMEMBER THESE GUYS!
THE MOST ENJOYABLE PART OF MAKING MANGA IS CREATING CHARACTERS.
SO THAT'S HOW I CREATED THIS MANGA.
I WANT TO DO MY BEST FOR ALL MY FANS AND FOR MYSELF TOO!
SEE YOU LATER!
OKAY, MY ASSIS-TANTS!!
LET'S DO OUR BEST!!
GO, GO, GO!!
YOU HUNGRY ?
YEAH.
SHALL WE GO GET SOME-THING?
fwp
Funny.

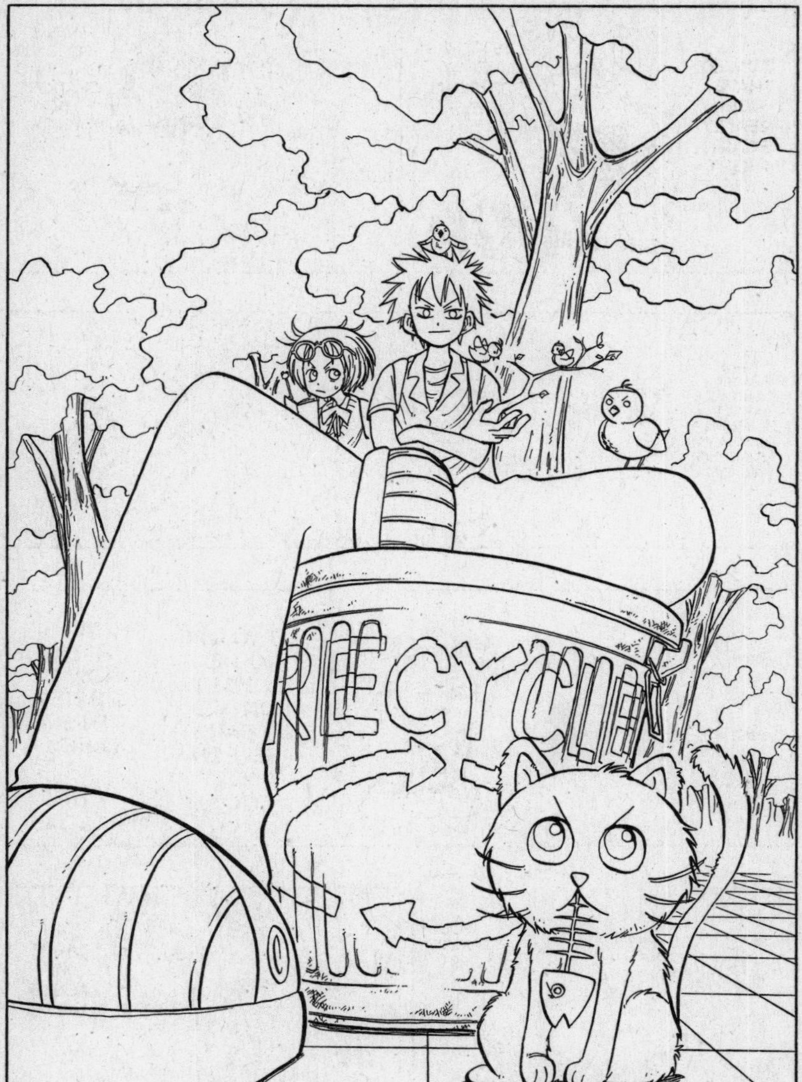

scribble
—scribble
creator
SNORE

When I was a kid, I used to draw
all sorts of characters. They could
fly around, I would create allies for
them, and they'd fight against the
bad guys. It'd be great if I get to
draw characters like that for this
manga.

DIFFERENT LAWS

THE LAW THAT STATES THAT YOU GET SLEEPY AS SOON AS YOU PICK UP A PEN.
sleepy ME sleepy
A CLOSE UP OF UEKI SHOULD GO HERE.
UEKI'S FACE...
Hey, Mori!
DUH!
A FEW MINUTES LATER.
MORI!
Hey, Mori!
ARRRGH!!!!
Assistants!!!
WHAT'S WRONG ?!

The Law of Ueki ①

STORY AND ART BY TSUBASA FUKUCHI
VIZ Media Edition

Translation & Adaptation/Yoshiko Tokuhara
and Filomila Papakonstantinou
Touch-up Art & Lettering/Avril Averill
Cover Design & Graphic Layout/Amy Martin
Editor/Andy Nakatani

Managing Editor/Annette Roman
Editorial Director/Elizabeth Kawasaki
Editor in Chief/Alvin Lu
Sr. Director of Acquisitions/Rika Inouye
Senior VP of Marketing/Liza Coppola
Exec. VP of Sales & Marketing/John Easum
Publisher/Hyoe Narita

Printed in the U.S.A.

Published by VIZ Media, LLC
P.O. Box 77010
San Francisco, CA 94107

VIZ Media Edition
10 9 8 7 6 5 4 3 2 1
First printing, August 2006

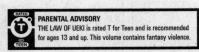

www.viz.com

store.viz.com

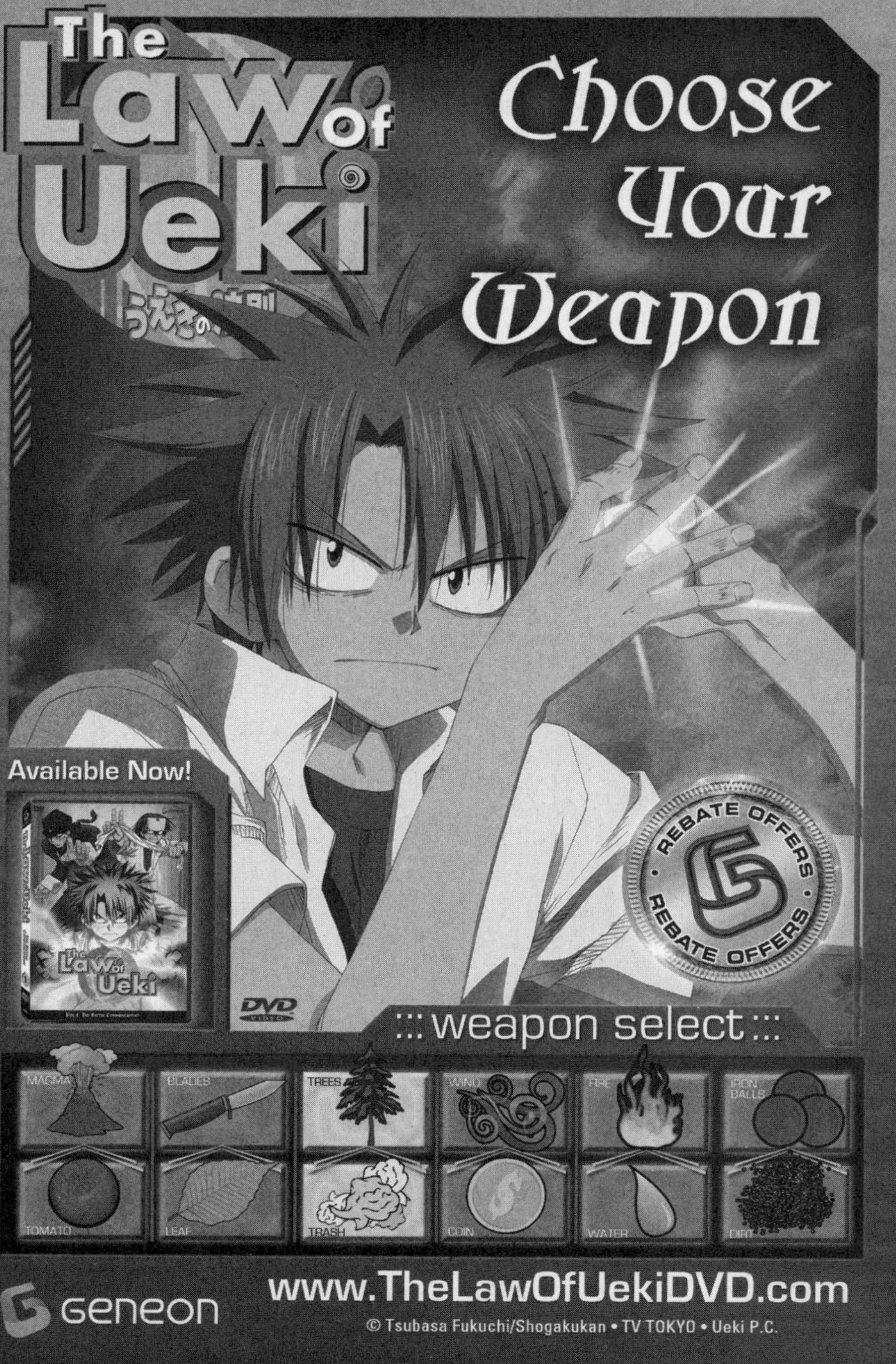
The Law of Ueki
Choose Your Weapon
Available Now!
DVD
REBATE OFFERS
::: weapon select :::
MAGMA
BLADES
TREES
WIND
FIRE
IRON BALLS
TOMATO
LEAF
TRASH
COIN
WATER
DIRT
www.TheLawOfUekiDVD.com
GENEON
© Tsubasa Fukuchi/Shogakukan • TV TOKYO • Ueki P.C.

Half Human, Half

When Kagome discovers a well that transports her to feudal era Japan, she unwittingly frees a half-demon, Inuyasha, and shatters the sacred Jewel of Four Souls. Now they must work together to restore the jewel before it falls into the wrong hands...

INUYASHA

The manga that inspired a phenomenon!

FULL COLOR adaptation of the TV series!

Only $9.95!

Only $11.95!

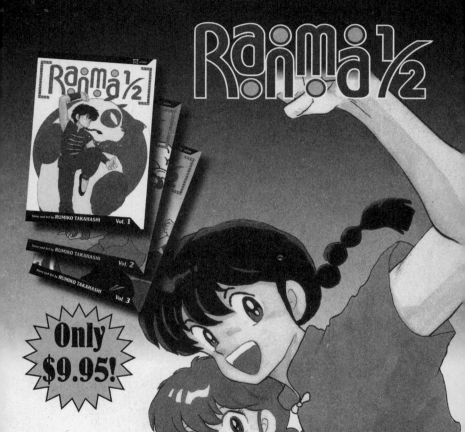

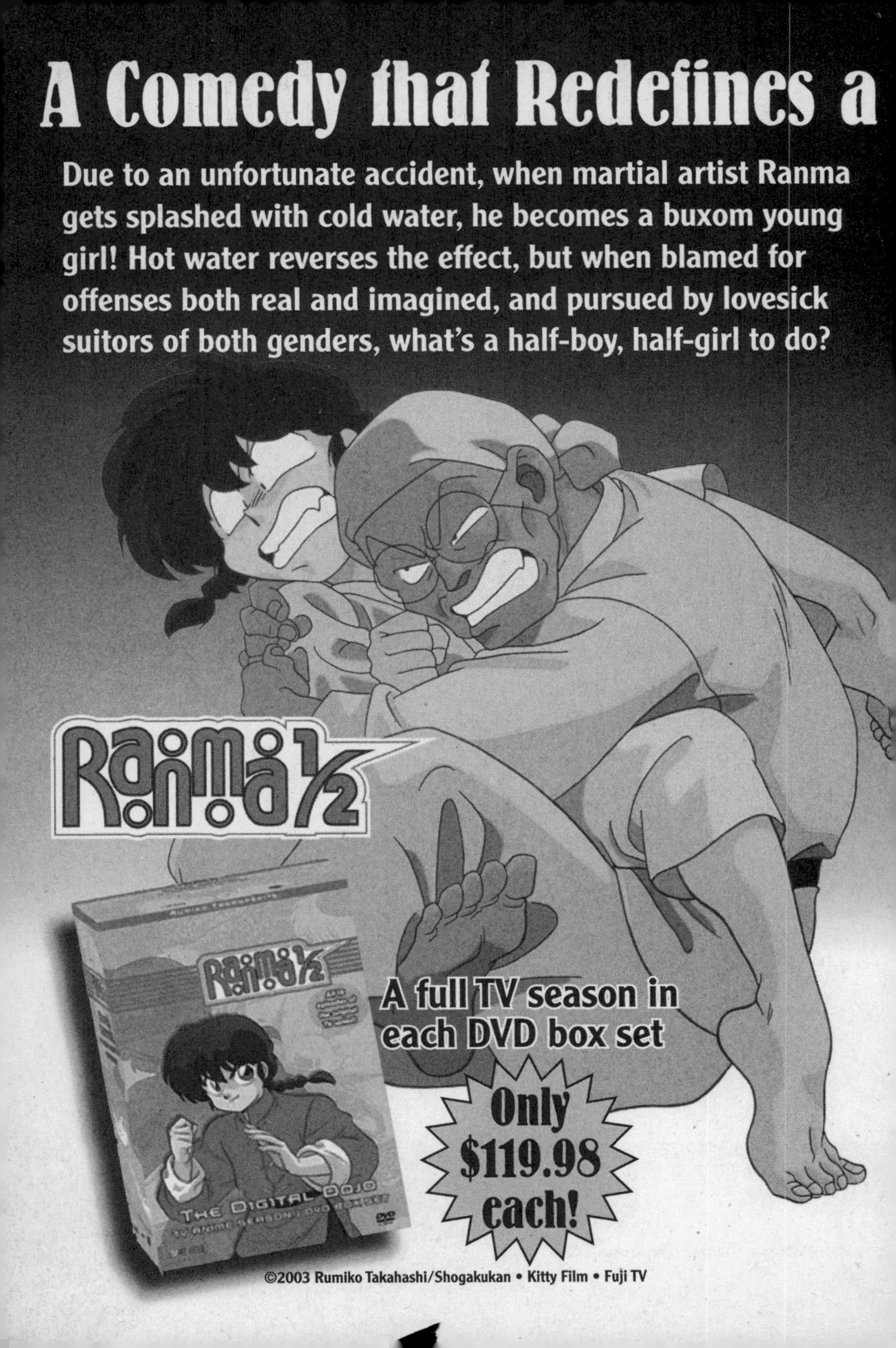
A Comedy that Redefines a
Due to an unfortunate accident, when martial artist Ranma gets splashed with cold water, he becomes a buxom young girl! Hot water reverses the effect, but when blamed for offenses both real and imagined, and pursued by lovesick suitors of both genders, what's a half-boy, half-girl to do?
Ranma 1/2
The Digital Dojo
A full TV season in each DVD box set
Only $119.98 each!
©2003 Rumiko Takahashi/Shogakukan • Kitty Film • Fuji TV

LOVE MANGA?
LET US KNOW WHAT YOU THINK!